Modern Theories and Practices for Cyber Ethics and Security Compliance

Winfred Yaokumah
University of Ghana, Ghana

Muttukrishnan Rajarajan
City University of London, UK

Jamal-Deen Abdulai
University of Ghana, Ghana

Isaac Wiafe
University of Ghana, Ghana

Ferdinand Apietu Katsriku
University of Ghana, Ghana

A volume in the Advances in Information Security, Privacy, and Ethics (AISPE) Book Series

Published in the United States of America by
    IGI Global
    Information Science Reference (an imprint of IGI Global)
    701 E. Chocolate Avenue
    Hershey PA, USA 17033
    Tel: 717-533-8845
    Fax: 717-533-8661
    E-mail: cust@igi-global.com
    Web site: http://www.igi-global.com

                            Library of Congress Cataloging-in-Publication Data

Names: Yaokumah, Winfred, editor.
Title: Modern Theories and practices for cyber ethics and security compliance /
    Winfred Yaokumah [and 4 others], editors.
Description: Hershey, PA : Information Science Reference, an imprint of IGI
    Global, [2020] | Includes bibliographical references and index. |
    Summary: "This book examines concepts, models, issues, challenges,
    innovations, and mitigation strategies needed to improve cyber security,
    cyber safety, and cyber ethics"-- Provided by publisher.
Identifiers: LCCN 2019048523 (print) | LCCN 2019048524 (ebook) | ISBN
    9781799831495 (hardcover) | ISBN 9781799857525 (paperback) | ISBN
    9781799831501 (ebook)
Subjects: LCSH: Internet--Security measures. | Internet--Safety measures. |
    Internet--Moral and ethical aspects.
Classification: LCC TK5105.59 .H3528 2020 (print) | LCC TK5105.59 (ebook)
    | DDC 005.8--dc23
LC record available at https://lccn.loc.gov/2019048523
LC ebook record available at https://lccn.loc.gov/2019048524

This book is published in the IGI Global book series Advances in Information Security, Privacy, and Ethics (AISPE) (ISSN:
1948-9730; eISSN: 1948-9749)

British Cataloguing in Publication Data
A Cataloguing in Publication record for this book is available from the British Library.

All work contributed to this book is new, previously-unpublished material. The views expressed in this book are those of the
authors, but not necessarily of the publisher.

For electronic access to this publication, please contact: eresources@igi-global.com.

Advances in Information Security, Privacy, and Ethics (AISPE) Book Series

Manish Gupta
State University of New York, USA

ISSN:1948-9730
EISSN:1948-9749

MISSION

As digital technologies become more pervasive in everyday life and the Internet is utilized in ever in-creasing ways by both private and public entities, concern over digital threats becomes more prevalent.

The **Advances in Information Security, Privacy, & Ethics (AISPE) Book Series** provides cutting-edge research on the protection and misuse of information and technology across various industries and settings. Comprised of scholarly research on topics such as identity management, cryptography, system security, authentication, and data protection, this book series is ideal for reference by IT professionals, academicians, and upper-level students.

COVERAGE

- Cyberethics
- Global Privacy Concerns
- Privacy-Enhancing Technologies
- IT Risk
- Network Security Services
- Technoethics
- CIA Triad of Information Security
- Device Fingerprinting
- Internet Governance
- Tracking Cookies

IGI Global is currently accepting manuscripts for publication within this series. To submit a pro-posal for a volume in this series, please contact our Acquisition Editors at Acquisitions@igi-global.com or visit: http://www.igi-global.com/publish/.

Titles in this Series

For a list of additional titles in this series, please visit:
http://www.igi-global.com/book-series/advances-information-security-privacy-ethics/37157

Blockchain Applications in IoT Security
Harshita Patel (KLEF, Vaddeswaram, Guntur, Andhra Pradesh, India) and Ghanshyam Singh Thakur (MANIT, Bhopal, Madhya Pradesh, India)
Information Science Reference • © 2020 • 300pp • H/C (ISBN: 9781799824145) • US $215.00

Handbook of Research on Multimedia Cyber Security
Brij B. Gupta (National Institute of Technology, Kurukshetra, India) and Deepak Gupta (LoginRadius Inc., Canada)
Information Science Reference • © 2020 • 372pp • H/C (ISBN: 9781799827016) • US $265.00

Security and Privacy Applications for Smart City Development
Sharvari C. Tamane (MGM's Jawaharlal Nehru Engineering College, India)
Information Science Reference • © 2020 • 300pp • H/C (ISBN: 9781799824985) • US $215.00

Cyber Security of Industrial Control Systems in the Future Internet Environment
Mirjana D. Stojanović (University of Belgrade, Serbia) and Slavica V. Boštjančič Rakas (University of Belgrade, Serbia)
Information Science Reference • © 2020 • 374pp • H/C (ISBN: 9781799829102) • US $195.00

Digital Investigation and Intrusion Detection in Biometrics and Embedded Sensors
Asaad Abdulrahman Nayyef (Sultan Qaboos University, Iraq)
Information Science Reference • © 2020 • 320pp • H/C (ISBN: 9781799819448) • US $235.00

Handbook of Research on Intrusion Detection Systems
Brij B. Gupta (National Institute of Technology, Kurukshetra, India) and Srivathsan Srinivasagopalan (AT&T, USA)
Information Science Reference • © 2020 • 407pp • H/C (ISBN: 9781799822424) • US $265.00

Applied Approach to Privacy and Security for the Internet of Things
Parag Chatterjee (National Technological University, Argentina & University of the Republic, Uruguay) Emmanuel Benoist (Bern University of Applied Sciences, Switzerland) and Asoke Nath (St. Xavier's College, University of Calcutta, India)
Information Science Reference • © 2020 • 315pp • H/C (ISBN: 9781799824442) • US $235.00

701 East Chocolate Avenue, Hershey, PA 17033, USA
Tel: 717-533-8845 x100 • Fax: 717-533-8661
E-Mail: cust@igi-global.com • www.igi-global.com

Table of Contents

Detailed Table of Contents

Riza Azmi, University of Wollongong, Australia
Kautsarina Kautsarina, University of Indonesia, Indonesia
Ima Apriany, University of Wollongong, Australia
William J. Tibben, University of Wollongong, Australia

The term "cyber" has been used widely in recent times and in particular in the context of security. Given the wide usage in formal and informal contexts, it is possible that its origin and true meaning will not be fully appreciated and understood. The Cooperative Cyber Defense Center of Excellence (CCDCE) has made available a range of various definitions. The term cyber has become very prevalent and appeared in many national and international statements and in some cases having contradictory interpretations. This chapter aims to revisit the term cyber by walking through its use in various contexts. It starts from the context of the word's origin; what is really entailed in the cyber world; and definitions portraying the understanding of the term from academics, national, and international organizations. Finally, the chapter combines the different interpretations into a single abridged definition from the various accumulated perspectives.

Winfred Yaokumah, University of Ghana, Ghana
Ferdinard Katsriku, University of Ghana, Ghana
Jamal-Deen Abdulai, University of Ghana, Ghana
Kwame Okwabi Asante-Offei, Ghana Institute of Management and Public Administration,
   Ghana

Application security measures are the controls within software systems that protect information assets from security attacks. Cyber attacks are largely carried out through software systems running on computing systems in cyberspace. To mitigate the risks of cyber attacks on software systems, identification of entities operating within cyberspace, threats to application security and vulnerabilities, and defense mechanisms are crucial. This chapter offers a taxonomy that identifies assets in cyberspace, classifies cyber threats into eight categories (buffer overflow, malicious software, input attacks, object reuse, mobile code, social engineering, back door, and logic bomb), provides security defenses, and maps security measures to control types and functionalities. Understanding application security threats and defenses will help IT security professionals in the choice of appropriate security countermeasures for setting up strong defense-in-depth mechanisms. Individuals can also apply these safeguards to protect themselves from cyber-attacks.

Chapter 3

Paul Danquah, Heritage Christian College, Ghana
Olumide Babatope Longe, American University of Nigeria, Nigeria
Jojo Desmond Lartey, Heritage Christian College, Ghana
Peter Ebo Tobbin, Center for IT Professional Development, Ghana

Socially engineered cyber deception and theft seems to have gained prominence in cybercrime. Given the contextual background of inadequate theoretical explanations of socially engineered cyber deception and theft cybercrime, there is the need for theory to better explain and possibly predict activities involved in socially engineered cyber deception and theft. This chapter proposes a theory of socially engineered cyber deception and theft (SECT), with routine activity theory, crime displacement theory, the space transition theory, and empirical review as its foundation. It iteratively combines deductive and inductive approaches to infer the occurrence of socially engineered cyber deception and theft. While the deductive approach serves the deduction leading to the inference, the inductive approach extracts and suggests empirical evidence for a deterministic prediction of the crime occurrence. It is recommended that the theory is further validated to test its applicability.

Chapter 4

Kwasi Danso Dankwa, University of Reading, UK

The use of computers and sophisticated technologies are on the rise, and organizations are constantly looking for ways to invest in technologies to stay ahead of the competitive market. As such, cyber security and safety measures have been put in place by the organizations to protect them from attacks and to ensure that products and services are safe. However, managing cyber security and safety is becoming more challenging in today's business because people are both a cause of cyber security incidents as well as a key part of the protection from them. It is however that non-compliance with policies and directives are major security breaches. What is not well known, however, are the reasons behind the non-compliance behaviours. This chapter seeks to explore the reasons behind the non-compliance behaviours by use of compliance assessment model (CAM). The chapter reviews a case study in a health centre and systematically assesses the reasons behind the non-compliance behaviour by using the CAM model.

Chapter 5

Nana Assyne, University of Jyväskylä, Finland

Software growth has been explosive as people depend heavily on software on daily basis. Software development is a human-intensive effort, and developers' competence in software security is essential for secure software development. In addition, ubiquitous computing provides an added complexity to software security. Studies have treated security competences of software developers as a subsidiary of security engineers' competence instead of software engineers' competence, limiting the full knowledge of the security competences of software developers. This presents a crucial challenge for developers, educators, and users to maintain developers' competences in security. As a first step in pushing for the developers' security competence studies, this chapter utilises a literature review to identify the security competences of software developers. Thirteen security competences of software developers were identified and mapped to the common body of knowledge for information security professional framework. Lastly, the implications for, with, and without the competences are analysed and presented.

Chapter 6

   Enoch Agyepong, Cardiff University, UK
   Yulia Cherdantseva, Cardiff University, UK
   Philipp Reinecke, Cardiff University, UK
   Pete Burnap, Cardiff University, UK

Cyber security operations centres (SOCs) are attracting much attention in recent times as they play a vital role in helping businesses to detect cyberattacks, maintain cyber situational awareness, and mitigate real-time cybersecurity threats. Literature often cites the monitoring of an enterprise network and the detection of cyberattacks as core functions of an SOC. While this may be true, an SOC offers more functions than the detection of cyberattacks. For example, an SOC can provide functions that focus on helping an organisation to meet regulatory and compliance requirement. A better understanding of the functions that could be offered by an SOC is useful as this can aid businesses running an in-house SOC to extend their SOC capabilities to improve their overall cybersecurity posture. The goal of this chapter is to present the basics one needs to know about SOCs. The authors also introduce readers and IT professionals who are not familiar with SOCs to SOC concepts, types of SOC implementation, the functions and services offered by SOCs, along with some of the challenges faced by an SOC.

Chapter 7

   Isaac Wiafe, University of Ghana, Ghana
   Winfred Yaokumah, University of Ghana, Ghana
   Felicia Amanfo Kissi, Ghana Institute of Management and Public Administration, Ghana

Cyber ethical decisions have grave moral, legal, and social consequences on individuals, organizations, and societies at large. This chapter examines the extent of cyber unethical intentions among students on cyber piracy, cyber plagiarism, computer crime and abuses, and cyber privacy infringement. Using frequency analysis and the t-test of independent samples, the results showed that almost 24% of the respondents have intentions to engage in cyber piracy and about 13% would infringe on others privacy in cyberspace. More respondents have intentions to commit cyber piracy as compared to other cyber ethic issues, while cyber privacy infringement was the least observed. Almost 30% of respondents had intentions to commit software piracy, and 18.6% would engage in hacking activities. Also, cybercrime and computer abuse were more common among males than females. Cyber plagiarism was significantly higher among foreign students when compared to local students. Cyber piracy, cyber plagiarism, computer crime, and cyber privacy infringement were significantly higher in public universities.

Rizwan Ur Rahman, Maulana Azad National Institute of Technology, Bhopal, India
Deepak Singh Tomar, Maulana Azad National Institute of Technology, Bhopal, India

Research into web application security is still in its initial phase. In spite of enhancements in web application development, large numbers of security issues remain unresolved. Login attacks are the most malevolent threats to the web application. Authentication is the method of confirming the stated identity of a user. Conventional authentication systems suffer from a weakness that can compromise the defense of the system. An example of such vulnerabilities is login attack. An attacker may exploit a pre-saved password or an authentication credential to log into web applications. An added problem with current authentication systems is that the authentication process is done only at the start of a session. Once the user is authenticated in the web application, the user's identity is assumed to remain the same during the lifetime of the session. This chapter examines the level login attacks that could be a threat to websites. The chapter provides a review of vulnerabilities, threats of login attacks associated with websites, and effective measures to counter them.

Felix Nti Koranteng, University of Education, Winneba, Kumasi Campus, Ghana
Richard Apau, Kwame Nkrumah University of Science and Technology, Ghana
Jones Opoku-Ware, Kwame Nkrumah University of Science and Technology, Ghana
Akon Obu Ekpezu, Cross River University of Technology, Cross River, Nigeria

There is a long-held belief that deterrence mechanisms are more useful in developing countries. Evidence on this belief is anecdotal rather than empirical. In this chapter, individual compliance to information system security policy (ISSP) is examined through the lenses of deterrence theory. The effects of certainty of detection and severity of punishment on attitude towards compliance and also ISSP compliance behaviour are investigated. A survey questionnaire was distributed to gather responses from 432 individuals who are staff of a public university in Ghana. The data was analysed using partial least square structural equation modelling (PLS-SEM). The results indicate that severity of punishment has a positive effect on attitude towards compliance and ISSP compliance behaviour. However, certainty of detection neither affected attitude towards compliance nor ISSP compliance behaviour. It is recommended that organizations enhance the severity of sanctions imposed on those who violate ISSPs. Future studies should explore how users apply neutralization techniques to evade sanctions.

    Kwame Simpe Ofori, School of Management and Economics, University of Electronic Science and Technology of China, China
    Hod Anyigba, Nobel International Business School, Ghana
    George Oppong Appiagyei Ampong, Department of Management, Ghana Technology University College, Ghana
    Osaretin Kayode Omoregie, Department of Finance, Lagos Business School, Pan-Atlantic University, Nigeria
    Makafui Nyamadi, Department of Operations and Information Systems, Business School, University of Ghana, Ghana
    Eli Fianu, Ghana Technology University College, Ghana

One of the major concerns of organizations in today's networked world is to unravel how employees comply with information security policies (ISPs) since the internal employee has been identified as the weakest link in security policy breaches. A number of studies have examined ISP compliance from the perspective of deterrence; however, there have been mixed results. The study seeks to examine information security compliance from the perspective of the general deterrence theory (GDT) and information security climate (ISC). Data was collected from 329 employees drawn from the five top-performing banks in Ghana and analyzed with PLS-SEM. Results from the study show that security education training and awareness, top-management's commitment for information security, and peer non-compliance behavior affect the information security climate in an organization. Information security climate, punishment severity, and certainty of deterrent were also found to influence employees' intention to comply with ISP. The implications, limitations, and directions for future research are discussed.

    Akon Obu Ekpezu, Cross River University of Technology, Cross River, Nigeria
    Enoima Essien Umoh, Cross River University of Technology, Nigeria
    Felix Nti Koranteng, University of Education, Winneba, Kumasi Campus, Ghana
    Joseph Ahor Abandoh-Sam, Valley View University, Ghana

Due to the sensitivity and amount of information stored on mobile devices, the need to protect these devices from unauthorized access has become imperative. Among the various mechanisms to manage access on mobile devices, this chapter focused on identifying research trends on biometric authentication schemes. The systematic literature review approach was adopted to guide future researches in the subject area. Consequently, seventeen selected articles from journals in three databases (IEEE, ACM digital library, and SpringerLink) were reviewed. Findings from the reviewed articles indicated that touch gestures are the predominant authentication technique used in mobile devices, particularly in android devices. Furthermore, mimic attacks were identified as the commonest attacks on biometric authentic schemes. While, robust authentication techniques such as dental occlusion, ECG (electrocardiogram), palmprints and knuckles were identified as newly implemented authentication techniques in mobile devices.

    Abigail Wiafe, University of Eastern Finland, Finland
    Pasi Fränti, University of Eastern Finland, Finland

Affective algorithmic composition systems are emotionally intelligent automatic music generation systems that explore the current emotions or mood of a listener and compose an affective music to alter the person's mood to a predetermined one. The fusion of affective algorithmic composition systems and smart spaces have been identified to be beneficial. For instance, studies have shown that they can be used for therapeutic purposes. Amidst these benefits, research on its related security and ethical issues is lacking. This chapter therefore seeks to provoke discussion on security and ethical implications of using affective algorithmic compositions systems in smart spaces. It presents issues such as impersonation, eavesdropping, data tempering, malicious codes, and denial-of-service attacks associated with affective algorithmic composition systems. It also discusses some ethical implications relating to intensions, harm, and possible conflicts that users of such systems may experience.

Chapter 13

Users are considered the weakest link in ensuring information security (InfoSec). As a result, users' security behaviour remains crucial in many organizations. In response, InfoSec research has produced many behavioural theories targeted at explaining information security policy (ISP) compliance. Meanwhile, these theories mostly draw samples from employees often in developing countries. Such theories are not applicable to students in educational institutions since their psychological orientation with regards to InfoSec is different when compared with employees. Based on this premise, the chapter presents arguments founded on synthesis from existing literature. It proposes a students' security compliance model (SSCM) that attempts to explain predictive factors of students' ISP compliance intentions. The study encourages further research to confirm the proposed relationships using qualitative and quantitative techniques.

Chapter 14

Small businesses employ 29% of New Zealand's private sector workforce and account for more than a quarter of its gross domestic product. Thus, a large-scale attack on small businesses could prove to be catastrophic to the economy. This chapter, which is framed by the protection motivation theory, explores 80 small business owners' IT security decision-making via an online survey. The findings revealed that 21% of small businesses were affected by ransomware. Fifty-one percent of the respondents did not have any anti-malware and none of the respondents used data classification, which means all information was regarded as the same. Since they managed to recover their backup information, they did not perceive the threat of ransomware as imminent. In terms of coping appraisal, it is assumed that if the business owner-managers believe that the capability of IT security investment averts threats in their organizations, they will be more inclined to develop an intention to invest in it.

Chapter 15

Daniel Kobla Gasu, Department of Computer Science, University of Ghana, Ghana

The internet has become an indispensable resource for exchanging information among users, devices, and organizations. However, the use of the internet also exposes these entities to myriad cyber-attacks that may result in devastating outcomes if appropriate measures are not implemented to mitigate the risks. Currently, intrusion detection and threat detection schemes still face a number of challenges including low detection rates, high rates of false alarms, adversarial resilience, and big data issues. This chapter describes a focused literature survey of machine learning (ML) and data mining (DM) methods for cyber analytics in support of intrusion detection and cyber-attack detection. Key literature on ML and DM methods for intrusion detection is described. ML and DM methods and approaches such as support vector machine, random forest, and artificial neural networks, among others, with their variations, are surveyed, compared, and contrasted. Selected papers were indexed, read, and summarized in a tabular format.

Preface

OVERVIEW OF THE BOOK

There is no ambiguity on the fact that the introduction of the Internet has made remarkable contributions to today's organizations, humans and the general society. It breaks geographical boundaries and facilitates information distribution, knowledge sharing (Koranteng & Wiafe, 2018), commerce, (Kraemer & Dedrick, 2002; Kuoppamäki, Taipale, & Wilska, 2017) communication (Kuzlu, Rahman, Pipattanasomporn, & Rahman, 2017; Perry, Taylor, & Doerfel, 2003), collaboration (Koranteng, Wiafe, & Kuada, 2018; Wu, Wu, & Si, 2016), entertainment (Kuoppamäki et al., 2017) and data storage (Cai, Xu, Jiang, & Vasilakos, 2016; Liono, Jayaraman, Qin, Nguyen, & Salim, 2019). It has created a virtual space or environment where communication between computing devices or networks occurs. This is known as cyberspace. The globalized world, businesses, and governments rely on cyber technology for protecting essential information, sensitive data, and critical infrastructure. The volume of interactions within the cyberspace and the lack of strict controls on how communications occur within this space present security and ethical challenges to organizations and the general public (Yaokumah, 2020).

In particular, solutions for issues and challenges regarding the availability of critical information infrastructure such as power generation, distribution systems, transportation control networks, and business data integrity (including financial data) are limited. Again, issues on the confidentiality of sensitive business data such as medical records and trade secrets have also been identified to be worrying (Caputo, Maloof, & Stephens, 2009). Current limitations and gaps in knowledge is a concern to civil society, businesses, governments, security professionals, and researchers across the globe (Siponen & Oinas-Kukkonen, 2007; Yaokumah, 2013).

The complex and multifaceted nature of the cyber world, the wide range of cyber-attacks and cybercriminal activities, and the broad scope of cyber-attacks targeting businesses, governments, and the society call for improvements in current cyber security mitigation strategies. The need to focus on established theories that have been empirically substantiated, approved and accepted, to provide practical guidelines that deal with cyber risks cannot be overemphasized. These risks emanate from existing and newer cyber-attacks. A multi-disciplinary approach that includes technical, behavioral, philosophical and managerial perspective is required to mitigate these cyber-related vulnerabilities and its associated attacks.

Accordingly, the Modern Theories and Practices for Cyber Ethics and Security Compliance provides information systems professionals and researchers a holistic and global view that consist of current research on cyber security challenges, mitigation strategies, concepts, tools, methodologies, and practical guidelines for combating the prevailing and emerging cyber threats. Specifically, it seeks to enhance theoretical and practical knowledge in cyber security, cyber safety, and cyber ethics.

Cyber security protects information systems from threats to confidentiality, integrity, and availability in cyberspace. It involves the understanding of threats, risks to systems and data, and taking appropriate actions to manage, treat and monitor the risks. The cyberspace is a complex virtual environment characterized by interactions of people, software and services on the Internet through technology devices and connected networks. While cyber security research attempts to understand the challenges that the society, businesses, and governments encounter in the cyberspace, there seem to be inadequate protection and mitigation strategies to maintain cyber safety and response to cyber-attacks appropriately.

The average annual cost of cybercrime is expected to reach US$6 trillion by 2021 (Morgan, 2017). Thus, the threat is imminent, and it puts businesses, government agencies, schools, hospitals, and critical public infrastructure, public safety and national security at risk. The actions that users of IT systems and applications can take to protect themselves from cyber threats and vulnerabilities, risks to their computing devices, and personal data (i.e. cyber safety) must be considered. Attention must be given to protecting the privacy of users as well as preventing cyber harassment, cyberbullying and scams (including those that are perpetuated through cyber-dating). Undoubtedly, today's society is concerned (Carvalho, Rocha, Abreu, & Victor, 2020; Oreku & Mtenzi, 2017) and aware (Ismailova et al., 2019) of the ethical and security challenges, introduced by cyberspace.

However, the legitimacy of what actions are right, just, and fair when using the cyberspace remains a challenge. Hence, there is the need to examine the moral, legal and social issues relating to the development and use of cyber technology. In other words, there is a need for cyber ethical concerns to be addressed. The scope of ethical conduct includes cyberspace psychology, privacy, Internet safety, responsible computing, harassment, cyberbullying, hate speech, hacking, netiquette, cyber-citizenship and computer ethics. Additionally, issues on intellectual property rights, confidentiality and privacy of information, data security, plagiarism, and cyber safety must be considered.

To address these concerns, the research community must double its effort to propose applicable solutions. There is, therefore, an urgent need for an aggregated collection of studies that present theoretical and empirical findings on the concepts, models, issues, challenges, innovations and mitigation strategies for improving cyber security, cyber safety, and cyber ethics practices. This will provide the requisite knowledge for professionals, individuals, civil society, businesses, organizations, governmental organizations, and researchers to facilitate the appropriate behavior of users within the cyberspace. It will also offer practical guidelines to users. Accordingly, this book is in-depth collection of current research that provides guidelines to protect and safeguard data and cyber infrastructure from cyber-attacks.

The Modern Theories and Practices for Cyber Ethics and Security Compliance is written to meet the need of researchers, practitioners, governments, legal practitioners and civil society who are concerned with cyber security, cyber safety, and cyber ethics issues. It provides the theoretical foundation needed for researchers to conduct further investigations. Also, it serves as a guide with practical insights to support civil society and individuals for protecting themselves from cyber-attacks. It offers legal practitioners' knowledge of cyber-related issues and provides governments with strategies that can be used to guide the development of cyber policies.

OVERVIEW OF THE CHAPTERS

The book is organized into 15 chapters and each of them seeks to address one or more of the above-mentioned challenges. Below are briefings of what each chapter contributes.

Chapter 1 seeks to define and explain *cyber* from various perspectives as presented by international, national, states, and diverse organizations. The authors explore the various definitions by examining its usage from multiple perspectives. Particular interest is given to linguistic genealogy, the context of the cyberworld, and the use of cyber in context. The chapter combines the various interpretations into an abridged definition that considers various perspectives. This study, therefore, is significant as it provides policymakers with a concise and unambiguous definition.

Chapter 2 offers a taxonomy of current and emerging application security threats and proposes applicable countermeasures that can be used to mitigate such threats. It identifies cyberspace assets and vulnerabilities by classifying application cyber security threats into eight categories. These categories are buffer overflows, malicious software, input attacks, object reuse, mobile codes, social engineering, back doors, and logic bombs. It proposes security defenses that are needed to mitigate these threats. The authors provide control measures for InfoSec professionals that can be used to facilitate the selection of security countermeasures for setting up strong defense-in-depth mechanisms. In addition, it proposes practical guidelines that enable individuals to safeguard themselves from cyber-attacks.

Chapter 3 presents a theoretical explanation for better understanding and prediction of activities involved in socially engineered cyber deception and cyber theft. The authors propose a Socially Engineered Cyber Deception and Theft (SECT) theory. The theory is based on the Routine Activity Theory, Crime Displacement Theory, and the Space Transition Theory. Similar to the other chapters, this chapter has significant research implications relating to understanding cyber deception and theft cybercrime.

Chapter 4 explains the myth about non-compliance to cyber security policy by considering the reasons behind non-compliance and its impact on cyber safety and security. It presents discussions on the potential impact of security and safety breaches on patient treatments and other relevant stakeholders within the healthcare sector. The author argues that in most cases, non-compliance occurs because stakeholders do not understand the importance and usefulness of rules and regulations of the organization. Many non-compliances instances are due to individual's lack of knowledge on the role they play in security and safety architecture, adoption and use of technology or resources available, and the impact of their non-compliance behaviour on safety and quality of treatment of patients.

Chapter 5 presents an in-depth review on identifying the security competences of software developers. The study identifies thirteen security competences of software developers and maps them to the Common Body of Knowledge of Information Security professional's framework. The competencies identified and the linkages provided between the security competency of software developers and the information security professional framework serves as a basis for the development of security competencies of software developers. This study is relevant since the security competence of software developers affects the security of applications developed.

Chapter 6 explains the need for Cyber Security Operations Centres (SOC). SOC plays a vital role in helping businesses to detect cyberattacks, maintain cyber situational awareness, and mitigate real-time cybersecurity threats. The authors discuss several functions and benefits of SOC, including monitoring of an enterprise network, detection of cyberattacks, and helping organisations to meet regulatory and compliance requirement. The chapter provides a better understanding of several useful functions that SOC offers, with the aim of helping businesses running an in-house SOC to extend their SOC capabilities to improve their overall cybersecurity posture. Moreover, the authors introduce readers and IT professionals who are not familiar with SOCs to SOC concepts, types of SOC implementation, the functions and services offered by SOCs, along with some of the challenges faced by a SOC.

Chapter 7 argues that users' cyber ethical decisions may have grave moral, legal, and social consequences on society, organizations, and individuals. The authors examine the extent of cyber ethical practices among students with regards to cyber piracy, cyber plagiarism, computer crime and abuses, and cyber privacy infringement. It ascertains students' intentions of cyber ethical choices for cyberpiracy, plagiarism, computer crime and abuses, and cyberprivacy infringement. It also examined the differences in intention on cyber piracy, plagiarism, computer crime and abuses, and cyber privacy violation between genders, nationalities, and universities. The chapter concludes by proposing appropriate ways in which ethical behaviour can be encouraged.

Chapter 8 contends that conventional authentication methods in web-based applications suffer defense limitations. The chapter explains that an attacker can exploit a pre-saved password or an authentication credential to log into web applications. The challenge with current authentication systems is that the authentication process is done "only" at the start of a session. Thus, once a user is authenticated in a web application, the user's identity is assumed to remain the same during the session lifetime. The authors examine login attacks that are threats to websites, review associated vulnerabilities, and provide effective measures for countering them.

Chapter 9 scrutinizes the proposition that deterrence mechanisms are effective in influencing Information System Security Policy (ISSP) compliance in developing countries because many of these countries are collectivist. This assertion is based on anecdotal evidence rather than empirical. Consequently, the authors examine ISSP compliance in a developing country by using Deterrence Theory. It investigates the direct effects of the severity of punishments and certainty of detection on ISSP compliance intention and also how the attitude toward compliance mediates these relationships. The study makes a significant contribution in explaining the effectiveness of deterrent mechanisms in ensuring ISSP compliance in developing countries.

Chapter 10 provides a systematic insight of the factors affecting information security policy compliance by highlighting key antecedent factors influencing policy compliance behavior. It seeks to examine information security compliance from the perspective of the General Deterrence Theory (GDT) and Information Security Climate (ISC). Collecting data from employees from the five top-performing banks in Ghana, the authors found that security education training and awareness, top-management's commitment for information security, and peer non-compliance behavior affect the information security climate in the selected organizations. Information security climate as well as punishment severity and certainty of deterrent are also found to influence employees' intention to comply with ISP. The chapter offers current findings in the area of security compliance that enhance organizational capabilities of safeguarding systems and cyber security.

Chapter 11 presents a holistic systematic literature overview on biometric authentication in mobile devices that guides future researches in the domain. It argues that mobile devices represent a unique environment that requires a secured, reliable and robust authentication mechanism. Accordingly, many authentication approaches have been implemented. Yet, these authentication systems provide limited security and privacy solutions. The authors suggest that new methods must be explored: methods that integrate multiple characteristics to combat internal and external attacks. The chapter further discusses various biometric techniques, resilient attacks, sensors in mobile devices, classifiers, extracted features and performance measurements. The study identifies current research trends in biometric authentication systems on mobile devices.

Chapter 12 discusses security challenges and threats associated with the fusion of affective algorithmic composition (AAC) and smart spaces. It is motivated by the suspicion that formalized music and AAC has not explicitly confronted issues in cyber security. Hence, the chapter seeks to provoke thinking in research and practice in the use of AACs in smart spaces. The authors present issues such as impersonation, eavesdropping, data tampering, malicious codes and denial-of-service attacks associated with AAC systems. It also discusses some ethical implications relating to harm and possible conflicts that users of such systems may experience.

Chapter 13 argues that many behavioral theories are targeted at explaining Information Security Policy (ISP) compliance of employees in organizations. Most of these theories often draw samples from organizational employees. Such theories do not apply to students in educational institutions since their psychological orientation with regards to InfoSec is different when compared with employees. Based on this premise, the study presents arguments founded on synthesis from existing literature. The chapter proposes a Students' Security Compliance Model (SSCM) that explains predictive factors of students' ISP compliance intentions.

Chapter 14 explores eighty small business owners' IT security investment decision-making in New Zealand via an online survey. The chapter reveals alarming rates of ransomware and the lack of investment in anti-malware for protecting sensitive data. The chapter proposes a conceptual framework that assists managers in redesigning IT strategies based on vulnerability-threat assessment and analysis. It extends studies on small businesses' IT security decision-making literature and also provides relevant insights into the current state of management accounting consideration in owner-managers' investment decisions. In terms of practical managerial significance, the chapter provides insight into the challenges and dilemmas faced by owner-managers in balancing the cost of investment required, and the need to protect businesses against security threats. It encourages managers to consider IT security as a strategic resource rather than outflow expenditure of budget.

Chapter 15 is a literature survey of machine learning (ML) and data mining (DM) methods for cyber analytics in support of intrusion detection and cyber-attack detection. Key literature on ML and DM methods for intrusion detection is presented. ML and DM methods and approaches including Support Vector Machine, Random Forest and Artificial Neural Networks among others and their variations are surveyed, compared and contrasted. The chapter discusses challenges of intrusion detection and threat detection schemes including low detection rates, high rates of false alarms, adversarial resilience and big data issues.

CONCLUSION

The Modern Theories and Practices for Cyber Ethics and Security Compliance provides you a collection of research on contemporary concepts, models, issues, challenges, innovations and mitigation strategies needed to improve cyber protection. It focuses on a broad range of topics including cyber-attack detection and monitoring, cyber deception and theft, cryptography, secured authentication methods, intrusion detection and prevention techniques, cyber security operations, cyber security investment, cyber security and privacy, and cyber security policy and compliance. Accordingly, the Modern Theories and Practices for Cyber Ethics and Security Compliance provides guidelines for protection, safety, ethics, and security of business data and national infrastructure from cyber-attacks. It is envisaged that the various chapters shall feed security analysts, law enforcers, researchers, legal practitioners, policymakers, business professionals, governments, strategists, educators and students with the relevant background needed for research, practice, and policymaking relating to cyber security, safety and ethical issues.

Winfred Yaokumah
University of Ghana, Ghana

Muttukrishnan Rajarajan
City University of London, UK

Jamal-Deen Abdulai
University of Ghana, Ghana

Isaac Wiafe
University of Ghana, Ghana

Ferdinand Apietu Katsriku
University of Ghana, Ghana

REFERENCES

Cai, H., Xu, B., Jiang, L., & Vasilakos, A. V. (2016). IoT-based big data storage systems in cloud computing: Perspectives and challenges. *IEEE Internet of Things Journal*, *4*(1), 75–87. doi:10.1109/JIOT.2016.2619369

Caputo, D., Maloof, M., & Stephens, G. (2009). Detecting insider theft of trade secrets. *IEEE Security and Privacy*, *7*(6), 14–21. doi:10.1109/MSP.2009.110

Carvalho, J. V., Rocha, Á., Abreu, A., & Victor, A. (2020). Portuguese Concerns and Experience of Specific Cybercrimes: A Benchmarking with European Citizens. In Developments and Advances in Defense and Security (pp. 39–50). Springer. doi:10.1007/978-981-13-9155-2_4

Ismailova, R., Muhametjanova, G., Medeni, T. D., Medeni, I. T., Soylu, D., & Dossymbekuly, O. A. (2019). Cybercrime risk awareness rate among students in Central Asia: A comparative study in Kyrgyzstan and Kazakhstan. *Information Security Journal: A Global Perspective, 28*(4–5), 127–135.

Koranteng, F. N., & Wiafe, I. (2018). Factors that Promote Knowledge Sharing on Academic Social Networking Sites: An Empirical Study. *Education and Information Technologies*, 1–26. doi:10.100710639-018-9825-0

Koranteng, F. N., Wiafe, I., & Kuada, E. (2018). An Empirical Study of the Relationship Between Social Networking Sites and Students' Engagement in Higher Education. *Journal of Educational Computing Research*. doi:10.1177/0735633118787528

Kraemer, K. L., & Dedrick, J. (2002). Strategic use of the Internet and e-commerce: Cisco Systems. *The Journal of Strategic Information Systems*, *11*(1), 5–29. doi:10.1016/S0963-8687(01)00056-7

Kuoppamäki, S.-M., Taipale, S., & Wilska, T.-A. (2017). The use of mobile technology for online shopping and entertainment among older adults in Finland. *Telematics and Informatics*, *34*(4), 110–117. doi:10.1016/j.tele.2017.01.005

Kuzlu, M., Rahman, M. M., Pipattanasomporn, M., & Rahman, S. (2017). Internet-based communication platform for residential DR programmes. *IET Networks*, *6*(2), 25–31. doi:10.1049/iet-net.2016.0040

Liono, J., Jayaraman, P. P., Qin, A. K., Nguyen, T., & Salim, F. D. (2019). QDaS: Quality driven data summarisation for effective storage management in Internet of Things. *Journal of Parallel and Distributed Computing*, *127*, 196–208. doi:10.1016/j.jpdc.2018.03.013

Morgan, S. (2017). *Cybercrime Report, 2017*. Cyber Security Ventures.

Oreku, G. S., & Mtenzi, F. J. (2017). Cybercrime: Concerns, Challenges and Opportunities. In Information Fusion for Cyber-Security Analytics (pp. 129–153). Springer.

Perry, D. C., Taylor, M., & Doerfel, M. L. (2003). Internet-based communication in crisis management. *Management Communication Quarterly*, *17*(2), 206–232. doi:10.1177/0893318903256227

Siponen, M. T., & Oinas-Kukkonen, H. (2007). A Review of Information Security Issues and Respective Research Contributions. *The Data Base for Advances in Information Systems*, *38*(1), 60–80. doi:10.1145/1216218.1216224

Wu, J., Wu, Z., & Si, S. (2016). The influences of Internet-based collaboration and intimate interactions in buyer–supplier relationship on product innovation. *Journal of Business Research*, *69*(9), 3780–3787. doi:10.1016/j.jbusres.2015.12.070

Yaokumah, W. (2013). Evaluating the effectiveness of information security governance practices in developing nations: A case of Ghana. *International Journal of IT/Business Alignment and Governance*, *4*(1), 27–43. doi:10.4018/jitbag.2013010103

Yaokumah, W. (2020). Predicting and Explaining Cyber Ethics with Ethical Theories. *International Journal of Cyber Warfare & Terrorism*, *10*(2), 46–63. doi:10.4018/IJCWT.2020040103

Chapter 1
Revisiting "Cyber" Definition:
Context, History, and Domain

Riza Azmi
University of Wollongong, Australia

Kautsarina Kautsarina
University of Indonesia, Indonesia

Ima Apriany
University of Wollongong, Australia

William J. Tibben
University of Wollongong, Australia

ABSTRACT

The term "cyber" has been used widely in recent times and in particular in the context of security. Given the wide usage in formal and informal contexts, it is possible that its origin and true meaning will not be fully appreciated and understood. The Cooperative Cyber Defense Center of Excellence (CCDCE) has made available a range of various definitions. The term cyber has become very prevalent and appeared in many national and international statements and in some cases having contradictory interpretations. This chapter aims to revisit the term cyber by walking through its use in various contexts. It starts from the context of the word's origin; what is really entailed in the cyber world; and definitions portraying the understanding of the term from academics, national, and international organizations. Finally, the chapter combines the different interpretations into a single abridged definition from the various accumulated perspectives.

DOI: 10.4018/978-1-7998-3149-5.ch001

INTRODUCTION

The term *cyber* is commonly used jargon to describe computers, networks, the Internet and its associated "virtual" environments (Merriam-Webster, 2020; Oxford Dictionary, 2020). Despite its prevalence in the media, conversations and official statements, this term is still understood in different ways (CCDCE, 2017; Lehto, 2015). In this chapter, we investigate the term *cyber* and its definition to see how various scholars interpret the word. In doing so, this chapter aims to bring together the definitions of *cyber* to enable better comprehension of the term as it is used today.

In investigating the definition of *cyber*, we explore several contexts in order to develop a working definition of the term. In section 2 we start by discussing the diverse perspectives which includes the differences between its use as an adjective vs. a noun, as well as the confusion of the word in other domains reflected in the two common terms *information security* vs. *cyber security*. In Section 3, we will explore the use of the term by seeing it used from multiple perspectives: linguistic genealogy, the context of the cyber world, and the use of the word in today's context, which we find varies considerably. In Section 4, we will combine these different perspectives to advance a single abridged definition which is suitable for today.

"Cyber": Jargon and the Divergence of Understanding

Although *cyber* is used as common jargon in modern societies, a singular meaning is elusive. Until now, *cyber* has been understood in differing ways across the domains of time and disciplines. Interestingly, an association with computers or the Internet is not a perquisite for understanding this term which can be readily grasped by referring to a common dictionary (Merriam-Webster, 2020; Oxford Dictionary, 2020). Despite this, there is currently no consensus on a definition. We found that there are several diverging understandings, such as on the semantic discussion (adjective vs. noun), and domain (such as the confusion between information security and cyber security).

Semantic Debate: Noun vs. Adjective

In a semantic debate, *cyber* is often used as an adjective that emphasizes its corresponding domain, such as the use of terms *cyber space* and *cyber security*. In these cases, the word modifies "space," which refers to a virtual room, and adds meaning "security" in the cyber space (see semantic discussion in Bayuk et al., 2012; and Ramirez & Choucri, 2016). The term *cyber* is also used as a noun to combine with its corresponding domain, such as in the use of *cyberspace* and *cybersecurity*.

The use of *cyber* as a noun is usually used and recognized with US English, while the use of *cyber* as an adjective is used globally and is recognized with UK English. However, this claim is not entirely valid since some organizations in Europe use the US style of English. One example of different uses, for instance Oxford University (GCSCC, 2014) uses the term "Cyber Security" (with a space), while the International Telecommunication Union (ITU, 2012), and the International Organization for Standardization and the International Electrotechnical Commission (ISO/IEC, 2012) uses the term "Cybersecurity."

While the use of *cyber* as noun and adjective are interchangeably used in modern statements, the open compound word "cyber security" is often used as a noun, and the closed compound word "cybersecurity" is commonly used as an adjective. The actual definition of each variation in order to attain a better understanding of the fact that the terms are defined differently through this approach on "cyber security" and "cybersecurity," we consider these sample sentences:

Cyber security is vital for the reliability and availability of the fundamental infrastructure.

Start developing a cybersecurity roadmap for your organization.

There are arguments which show the different uses of its noun and adjective forms. The semantic debate seems superfluous due to the fact that the jargon *cyber* is commonly understood as a virtual space (Bayuk et al., 2012). Ramirez and Choucri (2016) argue that a term should follow a linguistic basis, such as a clear etymology, enjoy the widespread and historical usage by the global community based on its trends, search ability, and definition. A clear etymology would mean a phonological change to language and the systematic nature to past word forms (including ancient Latin, Greek, and Indo-European languages), which would allow for a more widespread and historical usage of the term by the global community, and an improved search-ability and overall definition. Global community trends on Google show that from 2004 onward (see Figure 1), the terms *cybersecurity* and *cyberspace* are multiplying, with the word *cyber* being continuously used as an adjective rather than a noun.

Figure 1. "Cybersecurity" vs. "Cyber Security" trends on Google between 2004 onward

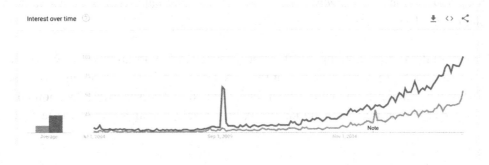

Domain

Cyber jargon is used interchangeably with other security domains, such as cyber security and information security (Luiijf, Besseling, & de Graaf, 2013). While in contrast to the CIA Triad[1] of Information Security (or McCumber's cube, 1991), which directly describes what underpins information security, the domain of cyber security is vague. For example, the ITU (2012) and the ISO/IEC (2012) use the term *cyber security* and *information security* as an interchangeable domain without any clear distinction.

The ITU (2012) defines cyber security in conjunction with information security, of which the main aim is to attain and maintain the security properties of confidentiality, integrity, and availability of information. The distinctions are information security started in its stand-alone and not traverse into other jurisdictions. This implies that information security is only focused on securing its internal organization system's perimeter, while cyber security is defined as a global challenge.

From another perspective, the ISO/IEC defines cyber security as seemly intertwined with information security (ISO/IEC, 2012). To distinguish these two domains as two separate aspects, the ISO/IEC has defined two different standards: the information security standard and the cyber security standard. The Information Security (see ISO/IEC, 2013) focuses more on how to manage a single organization's information security, while Cyber Security (see ISO/IEC, 2012) focuses more on how to collaborate and to address issues globally on security domains within cyberspace. Furthermore, in the ISO/IEC 27032 (ISO/IEC, 2012), the term "security" is classified into six domains, of which cyber security acts as the tip or center of the other five domains: Information Security, Application Security, Network Security, Internet Security, and Critical Information Infrastructure Protection.

In various policy statements, such as one from the National Cyber Security Strategy (NCSS), these two domains (information security and cyber security) appear to be intertwined. For example, according to the NCSS of Afghanistan and Croatia, cyber security is defined as:

Protection of information systems that protect the cyber space from attacks, ensuring the confidentiality, integrity, and accessibility of the information being processed in this space, detection of attacks and cyber security incidents; putting into force the countermeasures against these incidents and then putting these systems back to their original states prior to the cyber security incident. National Cyber Security Strategy of Afghanistan (Wafa, 2014)

Cyber security encompasses activities and measures for achieving the confidentiality, integrity, and availability of information and systems in cyberspace. The National Cyber Security Strategy of the Republic of Croatia (The Republic of Croatia, 2015)

The above definitions certainly imply that cyber security and information security are intertwined, and that cyber security borrows the principle of the CIA Triad of information but in cyberspace.

According to a recent definition by the Joint Task Force on Cybersecurity Education (JFT), cyber security is defined as covering broad and interdisciplinary fields, spanning from the technological to the non-technological:

Cyber security is a computing-based discipline involving technology, people, information, and processes to enable assured operations. It involves the creation, operation, analysis, and testing of secure computer systems. It is an interdisciplinary course of study, including aspects of law, policy, human factors, ethics, and risk management in the context of adversaries (JFT, 2017).

Since these two domains (information security and cyber security) are defined as interrelated, they can be used interchangeably. The term *cyber*, even though widely used, seems to be used in diverse ways. Through those diverging views of the definition of *cyber*, in the next chapter we try to untangle this definition. We start by elucidating this term from its origin to the context of current use. We also see the common theme on the use of the definition by different organizations. This will be discussed in the following sections.

REVISITING THE TERM CYBER

Context 1: History of the Word Cyber

When the term cyber is traced back to its original context, we can discover that it has strayed from its original meaning. In linguistic genealogy, the word *cyber* is rooted in the ancient Greek word "kybereo" (κυβερεω), which means "to assist," "to steer," "to guide," "to control," or "to govern" (Lehto, 2013; Maathuis, Pieters, & Van Den Berg, 2017).

The earliest use of this word can be found in the dialog between Plato and Alcibiades (see Alcibiades I) "kybernetikes" (κυβερνητικης), meaning a steersman, pilot, or governor (Liddell & Scott, 1940). Plato used this word to highlight the importance of skill in navigation (Johnson, 2015):

Socrates: Or again, in a ship, if a man having the power to do what he likes, has no intelligence or skill in navigation [αρετης κυβερνητικης, aretes kybernetikes], do you see what will happen to him and to his fellow-sailors? (Plato, 2014, Alcibiades I, translated by Benjamin Jowett)

Two millennia after, in 1843, André-Marie Ampère coined the word *"La cybernétique"* in the France language. According to the essay "Essai sur la philosophie des sciences, ou, Exposition analytique d'une classification de toutes les connaissances humaines," he wrote that "the future science of government should be called 'la cybernétique'" (Ampère, 1843, pp. 140–141). Etymologically, this word was adopted from the Greek to the France language.

In 1948, Norbert Wiener aspired to use the word *cyber* in his seminal work entitled "Cybernetics: or Control and Communication in the Animal and the Machine" to introduce the new field study in communication and control (as he previously used the term *"angelos"* (messenger) but finally settled on "cybernetics," which express the same meaning (Johnson, 2015).

The term cybernetics, which is a derivative of the word kybernetikes (steersman) or cybernétique (to govern), became widely known since the Wiener's seminal work was published. Cybernetics, as Wiener described, is the science of control and communication in the animal and the machine. It also refers to the science of automated control systems in both machines and living things that require "communication" and "feedback" (Ashby, 1957; Johnson, 2015; Wiener, 1948). Back in 1940's, this idea was peculiar since non-living (machines) things couldn't have "a purpose" (Pangaro, 2013).

Three decades after on 1980's, the term *cyber* first appears, and was borrowed from the word cybernetics (Johnson, 2015; Ottis & Lorents, 2010; Solomon, 2007). Gibson (1984), in the early 1980s used this word and brought a new term that we now widely use (Solomon, 2007). He introduced the term *cyberspace* in his science fiction novel, Neuromancer, which is something that represents a virtual environment and an alternative situation, which strayed from its original context (i.e., to govern, or steermanship). The term cyberspace in his book is described as:

...a graphic representation of data abstracted from banks of every computer in the human system. Neuromancer (Gibson, 1984)

However, the term *cyber* is also widely misunderstood as the integration between the biological and non-biological thing which further brings a new thought of the possibility to integrate human and machine (Ottis & Lorents, 2010). It is since the prefix "cyb" in cybernetics is widely understood as referring to the term "cyborg," or a robot/android (Pangaro, 2013).

Although it strays from its original context, the term "cyber" has entered common usage, including in information system's studies (Ottis & Lorents, 2010). The use of this term began to rise in academia in 1990 (Ramirez & Choucri, 2016), and has continued to do so up until now in current conversations and statements.

While the word *cyber* has strayed from its original roots, the notion of cyberspace is introduced, not just a concept of an abstract representation of the environment, but to the development of the interaction between entities inside cyberspace. This brings about a new study of the social structure of the cyber world. In the next section, we will discuss the social context of the cyber world.

Context 2: The Social Structure of the Cyber World

As discussed in the previous section, the word *cyber* in the contemporary context is widely understood as the abstract and alternative environment enabled by the internet and computer. It is also understood as referring to the terms cyborg and robot, or to the integration between biological and non-biological things (Pangaro, 2013). *Consequently, this raises the question of what is inside this virtual world, a question which implies a necessary understanding of the structure of the abstract world.*

There are some views that capture this abstract world that the authors characterize as the cyber world, into two characteristics. First, the cyber world is interdependent on the physical world (Kuusisto & Kuusisto, 2015, p. 33). Second, the cyber world is built by the interaction between each node connected to the internet (Kuusisto & Kuusisto, 2015; WEF, 2014).

The cyber world is tied to the physical world, and transgressions in the cyber world may affect the physical world and vice versa. For example, at the end of 2017, Bitcoin hacking, although the asset was virtual and happened in a virtual space, caused people to lose investments in real life, and an estimated value of 64 million dollars was stolen (Gibbs, 2017; Khatwani, 2017). Furthermore, a transgression in the physical world may trigger the cyber world. For example, the crisis between Georgia and Russia made Georgia creating national cyber policy to improve their national cyber defence. Another example is how South Korea and Japan avail their cyber defense unit to address regional tension (Azmi, Tibben, & Win, 2016).

Figure 2. The border between the cyber world and the physical world

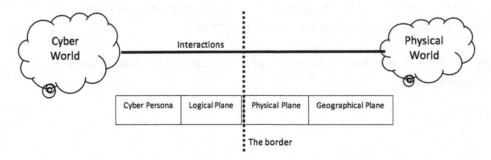

In relation with the tangled system between these two worlds, the border between the cyber world and the physical world can be distinguished into four layers (Kuusisto & Kuusisto, 2015; Fanelli & Conti, 2012; Lehto, 2015; Raymond, Conti, Cross, & Fanelli, 2013; Raymond, Cross, Conti, & Nowatkowski, 2014). These layers are the Cyber Persona, Logical Plane, Physical Plane, and the Geographical Plane (see Figure 2). The Cyber Persona refers to a plane of identity in the cyber world. The persona is attached to every entity connected to the cyber world, and can be referred to as an individual, an ego, a group of people, an animal, a machine, an autonomous system, [or] a software, which may hinder real identity anonymously. For example, people can create a social media account (i.e. Instagram profile) for their pet, which considers as a persona in cyberspace. The pet account together with other accounts is considered a cyber persona. While in the real life each of persona is referred to different objects, in cyberspace all objects/personas are in the same social level, which is represented by account name that describe who are us in cyberspace. The Logical Plane consists of software, operating systems, applications, and any logical systems. The Physical Plane is the information infrastructure that is one of the pillars of the cyber world. This can be hardware, a router, switches, or electricity. The Geographical Plane is the location in the real world that affects the operations of cyberspace.

Another characteristic of the cyber world is that it is consists of a collection of nodes connected to the internet (which is described as a persona). There are two views on this idea, which are in the perspective of Complex Adaptive System and in the perspective of the Social Network Theory.

The first view is the philosophical perspective, wherein Kuusisto & Kuusisto (2015) captures the cyber-world using the perspective of the Complex Adaptive System (CAS) to describe the social structure and environment of the cyber world. In Kuusisto's (Kuusisto & Kuusisto, 2015) view, the cyber world appears as a complex collective behavior, while any change of action in the cyber world cannot be seen as a product of a single actor in the cyber world. Within this context, the overall social structure that builds the cyber world may be perceived as a co-evolution with other related systems rather than an adaptation of the cyber environment (Chan, 2001).

In this context, the structure of the cyber-world perceived by CAS is understood in the broad sense (macro-perspective), and assumes that the cyber world is a single emerged phenomenon (Kuusisto & Kuusisto, 2015). However by using this view, it is puzzling to explain particular events inside the cyber world, since cyber world is only perceived as a single persona expressing a big group of people or an organization in the cyber world, and hinders the particular behavior of a single actor in the cyber world as well as their connections to each other in the cyber world. The interaction between actors may detract a view that cyberspace is a *hyper-connected* environment.

The second view outlines the social structure of the cyber world context and is known as the Social Network Theory. This view has been adapted by the World Economic Forum (WEF) in order to view the cyber world. The WEF perceives the cyber world as a hyper-connected environment. It also considers that the structural relationship has been changed from a hierarchical relationship (i.e. one is higher than the others) to a flat structure (i.e. we all are same in cyberspace). This means that no hierarchy when connected to cyberspace. Every single object joined in cyberspace acts as an entity with the same social level, including humans, animals, machines, and any other purposes.

Table 1. Cyber Definitions

ID	Term	Definition	Source
(1)	Cyber	*"Cyber refers to the interdependent network of information technology infrastructure, and includes technology "tools," such as the Internet, telecommunications networks, computer systems, and embedded processors and controllers in critical industries."*	WEF (2012)
(2)	Cyber	*"The word cyber is almost invariably the prefix for a term or the modifier of a compound word, rather than a stand-alone word. Its inference usually relates to electronic information (data) processing, information technology, electronic communications (data transfer), or information and computer systems. Only the complete term of the compound word (modifier+head) itself can be considered to possess actual meaning. The word cyber is generally believed to originate from the Ancient Greek verb κυβερεω (kybereo) meaning "to steer," "to guide," and "to control.""*	Finland (2013)
(3)	Cyber	*"Cyber is defined as anything relating to, or involving, computers or computer networks (such as the Internet)."*	Montenegro (2013)
(4)	Cyberspace	*"Cyberspace is the global environment that created through the interconnection of communication and information systems. The cyberspace includes physical and virtual computer networks, computer systems, digital media, and data."*	Belgium (2012)
(5)	Cyberspace	*"Cyberspace is the electronic world created by interconnected networks of information technology and the information on those networks. It is a global common where more people come together to exchange ideas, services, and friendship."*	Canada (2010)
(6)	Cyberspace	*"Cyber space refers to the digital environment, enabling the creation, process, and exchange of information created by information systems, services and electronic communication networks."*	Czech Republic (2015)
(7)	Cyberspace	*"Cyberspace is a space in which communication among information systems takes place, In the context of strategy, it encompasses the Internet and all the systems connected to it."*	Croatia (The Republic of Croatia, 2015)
(8)	Cyberspace	*"Cyberspace is the virtual space of all IT systems linked at the data level on a global scale. The basis for cyberspace is the Internet as a universal and publicly accessible connection and transport network, which can be complemented and further expanded by any number of additional data networks. IT systems in an isolated virtual space are not part of cyberspace."*	Germany (2011)
(9)	Cyberspace	*"Cyberspace is a complex environment consisting of interactions between people, software, and services, supported by the worldwide distribution of information and communication technology (ICT) devices and networks."*	India (2013)
(10)	Cyberspace	*"Cyberspace is the physical and non-physical domain that is created or composed of part of or all of the following components: mechanized and computerized systems, computer and communications networks, programs, computerized information, content conveyed by computers, traffic, and supervisory data and those who use such data."*	Israel (2011)
(11)	Cyberspace	*"Cyberspace refers to the complexity of all interconnected ICT hardware and software infrastructure, to all data stored in and transferred through the networks and all connected users, as well as to all logical connections established among them. Cyberspace therefore encompasses the Internet and all communication cables, networks, and connections that support information and data processing, including all mobile Internet devices."*	Italy (2013)
(12)	Cyberspace	*"Cyberspace is an artificial domain for the free exchange of ideas without regard to national borders; it is a digital frontier of infinite values generated by intellectual creations and innovations inspired by ideas globally exchanged. Cyberspace is a multi-dimensional space composed of various stakeholders' activities in a variety of layers."*	Japan (2015)
(13)	Cyberspace	*"Cyberspace is the notional environment in which communication over computer networks occurs."*	Kenya (2014)
(14)	Cyberspace	*"Cyber space is an interactive environment that includes users, networks, computing technology, software, processes, the information in transit or storage, applications, services, and systems that can be connected directly or indirectly to the Internet, telecommunications, and computer networks. Cyber space has no physical boarders."*	Latvia (2014)
(15)	Cyberspace	*"Cyberspace is more than the Internet; it includes not only hardware, software, and information systems, but also people and social interaction within these networks."*	Montenegro (GoM, 2013)
(16)	Cyberspace	*"Cyberspace is an interdependent network of critical and non-critical national information infrastructure, the convergence of interconnected information and communication resources through the use of information and communication technologies. It encompasses all forms of digital engagements, interactions, socializations, and transactional activities, contents, contacts, and resources deployed through interconnected networks."*	New Zealand (2011)
(17)	Cyberspace	*"Cyberspace is a space of processing and exchanging information created by the ICT systems."*	Poland (2013)
(18)	Cyberspace	*"Cyberspace is virtual or electronic environment that results from the interdependent network of information and communications technology (e.g., the Internet, telecommunications networks, computer systems, and embedded processors and controllers) that link people with services and information."*	Qatar (2013)
(19)	Cyberspace	*"Cyberspace refers to a physical and non-physical terrain created by and/or composed of some or all of the following: computers, computer systems, networks, and their computer programs, computer data, content data, traffic data, and users."*	South Africa (2012)
(20)	Cyberspace	*"Cyberspace integrates a number of capabilities, such as sensors, signals, connections, transmissions, processors, and controllers, and generates a virtual interactive experience accessed for the purpose of communication and control regardless of a geographic location. Cyberspace allows the interdependent network of information technology infrastructure and telecommunications networks, such as the Internet, computer systems, integrated sensors, system control networks, and embedded processors and controllers typical to global control and communications."*	Trinidad & Tobago (2012)
(21)	Cyberspace/ National cyberspace	*"Cyberspace is an environment consisting of information systems that span across the world, including the networks that interconnect with these systems." "National cyberspace is the environment consisting of the information systems that belong to public organizations, natural and legal persons."*	Turkey (2013)
(22)	Cyberspace	*"Cyberspace is an interactive domain made up of digital networks that are used to store, modify, and communicate information. It includes the internet, but also other information systems that support businesses, infrastructure, and services."*	United Kingdom (2011)
(23)	Cyberspace	*"Cyberspace is composed of hundreds of thousands of interconnected computers, servers, routers, switches, and fiber optic cables that allow our critical infrastructure to work."*	United States (2015)
(24)	Cybersecurity/ cyber	*"The term "cybersecurity" and the prefix "cyber" do not appear because of their focus on the economic and social objectives of the public and private organizations. Instead, we can use term "digital security" that can be approached from several perspectives, such as technology, law enforcement, national and international security, and economic and social prosperity. Moreover, the term "digital security risk" as the expression describing a category of risk related to the use, development, and management of the digital environment of any activity. This includes aspects related to the digital and physical environments, the people involved in an activity, and the organizational process supporting it."*	OECD (2015)
(25)	Cybercrime	*"The term "cybercrime" refers to two categories of offences: 1) Offences where a computer system is the target of a criminal act; and 2) Offences where traditional crimes are committed via the means of a computer system."*	Singapore (2019)
(26)	Cybercrime	*"Cybercrime is substantive criminal offence acts which affect the confidentiality, integrity, availability, and survival of information and communication technology systems, the data they process and the underlying network infrastructure."*	African Union (draft, 2014)

Context 3: Cyber in the Contemporary Context

From the previous section where we examined the context of the term *cyber* from the words history and its originally intended meaning, in this section we will discuss the term *cyber* as it has been used in recent conversations and statements. Table 1 consists of a collection of definitions of the terms *cyber, cyberspace, cybersecurity,* and *cybercrime.*

From those definitions, we can see that the terms cyber, cyberspace, cybercrime and cybersecurity are relatively similar in many ways. However, in the broad sense, we can see that the term *cyber* can be related to the following five areas, which are also further explored in Table 2:

1. Physical Infrastructure:
   Cyber needs IT infrastructure, such as hardware and software infrastructure, and also physical networks, such as fiber optic. *Cyber* is tightly related to critical information infrastructure.

2. Communication/Network:
   Cyber is related to communications or networks, and the Internet that links each actor on the environment.

3. System:
   Cyber covers information systems that support business, infrastructure, and services.

4. Devices:
   Cyber is also related to IT devices, such as computers, servers, routers, and more that have connectivity to the internet directly or indirectly in the environment.

5. Virtual Environment:
   Cyber refers to complex electronic or digital environments that relate to national space and territory.

Table 2. The Term Cyber Related

Related to	ID of Reference
Physical/IT Infrastructure	(1), (4), (5), (7), (9), (10), (11), (14), (16), (17), (18), (19), (20), (22), (23)
Communication/Network	(1), (2), (3), (4), (5), (6), (8), (9), (10), (11), (12), (13), (14), (15), (16), (17),(18), (20), (21), (22), (23), (26)
System	(1), (4), (6), (7), (8), (9), (10), (11), (12), (13), (14), (15), (16), (17), (18), (19), (20), (22), (25), (26)
Devices	(1), (3), (4), (8), (9), (10), (11), (13), (14), (15), (17), (18), (19), (20), (22), (23)
Virtual Environment	(2), (4), (5), (6), (8), (9), (10), (11), (12), (13), (14), (15), (16), (17), (18), (19), (20), (21), (22), (24)

DISCUSSIONS

In the previous section, we have seen that the definition of *cyber* has strayed from its original meaning, from "steermanship" (Plato, 2014), and "to govern" (Ampère, 1843), to "the alternative environment" (Gibson, 1982). The root of the word discusses the integration between human or animal and non-living things (just as the word cyborg) and is a study about autonomous systems closely related to (or may be broader than) the study of AI.

Although the definition of *cyber* has been scattered in many different perspectives and seems to have no agreed upon consensus of use, we can grasp the fact that the meaning of *cyber* is related to five categories: IT Infrastructure, Communication/Network, Systems, Devices, and Virtual Environment. We also see that cyberspace is a "virtual space" tied to "real life." In this section, we try to bridge together the different perspectives by consolidating the various points of view of the various definitions into one abridged definition.

Semantic Use of Cyber

From a semantic perspective, the four linguistic bases discussed in Section 1 can be used to gain a consensus on the term *cyber* (i.e., clear etymology, a widespread and historical usage by the global community based on its trends, search ability, and definition) (Ramirez & Choucri, 2016). For example, the terms "cyber security" vs. "cybersecurity" are used mainly interchangeably, and both are acceptable. However, the term "cyber security" is more acceptable (Ramirez & Choucri, 2016). Furthermore, some words containing *cyber* can be used in a combined style (noun word), such as cyberspace, while other new jargon recommends the use of the adjective style (cyber<space>[domain]). Etymologically, separating the word *cyber* is also favored in most forms (Ramirez & Choucri, 2016). The semantic suggestion is shown in Table 3.

Table 3. Semantic Uses of the term Cyber

Style	Favorable	Unfavorable
Combined style (noun word)	Cybernetics	
	Cyberspace	Cyber Space
Adjective style	Cyber Security	Cybersecurity
	Cyber<space>[domain] Example: cyber world, cyber culture, cyber attack, cyber warfare, cyber terrorism	

Context of Cyber

As we can see from the previous discussion, the domain of *cyber* is found to vary, especially in the security domain. Some organizations and Governments use cyber security, information security, network security, internet security, and critical information infrastructure security as interrelated domains (ISO/ IEC, 2012; see ITU-T X.1205 ITU, 2009; Microsoft, 2013, p. 4; NIST, 2014; The Republic of Croatia,

2015; Wafa, 2014). As such, cyber security is comprised of confidentiality, integrity, and availability of all aspects inside cyber space (McCumber, 1991). Other entities escalate the domain of cyber security as not only on securing their own security perimeter, just like in securing other security domains, but beyond that. Cyber security is intended to secure the virtual hyper-connected environment including the interaction between entities, as stated in the following definition:

Cybersecurity is information security with jurisdictional uncertainty and attribution issues. ITU National Cybersecurity Strategy Guide (ITU, 2012)

Cyberspace can be described as a virtual environment, which does not exist in any physical form, but rather, a complex environment or space resulting from the emergence of... [several entities]. Cyberse-curity is about the security of this virtual world. ISO/IEC Cybersecurity Guidelines (ISO/IEC, 2012)

To distil the various perspectives, we first try to disentangle the security domains between cyber security and any other security domains (i.e., information security, critical infrastructure, and network security) using the perspective of von Solms and van Niekerk (2013), which states that cyber security is the securing of all assets in the online form, including information and non-information assets. When we take into account the domain of cyber security, we can say that cyber security is more global and provides a hyper-connected environment in which there are interactions between each entity in the virtual environment. Therefore, consolidated from the various perspectives, we can abridge the term cyber security as follows:

"Securing a virtual environment, including <u>its assets</u> (i.e., information and non-information based), <u>entities</u> (such as end-users, organizations, governments, societies, machines, and software), and <u>its interactions</u> (enabled by IT Infrastructure, Communication/Networks, Systems, and Devices)."

Therefore, we can imply that cyberspace is orchestrated by three parts – entities (nodes), interactions (lines), and assets (illustrated in Figure 3).

Legend:
  Nodes: represent entities in cyberspace, such as end-users, organizations, governments, societies, machines, and software.
  Lines: represent interactions in cyberspace enabled by technology, systems, and networks.
  Assets: represent something that needs to be protected and is valuable, whether inside the entity or information crossing the interaction.

The entities refer to every object connected to cyberspace. In the perspective of ISO/IEC (ISO/IEC, 2012), this entity refers to "providers" and "consumers," while others refer to this as stakeholders, i.e., governments and private and public societies (ITU, 2012; "National Cyber Security Framework Manual," 2012; OAS, 2004; WEF, 2012a). In order to abridge various perspectives in this context, we favor the use of the term "entity," which is represented as a node in Figure 3. In this context, we recite the term used in the CCDCE, "the 3 Dimensions" which refers to the Government (the central), the national (all actors related to cyber space), and the international. However, the term "entity" is preferred and helps illustrate that the entity is more global while also emphasizing the flattening concept of end users and nodes in cyberspace. This also shows the nature of the relationship in cyber space has changed from a hierarchical system to a flattened and hyper-connected relationship (see the WEF concept).

Figure 3. Illustration of Cyberspace

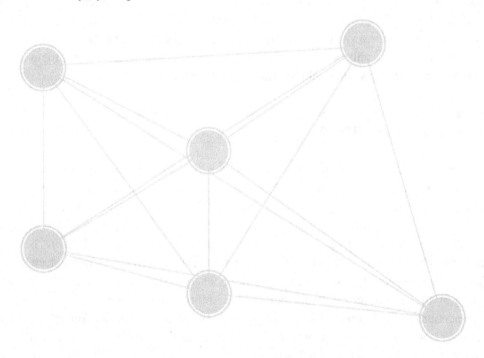

Since those entities live in a hyper-connected environment (Kuusisto & Kuusisto, 2015; WEF, 2012a, 2012b, 2014, 2015), they naturally have interactions. These <u>interactions</u> between the entity in cyberspace is illustrated as connected lines between one another in Figure 3, which shows this from the perspective of CAS or the Social Network Theory. These interactions are enabled by IT Infrastructure, Communications/Networks, Systems, and Devices (see Table 2 for the discussion).

The last aspect of the cyber world is its assets. <u>Assets</u> are something of value that needs to be protected, whether inside the entity or information crossing the interaction. Since assets differ from one organization to another, defining how valuable they are depending on how the entity views it. Unlike the information asset, which, if it is stolen the information still resides in the owner, the transgression of the cyber asset (or non-information asset as described by von Solms et al. (von Solms & van Niekerk, 2013) means to remove the ownership of the asset virtually.

FUTURE RESEARCH DIRECTION

This work may contribute in several ways. First, policymakers in their recent conversations and statements can revisit the context and definition of *cyber* and realign the focus. For example, discussing information security and cyber security, although they overlap, they are on different domains. Second, researchers may benefit from refocusing the subject of their research. Furthermore, the interaction discussed in this paper may illuminate a new study of the social structure of the cyber world.

CONCLUSION

This chapter began with the aim of revisiting the term *cyber* by exploring its use in various contexts. On revisiting the term, this paper started with the history of the word and explained what is inside the cyber world, and the modern context of this term from the perspectives of various organizations and governments. Abridging the various definitions, we can grasp that the context of the term shifted from not only describing the Internet and its virtual environment, but also its entities, its interactions, and assets, all of which are interdependent on the physical world.

ACKNOWLEDGMENT

This article was supported by Centre for Research and Development of Postal and Information Technology Resources, Equipment and Services (PITRES) 2020, Research and Human Resources Development Agency, Ministry of Communication and Informatics, Republics of Indonesia.

REFERENCES

Ampère, A.-M. (1843). *Essai sur la philosophie des sciences, ou, Exposition analytique d'une classification de toutes les connaissances humaines*. Academic Press.

Ashby, W. R. (1957). An Introduction to Cybernetics (2nd ed.). London: Chapman & Hall Ltd.

Azmi, R., Tibben, W., & Win, K. T. (2016). Motives behind Cyber Security Strategy Development: A Literature Review of National Cyber Security Strategy. In *Australasian Conference on Information Systems*. Wollongong: University of Wollongong.

Bayuk, J. L., Healey, J., Rohmeyer, P., Sachs, M. H., Schmidt, J., & Weiss, J. (2012). Cyber Security Policy Guidebook. doi:10.1002/9781118241530

BMI (Bundesministerium des Innern - Germany). (2011). *Cyber Security Strategy for Germany*. Berlin: Federal Ministry of the Interior.

CCDCE (Cooperative Cyber Defence Centre of Excellence). (2017). *Cyber Definitions*. https://ccdcoe.org/cyber-definitions.html

Chan, S. (2001). Complex Adaptive Systems. In ESD.83 Research Seminar in Engineering Systems (Vol. 31). doi:10.1002/cplx.20316

CO. (2011). *The UK Cyber Security Strategy: Protecting and Promoting the UK in a digital world*. Author.

DoD. (2015). The DoD Cyberstrategy. doi:10.1017/CBO9781107415324.004

Fanelli, R., & Conti, G. (2012). A methodology for cyber operations targeting and control of collateral damage in the context of lawful armed conflict. *2012 4th International Conference on Cyber Conflict (CYCON)*, 1–13.

Finland. (2013). *Finland´s Cyber security Strategy*. Academic Press.

GCSCC (Global Cyber Security Capacity Centre). (2014). Cyber Security Capability Maturity Model (CMM) (Version 1). Oxford: Global Cyber Security Capacity Centre (GCSCC), University of Oxford.

Gibbs, S. (2020, December). Bitcoin: $64m in cryptocurrency stolen in "sophisticated" hack, exchange says. *The Guardian Online.* https://www.theguardian.com/technology/2017/dec/07/bitcoin-64m-cryptocurrency-stolen-hack-attack-marketplace-nicehash-passwords

Gibson, W. (1982). *Burning Chrome.* Omni.

Gibson, W. (1984). Neuromancer. New York: Ace Books.

GoB (The Government of Belgium). (2012). *Cyber Security Strategy: Securing Cyberspace.* Author.

GoJ (The Government of Japan). (2015). *Cybersecurity Strategy (Provisional Translation).* Author.

GoM (The Government of Montenegro). (2013). *National Cyber Security Strategy.* Author.

IMCCS (Inter-Ministerial Committee for Cyber Security - the Republic of Trinidad & Tobago National). (2012). *Government of the Republic of Trinidad & Tobago National Cyber Security Strategy.* Author.

ISO/IEC (International Organization for Standardization/International Electrotechnical Commission). (2012). *ISO/IEC 27032:2012 Information technology — Security techniques — Guidelines for cybersecurity.* Geneva: ISO.

ISO/IEC (International Organization for Standardization/International Electrotechnical Commission). (2013). *ISO/IEC 27001:2013 - Information Security Management.* Geneva: ISO.

ITU (International Telecommunication Union). (2009). *Definition of cybersecurity.* ITU.

ITU (International Telecommunication Union). (2012). ITU National Cybersecurity Strategy Guide (F. Wamala, Ed.). Geneva: ITU.

Johnson, C. (2015). "French" cybernetics. *French Studies, 69*(1), 60–78. doi:10.1093/fs/knu229

Khatwani, S. (2017, November). Biggest Bitcoin Hacks Ever. *CoinSutra.*

Kuusisto, T., & Kuusisto, R. (2015). Cyber World as a Social System. In M. Lehto & P. Neittaanmäki (Eds.), *Cyber Security: Analytics* (pp. 31–44). Technology and Automation. doi:10.1007/978-3-319-18302-2_2

Lehto, M. (2013). The Cyberspace Threats and Cyber Security Objectives in the Cyber Security Strategies. *International Journal of Cyber Warfare & Terrorism, 3*(3), 1–18. doi:10.4018/ijcwt.2013070101

Lehto, M. (2015). Phenomena in the Cyber World. In M. Lehto & P. Neittaanmäki (Eds.), *Cyber Security: Analytics* (pp. 3–29). Technology and Automation. doi:10.1007/978-3-319-18302-2_1

Liddell, H. G., & Scott, R. (1940). *A Greek-English Lexicon.* Oxford: Clarendon Press.

Lucas, C. (2004). *Cybernetics and Stochastic Systems. The Complexity & Artificial Life Research Concept for Self-Organizing Systems.* http://www.calresco.org/lucas/systems.htm

Luiijf, E., Besseling, K., & de Graaf, P. (2013). Nineteen national cyber security strategies. International Journal of Critical, 2–31. doi:10.1504/IJCIS.2013.051608

Maathuis, C., Pieters, W., & Van Den Berg, J. (2017). Cyber weapons: A profiling framework. *2016 IEEE International Conference on Cyber Conflict*, CyCon U.S. 10.1109/CYCONUS.2016.7836621

MADISA (Ministry of Administration and Digitisation, Internal Security Agency - Republic of Poland). (2013). *Cyperspace Protection Policy of the Republic of Poland*. Warsaw, Poland: Author.

McCumber, J. R. (1991). Information System Security: A Comprehensive Model. *14th National Computer Security Conference*. Washington, DC: National Institute of Standards and Technology, National Computer Security Center.

MCIT (Ministry of Information and Communications Technology - India). (2013). *National Cyber Security Policy 2013 (NCSP-2013)* (No. 2(35)/2011-CERT-In). Author.

MED (Ministry of Economic Development - New Zealand). (2011). *New Zealand's Cyber Security Strategy*. Author.

Merriam-Webster. (2020). Cyber. In *Merriam-Webster.com dictionary*. Retrieved January 14, 2020, from https://www.merriam-webster.com/dictionary/cyber

Microsoft. (2013). Developing a National Strategy for Cybersecurity: Foundations for Security, Growth, and Innovation (C. F. Goodwin & J. P. Nicholas, Eds.). Redmon: Microsoft.

MICT (Ministry of Information and Communications Technology - Kingdom of Qatar). (2013). *National Cyber Security Strategy*. Author.

MICT (Ministry of Information Communications and Technology - Republic of Kenya). (2014). *Cybersecurity Strategy*. Author.

MOD (Ministry of Defence - Republic of Latvia). (2014). *Cyber Security Strategy of Latvia 2014 - 2018*. Riga, Latvia: Ministry of Defence - Republic of Latvia.

MPS. (2010). *Canada's Cyber Security Strategy*. Ottawa: Ministry of Public Safety.

National Cyber Security Framework Manual. (2012). The NATO Science for Peace and Security Programme.

NCKB (National Cyber Security Centre - The Czech Republic). (2015). *National Cyber Security Centre of The Czech Republic for the Periode from 2015 to 2020*. Czech: National Cyber Security Centre (NCKB) - The Czech Republic.

NIST (National Institute of Standards and Technology). (2014). Framework for Improving Critical Infrastructure Cybersecurity. In National Institute of S (Version 1). New York: National Institute of Standards and Technology.

OAS (Organization of American States). (2004). A Comprehensive Inter-American Cybersecurity Strategy: a Multidimensional and Multidisciplinary Approach to Creating a Culture of Cybersecurity. In Inter-Americaan Committee Against Terrorism (CICTE) (Ed.), AG/RES. 204 (XXXIV-O/04) on Adoption of Comprehensive Inter-American Strategy to Combat Threats to Cybersecurity: A Multidimensional and Multidisciplinary Approach to Creating a Culture of Cybersecurity. Montevideo, Uruguay: Organization of American States (OAS).

Ottis, R., & Lorents, P. (2010). Cyberspace: Definition and Implication. In *Proceeding of the 5th International Conference Information Warfare and Security*, (pp. 267–269). The Air Force Institute of Technology.

Oxford Dictionary. (2020). Cyber. In *OxfordEnglishDictionary.com*. Retrieved January 14, 2020, from https://www.lexico.com/definition/cyber

Pangaro, P. (2013). *Cybernetics - A Definition*. Accessed January 14, 2020, from https://www.pangaro.com/definition-cybernetics.html

Pangaro, P. (2017). Cybernetics as Phoenix: Why Ashes, What New Life. In L. C. Werner (Ed.), *Conversations. Cybernetics: State of the Art*. doi:10.1007/978-3-642-01310-2_2

PCM (Presidency of the Council of Ministers - Italian Republic). (2013). *The National Plan for Cyberspace Protection and ICT security*. Rome, Italy: Presidency of the Council of Ministers - Italian Republic.

Plato. (2014). *The First Alcibiades (B. Jowett, Trans.)*. Bloomsbury Academic.

PMO (Prime Minister's Office of Israel). (2011). *Advancing National Cyberspace Capabilities: Resolution No. 3611 of the Government of August 7, 2011*. Author.

Ramirez, R., & Choucri, N. (2016). Improving Interdisciplinary Communication With Standardized Cyber Security Terminology: A Literature Review. *IEEE Access: Practical Innovations, Open Solutions*, *4*, 2216–2243. doi:10.1109/ACCESS.2016.2544381

Raymond, D., Conti, G., Cross, T., & Fanelli, R. (2013). A Control Measure Framework to Limit Collateral Damage and Propagation of Cyber Weapons. *5th International Conference on Cyber Conflict (CyCon)*, 1–16.

Raymond, D., Cross, T., Conti, G., & Nowatkowski, M. (2014). Key terrain in cyberspace: Seeking the high ground. *International Conference on Cyber Conflict, CYCON*, 287–300. 10.1109/CYCON.2014.6916409

Republic of Turkey. (2013). *National Cyber Security Strategy and 2013-2014 Action Plan*. Author.

Solomon, D. (2007, August). Back From the Future: Questions for William Gibson. *The New York Times Magazine*.

The Republic of Croatia. (2015). *The National Cyber Security Strategy of the Republic of Croatia* (Vol. 2015). Zagreb: Republic of Croatia.

von Solms, R., & van Niekerk, J. (2013). From information security to cyber security. *Computers & Security*, *38*, 97–102. doi:10.1016/j.cose.2013.04.004

Wafa, Z. (2014). National Cyber Security Strategy of Afghanistan (NCSA) (2nd ed.). Kabul, Afghanistan: Ministry of Communications and IT - Islamic Republic of Afghanistan.

WEF. (2012a). *Partnering for Cyber Resilience: Risk and Responsibility in a Hyperconnected World - Principles and Guidelines*. Geneva, Switzerland: World Economic Forum (WEF).

WEF (World Economic Forum). (2012b). *Risk and Responsibility in a Hyperconnected World: Pathways to Global Cyber Resilience*. WEF.

WEF (World Economic Forum). (2014). Risk and responsibility in a hyperconnected world: Implications for enterprises. In J. Kaplan, A. Weinberg, & D. Chinn (Eds.), *World Economic Forum In collaboration with McKinsey & Company*. Geneva, Switzerland: WEF.

WEF (World Economic Forum). (2015). *Partnering for Cyber Resilience: Towards the Quantification of Cyber Threats*. Geneva: World Economic Forum (WEF).

Wiener, N. (1948). Cybernetics: Control and Communication in the Animal and the Machine (2nd ed.). Cambridge, MA: The MIT Press.

ENDNOTES

[1]   CIA Triad: Confidentiality, Integrity, and Availability (McCumber, 1991).

Chapter 2
Taxonomy of Cyber Threats to Application Security and Applicable Defenses

Winfred Yaokumah

https://orcid.org/0000-0001-7756-1832

University of Ghana, Ghana

Ferdinard Katsriku

University of Ghana, Ghana

Jamal-Deen Abdulai

University of Ghana, Ghana

Kwame Okwabi Asante-Offei

Ghana Institute of Management and Public Administration, Ghana

ABSTRACT

Application security measures are the controls within software systems that protect information assets from security attacks. Cyber attacks are largely carried out through software systems running on computing systems in cyberspace. To mitigate the risks of cyber attacks on software systems, identification of entities operating within cyberspace, threats to application security and vulnerabilities, and defense mechanisms are crucial. This chapter offers a taxonomy that identifies assets in cyberspace, classifies cyber threats into eight categories (buffer overflow, malicious software, input attacks, object reuse, mobile code, social engineering, back door, and logic bomb), provides security defenses, and maps security measures to control types and functionalities. Understanding application security threats and defenses will help IT security professionals in the choice of appropriate security countermeasures for setting up strong defense-in-depth mechanisms. Individuals can also apply these safeguards to protect themselves from cyber-attacks.

DOI: 10.4018/978-1-7998-3149-5.ch002

INTRODUCTION

Cyberspace represents the virtual environment that allows interaction of people, devices, software, networks, information, applications, critical information infrastructures, and services on the Internet using computing devices and telecommunication networks (ISO/IEC 27032, 2012). It is a complex environment of diverse entities and resources, comprising of stakeholders and their roles, cyberspace assets, threat agents and threats, vulnerabilities, and cybersecurity controls. Cyber threats are emerging risks posing a range of challenges to users of cyberspace (Marotta & McShane, 2018). Cybercriminals use cyberspace to launch attacks on information assets and critical information infrastructures. In 2018, it was estimated that cyberattacks cost the world economy some $45 billion (SecurityMagazine, 2019). The main medium by which cyber-attacks are carried out is via vulnerabilities in software applications and operating systems over communications networks. Thus, information technology (IT) security professionals are most concerned about threats to software systems, such as phishing and ransomware (Kerner, 2017). Though cyber-attacks may be detected, it often takes much time to recover from them (Kerner, 2017). According to a recent report, ransomware alone costs businesses more than $75 million per year (Oberly, 2019). It is suggested that cybersecurity threats will grow in importance, in particular, as the Internet-of-Things (IoT) becomes widespread (Rash, 2015).

With the aim of mitigating cyber-attacks, ISO/IEC 27032:2012 Guidelines for Cybersecurity provides guidance for reducing cyber risks. The standard describes cybersecurity practices and the roles of stakeholders in cyberspace, outlines guidelines for resolving common cybersecurity issues, and provide a framework for stakeholders to collaborate to resolve cybersecurity issues (ISO/IEC 27032, 2012). The standard identifies the following four major areas; a) information security, b) network security, c) Internet security, and d) critical information infrastructure protection (CIIP) (ISO/IEC 27032, 2012). According to Kerner (2017), though cybersecurity standards and practices have helped in the decline of network and client vulnerabilities, server vulnerabilities have increased by 34 percent. Apparently, organizations are losing the cyber-war due to overdependence on humans to protect computer systems (Needle, 2017). A recent studies and report note that human failure to comply with security policies (Yaokumah, Walker, Kumah, 2019), such as updating security patches, has led to the theft of 145.5 million credit cards and personal information (Anwar, 2019). Also, data breaches of 450 million records in 2018 and nearly 773 million passwords and email addresses were stolen in 2019 (Anwar, 2019).

Data breaches are carried out through software systems running on networks. Software systems security, often referred to as application security, is among the most important aspect of cyberspace security (McGraw, 2013). The International Information System Security Certification Consortium (ISC)[2] Common Body of Knowledge (CBK) defines the key areas of knowledge for application security as:

The controls that are included within systems and application software and the steps used in their development. Applications refer to agents, applets, software, databases, data warehouses, and knowledge-based systems. These applications may be used in distributed or centralized environments (Gregory, 2010, p.78).

Application security is one of the most important means of securing the cyberspace (McGraw, 2013). Threats to software systems can be malicious (such as distributed denial-of-service [DDoS] and injection attacks) or non-malicious (such as system crashes and Internet connection failures) (Refsdal et al., 2015). Malicious attacks are designed to steal information, deny access to, degrade, or destroy critical information systems (DHS, 2017). Therefore, software systems should be engineered so that they can continue to function correctly under malicious attacks (McGraw, 2013).

This chapter offers a taxonomy that provides better understanding of cybersecurity landscape with regards to application security by a) categorizing cybersecurity based on control types, b) identifying cyber threat agents and cyberspace assets, c) presenting threats to application security, d) providing application security defenses, and e) maps application security measures to security control types and functionalities. Since cybersecurity is largely in the domain of computer experts (Nye, 2013), understanding entities in the cyberspace, cyber threats and agents, vulnerabilities, attack types, and defenses will help IT security professionals in the choice of appropriate security countermeasures for deploying strong defense-in-depth mechanisms. It will also guide individuals in applying safe security practices in cyberspace.

BACKGROUND

Scope of Cyber Security Controls

A control is a technology, a process, or a policy designed and implemented as a response against the actual threats and attack vectors present in any given application, system or environment (Muckin & Scott, 2019). It is any potential mechanism that protects information assets from unauthorized access, which is intended to reduce the risk of cyber-attacks. Controls are often referred to as safeguards or countermeasures put in place to remove or mitigate the risk to information assets (Solomon & Chapple, 2005). Security controls include security policies, procedures, techniques, methods, solutions, plans, actions, or devices designed to help accomplish security goals (Walkowski, 2019). They are classified into three: Administrative, Technical, and Physical. Figure 1 shows the three types of cybersecurity controls. Understanding these controls is helpful when implementing defense-in-depth. Defense-in-depth requires a combination of various control types in a layered manner to protect information assets.

Administrative controls are referred to as management, operational, or soft controls. These controls are managerial in nature and focus primarily on protecting the organization from loss through the actions of its own employees (Wilson, 2017). Administrative controls consist of policies, standards, procedures, and guidelines that define leadership support for security and how employees are expected to behave; how organizational systems should be configured and used; and how the organization intends to respond to security incidents (Yau, 2014). Administrative controls span personnel recruitment strategies, background verification (Kumah, Yaokumah, Buabeng-Andoh, 2018), interview, rotation of jobs, mandatory vacations, separation of duties, data classification, risk analysis, and business impact analysis (McAlaney et al, 2018), and security awareness training for employees (Walkowski, 2019).

Technical controls (also known as logical controls) are the safeguards integrated into computer hardware, operations or application software, communication hardware and software, and other related devices (Tipton & Krause, 2007). Technical controls use software systems as a basis for controlling access and usage of sensitive data throughout a physical structure and over a network. Technical controls are logical in the sense that once a *control* is installed and configured, it automatically provides the required protection (Wilson, 2017). They include technologies such as encryption, antivirus software, smart cards, network authentication, firewalls, access control lists, file integrity auditing software, and intrusion detection systems.

Figure 1. Cyber Security Control Types

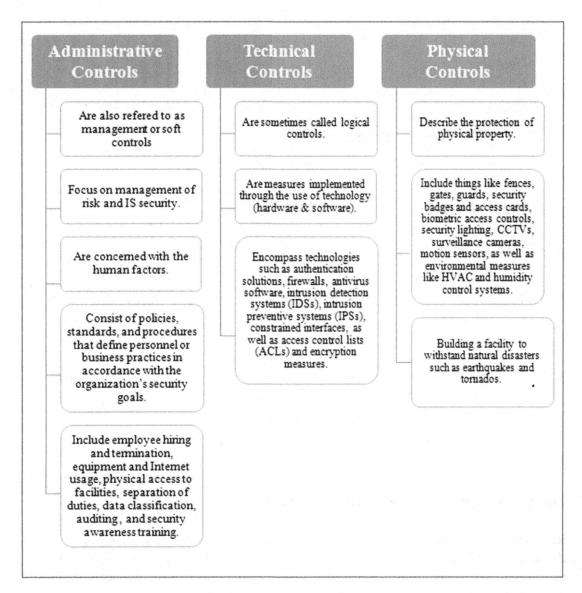

Physical controls are the protection of personnel, data, hardware, software, and other information assets from physical threats that could harm, damage, or disrupt business operations or impact the confidentiality, integrity, or availability of systems (LBMC, 2020). Such controls include fencing, gates, video surveillance, closed-circuit television (CCTV), motion detection systems, biometric access controls, security guards and dogs, as well as environmental measures like air filtration, humidity control systems, and fire suppression systems. The design of a facility itself, as to whether it is built to withstand natural disasters like earthquakes and tornados, is also considered under physical control (Wilson, 2017).

Figure 2. Cyber Agents and Assets

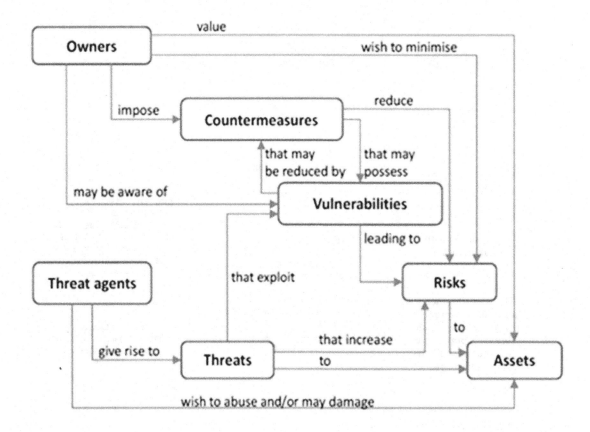

Cyberspace Agents and Cyberspace Assets

Figure 2 presents cyberspace assets and the agents (entities) that interact with the assets. ENISA Threat Landscape (2013) classifies cyber agents as *friendly* or *hostile*. The friendly agents (such as researchers, security agents, and law enforcement agents) use cyberspace without any ulterior motives, while hostile agents (such as cyber terrorists and cyber criminals) have malicious intents. Intention of the cyber agent distinguishes between friendly and hostile agent. For example, both cybercriminals and intelligence agencies of nations may exploit software vulnerabilities (Kumar & Kumar, 2014), but intelligence agencies may do so with the intent to find ways to mitigate software vulnerabilities. For cybercriminals, the motive may be for fraudulent financial gain, intellectual property theft, espionage, and for terrorism (Warikoo, 2014). In particularly, cybercriminals often target vulnerabilities in software systems (PandaLabs, 2012) to perpetuate nefarious activities.

Interrelationship among Threats, Vulnerabilities and Countermeasures in Cyberspace

The cyberspace consists of assets (servers, communication networks, data, software systems); asset owners (individuals, organizations, service providers, governments); threats agents (cybercriminals, hackers, state agencies); vulnerabilities (weaknesses in cyber assets); exposure of the assets to risk (the chance that the threats agents may exploit the vulnerabilities in the assets and its impact on the asset owners), and the countermeasures (controls or safeguards put in place to mitigate the impact of the threat). Figure 3, adopted from ISO 15408:2005, illustrates the interaction of various entities in the cyberspace (ISO 15408, 2005). As can be observed in figure, the threat agents deploy threats and attempt to exploit vulnerabilities in the asset so as to harm or take over the asset (ENISA Threats Landscape, 2013). The asset owner implements security measures to protect or safeguard the asset in order to reduce or eliminate the negative effects of the threat (ENISA Threats Landscape, 2013). The probability that the threat would actually exploit the vulnerability in the asset and the impact that it makes on the asset owner is the risk.

Figure 3. Entities in Cyberspace and their Relationships
Source: ISO 15408:2005

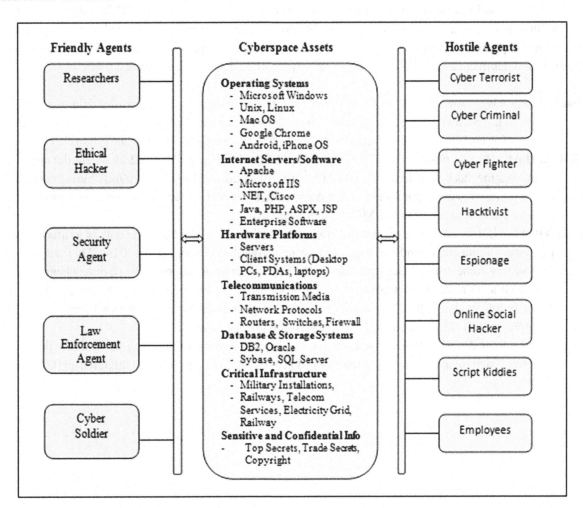

TAXONOMY OF APPLICATION SECURITY THREATS

Vulnerabilities in software systems are among the major sources of risk to cybersecurity. Kumar and Kumar (2014) observe that configuration errors and vulnerabilities in most popular software enable malicious users to disrupt systems and the integrity of sensitive information over the Internet. This section presents a taxonomy of threats to application security and the following section provides applicable countermeasures. Through an in-depth review of both scholarly and practitioner literature, Figure 4 shows a taxonomy of threats to application security. Though the list may not be exhaustive, the threats identified are classified as: Buffer overflow, malicious software, input attacks, object reuse, mobile code, social engineering, back door, and logic bomb.

Buffer Overflow

Software applications usually function by accepting input from the user (or from another other applications) through an interface. An attacker can disrupt the function of a software application by providing more data to the application than it was designed to handle. A buffer overflow (or buffer overrun) occurs when the amount of data entered into the buffer is more than it was designed to handle. As a result, the extra information gets overflowed and overwrites other memory locations (Maheshwari, 2018). Depending upon the hardware and software architecture of the program, this can lead to an unexpected change in the program's behaviour. A buffer overflow exploitation allows an attacker to take control of the system (Chaim et al., 2019). There are several types of buffer overflow attacks:

Stack Buffer Overflow. The buffer overflow occurs when a program, while writing data to a buffer, overruns the buffer's boundary and overwrites adjacent memory locations (Nicula & Zota, 2019). This causes corruption of other data in the stack, which results in the program's malfunction.

NOP Sled Attack. The no-operation (NOP) sled attack is a specific stack overflow where the attacker overflows the stack with harmless NOP (no-op) instructions (Gregory, 2010). A buffer overflow attack is crafted using a combination of a no-operation instruction sled, an executable payload, and a return address pointing to the NOP sled or payload.

Heap Overflow. It happens when a chunk of memory is allocated to the heap and data is written to this memory without any bound checking being done on the data (Huang et al., 2019). This can lead to overwriting some critical data structures in the heap (such as the heap headers), or any heap-based data such as dynamic object pointers, which in turn can lead to overwriting the virtual function table (Huang et al., 2019). The exploit of heap overflow vulnerabilities may lead to hijacking of a program control flow and arbitrary code execution (Huang et al., 2019).

Jump-to-Register Attack. In this attack, the return pointer is overwritten with a value that will cause the program to jump to a known pointer stored in a register that points to the input buffer (Gregory, 2010).

Figure 4. Taxonomy of Application Security Threats

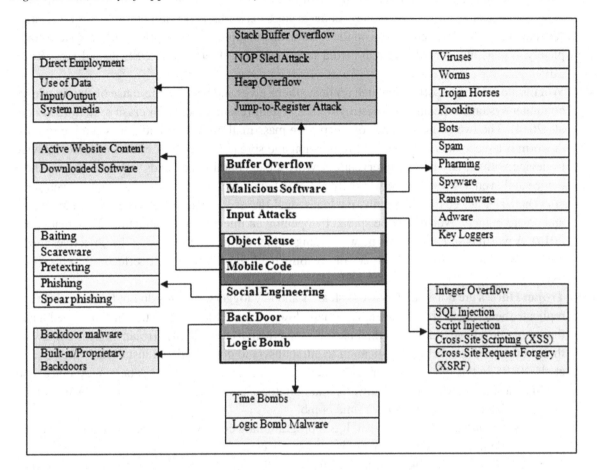

Malicious Software

Malware is a malicious software that is programmed with an intention to do harm (Shahriar et al., 2018). Malware may include software that gathers user information without permission. It is a malicious code that propagates over the network (Okereke & Chukwunonso, 2018). Malware can be written to disrupt normal functioning, bypass access controls, gather sensitive information, display unwanted advertising, or get control of the device without user's knowledge (Qamar et al., 2019). Malware can be classified according to its functions and purposes. It can be divided into four categories according to the types of behaviour – propagation, infection, persistence and payload (Kara, 2019). There are different types of malware, including the following:

- **Viruses** are computer code fragments that attach themselves to a legitimate program file on a computer. The virus can only run when a legitimate program is run (Mirza et al., 2014). There are several types of viruses, including master boot record (MBR) viruses, file infector viruses, and macro viruses. Viruses propagate in the system with the help of documents, script files, and from vulnerabilities in web applications. In some cases, viruses depend on human activities to launch themselves by opening any infected file or through running a program. Viruses cause different types of attacks such as steal money, damage host networks and computers, control activities (Qamar et al., 2019), deleting files on the system, and stopping the operations of the system completely. It generally spreads through media such as CD/DVD, email and USB flash drives (Kara, 2019).

- **Worms** are malicious software which replicate themselves and become the cause of slowing down computer systems especially by destroying the system resources or even crash system (Mirza et al., 2014). The two common types of worms are mass mailing worms and port scanning worms. A worm is a piece of code capable of replication and spread over computer networks from device to device without any human intervention. Worms can contain "payloads" that damage the host device and even destroy host networks by utilizing bandwidth and create congestion on web servers (Qamar et al., 2019). Generally, payloads steal the user's data, delete files from the system and create botnets. Worms can be spread by opening an infected email attachment (Qamar et al., 2019). A worm is spread over the network using vulnerabilities in the system. Its objectives might include consuming network resources or creating a denial of service by overloading web servers (Kara, 2019).

- **Trojan Horses** are normally password stealers and key loggers. Trojans do not have the ability to replicate themselves. Trojan travels via email, downloadable files or data transmission media and they generate a huge traffic until the link is crashed (Mirza et al., 2014). Trojan horse is a malware that shows itself as a benign application to attract users to download and install malware (Qamar et al., 2019). In this type of malware, attackers gain remote access to steal data, money, delete and modify files, create variants of malware, and monitor user activities and their logs (Qamar et al., 2019). Trojan can be logic bomb or time bomb.
  ○ *Logic Bomb* is a kind of Trojan. It is a programming code, which is very dangerous and can explode important data e.g. letter bomb (Mirza et al., 2014).
  ○ *Time Bomb* works like a timer and triggers off when the time strikes on a particular date (Mirza et al., 2014).

- **Rootkits** are hidden computer programs designed to provide continued privileged access to a computer while actively hiding its presence. This is designed to enable remote access of the system without being noticed by the user. The main aim of a rootkit is to change system software so as to obscure the presence of both, itself and also of an accompanying virus (Messier, 2016). Also, rootkits can obtain and maintain root level access on a system. If a rootkit runs successfully, it can perform many operations in the system, for example uploading files, installing programs, modifying system files or disabling programs such as anti-virus (Kara, 2019). It can gain administrative access to install different malicious activities such as steal information, disturb normal routine of the system, apply changes in the system, and alter system configuration. Once the rootkit is installed in the computer, it runs on every bootup. Due to the secret operations of the rootkit, it is difficult to identify and remove from the system (Qamar et al., 2019). Rootkit uses obfuscation to hide their presence and can remain in the system for a long duration (Qamar et al., 2019).

- **Bots** (short for robots). Bot malware is typically used to exploit the computing power of the system in large-scale attacks (Kara, 2019). It is evolving to become a severe security threat because botnets can launch distributed denial of service (DDoS) attacks (Qamar et al., 2019). Bots are also referred to as spiders, crawlers, and web bots. While they may be utilized to perform repetitive jobs, such as indexing a search engine, they frequently come in the form of malware. Malware bots are used to gain total control over a computer (Okutan & Çebi, 2019) and are difficulty to detect (Larson, 2016).

- **Spam** is a major tool for criminals to conduct illegal activities on the Internet, such as stealing sensitive information, selling counterfeit goods, and distributing malware (Dinh et al., 2015). Spam is the abusive use of email and messaging technologies to flood users with unsolicited messages. It is time-consuming and costly for spam recipients and service providers in terms of network bandwidth and storage (ENISA Threat Landscape, 2013). One way cybercriminals exploit the vulnerabilities of new technologies and potential victims is the use of deceptive emails on a massive scale (Alazab & Broadhurst, 2017).

- **Pharming** is an internet swindling practice in which malicious code is installed on users computers or server misdirecting users to fraudulent website without their knowledge or consent (Alfayoumi & Barhoom, 2015). Pharming attacks can be performed at the client-side or via the internet.

- **Spyware** is very dangerous as it collects data from any specific location. It travels on the internet via emails, software or come with legitimate applications. It is also called tracking software and once it is installed on the system, it is hard to stop (Mirza et al., 2014). It is designed to collect information without the users knowledge and without being noticed (Mirza et al., 2014). If the system is infected, it records the user's keystrokes, file operations and important information such as usernames, passwords and credit cards saved in the Internet browser (Kara, 2019). Spyware creates interference in network settings by changing its security operations.

- **Adware** is software that automatically generates advertisements. Though it is not defined as malicious software in itself, it can be transformed into a relatively more damaging type of software for stealing user information and capturing movements in the system when used together with a type of spyware (Kara, 2019).

- **Ransomware** is the fastest-growing type of cyber threat faced by businesses in recent years. Ransomware activities increased by 82% in 2016 (Oberly, 2019). A type of malware that would not release computer resources until the victim pays some money as ransom. After payment, ransomware malware releases the system (Qamar et al., 2019). Ransomware self-proliferates and encrypts data inside its environment.

- **Key Loggers** record what users type on the keyboard so as to gather users' log-in details and other information and send it to the key-logging program (Okutan & Çebi, 2019). Key-loggers are typically used by various organizations to obtain information relating to computer usage (Qamar et al., 2019). They are also known as keystroke loggers. Key loggers will record every keystroke or those made in specific application (Okutan & Çebi, 2019).

Input Attacks

Applications often request input from users. Input validation attacks refer to those inputs that bypass validation procedures in order to exploit web application vulnerabilities. The strategy of such attacks is to send a specially crafted request exploiting vulnerabilities in web servers or client applications. Input attacks are sometimes called malformed input attacks or injection attacks. They are designed to exploit weaknesses in the application by causing unexpected behaviour. Several types of input attacks can be launched against an application, including:

- **Buffer Overflow** is currently one of the most hostile vulnerability in information storage and processing (Chatole, 2018). The characteristics that make buffer overflows so threatening is that it runs inside the target program with all its privileges.
- **Structured Query Language (SQL) Injection** technique is the exploitation of vulnerabilities in a database that does not perform filtering properly and allows database commands to be injected and executed, leading to leakage of information (Chiew et al., 2018). This is done through injection of SQL commands into an SQL statement or query through a webpage input to alter the original intent of the statement (Patil & Patil, 2015). The injected code is concatenated with the SQL commands through the user-input variables and this dynamic SQL command is then executed. This attack gives the attacker control over the database. This happens because of a bug in the software that allows attacker input to be treated as code to execute rather than data to store (Zabicki & Ellis, 2017)
- **Script Injection** is similar to SQL injection. An attacker inserts script language into an input field in the hopes that the scripting language will be executed (Gregory, 2010).
- **Cross-Site Scripting (XSS)** is an attack which occurs when a web application gathers malicious data from a user. The data is usually gathered in the form of a hyperlink which contains malicious content within it. Malicious injection of the code within vulnerable web applications will trick users and redirect them to untrusted websites (Ayeni et al., 2018). XSS may occur even when the servers and database engine contain no vulnerability themselves, and it is one of the most predominant web application exposures today.
- **Cross-Site Request Forgery (XSRF)** is an attack where malicious HTML is inserted into a web page or e-mail that, when clicked, causes an action to occur on an unrelated site where the user may have an active session (Gregory, 2010).

Object Reuse

Many system resources are shared in multiprocessing systems, including memory, databases, file systems, and paging space (Gregory, 2010). When one process utilizes a resource, the process may write some information to the resource temporarily. Operating systems (OS) generally zero out or overwrite memory used by a previous process before allocating it to another process (Gregory, 2010). But a flaw in the design of an OS may make it possible for a process to discover the residual data left by a process that previously occupied a particular part of memory. This flaw is known as object reuse. There are two aspects of application object reuse: the direct employment of the object or the use of data input/output from the object (Tipton & Henry, 2007). In the case of object use, it is necessary for the system providing the object to verify the requesting entity. In the event of object data use, if not all cases, the system should clear all residual data prior to assigning the object to another process, ensuring that no process intentionally or unintentionally inherits or reads the data of another process (Tipton & Henry, 2007).

Many systems allow several processes to execute in memory simultaneously. Sections of memory may be allocated to one process for a while, then deallocated, then reallocated to another process. The constant reallocation of memory is a potential security vulnerability, because residual information may remain when a section of memory is reassigned to a new process after a previous process is completed (Tipton & Henry, 2007). Object reuse is also applicable to system media, such as hard drives, magnetic media, or other forms of data storage. The success of code-reuse attacks depends on the availability of useful gadgets on the target platform and the complexity of the code the attacker wants to run (Follner & Bodden, 2016). In practice, however, most systems are vulnerable to such code-reuse attacks.

Mobile Code

Also known as executable code, active content, and downloadable content, mobile code is any software program designed to move from computer to computer and network to network, in order to intentionally modify computer systems without the consent of the owner or operator (Grimes, 2001). Examples of mobile code include active website content and downloaded software. It is software that is transmitted across a network from a remote source to a local system and is then executed on that local system, often without explicit action on the part of the user. The local system is often a personal computer, but can also be a smart device – PDA, mobile phone, and Internet appliance. Mobile code differs from traditional software in that it needs not be installed or executed explicitly by the user (Gregory, 2010). Examples of mobile code include:

- **Active website content**. This includes ActiveX, Java, JavaScript, Flash, and Shockwave. This content originates on a Web server and executes on a user's workstation (Gregory, 2010). Depending on the technology associated with the downloaded content, this mobile code may have restricted access to the end user's system or may have full control over it.
- **Downloaded software**. This includes software of every kind from legitimate sites (Gregory, 2010). Some of this software may be genuinely harmless, but others can be Trojan horse programs and worse.

Mobile code, if left unchecked, can be used to track user activity, access vital information, or be leveraged to install other applications without alerting the user (Tipton & Henry, 2007). The issue worsens if the user is remotely accessing corporate resources. Data can be copied to the local system, which may be exposed to unwanted threats, access credentials may be captured and later used by an attacker, or the communication can be used to inject malicious software into the organization (Tipton & Henry, 2007). Mobile code can range from a system nuisance, such as Web sites tracking Internet activity, to highly problematic situations, such as spyware that can be used in identity theft (Tipton & Henry, 2007).

Social Engineering

Social engineering is the term used to describe a broad range of malicious activities accomplished through human interactions. It uses psychological manipulation to trick users into making security mistakes or giving away sensitive information (Okutan & Çebi, 2019). The focus of social engineering is to divert the victim from making rational choices, which leads the victim to make emotional choices instead (Goel et al., 2017). Examples of such emotions are fear, greed, curiosity, anger, friendship, patriotism, vanity, altruism, community belonging, sense of duty, and authority.

Social engineering attacks come in many different forms and can be performed anywhere human interaction is involved. The following are the five most common forms of digital social engineering assaults:

- **Baiting**. As its name implies, baiting attacks use a false promise to temper a victim's greed or curiosity. The most reviled form of baiting uses physical media to disperse malware. For example, attackers leave the bait – typically malware-infected flash drives at inconspicuous areas where potential victims are certain to see them (e.g., bathrooms, elevators, the parking lot of a targeted company). Victims pick up the bait out of curiosity and insert it into the computer, resulting in automatic malware installation on the system (Alsmadi & Alsmadi, 2019). Baiting scams do not necessarily have to be carried out in the physical world.

- **Scareware**. Scareware is a form of malicious software that uses social engineering to cause shock, anxiety, or the perception of a threat in order to manipulate users into buying unwanted software (Ayala, 2016). Scareware is also referred to as deception software, rogue scanner software and fraud ware. A common scareware example is the legitimate-looking pop-up banners appearing in browsers while surfing the web, displaying such text as, "Your computer may be infected with harmful spyware programs." Scareware is also distributed via other tactics such as sending out spam mail, and once the email is opened, victims are then fooled into buying worthless services (Alsmadi & Alsmadi, 2019).

- **Pretexting**. Here an attacker focuses on creating a good pretext, or a fabricated scenario, that the attacker uses to try and steal the victims' personal information. The scammer pretends to need sensitive information from a victim so as to perform a critical task (Bisson, 2019). The attacker usually starts by establishing trust with their victim by impersonating co-workers, police, bank and tax officials, or other persons who have right-to-know authority (Bisson, 2019). The *pretexter* asks questions that are seemingly required to confirm the victim's identity, through which they gather important personal data. All sorts of pertinent information and records are gathered using this scam, such as social security numbers, personal addresses, phone numbers, phone records, staff vacation dates, and bank records (Alsmadi & Alsmadi, 2019).

- **Phishing**. A phishing process can be divided into five steps: reconnaissance, weaponization, distribution, exploitation, and exfiltration (Das et al., 2019). It starts with the attacker, disguised as a legitimate entity (reconnaissance). The attacker hosts a website similar to the target (weaponization) and sends an attack vector (usually an email) to the victim (distribution). The attacker may also spread such links using social networking sites and instant messaging applications. The attackers use innovative methods to exploit the weakness of humans to make them think the fraudulent websites are legitimate (exploitation). In the last step, the attacker collects the sensitive information exposed by victims (exfiltration) (Das et al., 2019). Thus, phishing at its most basic is taking advantage of human weaknesses to gather information (Faircloth, 2017). That information could be in the form of usernames and passwords for a system or even something as simple as finding out more about a target company's organization structure for future penetration testing.

- **Spear phishing (whaling)** is a targeted attack against an individual, a group or an organization (Alsmadi & Alsmadi, 2019). Spear phishing has become the popular choice by phishers over the conventional phishing using mass and random email phishing (Chiew et al., 2018). This is because of the high success rate compared to the conventional ones. Spear phishing uses specially crafted email mimicking a sender whom the victim knows. The content of the email is relevant to the victim, which will not trigger any suspicion from the victim. The effectiveness of spear phishing is high because internet users will normally trust email or eFax from the website of a presumed organisation that they used before or have an account with (Chiew et al., 2018).

Back Doors

This is a type of malware that is intended to set grounds for other malware by opening a backdoor onto a device. It works as a helper to other malicious activities by providing them a network connection to enter and snip information (Qamar et al., 2019). The backdoor attack is the method of gaining trust of the victim's device through the pairing mechanism. It ensures that the attacker's device does not appear on the victims list of paired devices (Shahriar et al., 2018). In this way, the attacker can monitor the activities of the victim's device. The attacker can retrieve data from the victim's device and access services such as modems, Internet, Wireless Application Protocol (WAP) and General Packet Radio Service (GPRS) gateways without the concern of the victim (Shahriar et al., 2018).

Based on vulnerabilities, backdoors are classified into three types (Jyotiyana & Mishra, 2016):

Type-1: Tempering the source code by inserting malicious code to bypass programming logic (Authentication).

Type-2: Code insertion (as data) using buffer overflow. It may attack the stack section like in Stack smashing attack and Return oriented programming exploitation.

Type-3: Backdoor which attacks the data section - system events and internal states of authentication process, and the global variables that exist in data section. Example of such attack is return-to-got attack.

Logic Bombs (Time Bombs)

They are instructions deliberately placed in application code that perform some hostile action when a predetermined condition is met (Gregory, 2010). Typically, a logic bomb consists of code that performs some damaging action on a date in the distant future. A logic bomb works through a code that is inserted into existing software on a network or in a computer where it will lie dormant until a *trigger* occurs such as a date or time or other commands from the computer programmer (SpamLaws, 2019). When the bomb finally releases, the code can delete files, send confidential information to unauthorized parties, wipe out databases, and disable a network for a period of days. Triggers can be categorized as positive or negative. Logic bombs with positive triggers happen after a condition is met, such as the date of a major company event (Green, 2019). Negative triggers initiate a logic bomb when a condition is not met, such as an employee fails to enter the diffuse code by a certain time (Green, 2019). Either way, when the conditions become true, the logic bomb will go off and inflict its programmed damage.

Examples of logic bomb attacks include the following:

- Hackers might hide logic bombs in computer viruses, worms, and Trojan horses. Logic bomb viruses can hide arbitrary code that gives remote access to devices. The moment the user opens the malicious software the attackers will gain access and will be able to cause as much damage as they wish (Green, 2019).
- Some logic bombs can be designed to take effect on a specific date or a specific event. For example, Christmas, New Year, or Independence Day. Time bombs are a type of logic bomb that will continuously poll the system date in a dormant state until the author's predetermine appointment is reached. At this point, the program will activate and execute its code. These methods are also used commonly by valid software vendors to provide trial periods for evaluation (Anderson &

Anderson, 2010). An example of this would be an application that authorizes only 10 initializations before the program ceases to function.

- Programmers and malicious employees might plant a logic bomb in their company's system. This could have various effects. It could be set off the moment the employee is taken off a payroll (Green, 2019).
- Hackers could use a combination of spyware and logic bombs to steal personal information. For example, a logic bomb could secretly be waiting to be launched at a specific website, like an online banking site (Green, 2019). Once the user logs in, it would trigger a key logger. Now everything the user types in, including login details and passwords, will be sent straight to the hacker.

APPLICATION SECURITY DEFENSES

Figure 5 presents application security defences (countermeasures). The application security threats and the corresponding defenses are discussed in the following section.

Buffer Overflow Countermeasure

Due to multiple protection mechanisms enforced by the operating system, buffer overflow has become harder to exploit. Multiple bypass techniques are often required in order to successfully exploit the vulnerability and control the execution flow of the executable codes (Nicula & Zota, 2019). One of the security features designed as protection mechanisms is Data Execution Prevention (DEP). DEP can help prevent code execution from the stack, heap or memory pool pages by marking all memory locations in a process as non-executable unless the location explicitly contains executable code (Nicula & Zota, 2019). Another protection mechanism is the Address Space Layout Randomization (ASLR), which is often used in conjunction with DEP. This security feature randomizes the location where the system executables are loaded into memory. By default, modern day operating systems have these security features implemented (Nicula & Zota, 2019). Some mechanisms prevent overflows from occurring, while others react once overflows happen (Leon & Bruda, 2016). Thus measures to defend buffer overflow include choice a safe programming language, use of safe libraries, executable space protection, stack smashing protection, deep packet inspection, address space layout randomization, deep packet inspection, and executable space protection (Chatole, 2018).

Malware Countermeasures

Several measures are needed to block the ability of malware entering and running on a computer system. These countermeasures include anti-virus, anti-rootkits, anti-spyware, anti-spam, firewalls, decreased privilege levels, penetration testing, and hardening (Borky & Bradley, 2019). Anti-virus is a detection of malicious software by its signature and behaviour (Okutan & Çebi, 2019). Despite the use of anti-virus solutions, complicated anti-detection techniques allowed adversaries to bypass defense mechanisms. This fact points out to a need for improvements in malware detection. Anti-virus programs are found in many places in an organization as part of a defense-in-depth to prevent the unwanted consequences of malware (Campbell, 2016). Such places include end-user workstations, e-mail servers, file servers, web proxy servers and security.

Anti-rootkit software uses techniques to find hidden processes, hidden registry entries, unexpected kernel hooks, and hidden files in order to find rootkits that may be present on a system. Anti-rootkit software programs use various means to find these hidden objects in a system, generally through the use of directly examining the running operating system instead of using tools that the rootkit may have been able to manipulate (Gregory, 2010). Anti-spyware blocks spyware and adware in similar manner as anti-virus software. Anti-spyware monitors incoming files and examines them against a collection of signatures, and blocks those files that match known signatures (Okutan & Çebi, 2019). Like anti-virus software, anti-spyware can scan a hard drive to identify spyware, adware, and other unwanted programs, and remove them. Also, a firewall as a network security device can monitor incoming and outgoing network traffic and decide whether to allow or block specific traffic based on a defined set of security rules (Okutan & Çebi, 2019). For penetration testing, rather than simply relying upon security configuration settings, an organization should also test the settings by using tools to simulate a hacker's attempt to find weaknesses in a system. looks for security flaws to exploit. A typical penetration test would look for vulnerabilities that could lead to major security problems such as the ability to impersonate users, steal passwords, or delete all data in the system (Zabicki & Ellis, 2017).

Figure 5. Application Security Defenses

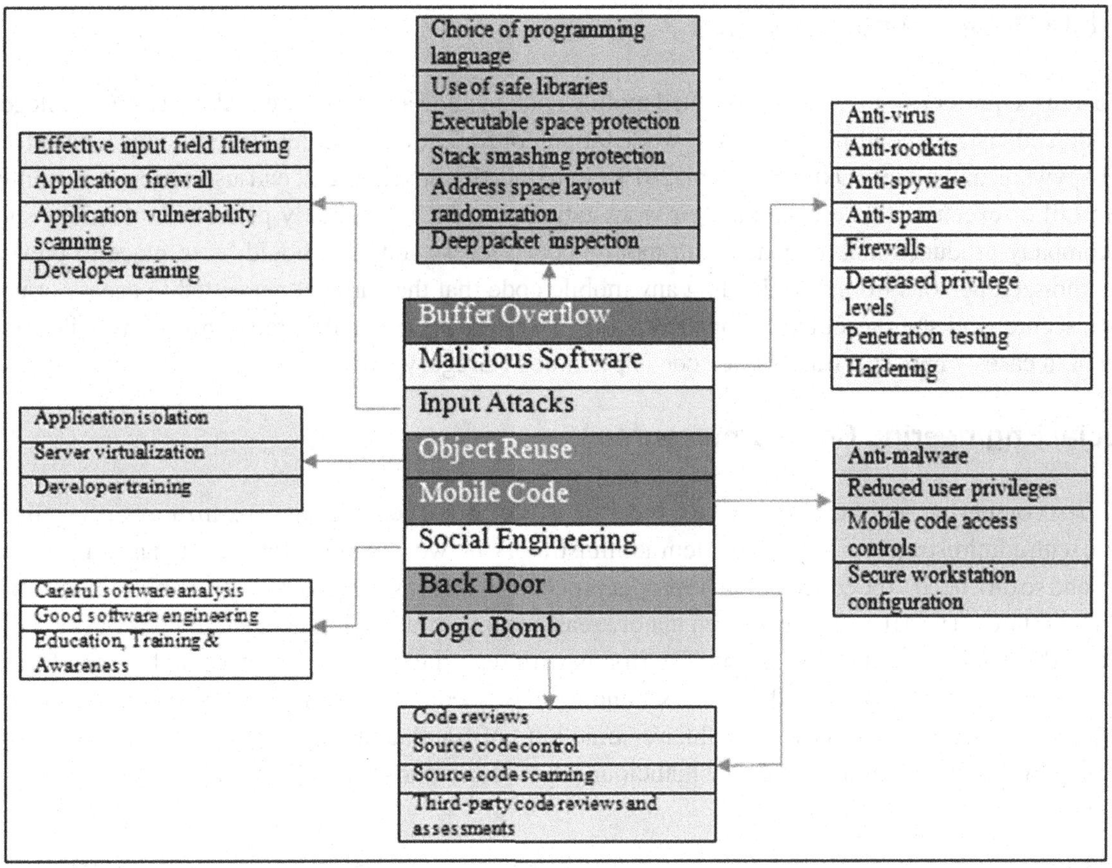

Input Attack Countermeasures

Measures that can be used to prevent input attacks include effective input field filtering, application firewall, application vulnerability scanning, and developer training. With effective input field filtering, input fields should be filtered to remove all characters that might be a part of an input injection (Gregory, 2010). Application firewall examines the contents of packets and blocks packets containing input attack code and other unwanted data. Application vulnerability scanning scans applications for input attack vulnerabilities in order to identify vulnerabilities. Importantly, developer training offers software developers training in secure application development techniques.

Object Reuse Countermeasures

Several measures should be taken to prevent object reuse vulnerabilities. Among these measures include application isolation, server virtualization, and developer training. Application isolation isolates to individual systems. Thus, applications are less likely to encounter residual information left by other applications. Server virtualization technology makes it more cost-effective to isolate applications by running them on virtual machines. Software developers can be trained to write secure software that does not leave residual code that can be used by other processes (Gregory, 2010).

Mobile Code Countermeasures

Measures to protect systems from unwanted mobile code include anti-malware, reduced user privileges, mobile code access controls, and secure workstation configuration. Anti-malware includes anti-virus, anti-spyware, and others (Okutan & Çebi, 2019). In reduced user privileges, end-users are not permitted to install or execute mobile code on their workstations, except in explicitly permitted situations such as company-produced mobile code. With mobile code, access controls should be in place to prevent unauthorized persons from downloading any mobile code that they are not permitted to access or use. Also, secure workstation configuration detects that workstations are configured to restrict mobile code, except in cases where specific mobile code is permitted (Gregory, 2010).

Social Engineering Countermeasures

The best countermeasure against social engineering is education. People in the organization, particularly those with administrative privileges (system administrators, network administrators, database administrators, and so on), need to be educated on the proper procedures for providing company sensitive information to others (Gregory, 2010). There are two major areas, where social engineering should be considered in system development and management. The first is with regard to the user interface and human factors engineering (Tipton & Henry, 2007). The second issue of social engineering is with regard to its use in malicious software. Most malware will have some kind of fraudulent component, in an attempt to get the user to run the program, so that the malicious payload can perform undetected.

Back Door Countermeasures

Back doors can be difficult to find. Routine functional testing and quality assurance testing may not reveal back doors. Instead, other means are required to find them, including code reviews, source code control, source code scanning, and third-party code reviews and assessments. Code reviews require that when one developer makes changes to a software application, one or more other developers should examine the software to identify and approve of all changes. Source code control is a formal source code management system that identifies and records all changes made to the code. Source code scanning are tools used to scan static source code for security vulnerabilities. Third-party code reviews and assessments entail that outside personnel should be contracted to examine static and running code in order to identify any vulnerabilities and undesired features such as back doors.

Logic Bomb Countermeasures

The countermeasures for logic bombs are the same as for back doors: Code reviews, source code control, source code scanning, and third-party assessments (Harris, 2013).

MAPPING THREATS TO CONTROL FUNCTIONALITIES AND TYPES

As discussed earlier, the three different types of security controls are administrative, technical and physical. It is imperative to classify control types according to their functionality. Control functionality examines the rationality for implementing a control. The functional use of a specific control type is the purpose or reason for choosing and implementing that control. The major rational behind a choice of security controls include *preventive, detective, corrective, deterrent, and recovery.* A better understanding of the various control functionalities affords us in making informed decisions about what controls will be best used in specific situations and in the implementation of defines-in-depth. Table 1 maps the application security defenses discussed in the previous section to their respective control types and functionalities.

- **Preventive.** This is intended to stop an incident from occurring. It is designed to be implemented prior to a threat event and reduce and/or avoid the likelihood and potential impact of a successful threat event (Virtue & Rainey, 2015). These measures are usually preferred over detective ones since they are designed to prevent unwanted events from occurring in the first place. A prevented event is far easier to deal with than a detected event. In a strict sense, a preventive control may absolutely prevent unwanted activity, or it may make the activity much more difficult to perform. Examples include malware protection and buffer overflow measures (see Table 1)
- **Detective.** This is designed to detect a threat event that is in progress and provide assistance during investigations and audits after the event has occurred (Virtue & Rainey, 2015). In Table 1 examples of application security that fall under detective control are application scanning and source code reviews.
- **Corrective.** This is designed to mitigate or limit the potential impact of a threat event once it has occurred and fixes components or systems after an incident has occurred (Harris, 2013). Generally, corrective measures are undertaken in order to prevent the recurrence of an unwanted event. Examples of technical corrective controls include patching a system, quarantining a vi-

rus, terminating a process, or rebooting a system. Putting an incident response plan into action and implementing a business continuity plan are examples of administrative corrective control (Walkowski, 2019). A corrective measure includes antivirus.

- **Deterrent.** This is designed to be highly visible and give persons the impression that any unauthorized activities will be stopped and/or apprehended. They are implemented to discourage intruders from attempting to trespass, steal, destroy, or cause any other unwanted event (Gregory, 2010). Examples of physical deterrent measures include the use of razor wires, lighting, guards and dogs, and the use of visible surveillance cameras and monitors. Controls that are labelled as a deterrent are usually also preventive or detective. A typical example of a deterrent control would be a sign that warns of guard dogs when no guard dogs actually exist.

- **Recovery.** This is intended to bring the environment back to regular operations (Harris, 2013). Like corrective controls, recovery controls take place after an incident has occurred. Recovery controls are activities that enable the restoration to normal operations after some event. It is designed to complement the work of corrective measures. Having an offsite facility is a physical recovery control. An example of an administrative recovery control is the restoration of system files after a virus infection that corrupted critical system data.

DISCUSSION AND RECOMMENDATIONS

Application security is very important for preventing financial loss, protecting organizations and individuals, defending critical information infrastructures, and limiting successful cyber-attacks. This chapter identified categories of cyber threats in software systems as well as the applicable defenses. It provided a taxonomy that divided cyber threats in software systems into eight: Buffer overflow, malicious software, input attacks, object reuse, mobile code, social engineering, back door, and logic bomb. Of great importance is the prevalence of malicious software. Malware threats continue to grow, multiply and evolve (Lemos, 2016). Though anti-virus, anti-spam, and anti-phishing are available, seemingly their effects have not reduced cyber attacks considerably. In particular, ransomware continues to escalate (Oberly, 2019) and the best way to deal with this is through regular backups (Oberly, 2019).

Deployment of artificial intelligence and machine learning techniques (Rash, 2019) can help detect novel malicious intrusions in software systems. They can harden the security of a platform to protect them from cybersecurity threats from hackers (Hernandez, 2017). Automatic and manual software code review can unravel flaws in software which can then be corrected. Building security into software systems at the design stage (McGraw, 2013) is important. Moreover, knowing the intent of the attackers may not be ascertained easily, therefore deploying defense-in-depth mechanisms should be based not only on control types alone (administration, technical, and physical) but also on control functionalities (preventive, detective, corrective, deterrent, recovery). Thus, to protect an information asset, the countermeasures employed for the defense-in-depth should combine several control functionalities. Therefore, protection against cybersecurity threats contains not only prevention but also recovery (Kerner, 2018). This means that if a control to deter the attacker fails, the control to prevent the attacks may succeed. According to Zilber (2018), cyber offensive and defensive operations should be performed to mitigate the threat of cyber-attacks, espionage, and sabotage.

Table 1. Mapping Threats to Control Functionalities and Control Types

Threat/Countermeasure	Control Functionalities					Control Type
	Preventive	Detective	Corrective	Deterrent	Recovery	
Malicious Software						
Anti-virus	✓		✓		✓	Technical/Logical
Anti-rootkits	✓					✓
Anti-spyware	✓					✓
Anti-spam	✓					✓
Firewalls	✓					✓
Decreased privilege levels	✓					✓
Penetration testing		✓				✓
Hardening	✓					✓
Buffer Overflow						
Choice of programming language	✓					Technical/Logical
Use of safe libraries	✓					✓
Executable space protection	✓					✓
Stack smashing protection	✓					✓
Address space layout randomization	✓					✓
Deep packet inspection		✓				✓
Mobile Code						
Anti-malware	✓					Technical/Logical
Reduced user privileges	✓					✓
Mobile code access controls	✓					✓
Secure workstation configuration	✓					✓
Input Attacks						
Effective input field filtering	✓					Technical/Logical
Application firewall	✓					✓
Application vulnerability scanning		✓				✓
Developer training	✓					Administrative
Back Door						
Code reviews	✓					Technical/Logical
Source code control	✓					Administrative
Source code scanning		✓				Technical/Logical
Third-party code reviews and assessments	✓					✓
Object Reuse						
Application isolation	✓					Technical/Logical
Server virtualization	✓					✓
Developer training	✓					✓
Logic Bomb						
Code reviews	✓					Technical/Logical
Source code control	✓					Administrative
Source code scanning		✓				Technical/Logical
Third-party code reviews and assessments	✓					✓
Social Engineering						
Education	✓					Administrative

CONCLUSION AND FUTURE WORK

The current era presents several threats to application security. There seems to be an indication that the number of threats that users in cyberspace will have to face may continue to grow. Therefore, understanding assets in cyberspace that need protection, cyber threats and vulnerabilities in software systems, and cyber defenses are important for cybersecurity and safety. The presented taxonomy of threats and applicable defenses is important for those who want to assess the risks of their IT environment. Based on the taxonomy, appropriate security measures can be selected for the protection of critical and sensitive cyberspace assets. As this current chapter focuses mainly on application security, future work will review security threats in other cybersecurity domains such as communications networks.

REFERENCES

AlazabM.BroadhurstR. G. (2017). Cyber-Physical Security. doi:10.1007/978-3-319-32824-9

Alfayoumi, I., & Barhoom, T. (2015). Client side pharming attacks detection using authoritative domain name servers. *International Journal of Computers and Applications*, *113*(10), 26–31. doi:10.5120/19862-1820

Ali, M., Shiaeles, S., Clarke, N., & Kontogeorgis, D. (2019). A proactive malicious software identification approach for digital forensic examiners. *Journal of Information Security and Applications*, *47*, 139–155. doi:10.1016/j.jisa.2019.04.013

Alsmadi, I., & Alsmadi, I. (2019). Cyber Threat Analysis. The NICE Cyber Security Framework. doi:10.1007/978-3-030-02360-7_9

Anderson, B. & Anderson, B. (2010). USB-based virus/malicious code launch, seven deadliest usb attacks. Doi:10.1016/B978-1-59749-553-0.00003-2

Anwar, Z. (2019). A new framework for preventing cyber attacks. *Security: Solutions for Enterprise Security Leaders*, *56*(7), 34–36.

Ayala, L. (2016). *Cybersecurity for hospitals and healthcare facilities: A guide to detection and prevention.* Apress.

Bakare, A.K., Junaidu, S.B., & Kolawole, A.R. (2018). Detecting Cross-Site Scripting in Web Applications Using Fuzzy Inference System. *Journal Computer Networks and Communications, 2018*, 8159548:1-8159548:10.

Banin, S., & Dyrkolbotn, G. O. (2018). Multinomial malware classification via low-level features. *Proceedings of the Digital Forensic Research Conference, DFRWS 2018 USA*. 10.1016/j.diin.2018.04.019

Bisson, D. (2019). *The State of Security*. Retrieved from https://www.tripwire.com/state-of-security/security-awareness/5-social-engineering-attacks-to-watch-out-for/

Borky, J. M., & Bradley, T. H. (2019). Effective Model-Based Systems Engineering. Effective Model-Based Systems Engineering. doi:10.1007/978-3-319-95669-5

Campbell, T. (2016). Practical Information Security Management. *Practical Information Security Management*, 155–177.

Chaim, M. L., Santos, D. S., & Cruzes, D. S. (2019). What Do We Know About Buffer Overflow Detection? *International Journal of Systems and Software Security and Protection, 9*(3), 1–33. doi:10.4018/IJSSSP.2018070101

Chatole, V. (2018). Buffer overflow : Mechanism and countermeasures. *International Journal of Advanced Research. IDeas And Innovations In Technology, 4*(6), 526–529.

Chiew, K. L., Yong, K. S. C., & Tan, C. L. (2018). A survey of phishing attacks: Their types, vectors and technical approaches. *Expert Systems with Applications, 106*, 1–20. doi:10.1016/j.eswa.2018.03.050

Das, A., Baki, S., El Aassal, A., Verma, R., & Dunbar, A. (2019). SoK: A Comprehensive Reexamination of Phishing Research from the Security Perspective. *IEEE Communications Surveys and Tutorials*, 1–39.

DHS. (2017). *Securing Federal Networks*. Accessed April 15, 2017, from https://www.dhs.gov/topic/securing-federal-networks

Dinh, S., Azeb, T., Fortin, F., Mouheb, D., & Debbabi, M. (2015). Spam campaign detection, analysis, and investigation. *Proceedings of the Digital Forensic Research Conference, DFRWS 2015 EU*. 10.1016/j.diin.2015.01.006

ENISA Threat Landscape. (2013). *ENISA Threat Landscape Report 2013*. Retrieved from https://www.enisa.europa.eu/

Faircloth, J. (2017). Client-side attacks and social engineering. Penetration Tester's Open Source Toolkit. doi:10.1016/B978-0-12-802149-1.00008-7

Follner, A., & Bodden, E. (2016). ROPocop - Dynamic mitigation of code-reuse attacks. *Journal of Information Security and Applications, 29*, 16–26. doi:10.1016/j.jisa.2016.01.002

Goel, S., Williams, K., & Dincelli, E. (2017). Got phished? Internet security and human vulnerability. *Journal of the Association for Information Systems, 18*(1), 22–44. doi:10.17705/1jais.00447

Green, E. (2019). The logic bomb: What it is and how to prevent it. *NordVPN*. Retrieved from https://nordvpn.com/blog/logic-bomb/

Gregory, P. (2010). *CISSP Guide to Security Essentials*. Course Technology, Cengage Learning.

Grimes, R. A. (2001). *Malicious Mobile Code: Virus Protection for Windows*. O'Reilly & Associates, Inc.

Harris, S. (2013). *CISSP Exams Guide (All-In-One)*. McGraw-Hill Companies.

Hernandez, P. (2017). Microsoft Hardens Windows Cloud Instances With AI-Enabled Controls. *EWeek*, 1–4.

Huang, N., Huang, S., & Chang, C. (2019). Analysis to Heap Overflow Exploit in Linux with Symbolic Execution. *IOP Conference Series: Earth and Environmental Science, 252*(4). 10.1088/1755-1315/252/4/042100

ISO/IEC 27032 (2012). *Information technology — Security techniques — Guidelines for cybersecurity.* Retrieved from https://www.iso.org/standard/44375.html

Jyotiyana, J. P., & Mishra, A. (2016). Secure Authentication: Eliminating Possible Backdoors in Client-Server Endorsement. *Procedia Computer Science, 85,* 606–615. doi:10.1016/j.procs.2016.05.227

Kara, I. (2019). A basic malware analysis method. *Computer Fraud & Security, 6*(6), 11–19. doi:10.1016/S1361-3723(19)30064-8

Kerner, S. M. (2017). Cisco Cyber-Security Report Finds Server Threats Increased in 2016. *EWeek,* 1.

Kerner, S. M. (2018). How IBM Helps Organizations to Improve Security with Incident Response. *EWeek,* 1–2.

Kumah, P., Yaokumah, W., & Buabeng-Andoh, C. (2018). Identifying HRM Practices for Improving Information Security Performance: An Importance-Performance Map Analysis. *International Journal of Human Capital and Information Technology Professionals, 9*(4), 23–43. doi:10.4018/IJHCITP.2018100102

Kumar, G., & Kumar, K. (2014). Network security – an updated perspective. *Systems Science & Control Engineering, 2*(1), 325–334. doi:10.1080/21642583.2014.895969

Larson, D. (2016). Distributed denial of service attacks - Holding back the flood. *Network Security, 2016*(3), 5–7. doi:10.1016/S1353-4858(16)30026-5

LBMC. (2020). *Three Categories of Security Controls.* Retrieved from https://www.lbmc.com/blog/three-categories-of-security-controls/

Lemos, R. (2016). Government Surveillance Poses Cyber-security Threats, ISPs Say. *EWeek, 1.*

Leon, E., & Bruda, S. D. (2016). Counter-Measures against Stack Buffer Overflows in GNU/Linux Operating Systems. *Procedia Computer Science, 83,* 1301–1306. doi:10.1016/j.procs.2016.04.270

Maheshwari, R. (2018). Ideology of Buffer Overflow Exploits. *International Research Journal of Engineering and Technology, 5*(5).

Mahjabin, T., Xiao, Y., Sun, G., & Jiang, W. (2017). A survey of distributed denial-of-service attack, prevention, and mitigation techniques. *International Journal of Distributed Sensor Networks, 13*(12). doi:10.1177/1550147717741463

Marotta, A., & McShane, M. (2018). Integrating a proactive technique into a holistic cyber risk management approach. *Risk Management & Insurance Review, 21*(3), 435–452. doi:10.1111/rmir.12109

McAlaney, J., Frumkin, L. A., & Benson, V. (2018). *Psychological and Behavioral Examinations in Cyber Security. IGI Global book series Advances in Digital Crime.* Forensics, and Cyber Terrorism. doi:10.4018/978-1-5225-4053-3

McGraw, G. (2013). Cyber War is Inevitable (Unless We Build Security In). *The Journal of Strategic Studies, 36*(1), 109–119. doi:10.1080/01402390.2012.742013

Messier, R. (2016). Malware. Operating System Forensics, 265–299. doi:10.1016/b978-0-12-801949-8.00010-6

Mirza, M. B., Arslan, M., Tahseen, S., Bokhari, F., Zafar, R., & Raza, M. (2014). Malicious Software Detection, Protection & Recovery Methods. *Survey (London, England)*, *2*(5), 14–23.

Muckin, M., & Scott, C. F. (2019). A Threat-Driven Approach to Cyber Security. *Lockheed Martin Corporation*. Retrieved from https://pdfs.semanticscholar.org/dc7e/99de96c622dea52701a1a70172e5 32969b89.pdf

Needle, D. (2017). Oracle Cloud Security Suites Automatically Detect, Foil Cyber-Threats. *EWeek, 6*.

Nicula, S., & Zota, R. D. (2019). Exploiting stack-based buffer overflow using modern day techniques. *Procedia Computer Science*, *160*, 9–14. doi:10.1016/j.procs.2019.09.437

Nye, J. S. Jr. (2013). From bombs to bytes: Can our nuclear history inform our cyber future? *Bulletin of the Atomic Scientists*, *69*(5), 8–14. doi:10.1177/0096340213501338

Oberly, D. J. (2019). Best practices for effectively defending against ransomware cyber attacks. *Intellectual Property & Technology Law Journal*, *31*(7), 17–20.

Okereke, A. O., & Chukwunonso, C. E. (2018). Malware analysis and mitigation in information preservation. *Journal of Computational Engineering*, *20*(4), 53–62. doi:10.9790/0661-2004015362

Okutan, A., & Çebi, Y. (2019). A framework for cyber crime investigation. *Procedia Computer Science*, *158*, 287–294. doi:10.1016/j.procs.2019.09.054

PandaLabs. (2012). *2012 annual report pandalabs*. Retrieved September 23, 2013, from http://press.pandasecurity.com/wp-content/uploads/2013/02/PandaLabs-Annual-Report-2012.pdf

Patil, D. R., & Patil, J. B. (2015). Survey on Malicious Web Pages Detection Techniques. *International Journal of U- and e-Service. Science and Technology*, *8*(5), 195–206.

Qamar, A., Karim, A., & Chang, V. (2019). Mobile malware attacks: Review, taxonomy & future directions. *Future Generation Computer Systems*, *97*, 887–909. doi:10.1016/j.future.2019.03.007

Rash, W. (2015). IT Managers Struggling to Keep Up With Cyber-Threats: Security Experts. *EWeek, 1*.

Rash, W. (2019). *Five Things Enterprises Need to Know About Threat Landscape. EWeek, N*. PAG.

Refsdal, A., Solhaug, B., & Stølen, K. (2015). *Cyber risk management* (1st ed.). SpringerBriefs. doi:10.1007/978-3-319-23570-7

SecurityMagazine. (2019). *Cyber Attacks Cost $45 Billion in 2018*. Retrieved from https://www.securitymagazine.com/articles/90493-cyber-attacks-cost-45-billion-in-2018

Shahriar, S., Das, S., & Hossain, S. (2018). Security threats in Bluetooth technology. *Computers & Security*, *74*, 308–322. doi:10.1016/j.cose.2017.03.008

Solomon, M. G., & Chapple, M. (2005). *Information Security Illuminated*. Jones and Bartlett Publishers, Inc.

SpamLaws. (2019). *What is Malicious Mobile Code and How Does It Work?* Retrieved from https://www.spamlaws.com/how-malicious-mobile-code-works.html

Tipton, H. F., & Henry, K. (2007). *Official (ISC)² Guide to the CISSP CBK*. Taylor & Francis Group, LLC. Retrieved from https://books.google.com.gh/books?id=RbihG-YALUkC&lpg=PA139&dq=object%20 reuse%20attack&pg=PP1#v=onepage&q&f=false

Virtue, T. & Rainey, J. (2015). Information Risk Assessment, HCISPP Study Guide, 131-166. doi:10.1016/ B978-0-12-802043-2.00006-9

Walkowski, D. (2019). What Are Security Controls? *Application Threat Intelligence*. Retrieved from https://www.f5.com/labs/articles/education/what-are-security-controls

Warikoo, A. (2014). Proposed Methodology for Cyber Criminal Profiling. *Information Security Journal: A Global Perspective, 23*(4-6), 172-178.

Wilson, D. (2017). 3 basic types of security controls to protect your business. *Concerned Nerds*. Retrieved from http://concernednerds.com/3-basic-types-of-security-controls-to-protect-your-business/

Yaokumah, W. (2020). Predicting and Explaining Cyber Ethics with Ethical Theories. *International Journal of Cyber Warfare & Terrorism, 10*(2), 46–63. doi:10.4018/IJCWT.2020040103

Yaokumah, W., Walker, D., & Kumah, P. (2019). SETA and Security Behavior - Mediating Role of Employee Relations, Monitoring, and Accountability. *Journal of Global Information Management, 27*(3), 102–121. doi:10.4018/JGIM.2019040106

Yau, H. K. (2014). Information Security Controls. *Adv Robot Autom, 3*, e118. doi:10.4172/2168-9695.1000e118

Zabicki, R., & Ellis, S. R. (2017). Penetration Testing. In *Computer and Information Security Handbook*. Elsevier Inc.; doi:10.1016/B978-0-12-803843-7.00075-2

Zilber, N. (2018). Hackers for Hire. *Foreign Policy*, (230), 60–64.

KEY TERMS AND DEFINITIONS

Adware Cookies: Web beacons and other means used to track individual Internet users and build behavior profiles for them.

Anti-Rootkit: Software that uses techniques to find hidden processes, hidden registry entries, unexpected kernel hooks, and hidden files in order to find rootkits that may be present on a system.

Anti-Spyware: Software that is designed to detect and remove spyware.

Anti-Virus Software: Software that is used to detect and remove viruses and other malicious code from a system.

Back Door: A feature in a program that allows access that bypasses security.

Bot: Malicious software that allows someone to remotely control someone else's computer for illicit purposes.

Cross-Site Scripting (XSS): An attack where an attacker can inject a malicious script into HTML content in order to steal session cookies and other sensitive information.

Firewall: A hardware device or software program that controls the passage of traffic at a network boundary according to a predefined set of rules.

Hardening: The process of configuring a system to make it more robust and resistant to attack.

Key Logger: A hardware or software component that records keystrokes on a computer.

Logic Bomb: Computer code placed in a system that is intended to perform some harmful event when certain conditions are met—usually a specific day or time in the future.

Rootkit: Malicious code that is designed to avoid detection by hiding itself by some means.

Side-Channel Attack: An attack on a system where a subject can observe the physical characteristics of a system in order to make inferences on its internal operation.

Spam: Unwanted e-mail that usually contains unsolicited commercial advertisements, pornography, or attempts to lure recipients into opening malicious attachments or visiting malicious web sites.

Spyware: Usually unwanted and sometimes malicious software that is used to harvest Internet usage information from a user's workstation.

Trojan Horse: Malicious computer code that claims to perform some benign function while actually performing some additional, malicious function.

Virus: Malicious code that attaches to a file, document, or master boot record (MBR).

Worm: Malicious code that has the ability to self-propagate and spread rapidly from system to system.

Chapter 3
Towards a Theory for Explaining Socially–Engineered Cyber Deception and Theft

Paul Danquah
Heritage Christian College, Ghana

Olumide Babatope Longe
American University of Nigeria, Nigeria

Jojo Desmond Lartey
Heritage Christian College, Ghana

Peter Ebo Tobbin
Center for IT Professional Development, Ghana

ABSTRACT

Socially engineered cyber deception and theft seems to have gained prominence in cybercrime. Given the contextual background of inadequate theoretical explanations of socially engineered cyber deception and theft cybercrime, there is the need for theory to better explain and possibly predict activities involved in socially engineered cyber deception and theft. This chapter proposes a theory of socially engineered cyber deception and theft (SECT), with routine activity theory, crime displacement theory, the space transition theory, and empirical review as its foundation. It iteratively combines deductive and inductive approaches to infer the occurrence of socially engineered cyber deception and theft. While the deductive approach serves the deduction leading to the inference, the inductive approach extracts and suggests empirical evidence for a deterministic prediction of the crime occurrence. It is recommended that the theory is further validated to test its applicability.

DOI: 10.4018/978-1-7998-3149-5.ch003

INTRODUCTION

Cybercrime is a generic terminology used for all sorts of crimes committed with computers (Katyal, 2001). Srinivasan (2008) defines cybercrime as criminal activities that are executed by the use of communication networks such as the Internet, satellite, mobile networks, telephone and wireless networks. Service interruption, virus transmission, and denial-of-service attack are a number of ways in which cyber criminals can invade systems and cause damage. Yar (2005) categorizes cybercrime into four different types, namely *cyber deception and theft, Cyber trespass, cyber violence and cyber pornography*. Cyber-trespass occurs when a perpetrator intentionally intrudes or enter computer resource, asset or property belonging to other people, without their expressed approved authorization or authentication, in order to gain right of access and privileges available on the computer with a motive to harm or steal (Reynolds, 2015; Yar, 2005). Typical examples are website defacement, spread of viruses and hacking. Cyber-deception and Theft also involves the use of computer technology to deceive and steal, usually electronically, and typical examples are theft of assets or money, such as intellectual property (IP) breach or violation, IP piracy and credit card fraud (Reynolds, 2015). Cyber-pornography refers to activities that breach laws on obscenity and decency. An example is child pornography. Cyber violence on the other hand involves the use of the Internet and related technologies to cause psychological harm or incites physical injury against others, thereby breaking laws relating to the protection of the individual. Typical instances of cyber violence are hated-speech, denial of service attack and cyber mistreatment and bullying (Reynolds, 2015).

Ngo and Jaishankar (2017) further highlighted Wall (2005, revised in 2010, p. 82) which addressed cybercrime from four perspectives. These include crime against machines, crimes using machines, and crimes within computer/system, content-related crimes, which may encourage viciousness and further stimulate relatively traditional crimes like stalking and personal pestering.

These different crimes, arguably, bear striking resemblances that are characteristically different from other known crimes. Among the unique characteristics of such cybercrimes include transnational, through the Internet, whereby the attack originates from a different country to another than that of the victims with clearly different jurisdiction, laws and perhaps culture (Brenner 2004; Reynolds, 2015). "Such modus operendi from foreign lands makes it difficult to detect and consequently retaliate them" (Reynolds, 2015). Also, these crimes do not require proximity, and neither are they limited by physical constraints; it has the potential to scale at a high velocity with multiple victimization, while the perpetuator may possibly maintain perfect anonymity. It was identified by Assarut, Bunaramrueang and Kowpatanakit (2019) that freedom and anonymity are key factors in the behavioural intention to commit cybercrime. Al-Suwaidi, Haitham and Jabeen (2018) argued the need for collaboration of space tradition theory and criminal opportunity theory to explain cybercrime since they incorporate not only cyber space but also population characteristics in different countries.

There are several applicable cybercrime related theories, notable ones are the Routine Activity Theory (RAT) by Cohen and Felson (1979), Crime Displacement Theory (CDT) by Cox, Johnson & Richards (2009), and the Space Transition Theory (STT) by Jaishankar (2008). Much as these theories are applicable to cybercrime They all generalize their applicability for the purpose of either explaining the phenomena or predicting it. The STT focuses on cybercrime but again generally postulates as applicable to all the mentioned types of cybercrime. Socially engineered cyber deception and theft (SECT) is a subset of the cyber deception and theft category of cybercrime, a form of cybercrime that involves a perpetrator using computer system to leverage on gained-trust from a victim and subsequently fraudulently exploiting the victim (Danquah, 2015). The extant literature does refer to socially engineered cyber deception and theft as either cyber fraud or Internet fraud. Further, there are other forms of cyber deception and theft that may not be socially engineered, such as intellectual property violation and piracy. Typical examples of the socially engineered cyber deception and theft are online love scams that end up in theft, phishing that ultimately leads to theft and online gold scams. These terminologies describe the cyber deception and theft from a rather more generalized perspective.

BACKGROUND

Despite several empirical investigations to test the utility of Routine Activity Theory (RAT), Crime Displacement Theory (CDT), Space Transition Theory (STT) and their applicability and insights to address the cybercrimes, the unique characteristics of SECT has not been comprehensively synthesized and theorized for explanation or deterministic purposes. Scholars who tested the space transition theory have criticized that some of its propositions are rather difficult to test and may be specific to certain forms of cybercrimes (Holt, Bossler, & Spellar, 2015; Holt & Bossler, 2016). Additionally, other scholars have shown via empirical tests that some aspects of the STT theory do not apply in certain contexts (Danquah & Longe, 2011).

Jansen. & Leukfeldt (2016), in their research results suggested, in line with literature that everyone is susceptible to some degree of online fraud victimization and as a result research is needed mitigate the phenomena. Given the outlined contextual background of inadequate theoretical explanations of cybercrime as a unique explanation for the phenomenon of socially engineered cyber deception and theft, there is the need for theory to better explain and possibly predict activities involved in socially engineered cyber deception and theft. This paper proposes SECT as a theory that explains and therefore predicts the occurrence of socially engineered cyber deception and theft.

METHODOLOGY

Kerlinger (1979), defined theory as "a set of interrelated variables, definitions, and propositions that presents a systematic view of phenomena by specifying relations among variables, with the purpose of explaining natural phenomena." Theories abound in scientific research, and computer science is no exception, where it is explained that the seal of theory is the construct hypothetical statements, universal in focus and which can be confirmed or proved false (Gregor 2006). Two different types of theories can be identified: *predictive theories* – theories which can be tested deterministically using logical propositions, and *explanatory theories* – those theories that non-deterministically explain phenomena (Horne, Ahmad & Maynard, 2016). However, arriving at the theory may be through any or a combination of three possible alternative approaches of inductive, deductive and abductive reasoning (Christenson, 2015), with the first two approaches combined to serve this study its basis to develop the SECT Theory.

While the deductive reasoning entails working from a general perspective to the a more specific focus, the inductive reasoning, in contrast, starts from specific focus to a generalized one by collecting data on the specific perspective, describe the observation derived from patterns present in the data and then make a generalized conclusion (Blaikie, 2009; Christenson, 2015). Deductive reasoning has been observed to be most commonly applied to theories pertaining to specific occurrences and human behaviors, resulting in extensions to existing models or theories. This inspires it application to the current theory being proposed, given its application to human behavior of deception, and crime. Inductive approach on the other hand, is based on observations consistent with observed data patterns and which are then then captured into new models, frameworks or theories that builds on the existing ones (Blaikie, 2009; Christenson, 2015). Abductive approach entails leveraging on an incomplete set of observations that proceeds to the likeliest possible explanation for the group on the basis of the observations.

It is imperative, from the foregone, that deductive approach requires several theoretical different yet related works to feed on, before data are collected in order to arrive at a conclusion (Blaike, 2009). The theories applied may emanate from single or multiple sources with relevant constructs as models to be combined in order to generate a novel testable framework. On the other hand, and contrarily, inductive reasoning starts with data collection and ends with explanations and descriptions of consistent and inconsistent patterns in the data (Blaikie, 2009).

In this article/paper/research we adopt the deductive-inductive iteration approach. Inductive reasoning is employed to understand and apply empirical research findings related to socially engineered cyber deception and theft. The deductive aspect, however, is used to hypothesize statements that constitute SECT, according to three previous different theories of Routine Activity, Space Transition Theory and Crime Displacement Theory. The deductive method used in this study is syllogism; it is applied in deducing the relevant constructs of that are applicable to SECT. Inductive reasoning makes broad generalizations from specific observations, a review of many observations is made, a pattern is discerned and on that basis a generalization is inferred. These adoptions are in conformity with application of deductive approach to reasoning. Figure 1 diagrammatically illustrates the iterations in the deductive-inductive iteration approach.

Figure 1 shows a three-stage theoretical framework that develops SECT Theory. Observe the sequential stages with the first being a combination of both inductive and deductive philosophy, while the second stage involves precise activities implemented in the philosophical approaches, this involves reviewing empirical data and reviewing existing theory as inductive and deductive approaches respectively. The third, and last, stage of process involves merging results and findings from stage two as output that culminates in the development of SECT Theory.

DEDUCTIVE REVIEW

Routine Activity Theory (Crime Theory)

The Routine Activity Theory (RAT), is a generic criminological theory that was proposed by Cohen and Felson (1979), suggested that for any crime to be successfully committed then the following must be simultaneously extant:

(a)   A suitable target is available: This denotes an individual/people, object(s) or place(s).
(b)   Lack of a suitable guardian to prevent the crime from occurring: A suitable guardian denotes a restrictive or deterrent solution like police patrols, security guards, CCTV systems and vigilant friends or colleagues.
(c)   A motivated offender is present: This presumes it is only possible to have a victim if the perpetrator is motivated and intentionally acts.

Figure 1. Iterative methodology for using deductive and inductive reasoning
Source: Author

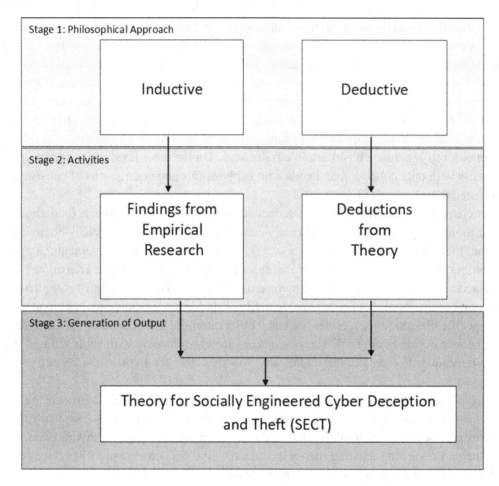

On the premise of syllogism approach, the postulates of the routine activity theory apply to all forms of crime irrespective of the type. On the basis of socially engineered cyber deception and theft being a crime, it can therefore be inferred that all postulates of the routine activity theory automatically applies to SECT. RAT applies to all forms of cybercrime; a crime would only occur when there is an opportunity to do so. Available opportunity is indeed a root cause of the crime. RAT has, however, been tested and confirmed by the cybercrime research community in on-line activities, guardianship, and malware infection; and the reader is referred to the works of Bossler and Holt (2009) for instance. The essential takeaway from RAT, in this study to generate SECT, is that any socially engineered cyber deception and theft will thrive provided all these conditions exist – suitable target, lack of a suitable guardian and the motivated offender.

Crime Displacement Theory

This theory suggests countering crime, as a solution to crime occurrences (Cox, Johnson & Richards, 2009), by focusing primarily on crime reduction via opportunity reduction in crime commission. The approach proposed by the theory involves simply displacing or moving the crime from one locale to the other, and such displacement may involve the following:

Geographical: Crime moved from one place to another location
Temporal: Moving Crime from a specific period to another time
Target: Moving Crime from one suitable target to another
Tactical: Altering the method of committing crime from one to another
Crime type: Changing the type of crime that is to be committed.

In the context of crime displacement theory and SECT, the inference from the crime displacement theory implies that, crime reduction is via opportunity reduction in crime commission is the way to address crime. The approach proposed therefore implies that for any crime to be successful, the appropriate locale must be chosen and the opportunity must exist. Essentially, the element deduced from the crime displacement theory is the need for an adequate locale for successful crime commission. Further to this, the application of this deduction is equally relevant for all forms of crime hence, it is applicable to socially engineered cyber deception and theft. Also, here the essential takeaway by SECT theory manage is the need for an appropriate locale to exist for the crime to be committed. Felson & Clarke (1998) further explained that the use of crime displacement as a method of decreasing crime may have unpredictable results which range from being positive, negative, neutral, even-handed to attractive.

Space Transition Theory

The most cybercrime specific theory is the Space Transition Theory STT propounded by Jaishankar (2008), and argues that, people behave differently when they move from one space to another. They postulate that:

1. Persons with repressed criminal behavior (in the physical space) have a propensity to commit crime in cyberspace, who, otherwise would not commit in physical space, due to their status and position.
2. Identity Flexibility, Dissociative Anonymity and lack of deterrence factor in the cyberspace provides the offenders the choice to commit cyber crime
3. Criminal behavior of offenders in cyberspace is likely to be imported to physical space which, in physical space may be exported to cyberspace as well.
4. Intermittent ventures of offenders into the cyberspace and the dynamic spatiotemporal nature of cyberspace provide the chance to escape.
5. (a) Strangers are likely to unite together in cyberspace to commit crime in the physical space. (b) Associates of physical space are likely to unite to commit crime in cyberspace.
6. Persons from closed society are more likely to commit crimes in cyberspace than persons from open society.
7. The conflict of Norms and Values of Physical Space with the Norms and Values of cyberspace may lead to cybercrimes (Jaishankar, 2007).

Tests carried out by Danquah and Longe (2011) and Danquah and Longe (2012) confirmed some postulates and disproved others. The research outcome indicated some precincts in the variety of cybercrimes committed and practiced in Ghana. It was also established that the Space Transition theory's postulates are not unequivocally applicable to all sorts of cybercrime. The essential deduction for the socially engineered cyber deception and theft is the second and third postulates which suggest that identity flexibility, dissociative anonymity, lack of deterrence factor and intermittent ventures of offenders in the cyberspace provides the offenders the choice to commit cybercrime and escape. An application of deductive syllogism in this context therefore suggests the applicable and extracted postulates are tenable constructs for the SECT being proposed.

Theoretical Deductions

Given the foregone review on the previous propounded theories, one can make relevant deductions, and in line with SECT, we now make the following critical yet very relevant deduction, outlined as deduced constructs in Table 1, towards the SECT Theory being proposed.

Table 1. Deduced Constructs from Reviewed Theories

No	Theory	Subjects
1	Routine Activity	1.1 Suitability of Target 1.2 Lack of a suitable guardian to prevent crime 1.3 A motivated offender to commit crime
2	Crime Displacement	2.1 Existence of a convenient and an appropriate locale
3	Space Transition	3.1 Identity flexibility 3.2 Dissociative anonymity 3.3 Lack of deterrence factor provides the offenders the choice to commit cybercrime 3.4 Intermittent ventures of offenders in the cyberspace provides the offenders the choice to escape after committing crime

INDUCTIVE REVIEW

Fundamental to the use of any empirical evidence as a basis for a theory is the need to employ the grounded theory approach. Grounded theory is an inductive reasoning based systematic methodology for the construction of theories through methodical gathering and analysis of data. The objective of grounded theory is to avoid gaps between theory and empirical research hence such the theory is built on empirical data (Martin and Turner, 1986). This section however references published empirical findings and behavioral patterns or approaches to committing socially engineered cyber deception and theft crimes. In 2017 Internet crime incidences reported by the American Federal Bureau of Investigation (FBI), and which were referred to the "Confidence/Romance Fraud" described a cybercriminal who deceived his victim into believing that a trust relationship in the form family, friendly or romantic exist between them. Given such belief, the victim is persuaded to send information about items of value – money, investment or other actions such as money laundering to the benefit of the criminal. However, researchers have made attempts at contributing to the understanding of cybercrime activities in the country from the microscopic perspective – "as it is on the ground".

The work of Longe et al. (2010), contributed to improved understanding of cyber activities with a focus on tracking cyber fraudsters. This, arguably, served Danquah & Longe, (2011) a launchpad to build upon the new knowledge gained to carry out an ethnographic study on cyber criminality in the country, while the sequel – Longe & Danquah (2012) specifically assessed socially engineered cyber deception and theft via an ethnographic study. Another sequel – Danquah, Ogunsanwo & Longe, (2013) did further work by investigating cyber deception and theft for which they delve into, and beyond, E-Mail header in socially engineered cyber deception and theft. Several cases assessed in the Longe et. al. (2010), Danquah & Longe (2011) and Danquah, Ogunsanwo & Longe, (2013) elaborated on the approach used by the fraudsters to socially engineer cyber deception and theft as elaborated in Table 2. Frauenstein & Flowerday (2016) also argued that constant user's information updates on social networking sites makes the user develop habituated clicking and distribution of links, such as liking posts, copying messages, pasting them, uploading and downloading media content, all of which results in information overload. This behavioral grooming, they argued, lead users to becoming more vulnerable to social engineering attacks/security breaches on social networks since these users do not cognitively process, they encounter during those clinking activities and messages, with security lenses.

Empirically, socially engineered cyber deception and theft is often referred to as internet fraud by the cyber research community. There have however been several research works focusing specifically on socially engineered cyber deception and theft, with the most prominent work being that of Danquah (2015) on cyber criminals involved, and which identified consistent pattern of behavior recorded in the Table 2. Some of the specific cases assessed and reported on to arrive at the pattern of behavior are namely the cases of Asare, Kwame, BKS, Dodoo, Yaw, Dela, Nii and Nana. Below is an induction from the approach of socially engineered cyber deception and theft perpetrators.

Inductions from Empirical Review

The consistent criminal behavioral pattern observed include (see Table 2):

i.   Attract Attention: The victim's attention is attracted by the perpetrator via e-mail, chat or text.

ii.   Collect/Exchange Information: The perpetrator communicates with the victim over a period during which information is exchanged between them.

iii.   Develop Cordial Relationship: A relationship is built between the perpetrator and the victim by regular communication which develops over time into a pleasant and hospitable relationship.

iv.   Establish Trust: Trust is developed between the victim and perpetrator through a myriad of means such as buying of gifts for the victim and acquainting victim with perpetrator's supposed family and close friends.

v.   Trigger a bait/Access Victim: Once trust is proven and established, victims incline to be willing to agree to various forms of help or sacrifice to the perpetrator.

vi.   Commit Offense: This typically delivers the perfect prospect for the perpetrator to launch the attack.

vii.   Clear Tracks (Optional): Some criminals are inclined to disappear from cyber space after successfully committing their offense whereas others continue until their victims are of no benefit to them again.

Table 2. Induced Constructs from Empirical Review

No	Crime	Empirical Induction (Electronically)
1	Socially Engineered Cyber Deception and Theft	1. Attract Attention 2. Exchange Information 3. Develop Cordial Relation. 4. Establish Trust 5. Trigger Bait/Access Victim 6. Commit Offence 7. Clear Tracks

These observations were confirmed by earlier works of various investigators, such as Boateng, Longe, Isabalija and Budu (2011); Warner(2011); Boateng, Longe, Mbarika, Avevor & Isabalija (2010); Wada, Longe and Danquah(2012), in their respective studies on approaches used by criminals who committed socially engineered cyber deception and theft. The work being done currently approached its investigation from a grounded theory perspective, as an attempt at theorizing induced pattern observed from perpetrated socially engineered cyber deception and theft. Given this approach, the arrived results, subsequently, cannot be considered pre-emptive one. This motivates the suggestion of the arrived SECT theory, in the next section, as a combination of the theoretical deductions and the inductions from empirical findings. Beyond this is a suggestion for testing the proposed SECT theory.

PROPOSED THEORY FOR SOCIALLY ENGINEERED CYBER DECEPTION AND THEFT (SECT)

For any socially engineered cyber deception and theft to be successful, the following conditions must be present within cyber or electronic space:

i. Suitability of Target
ii. Lack of a suitable guardian to prevent crime
iii. A motivated offender to commit crime
iv. Existence of an appropriate locale
v. There must be a conducive setting that makes it possible for Identity flexibility, Dissociative anonymity and Inadequate deterrence factor -
vi. There must be a condition that makes it possible for the perpetrator to Intermittently reside on the internet
vii. The perpetrator should be able to:
    a. Attract Attention
    b. Exchange Information
    c. Develop Cordial Relationship with victim.
    d. Establish Trust by victim
    e. Trigger Bait/Access Victim
    f. Commit Offence
    g. Clear Tracks (Optional)

The suitable target in this context is a person that becomes the victim of the socially engineered cyber deception and theft. The lack of a suitable guardian refers to the absence of a deterrence factor and the motivated offender is a criminal with the intentional malicious actions' executions. The existence of an appropriate locale refers to the option available for committing the crime. This may be geographical, temporal, target, or tactical. There is the need for an appropriate locale to exist for the crime commission. It is further required that these setting be conducive for the criminal to have identity flexibility to be optionally able to alter the identity, where the need be, dissociative anonymity to successfully remain unidentified by the victim. Lack of deterrence in this case is the absence of any activity or action that could deter the perpetrator from operating, while the existence of an electronic platform, that makes it possible for perpetrators to intermittently show up and disappear, must also be present for the commission of socially engineered cyber deception and theft.

Once all preceding conditions exist, the perpetrator would then approach the crime according to the sequence of actions: attract attention, exchanging information, developing a cordial relationship with the victim and establishing trust by the victim. These outlined actions are typically based on false pretense hence the deception component is experienced at these outlined stages. Beyond establishing trust, the perpetrator triggers a bait or accesses the victim to commit the offence. Typically this stage involves the theft component of the crime. Some perpetrators proceed to clear their tracks whereas others may not.

Mathematical Representation of Theory

A fundamental topic studied in discrete mathematics for computers science, among other fields that relies on mathematics as a tool to abstract constructs, is Sets Theory and we apply in this framework Axiomatic Set Theory (AST) in particular – to build the theoretical foundation that supports the proposed SECT theory for Socially Engineered Cyber Deception and Theft. The choice for AST, as appropriate candidate foundation for SECT, stems from three main considerations. First is the consideration that there must be key conditions necessary for a successful cyber deception and theft. Secondly these conditions, can be recognized as emanating from certain cliques of attributes, which are primitive in notion, yet very well suitable to constitute a well-defined idea. Thirdly no one clique is adequate to initiate a crime and that composite clique, and their respective entire memberships, must collectively interact in order to execute the crime.

From set theory perspective, "*a well define collection of objects*" defines a set (Jenkyn & Stephenson, 2013, p. 43), and here "well-defined" refers to any object or notion that can possibly be within the set identified for which there exist a way or approach for deciding whether the object or notion is in the set or not. Secondly the "collection" as well as "object" are primitive notions or terms that we do know their meanings. AST is applied to this definition to enforce the rule that we can adequately establish the properties characterizing the set and its membership relation, using rules of inference based on system of logic. Thirdly AST enforces three criteria that ensure: (1) consistency, (2) plausibility, (3) richness (Oliver, & Smiley, 2013). Consistency ensures impossible paradox in the characterization of the set's attribute – impossible to have both a statement and its negation in the same set. While the Plausibility criteria makes it possible to have intuitive beliefs or existence of a sets, the Richness criteria ensures that necessary results based on Cantorian set theory is derivable as a theorem – a collection of members as a group devoid of emptiness and singleness (Oliver, & Smiley, 2013).

Now consider *Routine Activity* (**R**), *Space Transition* (**S**) and *Crime Displacement* (**C**), as three main yet different cliques of attributes, constituting well-defined and the necessary conditions for a crime to be committed, as illustrated in Figure 2. **R, S,** and **C** therefore constitute three different non-disjoint sets – the clique of attributes have at least a commonality. Interaction among all the members from these sets define and culminates in the definition of *Electronic Activities* (E) – the actual crime being perpetuated. In this regard, the set *E* can be considered as the union of **R, S,** and **C** – the pool of necessary conditions to commit a cybercrime. Given that these conditions are non-disjoint, we are interested in identifying the number of emerging attributes, from the union, that can initiate a cybercrime. We proceed by formulating the relationship mathematically by first defining the following:

If **R** is a set, then n(**R**) is the number of identified attributes in the set **R**.
$R \cap C =$.**R** intersection **C**, i.e. a common attribute x .in both **R** and **C**
$R \cup C =$.**R** union **C**, i.e an attribute x .in **R** or in **C** or in both
$R \setminus C =$ .set difference between **R** and **C**, i.e. attribute x .is in *R* but not *in C*

Equation 1:

$$n(R \cup C \cup S) = n(R) + n(C) + n(S) - n(R \setminus (C \cap S)) - n(C \setminus (R \cap S)) - n(S \setminus (C \cap R)) + n(C \cap R \cap S).$$

Figure 2. Interaction of necessary conditions to guarantee a cybercrime
Source: Author

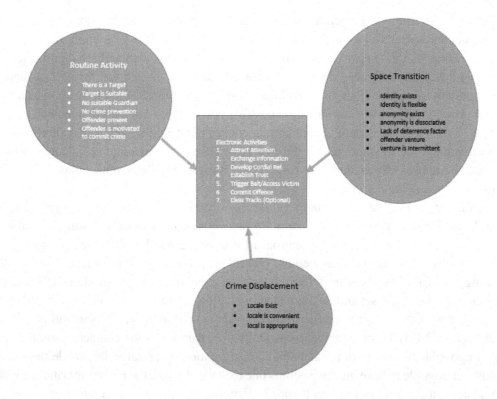

Rewriting equation 1, we obtain equation 2 as:

Equation 2:

$$n(C \cap R \cap S) = n(R \cup C \cup S) + n(R \setminus (C \cap S)) + n(C \setminus (R \cap S)) + n(S \setminus (C \cap R)) - n(R) - n(C) - n(S)$$

Observe from Equation 2 that the convergence of non-disjointed set members that must all be present to guarantee a crime is available only in the term $n(C \cap R \cap S)$ on the left-hand side of the equation 2. Thus, this constitutes the critical and necessary condition, contributed from all three sets – **R, S,** and **C**, that can successfully result in the cybercrime envisage.

Consequently, in identifying as well as preventing any cybercrime, this proposed framework suggests that unless those elements or member attributes in set $E = n(C \cap R \cap S)$ is isolated and immobilized the crime will be successfully committed. This is sure to vary from one event to the other, however it is determinable empirically and hence preventable, at least according to this proposed framework.

FUTURE RESEARCH DIRECTIONS

As indicated earlier, there have been several empirical investigations to test the utility of RAT, CDT, STT theories and their applicability and insights to address cybercrimes. SECT presents unique characteristics yet to be comprehensively synthesized for explanation or deterministic purposes. The theoretical and empirical foundations of SECT provide explanatory and deterministic components. It is therefore recommended that the theory is further validated via various tests to assess its viability and applicability.

CONCLUSION

Socially engineered cyber deception and theft tend to have gained prominence in cybercrime as a whole, emerging studies have tried to generalize cybercrime in theory with some level of success. This chapter proposes SECT theory – an explanatory and deterministic abductive framework arrived at via the combination of inductive and deductive study. Like most theories, mathematical tool of AST is used to abstract identified construct in the abductive framework, in the form of mathematical equation thereby serving as a scientific basis for establishing the SECT theory. Subsequently and given the inductive component of the theoretical basis, the proposed SECT theory is grounded on pre-validations and tested. The theoretical and empirical foundations of the theory respectively provided explanatory and deterministic components. It is however recommended that the theory is further validated via various tests to assess its viability and applicability, as an interesting sequel investigation to this work.

REFERENCES

Al-Suwaidi, N., Nobanee, H., & Jabeen, F. (2018). Estimating Causes of Cyber Crime: Evidence from Panel Data FGLS Estimator. *International Journal of Cyber Criminology*, *12*(2).

Assarut, N., Bunaramrueang, P., & Kowpatanakit, P. (2019). Clustering cyberspace population and the tendency to commit cyber crime: A quantitative application of space transition theory. *International Journal of Cyber Criminology*, *13*(1).

Blaike, N. (2009). *Designing social research.* Cambridge: Polity Press.

Boateng, R., Longe, O., Isabalija, R. S., & Budu, J. (2011). Sakawa - Cybercrime and Criminality in Ghana. *Journal of Information Technology Impact*, *11*(2), 85–100.

Boateng, R., Longe, O., Mbarika, V., Avevor, I., & Isabalija, R. S. (2010). Cyber Crime and Criminality in Ghana:Its Forms and Implications. *Americas Conference on Information Systems (AMCIS), Proceedings of the Sixteenth Americas Conference on Information Systems*, Lima, Peru.

Brenner, S. W. (2004b). Toward a criminal law for cyberspace, Distributed Security. *Boston University Journal of Science & Technology Law*, *10*(2).

Burgess, R. L., & Akers, R. L. (1966). A Differential Association-Reinforcement Theory of Criminal Behaviour. *Social Problems*, *14*(2), 128–147. doi:10.2307/798612

Christensen, L. B., Johnson, B., & Turner, L. A. (2015). *Research methods, design, and analysis.* Edinburgh: Pearson.

Cohen, L. E., & Felson, M. (1979). Social Change and Crime Rate Trends: A Routine Activity Approach. *American Sociological Review*, *44*(4), 588–608. doi:10.2307/2094589

Cox, Johnson, & Richards. (2009). Routine Activity Theory and Internet Crime. In F. Schmalleger & M. Pittaro (Eds.), *Crimes of the Internet,* (pp. 302-316). Pearson-Prentice Hall.

Danquah, P. (2015), *An Assessment of Cyber Criminal Behavioural Patterns* (PhD Thesis). Accra Institute of Technology Institutional Repository.

Danquah, P., & Longe, O. B. (2011). Cyber Deception and Theft: An Ethnographic Study on Cyber Criminality from a Ghanaian Perspective. *Journal of Information Technology Impact*, *11*(3), 169–182.

Danquah, P., & Longe, O. B. (2011). An Empirical Test Of The Space Transition Theory of Cyber Criminality: The Case of Ghana and beyond. *African Journal of Computing and ICT*, 38–48.

Danquah, P., Longe, O. B., & Totimeh, F. (2012). Just another Harmless Click of the Mouse? - An Empirical Evidence of Deviant Cyber Space Behaviour Using an Online Trap. *African Journal of Computing and ICT*, *5*(3), 49–56.

Diener, E., Fraser, S. C., Beaman, A. L., & Kelem, R. T. (1976). Effects of deindividuation variables on stealing among Halloween trick-or-treaters. *Journal of Personality & Social Psychology*, *33*, 178-183.

Drass, K. A. (1982). Negotiation and the structure of discourse in medical consultation. *Sociology of Health & Illness*, *4*(3), 320–341. doi:10.1111/1467-9566.ep10487982 PMID:10260462

Felson, M., & Clarke, R. V. (1998). *Opportunity makes the thief: Practical theory for crime prevention* (Police Research Series Paper No. 98). London: Research, Development and Statistics Directorate, Home Office. Retrieved from http://www.homeoffice.gov.uk/rds/prgpdfs/fprs98.pdf

Frauenstein, E. D., & Flowerday, S. V. (2016), Social network phishing: Becoming habituated to clicks and ignorant to threats, Information Security for South Africa. *Proceedings of the 2016 ISSA Conference*, 98-105.

Hirschi, T. (1969). *Causes of Delinquency*. Berkeley, CA: University of California Press.

Horne, C. A., Ahmad, A., & Maynard, S. B. (2016). A Theory on Information Security. *Australasian Conference on Information Systems.*

Jaishankar, K. (2008). Space Transition Theory of Cyber Crimes. In F. Schmalleger & M. Pittaro (Eds.), *Crimes of the Internet* (pp. 283–301). Upper Saddle River, NJ: Pearson-Prentice Hall.

Jansen, J., & Leukfeldt, R. (2016, January – June). Phishing and Malware Attacks on Online Banking Customers in the Netherlands: A Qualitative Analysis of Factors Leading to Victimization. *International Journal of Cyber Criminology*, *10*(1).

Jenkyn, T., & Stephenson, B. (2013). *Fundamentals of discrete math for computer Science a problem-solving primer*. London: Springer-Verlag. doi:10.1007/978-1-4471-4069-6

Katyal, N. K. (2001). Criminal Law in Cyberspace. *University of Pennsylvania Law Review*, 149.

Kerlinger, F. N. (1979). Behavioral research: A conceptual approach. New York: Academic Press.

Martin, P. Y., & Turner, B. A. (1986). Grounded Theory and Organizational Research. *The Journal of Applied Behavioral Science*, *22*(2), 141–157. doi:10.1177/002188638602200207

Ngo, F., & Jaishankar, K. (2017, January – June). Commemorating a Decade in Existence of the International Journal of Cyber Criminology: A Research Agenda to Advance the Scholarship on Cyber Crime. *International Journal of Cyber Criminology*, *11*(1).

Oliver, A., & Smiley, T. (2013). *Plural logic*. Oxford: University Press. doi:10.1093/acprof:oso/9780199570423.001.0001

Reynolds, G. W. (2015). *Ethics in Information Technology* (5th ed.). Cengage Learning Boston.

Srinivasan, M. L. (2008). *CISSP in 21 Days*. Packt Publishing.

Wada, F., Longe, O., & Danquah, P. (2012). Action Speaks Louder Than Words - Understanding Cyber Criminal Behavior Using Criminological Theories. *Journal of Internet Banking and Commerce*, *17*(1), 1–12.

Warner, J. (2011). Understanding Cyber-Crime in Ghana: A View from Below. *International Journal of Cyber Criminology*, *5*(1), 736–749.

Yar, M. (2005). The novelty of cybercrime: An assessment in light of routine activity theory. *European Journal of Criminology*, *2*(4), 407–427. doi:10.1177/147737080556056

KEY TERMS AND DEFINITIONS

Abductive Reasoning: Reasoning is used to obtain tacit knowledge to explain motives for orientations and actions. This relies on deductive and inductive iteration to arrive at theory.

Cyber Deception and Theft: A form of cybercrime that involves a perpetrator using computer system to gain trust from a victim and subsequently fraudulently exploiting the victim.

Deductive Reasoning: Reasoning based on theories or models, reasoning commences from premises contained in the theories or models and then draws conclusions.

Inductive Reasoning: Reasoning based on collected data and established patterns from observation. Reasoning commences with data collection and observation of data to establish patterns and signs.

Set: A well define collection of objects.

Social Engineering: The manipulation of victims to obtain trust for exploitation.

Theory: A proposition intended to explain a phenomenon or principles for a practice.

Chapter 4
Deciphering the Myth About Non–Compliance and Its Impact on Cyber Security and Safety

Kwasi Danso Dankwa
University of Reading, UK

ABSTRACT

The use of computers and sophisticated technologies are on the rise, and organizations are constantly looking for ways to invest in technologies to stay ahead of the competitive market. As such, cyber security and safety measures have been put in place by the organizations to protect them from attacks and to ensure that products and services are safe. However, managing cyber security and safety is becoming more challenging in today's business because people are both a cause of cyber security incidents as well as a key part of the protection from them. It is however that non-compliance with policies and directives are major security breaches. What is not well known, however, are the reasons behind the non-compliance behaviours. This chapter seeks to explore the reasons behind the non-compliance behaviours by use of compliance assessment model (CAM). The chapter reviews a case study in a health centre and systematically assesses the reasons behind the non-compliance behaviour by using the CAM model.

INTRODUCTION

The ubiquitous changes in the technological space require stringent measures to ensure that data integrity and security are not compromised. As a result, many rules and regulations have been enacted to manage the risk to stakeholders' interaction in the technological space. These regulations are not only limited to organizations and businesses, but countries have also put cyber security measures in place to protect their institutions and citizens. As a result of the increased regulations, set of harmonized and consolidated compliance controls have been adopted by organizations to promote operational transparency (Silveira et al., 2012). Importantly, organizations have put in systems and applied commensurate effort to aid compliance to relevant laws, policies, and regulations. This reduces unwanted replication

DOI: 10.4018/978-1-7998-3149-5.ch004

of effort and waste of resources while ensuring that all relevant governance stipulations are attained (Dankwa & Nakata, 2018).

Moreover, without relevant systems and processes that enable compliance knowledge, organizations may repeat and duplicate compliance breaches and even risk information leak or loss as they struggle to learn from the past non-compliance experiences (Caroline & Meyer, 2012). Despite systems and measures in place to curtail impact on security and safety, there are many instances within organizations where non-compliances have been reported. The cause of the non-compliances has been indicated to be multifactorial with different impact on people, organizations and even countries. Again, some questions remain unanswered although there is improved appreciation of how IT systems boost corporate execution (Kim & Kim, 2017). In addition, there is minimal information about the efficacy of the compliance support network in place, promoting the compliance intention of individual employees and thus enabling the assessment of compliance behaviour. Thus, this chapter seeks to address these questions:

a)   What are the reasons behind the non-compliance behaviours?
b)   How can understanding the reasons behind non-compliance behaviours help organizations to address and improve their systems?

The chapter proposes that the understanding and resolution of these questions will enable organizations to make compliance support systems that promote overall employee compliance intention and hence improve compliance behaviour. Consequently, the author seeks to explain the myth about non-compliance by considering the reasons behind non-compliance and the impact of it on safety and security. The author seeks to approach this paper from the potential impact of security and safety breaches on patient treatment and other relevant stakeholders within the health care sector. The author proposes that in most cases, non-compliance occurs because stakeholders do not understand the importance and usefulness of the rules and regulations in place. The study further argues that, many of the non-compliances are due to people not knowing their role in the security and safety architecture, their role in adoption and use of the technology or resource available and the impact of their failures on safety and quality of patient treatment.

The remainder of the chapter is organized as follows: Section 2 summarizes the background of previous research and studies within the field of cyber security and safety. This further considers the various gaps and factors that impede compliance to security and safety procedures, rules and regulations. In section 3, the chapter introduces the methodology that will be followed in this study to address the questions that were posed. Section 4 considers the rationale for the chosen model for the appraisal of the intentions behind the non-compliance behaviour. This is followed in section 5 by review of a case study in the health care sector using the chosen model. In section 6, the chapter discusses the outcome of the assessment and considers the limitation of the study and further work. Section 7 then concludes the whole chapter.

BACKGROUND

The quest for organizations to stay on top of the competitive market has led to the need for adoption of computer and internet technology to greatly improve the way businesses operate (Sikolia, 2013). This is not confined to the business world as the Health sectors have also implemented computers and other complicated information systems for better patient management. Importantly, the extended use of technologies, the advanced smart sensors and data gathering devices enable organizations to collect diversified data about consumers, organizations and other aspects that promotes better forecasting and business trending for future applications (Kim & Kim, 2017).

With the increased reliance on computers, internet and other smart devices and the complexity of these technologies for businesses and health care organizations, cyber security and safety has become critical. This is because, the sheer amount of data collected presents concerns about privacy and security (Christiansen, 2011) and need to be managed effectively and secured. Moreover, the risk to the confidentiality, integrity and availability of organizational data and Information security has become ever present concern for all organizations (Sikolia, 2013). According to Fielder et al. (2016), organizations are faced with the biggest concern of how they defend their operations from possible cyber-attacks and the prioritization of the means to actualize the defence. Thus, organizations must examine the risk of the most threats and implement measures to mitigate the many possible relevant vulnerabilities. This confirms a publication by Deloitte and NASCIO (2014), which indicated that most Chief Information Security Officers (CISOs) are not optimistic in accomplishing this particularly difficult task of dealing with the varying cyber threats. Essentially, with the increased sophistication of cyberattacks, innovative technologies designed by organizations to combat these threats have unwittingly presented novel and subtle fragilities. (Jalali, Siegel & Madnick, 2019). This shows how difficult it is to manage the threats to cyber security in businesses and many organizations. These cyber threats are not only related to organizations but are increasingly considered important risks to national and international stability and security (Van der Meer, 2015).

According to Gurusamy and Hirani (2018), there are two general categories of cyber security threats: actions targeted to damage cyber systems and actions that unlawfully utilize the cyber infrastructure without damaging or compromising that infrastructure. While cyber-attacks permit actions that destroy the computers capacities, cyber exploitation or utilization involves unlawful use of cyber systems to convey controversial messages, to commit fraud, to enlist and indoctrinate terrorists. Importantly, both categories indicate how far stretching cyber threats and impact on the cyber system can be. This supports Van der Meer (2015), who stated that cyber threats encompass a broad spectrum of illicit activities which include digital warfare, digital terrorism, digital espionage, digital activism and digital crime. It is evident that cyber threat can be across different technologies and lead to catastrophic impact on products and services. As such, it is essential to have cyber security and safety processes, controls and technologies that shields systems, networks, programs, devices and data from cyber-attacks.

The scope of the cyber security extends not only to security of IT systems within the enterprise but also extends to digital networks upon which the IT systems rely, i.e. cyber space and critical infrastructure (Gurusamy& Hirani, 2018). Essentially, the effective implementation of cyber security and safety measures lowers cyber-attack risks and protect unwarranted utilization of systems, networks and technologies (Schatz, Bashroush, & Wall, 2017). Therefore, by discouraging reactive approach and promoting understanding and the importance of proactive development in cybersecurity capabilities reduces failure rates and improve cost effectiveness of organizations (Kwon & Johnson, 2014).

Consequently, cyber security and safety systems have been implemented across organizations to address the organizational needs, ensuring that data and systems are not compromised. This requires implementation of these security measures is to meet policy requirements, rules and regulations. Gurusamy and Hirani (2018), indicated that cyber security in not only enforcement of national laws and cooperation of some international and regulation but also deals with secured private regulatory activity and defensive strategies and products. The standards and procedures implemented by organizations is to guide the users of these systems with reliance on the users following the procedures and processes as mandated by the organizations to ensure that customer needs are met, and regulatory standards are not flouted. Most IT Security Management approaches consist of checklist with a triage approach to categorizing threats which decision makers use to develop a coverage strategy. Moreover, threat impact analysis and other quantify IT security risk analysis have been used (Gurusamy & Hirani, 2018).

However, there has been indication that in many organizations, there may be different activities which impedes the organizations desires in meeting their goals. Some activities of staff can even be opposing the direction of the organization. Some of this may be employee attitude and or behaviour which can have a big impact on information security in organizations and can therefore not be ignored. According to Andersson and Reimers (2017), employees may take actions that ignore the best interests of organizational Information Security because they often do not see themselves as part of the drive to improve security. This may also be as a result of employees struggling to use or follow the cyber security and safety systems in place due to implementation constraints or difficulties in interpreting the procedures in place. As such, there is the need to understand the reasons behind non-compliances within organizations to follow cyber security and safety requirements with the view to improve compliance.

METHODOLOGY

In this study, the author proposes a structural model Compliance Assessment Model (CAM) based on the Technology Acceptance model and the Activity Theory. This model will be used for the assessment of the non-compliance behaviour. A systematic approach will be used for the assessment of a case study from the health sector. Here, an IT incident reported is assessed using the CAM model and results is discussed. The next section reviews the rationale for selection of CAM for the assessment of compliance behaviour and the assessment of the case study.

RATIONALE FOR USE OF THE COMPLIANCE ASSESSMENT MODEL

The use of computers and other digital devices demands the understanding of the adoption of these gadgets. To make the most of technology investments, research over the years have gained better understanding of technology adoption rates and implementation success (Venkatesh, Morris, Davis, & Davis, 2003). Lai (2017) stated that several theories that explain consumers' acceptance of new technologies and their intention to use have been proposed. This means user acceptance and use is an important component of technology acceptance. According to Dillon and Morris (1996), the apparent desire for the user group to use the information technology for the purpose it was designed for indicates the user acceptance of the technology. Thus, the theories of acceptance are more focused on understanding the factors that impacts the adoption of technologies as planned by the designers and less concerned with unintended uses of technologies. This adoption and implementation of technology has been shown to be influenced by the intention of the users' acceptance (Davis, 1989). As the use of technology and the correct use of the cyber security and safety measures are critical, it is incumbent on businesses and organizations that acceptance and use are well understood and documented. As such, many models like the Technology Acceptance Model (TAM) (Davis, Bogozzi & Warshaw, 1989), with the final version of (TAM) by Venkatesh and Davis (1996). Further, Venkatesh and Davis (2000) developed the Technology

Acceptance Model 2 (TAM2) and Venkatesh, Morris, Davis and Davis (2003) developed the Unified Theory of Acceptance and Use of Technology (UTAUT) and finally Technology Acceptance Model 3 (TAM3) Venkatesh and Bala (2008). These have been used to understand the acceptance of technology within organizations with the aim to predict what user behaviour (Lai, 2017).

However, in applying the technology involves subject manipulating the object to attain the set goal with this developing subject – object interaction (Kaptelinin, 2014). This subject - object interaction is mainly prompted by the desire to meet the needs of the subjects of activities. In this instance, the subject being the staff and the organization have a need to use the cyber security and safety systems to protect against the cyber threats. Essentially, the understanding of the acceptance of the technology alone is not enough as the routine use, and the technology should also be considered. Thus, there is the need to have a model that assesses the interaction of the subject with the object in using the technology to understand the observed compliance behaviour. Subsequently, the CAM model allows for the intention of the subject to be assessed by observing the subject and the object activities. Figure 1 shows the Compliance Assessment Model (CAM).

Figure 1. Compliance assessment Model (Dankwa & Nakata, 2018)

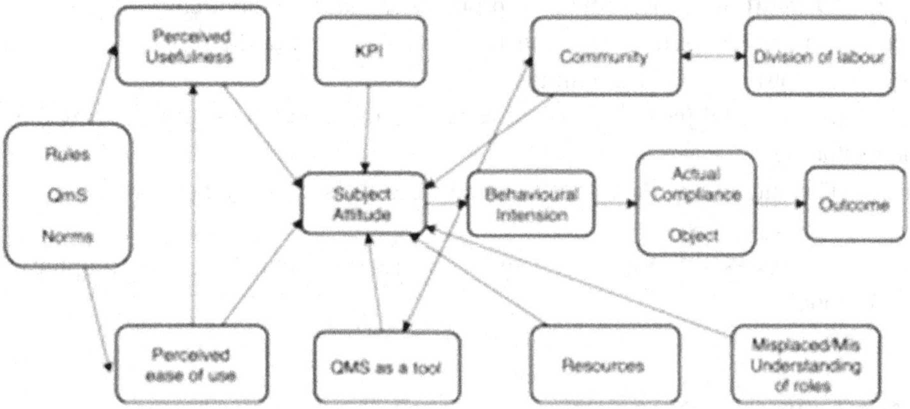

From the CAM model, the following constructs are observed:

- **Norms, Rules, QMS** - These are the external variables that affects the attitude of the subject in choosing the tool for the required interaction with the object.
- **Perceived Usefulness (PU)** –Is the degree to which a person believes that using a particular system would enhance their job performance (Davis, 1989). In other words, the subject perceiving the technology as useful for what they want to do.
- **Perceived Ease-Of-Use (PEOU)** – The degree to which the person using a particular system believes it to be free from effort (Davis, 1989). Looks at the ease with how the subject can use the technology.
- **Subject Attitude** - Is the individual's evaluation of an object and defined "belief" as a link between an object and some attribute and defined "behaviour" as a result or intention (Fishbien & Ajzen, 1975). This is the subject's settled way of thinking based on the evaluation of the technology.

- **QMS as a Tool** – Quality Management System which comprise all the procedures and processes in place for the subject to use. This involves the policies in place about the use of the technology. It acts as the means or tool for the subjects to interact with the object.

- **KPI** – This is the Key Performance Indicators that are in place to evaluate the success of an organization, employee in meeting objectives for performance. This may be part of the monitoring tool for the assessment of the subject's performance.

- **Resources** – This includes the staff numbers, the time available to perform task and all the relevant materials and equipment needed by the subject to use the technology as required.

- **Community** – The community involves the different sections that may exist within the department and how they interact with each other to achieve the outcome. This may promote the culture that exists within the department and by extension, the organization.

- **Division of Labour** – This is the hierarchy that exist within the department and the organization. This looks at the leadership and management structure and their interaction with the subject which influences their attitude.

- **Misplaced/Misunderstanding of Roles** – This looks at the various roles that exist within the department and how they complement each other in achieving the set goals. This also considers the role of other stakeholders within the organization whose activities impacts on the subject.

- **Behavioural Intention** – The subjective probability that an individual will perform a specified behaviour (Fishbein & Ajzen, 1975). This relates to the intent of the subject to perform the behaviour, especially towards others and things.

- **Actual compliance – Object** – This is the actual interaction with the object using the tool; in this case the technology

- **Outcome** – The outcome of the interactions between the subject and the object.

The next section assesses a case study to decipher the reasons behind the non-compliance behaviour using the CAM model.

ASSESSMENT OF COMPLIANCE

The health care provider manufacture blood components from whole blood donations collected from blood donors. To ensure that the blood components are safe for use, the testing department test blood samples for blood grouping and other viral markers to certify the components as appropriate for blood transfusion. The testing machines have in built security and safety measures to ensure that compliant results are released for patient treatment. It is believed that non-compliance occurs within the department due to many factors that requires investigation and the author propose the use of the CAM model for the assessment of the non-compliance.

Let us consider a case in the laboratory where a bottle of Abbott PRISM activator concentrate loaded onto Abbott Architect instead of Pre-trigger solution prior to testing on Saturday. This was noticed at the end of Testing on Monday when many samples have already been tested and results released.

The process of providing safe blood components for use involves the testing of the donation samples to confirm the blood groups and to ascertain microbiological status of the components. This being the object of the activity, the subject being the staff that are required to align with the values of the organization, are needed to complete the task. To so this, there are many factors that influences the attitude of the subject which subsequently can aid in assessing the behaviour intention of the staff thereby helping to assess the compliance behaviour. Due to the requirements to ensure that the components produced meet standards and regulations, Quality Management systems (QMS) have been implemented to act as the tool or the means to get the processing done. This entails the procedures for training and for processing, equipment maintenance and calibration and the appropriate storage of the reagents. This also ensures that the correct reagents are used for during the testing and appropriately checked when loaded unto the machine. Moreover, the policies and use of the safety measures are all documented with the procedures. For this incident, the wrong reagent was loaded but the systems in place failed to pick this up until it had been used to test samples for three days, which can have detrimental effect on patient safety but on this occasion, there was no impact.

In applying the procedures for the process, the subjects consider the perceived ease of use of the procedures and their interaction of the equipment. Here, the subject perceives the ease with which they can perform their task following the procedures in place. Although the subject is trained to check for the correct reagent and to scan the bar code of the reagents into the on-board computer system of the equipment to allow for use, they failed to follow the procedure. Moreover, the computer system on the equipment is to ensure safety of the process, but it was by-passed by the staff who scanned the bar code of the old bottle thinking they are the same. It is indicated that, the subject loaded the wrong reagent but scanned the bar code of the empty reagent bottle that was being replaced.

Also, there was confirmation that the reagents were not stored at the right location in the store room when it was fetched by the staff. The activator concentrate reagent was mixed up with the other reagents for the other machine. Consequently, the subject took the wrong reagent instead of the right one. Although the stock process requires the subjects to arrange the reagents following a clear and agreed system with signage, this was not followed. This is due to subject working in a 'pilot' mode due to the routine nature of the task and failing to see the need to follow the agreed process. As such, the failure led to the wrong bottle of reagent being taken from the store room and placed on the machine. Importantly, the security was breached as a result of failing to follow the procedure because the subject did not perceive the process to be easy.

Moreover, the perceived usefulness of the procedures and the systems in place to ensure the safety of the test was implicated in this incident. Although procedures were in place for safety of the process, the subject's perception of the usefulness of the procedures influenced the way the process was executed. They may have seen no need to follow the processes as prescribed in the procedure and therefore applied their own approach which led to the incident. Firstly, the requirement to follow agreed process of storing the reagents in the store room with all items for the same process being stored in one area was not followed as the subject didn't see the usefulness in doing that. Secondly, they failed to check the reagent against the requirement when it was picked from the shelf and transferred to the lab for use.

Lastly, appropriate checks were not performed as part of loading the machine and the wrong bar code was scanned which meant that the security system was by-passed. Despite the need for the subjects to follow the cyber security and safety measures in place to load the correct reagent and scan the reagent bar code for the on-board computer system to assess and confirm that the correct reagent is in use, the subject failed which led to the non-compliant test results. Essentially, because the subject did not perceive the usefulness of the cyber safety measures in place, they flouted it which led to the non-compliance behaviour.

From the CAM model, the perception of staff about the ease of use and usefulness of the procedures and processes are influenced by other factors like the norms. Five norms, namely, perceptual norms, cognitive norms, evaluative norms, behavioural norms and denotative norms (Liu, 2000), have been considered to control human behaviour and, in turn, organizational behaviour. The perceptual norms influence how people react to signals from their environment through their senses. Here, the norms and values are embedded in the physical structures and set up or lay out which influences the behaviour of the staff in the department. The cognitive norms enabled the staff to interpret what they perceived based on the beliefs and knowledge. The staff interpreted the procedures and processes based on the belief and knowledge that existed within the department. Although there is established rules and procedures, the acquired knowledge and beliefs coerced each staff differently to interpret the procedures which may lead to the non-compliant behaviour. The Evaluative norms aid in explaining the beliefs, values and objectives in the departments in the organization. The behavioural norms govern the behaviour of the staff within the departments. These behaviours are as a result of the norms that exist within the department and this influenced the non-compliant behaviour observed.

Finally, the denotative norms direct the choices of signs for signifying and these are culture dependent which influences the operation of staff within the department. These norm forms may have contributed to the failure in application of the procedures and processes and consequently the breach in the safety and security set up in the testing of the samples. Although there are procedures in place, the norms at the 'informal level' may have influenced the interaction of the subject with the on-board computer system of the equipment which led to the non-compliance behaviour.

While the norms have been shown to impact on the way the subject assessed the workload and the application of the procedures, the community in which the subject operates also influences their attitude and or their behaviour. The organization and by extension the department as a community, creates the culture within which the subjects operate which influences individual decision making (Vanhée, & Dignum, 2018) comprising compliance behaviour. According to Hofstede (2001), the community creates "collective programming of the mind" that influences the pattern on thinking, feeling and potential interactions and make groups unique. Essentially, the subjects operate in a department which in this case is the community for testing of samples that has an agreed way of dispatch of their duties, lay down of processes, with their actions guiding and directing each other as a group. Subsequently, although their decisions may not be documented in the procedures and policies, the informal agreement within the department influences how the subjects operate. According to Dankwa and Nakata (2016), the appropriateness and dispatch of responsibility by the subject is influenced by the established norms, practices and beliefs within the community which can either lead to compliance or non-compliance behaviour.

Consideration should also be given to the set up within the department in terms of supervision and managerial responsibilities which is referred to as the Division of Labour in the CAM model. Here, there is requirement on the part of the managers and supervisors to check and ensure that procedures are always followed for better outcome. They are required to check documentations, completed forms and statistical reports that are generated from test controls before certifying that the test results are compliant to be released. For this incident, the managers and supervisors failed to thoroughly check the control results before certifying for the subjects to continue with the testing process. The statistical report generated from the machine deviated from the expected results due to the wrong reagent on the machine, but the supervisors failed to identify the anomaly. Because they were informed by the subjects that the report was with consensus, they failed to check and verify the reports themselves.

This may be due to the reliance on the agreed norms, practices and the trust that is built within the community that indicates that if the subject states that the results are compliant then there is no need to verify. Although the procedure requires the supervisors and managers to verify the control results, the norms and beliefs within the department coerced the supervisors to act differently. According to Dankwa and Nakata (2016), in the organization, the responsibility is determined by the established common agreements or policies which leads to formation of 'life cycle' of responsibility which determines the role of each staff in the process. Essentially, each subject relies and trust on the output of the other subject that initiated the process and as such the supervisors failed to verify the report and act on the discrepancies which led to the release of the non-compliant results.

The CAM model also indicates the need to consider the Misplaced/Misunderstanding of Roles that may exist as a result of subjects working together in the department. Here, the subject think that other staff may check the outcome of their work and as such they fail to get it right the first time. Also, there is reliance on the quality assurance team to routinely check their controls and other aspects of the process so they failed to compliantly follow their process, thinking that any errors will be picked by the quality assurance team. For this incident, the quality assurance team did not review their output as they only perform sampling inspection of all the processes that are undertaken in the lab. Subsequently, the subjects failed to perform their task as required because of the misunderstanding of the role of the quality assurance team; they assumed that all their control results will be checked.

Moreover, in assessing the reasons for the non-compliance behaviour, the model also states that Key Performance Indicators (KPI) should be considered. The department are set KPI's from the senior management team for the operations within the department and subjects are required to work to ensure that KPI's are always met. Despite the need to have KPI's, there was indication that some of the KPI's tend to compete with the routine process and this may contribute to the non-compliance behaviour. In this incident, because the KPI requires the subjects to test number of samples within a given time, subjects were in a rush to get the samples tested and this led to failure to follow all the procedures in place to check reagents before loading and thoroughly checking the control report. Also, some of the KPI assesses the number of quality incidents and complaints raised within the section so staff may be reluctant to report incidents in order to meet the KPI requirements.

Further assessment considers the available resources for the subjects to complete their task. Although there was enough staff to perform the task, the space and equipment constraints meant that the subjects are constantly improvising to meet targets. Review of the reasons that led to the non-compliance revealed that the wrong reagent was mixed with the other reagents due to lack of space for storage. This led to the reagents for the prism and the architect machines being put together on the same shelf leading to the subject picking the wrong reagent. Moreover, although there was supposed to be two machines available for this test, one machine was in repairs and as such all the testing was required to be completed using the only available machine. As such, the subjects were in a rush to complete all the testing leading to failures to thoroughly check the labels on the reagent bottles and failing to scan the correct bar code before loading the bottle on the machine. Consequently, the security requirements of the machine were not followed with resultant release of testing results because the available resource for staff was inadequate.

DISCUSSION

From the assessment of the case study using the CAM model, it is evident that the non-compliance behaviour observed was due to many factors. In using the technology as prescribed, the CAM model indicated that the perceived ease of use was relevant to the technology on the equipment to be used as required. As stated by Davis (1989), Perceived Ease of Use refers to the extent to which the potential user believes the selected system to be effortless. In the case study, it was observed that, as the subjects perceived the instruction to arrange the reagents in a certain format and scan the bar codes of the bottle at any change of bottle not to be effortless, they failed to follow the procedure. Essentially, a stock management system that arranges stock as required and scans in the reagents unto the machine with little effort from the subject will improve the compliance behaviour. This supports Park and Jung (2003), who indicated that the possibility of non-compliance behaviour will increase if the procedures are so complicated that the operators cannot clearly understand the context of required actions specified in the procedures. Importantly, although procedures and systems are in place for the subjects to follow, the ease with which they are able to understand the procedures and what is required of them will enable compliance behaviour.

Moreover, the agreed procedures and processes in place influenced the subjects' behaviour as they perceived them not useful to what they aim to achieve. Davis (1989) defined perceived usefulness as the degree to which a person believes that using a particular system would enhance their job performance. As such, depending on what the subject perceives as useful, they either perform the behaviour of fail to perform as observed in the case study.

Although the subject acted as an individual, we noticed that their behaviour is influenced by the norms and the community they operated. This is because norms are developed through practical interaction and experience of people within the community. This have the ability of directing, coordinating and controlling the actions they take within the community which in this case, the department. According to Salter and Liu (2002), norms have been shown as the rules which determine how social organisms interact and control possible actions. As the subjects interact in the department, their behaviour patterns evolved over time and informs how they operate within the department. This was observed in the case study when subjects who were supposed to review the work of the staff who loaded the machine failed to do so. This supports Stamper, Hafkamp, and Ades (2000) who described norms as field of force that coerces the members of a community to think in a certain manner. Because these norms determine how the subject behave and act within the department and the seen as the standard to measure the behaviour of the subjects, they all acted to conform to the norms. Subsequently, the subjects in the department had a 'local' norm that controlled their operations different from the rest of the organization. Therefore, the subjects were able to use the knowledge gained through the norms to guide their actions in the department. Consequently, the attained knowledge of the norm was the non-compliant behaviour observed in the case study that was assessed.

Due to the differences that exist between different departments within the organization due to the different norms, there is creation of misunderstanding between stakeholders when discharging their duties. As observed in this case study, the subjects relied on other stakeholders like Quality Assurance team to review their output, which on this occasion did not materialize. Essentially, the misunderstanding of stakeholder roles led to the non-compliance behaviour that was observed. Again, as already eluded to, the 'life cycle' of responsibility that is created within the department led to the supervisors and managers failing to review the statistical report of the controls from that machine. This supports Dankwa and Nakata (2016), who indicated that due to the belief and trust that exists within the community, there is the understanding that the work of the subject at the start of the 'process chain' is sufficient enough to meet the requirements.

As compliance is an important requirement to meet the regulatory requirements and to ensure that patient needs are met, Read, West and Kelaher (2015) asserted that, it is not surprising that measuring the 'level of compliance' has emerged as a key performance indicator for success of many organizations world-wide. As a result, organizations have generally developed compliance performance indicators to facilitate analysis of compliance activities and its enforcement trends (Read, West, & Kelaher, 2015). This was evident in the case study as performance indicators were in place which the subject strives to achieve. This may have contributed to the non-compliance behaviour that was observed as there appear to be conflict between the agreed practice and what the requirements of the KPI. Essentially, because the model assesses the impact of the leadership team on the subjects, it is believed that the use of the model will support leadership strategic planning and setting clear KPIs that aligns efficiently with the work of the subjects. It will also help in creating clear roles for the subjects and provide the appropriate resources to aid the subjects in execution of their task. The model allowed for a holistic approach in assessment of the non-compliance behaviour by looking at the interaction between the subject and the object. The CAM model allows for the assessment of behavioural intention of the subject, which assist in assessing the non-compliance behaviour.

FUTURE RESEARCH DIRECTIONS

Although the CAM model seeks to explain and assess the reason behind the non-compliance behaviour, the author believes there may be other factors that led to the non-compliance behaviour observed that may not have been assessed as part of the CAM analysis. Moreover, despite the analysis allowing for the understanding of the reasons behind the non-compliance behaviour, the subjective nature of the analysis makes it difficult to generalize. The author proposes to conduct other research using other models and methods to aid in triangulation of the results.

CONCLUSION

This chapter sets out to decipher the reasons for non-compliance behaviour and its impact on security and safety. From the review of the case study, the author concludes that the increased requirements for improved cyber security and safety require the subjects operating within the organization to comply with the standards and procedures in place. Furthermore, there is indication that there are multiple factors that influence the behaviour of the subjects and these should be considered when implementing procedures and policies that support the application of technology within the organization. Moreover, the Compliance Assessment Model allows for a systematic approach to be followed when assessing the non-compliance behaviour. This may aid in predicting compliance outcome when the behaviour intention of the subjects is established.

REFERENCES

Christiansen, L. (2011). Personal privacy and Internet marketing: An impossible conflict or a marriage made in heaven? *Business Horizons, 54*(6), 509–514. doi:10.1016/j.bushor.2011.06.002

Dankwa, K., & Nakata, K. (2016). Making sense of non-compliance: A semiotic approach. In M. Baranauskas, K. Liu, L. Sun, V. Neris, R. Bonacin, & K. Nakata (Eds.), *Socially Aware Organisations and Technologies. Impact and Challenges. ICISO. IFIP Advances in Information and Communication Technology, 477*. Cham: Springer. doi:10.1007/978-3-319-42102-5_11

Dankwa, K., & Nakata, K. (2018). Getting it right: A model for compliance assessment. In K. Liu, K. Nakata, W. Li, & C. Baranauskas (Eds.), *Digitalisation, Innovation, and Transformation. ICISO. IFIP Advances in Information and Communication Technology, 527*. Cham: Springer. doi:10.1007/978-3-319-94541-5_23

Davis, F. D. (1989). Perceived usefulness, perceived ease of use, and user acceptance of information technology. *Management Information Systems Quarterly, 13*(3), 319–340. doi:10.2307/249008

DeloitteN. A. S. C. I. O. (2014). *Cybersecurity Study*. http://www.nascio.org/publications/documents/Deloitte-NASCIOCybersecurityStudy

Dillon, A., & Morris, M. (1996). User acceptance of new information technology: Theories and models. In M. Williams (Ed.), *Annual Review of Information Science and Technology, 31* (pp. 3–32). Medford, NJ: Information Today.

Fieldera, A., Panaousisb, E., Malacariac, P., Hankina, C., & Smeraldi, F. (2016). Decision support approaches for cyber security investment. *Decision Support Systems, 86*, 13–23. doi:10.1016/j.dss.2016.02.012

Gurusamy, V., & Hirani, B. (2018). *Cyber security for our digital life*. https://www.researchgate.net/publication/323605373_Cyber_Security_for_Our_Digital_Life

Hofstede, G. (2001). *Culture's Consequences: Comparing Values, Behaviours, Institutions, and organizations across nations* (2nd ed.). Thousand Oaks, CA: Sage Publications, Inc.

Jalali, M. S., Siegel, M., & Madnick, S. (2019). Decision-making and biases in cybersecurity capability development: Evidence from a simulation game experiment. *The Journal of Strategic Information Systems, 28*(1), 66–82. doi:10.1016/j.jsis.2018.09.003

Kaptelinin, V. (2014). Activity Theory. In M. Soegaard & R. F. Dam (Eds.), *The Encyclopedia of Human-Computer Interaction* (2nd ed.). Aarhus, Denmark: The Interaction Design Foundation. Retrieved from https://www.interactiondesign.org/encyclopedia/activity_theory.html

Kwon, J., & Johnson, M. E. (2014). Proactive versus reactive security investments in the healthcare sector. *Management Information Systems Quarterly, 38*(2), 451–471. doi:10.25300/MISQ/2014/38.2.06

Lai, P. C. (2017). The literature review of technology adoption models and theories for the novelty technology. *Journal of Information Systems and Technology Management, 14*(1), 21–38. doi:10.4301/S1807-17752017000100002

Lim, J. S., Chang, S., Maynard, S., & Ahmad, A. (2009). Exploring the Relationship between Organizational Culture and Information Security Culture. *7th Australian Information Security Management Conference*.

Liu, K., (2000). *Semiotics in Information Systems Engineering*. Retrieved from doi:10.1017/CBO9780511543364

Martins, E. (2012). Organizational and behavioural factors that influence knowledge retention. *Journal of Knowledge Management, 16*(1), 77–96. doi:10.1108/13673271211198954

Park, J., & Jung, W. (2003). The operators' non-compliance behavior to conduct emergency operating procedures - Comparing with the work experience and the complexity of procedural steps. *Reliability Engineering & System Safety, 82*(2), 115–131. doi:10.1016/S0951-8320(03)00123-6

Read, A. D., West, R. J., & Kelaher, B. P. (2015). Using compliance data to improve marine protected area management. *Marine Policy, 60*, 119–127. Retrieved from https://linkinghub.elsevier.com/retrieve/pii/S0308597X15001670

Reimers, K., Andersson, D. (2017). Post-secondary education network security: the end user challenge and evolving threats. *ICERI Proceedings,* 1787-1796.

Salter, A., & Liu, K. (2002). Using Semantic Analysis and Norm Analysis to Model Organizations. *ICEIS 2002 - Proceedings of the 4th International Conference on Enterprise Information Systems, 2,* 847-850.

Sang, S. K., & Yong, J. K. (2017). The effect of compliance knowledge and compliance support systems on information security compliance behavior. *Journal of Knowledge Management, 21*(4), 986–1010. doi:10.1108/JKM-08-2016-0353

Schatz, D., Bashroush, R., & Wall, J. (2017). Towards a more representative definition of cyber security. *Journal of Digital Forensics, Security and Law, 12*(2). doi:10.15394/jdfsl.2017.1476

Sikolia, D. (2013). "A thematic review of user compliance with information security policies literature" Annual ADFSL. *Conference on Digital Forensics, Security and Law, 2*. Retrieved from https://commons.erau.edu/adfsl/2013/tuesday/2

Silveira, P., Rodríguez, C., Birukou, A., Casati, F., Daniel, F., D'Andrea, V., ... Taheri, Z. (2012). Aiding Compliance Governance in Service-Based Business Processes. In S. Reiff-Marganiec & M. Tilly (Eds.), *Handbook of Research on Service-Oriented Systems and Non-Functional Properties: Future Directions.* doi:10.4018/978-1-61350-432-1.ch022

Stamper, R.., Liu, K., Hafkamp, M., & Ades Y. (2000). Understanding the Roles of Signs and Norms in Organizations. *Journal of Behaviour & Information Technology, 19*(1), 15–27.

Van der Meer, S. (2015). Enhancing international cyber security: A key role for diplomacy. *Security and Human Rights, 26*(2-4), 193–205. doi:10.1163/18750230-02602004

Vanhée, L., & Dignum, F. (2018). Explaining the emerging influence of culture, from individual influences to collective phenomena. *Journal of Artificial Societies and Social Simulation, 21*(4), 11. doi:10.18564/jasss.3881

Venkatesh, V., Morris, M. G., Davis, G. B., & Davis, F. D. (2003). User acceptance of information technology: Toward a unified view. *Management Information Systems Quarterly*, *27*(3), 425–478. doi:10.2307/30036540

KEY TERMS AND DEFINITIONS

Behavioural Intention: The subjective probability that an individual will perform a specified behaviour. This relates to the intent of the subject to perform the behaviour, especially towards others and things.

Community: The community involves the different sections that may exist within the department and how they interact with each other to achieve the outcome. This may promote the culture that exists within the department and by extension, the organization.

Division of Labour: This is the hierarchy that exist within the department and the organization. This looks at the leadership and management structure and their interaction with the subject which influences their attitude.

KPI: This is the key performance indicators that are in place to evaluate the success of an organization, employee in meeting objectives for performance. This may be part of the monitoring tool for the assessment of the subject's performance.

Misplaced/Misunderstanding of Roles: This looks at the various roles that exist within the department and how they complement each other in achieving the set goals. This also considers the role of other stakeholders within the organization whose activities impacts on the subject.

Norms, Rules, QMS: These are the external variables that affects the attitude of the subject in choosing the tool for the required interaction with the object.

Perceived Ease of Use: The degree to which the person using a particular system believes it to be free from effort (Davis, 1989). Looks at the ease with how the subject can use the technology.

Perceived Usefulness: Is the degree to which a person believes that using a particular system would enhance their job performance. In other words, the subject perceiving the technology as useful for what they want to do.

QMS as a Tool: Quality management system comprises all the procedures and processes in place for the subject to use. This involves the policies in place about the use of the technology. It acts as the means or tool for the subjects to interact with the object.

Resources: This includes the staff numbers, the time available to perform task and all the relevant materials and equipment needed by the subject to use the technology as required.

Chapter 5
Towards a Security Competence of Software Developers:
A Literature Review

Nana Assyne

https://orcid.org/0000-0003-0469-6642

University of Jyväskylä, Finland

ABSTRACT

Software growth has been explosive as people depend heavily on software on daily basis. Software development is a human-intensive effort, and developers' competence in software security is essential for secure software development. In addition, ubiquitous computing provides an added complexity to software security. Studies have treated security competences of software developers as a subsidiary of security engineers' competence instead of software engineers' competence, limiting the full knowledge of the security competences of software developers. This presents a crucial challenge for developers, educators, and users to maintain developers' competences in security. As a first step in pushing for the developers' security competence studies, this chapter utilises a literature review to identify the security competences of software developers. Thirteen security competences of software developers were identified and mapped to the common body of knowledge for information security professional framework. Lastly, the implications for, with, and without the competences are analysed and presented.

INTRODUCTION

The current explosive growth being observed in the software industry requires high-level corresponding software security. This is because "software vulnerabilities or flaws are often key entrance door for attackers" (Sametinger, 2013). They include buffer overflows, SQL injection, cross-site scripting, stack overflow, inconsistent error handling, and so on (McGraw, 2004). Previously, software security used to be an afterthought, but recently it is being addressed actively from the planning stage of software development. Additionally, in today's software development process, software testing includes security testing instead of only functional testing (Mano, Duhadway, & Striegel, 2006), thus making the security

DOI: 10.4018/978-1-7998-3149-5.ch005

competences of the developers more eminent in software development. Coupled with the fact that research work on software developers' competence is not lacking (Lenberg, Feldt, & Wallgren, 2015), the security competences of software developers should be well recorded in literature. But on the contrary, that is not the case. However, when they are recorded, they are recorded as a subsidiary of security engineers' competence instead of software engineers' competence, thus making it counterproductive to develop and maintain the security competences of software developers to the benefit of the possessors (developers), those who train the possessors of the competences (educators), and users of the competences (industry).

McGraw (2004) defines software security as "the idea of engineering software so that it continues to function correctly under malicious attack". And, Hazeyama & Shimizu (2012), goes further with the definition by stating that "software security deals with security during the whole software development process". On the other hand, software engineering competence is defined by the Institute of Electrical and Electronics Engineers (IEEE) as knowledge, skills, and attitudes of software developers to fulfil a given task in a software development project (IEEE, 2014). Thus, the author of this chapter defines security competence of software developers as those specific security competences required by a developer to deal with security during the whole software development process. An example is an SQL injection skills and security pattern skills.

As mentioned above, one cannot afford to leave software security as an afterthought; developers must strive to improve software security issues from the planning stage to the maintenance stage. The works of Cheng et al. (2008), Hilburn and Mead (2013), and Riehle and Nürnberg (2015) are studies that investigated methods to handle software security using the lifecycle of software development. It is also well established that vulnerabilities and flaws are the doors attackers exploit. Works such as Kaur and Kaur (2016), McGraw (2004), Park et al. (2010), and Wegerer and Tjoa (2016) confirm this assertion in literature. In addition, assailants of software systems are persons or entities, who are active and keep on improving their skills in attacking software systems to satisfy their desire (Cheng et al., 2008). However, the security competences of the developers of the software are not well established in literature.

Whilst introducing security engineering environment studies for software developers, Cheng et al. (2008) point out that there is urgent need to create an environment that integrates various tools and provides comprehensive facilities to the designers, developers, users, and maintainers of a software system (Cheng et al., 2008). The development and maintenance of such an environment requires knowledge of security competences of the developers to prepare and develop them to withstand the intrinsic difficulty of assailants of a software system (Cheng et al., 2008). This implies that security know-how of the developer is very crucial. Hazeyama and Shimizu (2012) and Hilburn and Mead (2013) reiterate the need for awareness to be channelled towards developers' skills regarding security. However, previous studies provide less concise and coordinated information on security competences of developers.

Summarily, these competences are scattered in several different studies. Thus, the following questions arise: *what are the security competences of software developers? How can they be improved?* As part of broader research on software developers' competences, we set our research question as *what are the security competences of a software developer that are available in literature?* The remainder of this work includes: Section 2 presents previous studies and background. Section 3 looks at the methodology used in this study. Section 4 looks at the results. Section 5 and 6 presents the discussion and conclusion.

PREVIOUS STUDIES AND BACKGROUND

In this section of the study, three literature review studies on software developers' competences are identified. These literature reviews are Cruz et al. (2015); Moustroufas et al. (2015) and Vishnubhotla et al. (2018). Two of the studies utilized systematic literature review methods and the last study employed a traditional literature review method. Cruz et al. (2015) and Vishnubhotla et al. (2018) that used systematic literature review, focused on specific areas of software developers' competence. Cruz et al. (2015) investigated the personality of software engineers and their roles in software development. Vishnubhotla et al. (2018) also presented the capability and competence measurement of software engineers, including team working in agile software development. Moustroufas et al. (2015) utilized a traditional literature review to evaluate the adequacy of software engineer competences and created a software competence profiling model for recruiting software engineers. Moustroufas et al. (2015) investigated and reviewed software developers' competence in general contrary to the first two that focused on specific areas. The software security competence of developers did not appear in any of the three studies, thus the need for this paper.

It is also worth mentioning that there are several efforts being made to improve security matters in the development of software. They include the development processes and the methods to reduce vulnerabilities and flaws in software. Hazeyama & Shimizu (2012) proposed a software security learning process using the traditional software development cycle. Cheng et al. (2008) reiterated for security engineering environment for software development since security requires continuous support. Thus, they make use of the lifecycle of software engineering for their solution which is based on International Organization for Standardization (ISO) and the International Electrotechnical Commission (IEC) standards. The work of Verdon (2006) and McGraw (2004) examined the security policies and best practices that are essential for software developers.

The Open Web Application Security Project (OWASP) that is OWASP top 10 -2017 that focused on software developers and designers stated that "insecure software is undermining our financial, healthcare, defense, energy, and other critical infrastructure." The increasing complexity and the connectedness of software, is making it more difficult in attaining an increase in application security. Additionally, we face the rapid process of developing software which increases our common security risks. This makes it impossible to accept simple security problems as listed in the OWASP top 10 – 2017. The top five on the list are (i) Injection, (ii) Broken Authentication, (iii) Sensitive Data Exposure, (iv) XML External Entities (XXE), and (v) Broken Access Control. The rest of the OWASP top 10 – 2017 are (vi) Security Misconfiguration, (vii) Cross-Site Scripting (XSS), (viii) -Insecure Deserialization, (ix) Using Components with Known Vulnerabilities, and (x) Insufficient Logging & Monitoring (OWASP, 2017). Such security problems require corresponding skills to handle them. Given this, software developers' need to develop their security competences. For them to be able to develop and maintain such competences, it requires that such competences are identified and placed in the appropriate domain. Thus, the need for this study.

A survey to identify the guidance available on the web to help software developers' to fix security matters was conducted by Acar et al. (2017). They concluded that not all the information on the web is readily made for fixing security issues (Acar et al., 2017). Therefore, it may require security competences of the developers' to adjust the available code to meet the security demand. Hilburn & Mead (2013), developed a software security assurance model by providing capabilities. The capability of the assurance model was addressed by utilizing the knowledge areas. The main knowledge areas of assurance model that were identified were: assurance across lifecycles, risk management, assurance assessment, assurance management, system security assurance, system functionality assurance and system operational assurance (Hilburn & Mead, 2013). Even though, this work focused on assurance in software security, it also provided some capabilities or knowledge areas that are useful for this paper. Work such as Meng et al. (2018); Miller and Heymann (2018) and Qian et al. (2018) provide some information on the security competences of software developers. Therefore, we employ these studies stated above and other existing studies to set the agenda for identifying the security competences of software developers and highlight the importance of software developers' security competences for further studies. Thus, this study seeks to employ traditional literature reviews to identify the security competences of software developers as the first step in broader research.

In presenting Common Body of Knowledge (CBK) for Information security professionals, Theoharidou & Gritzalis (2007) made a case for technical and behavioural skills for information security professionals. The framework was achieved using 135 academic intuitions from Africa, Asia, Australia, Europe, and South and North America to provide a skill set for information security professionals. The framework can be utilized in identifying and assessing the skills of information security professionals. The framework has three major areas: information communications technology skills area, security skills area and behavioural skills area. This study aimed at identifying the security competences of software developers from literature using traditional literature review and maps the result to the Common Body of Knowledge for information security professional skills framework (CBK). As a result, the CBK framework will be employed as a theoretical lens for this study.

METHODOLOGY

Primarily a literature review will be mainly employed in this study. Fink defines a research literature review as "a systematic, explicit and reproducible method for identifying, evaluating and synthesizing the existing body of completed and recorded work produced by researchers, scholars, and practitioners" (Fink, 2010, p. 3). In this section, an attempt is also made to distinguish between a traditional literature review and a systematic literature review. Systematic literature review is defined by Kitchenham and Charters as "a form of secondary study that uses a well-defined methodology to identify, analyse and interpret all available evidence related to a specific research question in a way that is unbiased and (to a degree) repeatable" (Kitchenham & Charters, 2007, p. vi, pp. 8). A traditional literature review is used to demonstrate a gap or a problem in an area one seeks to research without an explicit method for reviewing the literature (Moustroufas et al., 2015). Since this is the first step towards broader research, a traditional literature review will be utilized.

Given this, the IEEE database was used as the database to find studies that investigated software security. The identified competences were grouped into two areas: programming related competences and non-programming related competences. The detail of the classification is explained in the result section. The identified competences were then mapped to technical and behavioural skills of information security professionals' skill set framework. With regard to data collection, data was collected from the IEEE database. The search strings that were utilized for the search were: software engineers/developers' skills, competence, and security knowledge. This was done without any strict protocol. Only peer-review papers were employed for the study. The names of the competences were extracted, descriptions of the competences were recorded into an excel sheet for the next stage of the research. On data analysis, competences with the same meaning were group together. Different implications of the competences were analysed and recorded against the individual competences identified. Using conventional content analysis guideline of Hsieh & Shannon (2005), competences were classified into two areas. They are programming related competences and non-programming related competences. Lastly, the identified competences were mapped to the information security professional skills set framework.

RESULTS

The identified competences were categorized into two. They are programming related competences and non-programming related competences. Programming related competences are those that involve coding. Non-programming related competences are those that do not directly deal with coding. The competences were mapped to the common body of knowledge information security professional skills framework. Table 1 depicts the competence area, the competence name, the citation of the papers that the competences were extracted from and the CBK of information security professional's framework.

Table 1 shows the competences identified, their classifications, the literature from which the competence is extracted from and their relationship to CBK of information security professionals' framework. In all 13 competences were identified, nine competences were programming related and 4 competences were non-programming related. Seven of the competence maps to both information communication technology and security criterial and 6 maps to information communication technology. The next section provides the definition/descriptions of the competences and implications.

PROGRAMMING RELATED COMPETENCES

Secure Programming/Coding Skills

Description

The art of adopting a secure practice in the development of software. This includes the skill of being able to guide against vulnerabilities and flaws in software development. The majority of vulnerabilities and flaws in software appear when developers ignore secure practices in programming. More details of secure programming/coding competences can be found in the works of Mano et al. (2006); Miller & Heymann (2018) and Zainuddin & Normaziah (2011).

Implication

Without the adoption of secure coding, developers may create software with flaws and vulnerabilities. As pointed out by Sametinger (2013), vulnerabilities and flaws are the key entrants for attackers. Improving secure coding or programming will reduce security flaws. Secure coding must be part of a software development curriculum. There is a need to include fundamental security principles programming courses. Organizations must continue to introduce fresh courses on secure coding. In today's software development, secure coding must be started from the planning stage of the development to the end of the software development lifecycle. This implies that developers' competence in secure coding is essential.

Table 1. Security competences of software developers

Competence area	Competence name	Reference	CBK of information security professionals framework (Theoharidou & Gritzalis, 2007)
Programming related skills	Secure programming or coding skills	(Acar et al., 2017; Mano et al., 2006; Miller & Heymann, 2018; Qian, Lo, et al., 2018; Zainuddin & Normaziah, 2011)	Information communications technology/security
	Secure mobile software development skills	(Meng et al., 2018; Qian, Parizi, & Lo, 2018)	Information communications technology/security
	Secure socket layer/transport layer security (SSL/TLS) skills	(Verdon, 2006)	Information communications technology/security
	Web Application security development skills	(Qian, Lo, et al., 2018)	Information communications technology/security
	Integrated development environment (IDE) security skill	(Meng et al., 2018)	Information communications technology
	Code Analysis tools skills	(Meng et al., 2018)	Information communications technology
	Modelling SQL injection skills	(Kaur & Kaur, 2016; Wegerer & Tjoa, 2016)	Information communications technology/security
	Handling buffer overflow skills	(Park et al., 2010)	Information communications technology/security
	Security patterns skills	(Hazeyama & Shimizu, 2012)	Information communications technology/security
Non-Programming related skills	Software security policy skills	(Verdon, 2006)	Information communications technology
	Software security best practice and standard skills	(McGraw, 2004)(Hazeyama & Shimizu, 2012)(Cheng et al., 2008)	Information communications technology
	System Security assurance skills	(Hilburn & Mead, 2013)(Miller & Heymann, 2018)	Information communications technology
	Vulnerability assessment tool skills	(Miller & Heymann, 2018)	Information communications technology

As suggested by Mano et al. (2006), secured programming must be taught in the early part of a software program. It must also be recognized as important skill for software developers.

Secure Mobile Software Development Skills

Description

Mobile devices may have software applications that we utilize frequently or perhaps even daily. The process of developing apps for these devices differ from the main devices. Furthermore, the database and the storage for these devices also differ. Thus, requiring different programming and security competences for the development of mobile apps. More about secure mobile software development skills can be found in the works of Meng et al. (2018); Qian, Lo, et al. (2018); Qian, Parizi, et al. (2018).

Implication

Most of the developers of these apps lack the necessary skill for developing mobile apps, thereby creating vulnerabilities for attackers to exploit those devices. The common nature (maybe you could be more specific here?) of the devices makes them more vulnerable. Thus, delays in providing bug fixings for new versions of applications can provide a door for attackers. Un-updated operating systems (OS) on mobile devices can allow attackers to exploit the vulnerabilities on the OS to attack the software application. Developers must pay attention to secure mobile development skills since techniques used for developing mobiles are different from that of normal devices. Fundamentally the increased usage of mobile technology is putting pressure on mobile developers. Both the trainers and users of the security competence of developers must adopt modern techniques to upgrade the developers to withstand the modern attackers.

Secure Socket Layer Skills

Description

Communication – data transmission between devices - is important in the applications function. This requires developers' skills in standard cryptographic protocol and technology for communicating on the internet. More importantly the use of transport layer security (TLS). Developers need to have skills in socket programming to enable them to develop this type of communication. More details of secure socket layer skills can be found in the work of Verdon (2006)

Implications

Most attackers take advantage of eavesdropping on transmission and launch their attack. This happens when strong encryptions are not used. Developers are to have skills in SSL or TLS encryptions technology. This is because most devices use the internet as a means to transmit data. Without such skills will mean that most attackers can eavesdrop on the communication and launch attacks. Developers should understand and have skills in symmetric encryption.

Web Application Security Skills

Description

Skills to protect devices or applications against web attacks such as cross-site scripting, SQL injection, denial-of-service, etc. Most attackers use vulnerabilities of web applications to attack. It is important to know that web application security directly relates to websites, web applications and web services such as APIs. Again, one needs to distinguish between network security and web application security. Therefore, the competences may defer. More details of secure socket layer skills can be found in the works Anand & Ryoo (2017); Uskov (2013) and Uskov & Avenue (2013).

Implication

In today's world, most of our business is done using the internet. Thus, not having the skills of developing software that can reduce web vulnerability will mean that most businesses could face catastrophes in their dealings. There is the need to have developers who understand using up-to-date skills in proper authentication methods, encryptions and development of patching for discovered vulnerabilities.

Integrated Development Environment (IDE) Security Skills

Description

Most developers of software make use of IDE for the development of software. They are software applications that provide the environments for software development. Thus, they are attitude, skills, and knowledge for using IDE securities in developing software. More details of IDE security skills can be found in the work of Meng et al. (2018).

Implication

Such environments sometimes if not well protected, can leave vulnerabilities in the software being developed and can be exploited by attackers. Having the skills related to the security of the use of the said IDE provides the developer with an environment free of vulnerabilities and flaws. Security updates are important and other security in the transmission of data. Developers must understand such security environments and use them appropriately to avoid leaving vulnerabilities that can be taken advantage of attackers.

Code Analysis Tools Skills

Description

Code analysis tools are used during coding to aid in analysing the code of the developer. Such tools help in identifying bugs and guide the developer to fix them before deploying the applications. They are attitude, skills, and knowledge for performing code analytics in software development. More details of code analysis tools skills can be found in the work of Meng et al. (2018)

Implication

If developers do not have the skill of using code analysis tools it may mean that time to identify bugs during coding may be long. It can result in leaving bugs to be exploited by attackers. It is also important to note that most of these bugs are difficult to be identified by the human eye. Examples of such tools are PMD java and SonarQube.

Modelling SQL Injection Skills

Description

It is a code injection technique that attackers take advantage of data-driven applications using SQL statements. It mostly happens when user inputs are not well-typed. They are attitude, skills, and knowledge for developing software free of SQL injection. More detail of SQL injection skills can be found in the works of Kaur & Kaur (2016) and Wegerer & Tjoa (2016).

Implication

It allows attackers to use malicious SQL statements to attack. This can be used on websites and databases. This is done by using spoof identity to temper with existing data. Such attacks are known as vector. Without skills in SQL injection handling in web applications and applications using databases, it will give attackers the chance to attack just systems since such vulnerability is commonly committed by developers.

Handling Buffer Overflow Skills

Description

It happens when a program writing to the buffer, which is a memory area set aside to hold data overflow. Mostly, when malformed inputs are used. they are attitude, skills, and knowledge needed to avoid buffer overflows. More details of handling buffer overflow skills can be found in the work of Park et al. (2010).

Implication

This happens when programmers or developers assume that all inputs may be smaller, but this may not always be the case. In case there is an overflow, the system may write beyond the allocated size causing erratic in execution leading to access error or crashing of the system. There is the need to write code that has built-in protections in the programming codes. The possession of such skills may reduce buffer overflows in memory, since not all input size can be predicted well by the developer.

Security Patterns Skills

Description

Security patterns are applied during software development by developers to achieve security goals. Such security patterns are pre-defined to guide developers. Having such skills will enable developers to know what security pattern can be used to achieve a particular security goal. That is the protected system patterns for confidentiality and integrity of information and error detection/correction pattern for deducing errors for corrections. More detail of security patterns skills can be found in the work of Hazeyama & Shimizu (2012).

Implication

Without such patterns, developers are to start from scratch to develop such protections. Understanding or having such skills, they can also develop security patterns to meet a specific goal that is not available.

NON-PROGRAMMING RELATED SKILLS

Software Security Policy Skills

Description

A software security policy defines the specific rules of security that software to be developed must have. That means that developers must frequently reference to make sure that the software obeys such policy. Understanding software security policy as a skill will enable the developer to develop software that will meet the security policy of the organization, the state and the world in general. Thus, they are attitude, skills, and knowledge needed to develop software to meet software security policies of the organization, the state, and the international community. More details of software security policy skills can be found in the work of Verdon (2006).

Implication

If developers do not have the skill to understand security policies and cannot develop software to meet what the organization, the state, and the international community have set as their policy for software security, consumers may not trust those software products. Furthermore, software security policies are standards, established to help reduce security threats. This means that, without them, developers may develop software according to their skills. This can lead to a lower security standard for the software they develop.

Security Best Practice and Standard Skills

Description

Best practice and standard are what has been used, tested and agreed as the best way of handling security in software development. Security best practices and standards can guide developers in secure software development. Thus, they are the attitude, skills, and knowledge needed to develop software security best practices and standards. More details of software security policy skills can be found in the works Cheng et al. (2008); Hazeyama & Shimizu (2012) and McGraw (2004).

Implication

If developers do not have such skills, it will mean they may not follow the best way of developing secure software. Mostly, security best practices and standards serve as a guide, but also provide a means to develop to meet certain accepted way that leads to trust.

This will mean that software developed by such developers with security best practices and standards skills will develop secured software, thereby, reducing the vulnerabilities that an attacker can exploit.

System Security Assurance Tools Skills

Description

These are tools that help developers of software from protecting the data and resources controlled by the software. They are the first line in for defending the attackers and also assessing the software security. Thus, they are the attitudes, skills, and knowledge needed to use system security assurance tools when developing software. More details of system security assurance tools skills can be found in the works of Hilburn & Mead (2013) and Miller & Heymann (2018).

Implication

Mostly, the human resources of the developer alone may not be enough for handling the development of software. Therefore, tools are needed to support the development of secured software. System security assurance tools support developers in such a situation. Not having the skill of using such tools will require more human hand in the development process. Alternatively, they will develop software that does not provide the required assurance for the people.

Vulnerability Assessment Tool Skills

Description

Tools are needed to identify the threats and risks that may be in software during development. In using such tools developers will need some special skills. Thus, they are attitude, skills, and knowledge needed by developers to use vulnerability assessment tools during software development. More detail of vulnerability assessment tool skills can be found in the work of (Miller & Heymann, 2018)

Implication

Without such tools, the human factor is to be used for such identification of vulnerability and threats thus, making such skills important for developers. It is important to note that most of such vulnerabilities are difficult to be identified by the human eye, thus if developers have no skills in using these tools, it may mean suck vulnerabilities and threats may be left in the software for attackers to exploit.

DISCUSSIONS

As stated in the related works, there were three review papers on software developers' competences. Two made use of a systematic review and one used a traditional review. None of these reviews mentioned the security competences of software developers. Nevertheless, there are some similarities. The work of Moustroufas et al. (2015) also used a traditional review, which was the same method used by this paper.

The difference between this paper and Moustroufas et al. (2015) is that they looked at software developers competence in general, whereas this paper looked at is security competence of the developers which is a specific area in software developers' competence. On the other hand, the other two reviews also looked at specific areas of developers' competence similar to this paper but used a systematic literature review as a method. This paper agrees with these authors that competences of software developers are essential for software development and effort must be made to maintain them especially in academia.

In proposing a security engineering environment for software developers, Cheng et al. (2008) claimed that the tools and the developers must integrate for a secure engineering environment. We support their assertion, but their work falls short of the implication of not having such an environment. To add to their work, this paper has provided the security competences of the developers which are essential for the security engineering environment they proposed. Furthermore, this paper has responded to the call by Hazeyama and Shimizu (2012) and Hilburn and Mead (2013), that there is the need to pay attention to security competences of the developers'. This paper has provides some of the competences, therefore agreeing with Hazeyama and Shimizu (2012) and Hilburn and Mead (2013) that the security competences of the developers are an essential parts of software developers' competences. For that reason, we support their call for more research on security competences of software developers'.

Researchers such as Cheng et al. (2008); Hilburn & Mead (2013) and Riehle & Nürnberg (2015) have called for security competence development through the lifecycle of developers. We concede, we could not do that, but we have identified some security competences of the developer that can be used as a starting stage for security competences of the developers' studies. Acar et al. (2017)stated that not all web security resources can be used fully to solve security problems by developers. Therefore, with the identification of the security competences of software developers, industry players can add to such work (web resources) by using the competences they have. Thus, this chapter supports the work of Hilburn & Mead (2013) that, knowing those security competences of software developers will help the users, possessors, and educators. Meng et al. (2018); Miller and Heymann (2018) and Qian et al. (2018) provided individual security competences of software developers, though this paper could not provide a full list, the paper has provided the basis for more work to be done. Theoharidou & Gritzalis (2007) work identified the technical and behavioural competences of information security professionals. This assertion has been established in the literature. We did not identify any behavioural security competences of software developers. Nevertheless, we hold the belief that there are behavioural security competences of developers and that empirical work must be conducted to identify them.

CONCLUSION

This chapter proposes a security competence for software developers. It uses a literature review to identify and classify security competence of software developers. Thirteen security competences of software developers were identified. They were classified as programming related competence and non-programming related competence. The author agrees that the methodology used has some limitations. Nevertheless, the competence identified and the linkage provided between the security competence of software developers and the information security professional framework will serve as a base for the development of the security competence of software developers. Furthermore, this chapter also makes a call for empirical research to identify the security competence of software developers. By that, the author calls for a systematic literature review on the security competence of software developers. Again, there is the need also to identify those security competences using the lifecycle of the software development process.

REFERENCES

Acar, Y., Stransky, C., Wermke, D., Weir, C., Mazurek, M. L., & Fahl, S. (2017). *Developers Need Support, Too: A Survey of Security Advice for Software Developers. In 2017 IEEE Cybersecurity Development IEEE Secure Development Conference Developers* (pp. 22–26)., doi:10.1109/SecDev.2017.17

Anand, P., & Ryoo, J. (2017). Security Patterns As Architectural Solution - Mitigating Cross-Site Scripting Attacks in Web Applications. In *2017 International Conference on Software Security and Assurance (ICSSA)* (pp. 25–31). IEEE. 10.1109/ICSSA.2017.30

Cheng, J., Goto, Y., Morimoto, S., & Horie, D. (2008). A Security Engineering Environment Based on ISO / IEC Standards: Providing Standard, Formal, and Consistent Supports for Design, Development, Operation, and Maintenance of Secure Information Systems. In *2008 International Conference on Information Security and Assurance* (pp. 350–354). 10.1109/ISA.2008.106

Cruz, S., Fabio, Q. B., & Fernando, L. (2015). Forty years of research on personality in software engineering: A mapping study. *Computers in Human Behavior, 46*, 94–113. doi:10.1016/j.chb.2014.12.008

Fink, A. (2010). Conducting Research Literature Reviews: From the Internet to Paper (3rd ed.). SAGE.

Hazeyama, A., & Shimizu, H. (2012). Development of a Software Security Learning Environment. In *2012 13th ACIS International Conference on Software Engineering, Artificial Intelligence, Networking and Parallel/Distributed Computing* (pp. 518–523). IEEE. 10.1109/SNPD.2012.65

Hilburn, T. B., & Mead, N. R. (2013). Building Security In. *IEEE Security and Privacy, 11*(October), 89–92. doi:10.1109/MSP.2013.109

Hsieh, H.-F., & Shannon, S. E. (2005). Three Approaches to Qualitative Content Analysis. *Qualitative Health Research, 15*(9), 1277–1288. doi:10.1177/1049732305276687 PMID:16204405

IEEE. (2014). *Software Engineering Competency Model (SWECOM)*. IEEE. Retrieved from http://www.dahlan.web.id/files/ebooks/SWECOM.pdf

Kaur, N., & Kaur, P. (2016). Modeling a SQL Injection Attack. In *2016 3rd International Conference on Computing for Sustainable Global Development (INDIACom)* (pp. 77–82). Bharati Vidyapeeth.

Kitchenham, B., & Charters, S. (2007). Guidelines for performing Systematic Literature reviews in Software Engineering Version 2.3. Engineering (Vol. 45). doi:10.1145/1134285.1134500

Lenberg, P., Feldt, R., & Wallgren, L. G. (2015). Behavioral software engineering: A definition and systematic literature review. *Journal of Systems and Software, 107*, 15–37. doi:10.1016/j.jss.2015.04.084

Mano, C. D., Duhadway, L., & Striegel, A. (2006). A Case for Instilling Security as a Core Programming Skill. In *Proceedings. Frontiers in Education. 36th Annual Conference* (pp. 13–18). IEEE. 10.1109/FIE.2006.322347

McGraw, G. (2004). *Software Security*. IEEE Security & Privacy. doi:10.1109/MSECP.2004.1281254

Meng, X., Qian, K., Lo, D., & Wu, F. (2018). Secure Mobile Software Development with Vulnerability Detectors in Static Code Analysis. *2018 International Symposium on Networks, Computers and Communications (ISNCC)*, 1–4. 10.1109/ISNCC.2018.8531071

Miller, B. P., & Heymann, E. (2018). *Tutorial: Secure Coding Practices, Automated Assessment Tools and the SWAMP. In 2018 IEEE Cybersecurity Development (SecDev)* (pp. 124–125). IEEE; doi:10.1109/SecDev.2018.00025

Moustroufas, E., Stamelos, I., & Angelis, L. (2015). Competency profiling for software engineers: Literature review and a new model. In *Proceedings of the 19th Panhellenic Conference on Informatics* (pp. 235–240). Athens, Greece: ACM. 10.1145/2801948.2801960

OWASP. (2017). *OWASP Top 10 - 2017 The Ten Most Critical Web Application Security Risks*. OWASP.

Park, C. S., Lee, J. H., Seo, S. C., & Kim, B. K. (2010). Assuring software security against buffer overflow attacks in embedded software development life cycle. In *2010 The 12th International Conference on Advanced Communication Technology (ICACT)* (Vol. 1, pp. 787–790). IEEE.

Qian, K., Lo, D., Parizi, R., & Wu, F. (2018). Authentic Learning Secure Software Development (SSD) in Computing Education. *2018 IEEE Frontiers in Education Conference (FIE)*, 1–9.

Qian, K., Parizi, R. M., & Lo, D. (2018). OWASP Risk Analysis Driven Security Requirements Specification for Secure Android Mobile Software Development. In *2018 IEEE Conference on Dependable and Secure Computing (DSC)* (pp. 1–2). IEEE. 10.1109/DESEC.2018.8625114

Riehle, D., & Nürnberg, F.-A.-U. E. (2015). How Open Source Is Changing the Software Developer's Career. *Computer Practice*, *48*(5), 51–57. doi:10.1109/MC.2015.132

Sametinger, J. (2013). Software Security. In *2013 20th IEEE International Conference and Workshops on Engineering of Computer Based Systems (ECBS)* (p. 216). IEEE. 10.1109/ECBS.2013.24

Theoharidou, M., & Gritzalis, D. (2007). Common Body of Knowledge for Information Security. *IEEE Security & Privacy*, 64–67.

Uskov, A. V. (2013). Software and Web Application Security: State-of-the-Art courseware and Learning Paradigm. In *IEEE Global Engineering Education Conference (EDUCON)* (Vol. 0, pp. 608–611). 10.1109/EduCon.2013.6530168

Uskov, A. V., & Avenue, W. B. (2013). Hands-On Teaching of Software and Web Applications Security. 2013 3rd Interdisciplinary Engineering Design Education Conference, 71–78. 10.1109/IEDEC.2013.6526763

Verdon, D. (2006). *Security Policies and the Software Developer*. IEEE Security & Privacy. doi:10.1109/MSP.2006.103

Vishnubhotla, S. D., Mendes, E., & Lundberg, L. (2018). An Insight into the Capabilities of Professionals and Teams in Agile Software Development A Systematic Literature Review. In *ICSCA 2018* (pp. 10–19). Kuantan, Malaysia: ACM. doi:10.1145/3185089.3185096

Wegerer, M., & Tjoa, S. (2016). Defeating the Database Adversary Using Deception - A MySQL Database Honeypot. In *2016 International Conference on Software Security and Assurance (ICSSA)* (pp. 6–10). IEEE. 10.1109/ICSSA.2016.8

Zainuddin, H. N., & Normaziah, A. A. (2011). Secure Coding in Software Development. In *2011 Malaysian Conference in Software Engineering* (pp. 458–464). IEEE. 10.1109/MySEC.2011.6140716

KEY TERMS AND DEFINITIONS

Competence: A set of knowledge, skills, and attitudes for performing a task.

Non-Programming-Related Competences: Software security skills that do not directly deal with coding. For example, software security policy skills and system security assurance tools skills.

Programming Related Competences: Software security skills needed for coding. For example, secure programming/coding skills and secure mobile software development skills.

Security Competence of Developers: A set of specific security competencies required by a developer to deal with security during the whole software development process; For example, SQL injection skills, and security pattern skills.

Software Developer: Individuals who employ software development skills to design, construct, test, and maintain computer software.

Software Engineering Competence: A set of knowledge, skills, and attitudes of software developers to fulfill a given task in a software development project.

Software Security: An art of providing protection to software against hackers and attackers during the life cycle of the software.

Traditional Literature Review: A method used to demonstrate a gap or a problem in an area one seeks to research without an explicit method for reviewing the literature.

Chapter 6
Cyber Security Operations Centre Concepts and Implementation

Enoch Agyepong
Cardiff University, UK

Yulia Cherdantseva
Cardiff University, UK

Philipp Reinecke
Cardiff University, UK

Pete Burnap
Cardiff University, UK

ABSTRACT

Cyber security operations centres (SOCs) are attracting much attention in recent times as they play a vital role in helping businesses to detect cyberattacks, maintain cyber situational awareness, and mitigate real-time cybersecurity threats. Literature often cites the monitoring of an enterprise network and the detection of cyberattacks as core functions of an SOC. While this may be true, an SOC offers more functions than the detection of cyberattacks. For example, an SOC can provide functions that focus on helping an organisation to meet regulatory and compliance requirement. A better understanding of the functions that could be offered by an SOC is useful as this can aid businesses running an in-house SOC to extend their SOC capabilities to improve their overall cybersecurity posture. The goal of this chapter is to present the basics one needs to know about SOCs. The authors also introduce readers and IT professionals who are not familiar with SOCs to SOC concepts, types of SOC implementation, the functions and services offered by SOCs, along with some of the challenges faced by an SOC.

DOI: 10.4018/978-1-7998-3149-5.ch006

INTRODUCTION

Securing an organisation's network against cybercriminal activity remains one of the most challenging tasks for many businesses. In order for organisations to defend themselves against attacks, they need to understand current attack vectors and the specific threats that they face to put in place mitigation strategies. Traditionally, many organisations relied on security tools such as Firewalls, Intrusion Detection Systems (IDS), Intrusion Prevention Systems (IPS) and Anti-virus solutions to protect their networks, and secure their data against cyberattacks. However, recent cyberattacks have proven that deploying these defensive tools by themselves are no longer sufficient to fully protect an organisation and deal with the aftermath of a cyberattack (Chuan et al., 2019). For example, a Firewall can be hacked to behave differently by an attacker (Tuglular & Belli, 2008). Likewise, an Intrusion Prevention Systems (IPSs) can be evaded by some sophisticated attacks (Xia & Xu, 2017). The need to respond to such incidents in an efficient, coordinated and effective manner has led to organisations employing the services of a Security Operations Centre (SOC) (Majid & Ariffi, 2019).

A SOC can be defined as a centralised infrastructure, made up of people, processes and technology inside or outside an organisation that helps businesses to monitor their network and respond to cybersecurity threats and incidents (Mutemwa et al., 2019). A review of the literature shows that a SOC can also be referred to by other names, such as Security Intelligence Centre (SIC); Information Security Operations Centre (ISOC); Information Technology Operations Centre (ITOC) and Cyber Security Operations Centre (CSOC) (Brown et al., 2016; Miloslavskaya, 2018; Onwubiko & Ouazzane, 2019a). These terms are all used to denote the same meaning. In this chapter, we adopt and use the term SOC as it is the most commonly used term by many writers.

Since their inception in the '70s as coordinating centres for supporting governments or military organisations to protect their network against adversaries (Hewlett-Packard, 2013), SOCs have gradually evolved and are now being used in both the public and private sectors. According to Falk et al. (2017), the demand for SOC services is on the rise across all sectors. A threat report by researchers at McAfee, which surveyed over 400 companies in North America and across Europe found that 84% of commercial organisations and 94% of major companies use a SOC (Beek et al., 2016). Likewise, a publication by one of the world largest research store, Research and Markets on SOCs in 2019, reported that the global SOC market size is expected to grow from USD 372 million in 2019 to an estimated USD 1,137 million by 2024 US Dollars at a Compound Annual Growth Rate of 25% (Research and Markets, 2019). In fact, SOCs are being deployed by government agencies, universities and various corporations to defend their network and to identify malicious activities (Zhong et al., 2016). SOCs play a central role in the protection of an organisation's information communication systems and act as the custodian for monitoring, detecting and reacting to security incident (Onwubiko & Onwubiko, 2019). However, a SOC offers many more functions than the monitoring and detection of cyberattacks. For example, a SOC can be leveraged to support an organisation to address regulatory and compliance issues, like log retention and data privacy laws (Medeiros & Bygrave, 2015).

Similarly, a SOC can also offer a penetration testing function, which involves the simulation of an attack against an organisation's network to see how the business reacts (Schinagl et al., 2015). Other SOC functions include log collection and retention, policy management, compliance and vulnerability scans, risk management activities, performing business and technical audit through penetration testing, incident management activities, forensic and malware analysis, log analysis; threat identification and reporting of malicious activities. An understanding and appreciation of the functions of a SOC would be beneficial to organisations who may want to extend their SOC capabilities. Likewise, such understanding may help organisations outsourcing their SOC services to opt for additional SOC functions to improve their overall cybersecurity posture.

While SOCs offers many functions to support business operations, unfortunately, there are issues that can affect the overall effectiveness and efficiency of a SOC. A greater appreciation of some of these challenges and issues discussed in this chapter would help SOC stakeholders to work towards innovative ways to address some of these challenges. Addressing some of these issues would also help an organisation to reap the full benefit of a SOC.

This chapter provides the reader with an overview on the components of a SOC, the evolution of a SOC, the types of SOC implementation, functions offered by a SOC, along with some of the challenges faced by a SOC. The authors hope that IT professionals and readers who are not familiar with SOCs and how their functions can be leveraged in an enterprise would find this chapter useful.

THE COMPONENTS OF A SOC

A SOC operates through the harmonisation of three key components (people, processes and technology), as illustrated in Figure 1. A SOC needs a team of highly skilled IT professionals (*people*) to operate a wide range of technical and security controls needed to monitor and protect the network infrastructure of an organisation (Hámornik & Krasznay, 2017). An effective SOC also needs to adhere to a set of well-defined *processes* and must have access to adequate *technology* to identify a threat or perform functions such as compliance scans, analysis log and reporting of unusual activity. Underpinning these three components is the need for strong management support, as a bottom-up approach to running a SOC is bound to fail (Majid & Ariffi, 2019). The three key components are further described below.

People – Roles and Teams

Most SOCs will have multiple roles and teams to perform a wide range of activities, such as managing and maintaining deployed security controls. Key roles that exist in SOCs include SOC analysts, SOC engineers, SOC manager and in some cases, a chief information security officer (CISO) (Sundaramurthy et al., 2015). Amongst the roles, analysts are responsible for monitoring, detection, analysing and responding to all threats faced by an organisation (Sundaramurthy et al., 2015). Some SOCs operate a hierarchical tier structure for analysts and have roles such as *Level 1, Level 2* and *Level 3* analysts (Kokulu et al., 2019). *Level 1* analysts (also known as first line analysts) tend to be the less experienced, or junior analysts who are responsible for real-time monitoring of an organisation's network. *Level 1* analysts often perform initial analysis and triaging of alerts and escalate alerts to *Level 2* teams if they are unsure about a specific incident. An alert in this context denotes any observable occurrence originating from a computer system. An alert is classified as an incident if it poses a threat to a computer system. In addition, all unusual alerts are deemed as an incident (SANS Institute, 2018). *Level 2* analysts (also known as second line analysts) are expected to have much more in-depth knowledge and carry out in-depth analysis. Where a *level 2* analyst cannot resolve an incident, it would be escalated to a *level 3 team* (third line analysts), who are considered to have superior knowledge amongst the analysts. However, Mcevatt (2019) points out that some SOCs operates a single-tier structure for all analysts and rely on automation to carry out many of the manual tasks previously performed by *level 1* analysts.

Figure 1. The components of a SOC

SOC engineers are responsible for hardware and software maintenance. SOC engineers are responsible for configuring and collecting logs from devices being monitored by the SOC through a process known as onboarding (Onwubiko & Ouazzane, 2019a). SOC engineers are also responsible for ensuring optimal running of SOC toolings such as the Security Information and Event Management (SIEM) solution, scripting and automation of SOC processes. Professionals such as penetration testers, or pen-testers, may also operate in a SOC tasked with the function of occasional simulation of attacks on an organisation's network to see how the organisation responds. A SOC may also have forensic and malware specialists who are responsible for forensic analysis of logs in a manner that is acceptable by a court of law (Zimmerman, 2014). A SOC manager is responsible for providing leadership and direction of the SOC (Hámornik & Krasznay, 2017). A SOC manager is directly responsible for managing the individuals and teams within a SOC, including the manning, resourcing, budget, shift scheduling and tooling strategy. They run the day to day operations of the SOC and report directly to the Chief Information Security Officer (CISO) (Sundaramurthy et al., 2014). Although a CISO may not be physically present in the SOC, they are responsible for translating the business objectives into the security requirements and communicate this to SOC managers. They also offer strategic advice on the security posture of the organisation.

Processes

An effective SOC needs to follow a set of well-defined working processes. SOCs maintain standard operation procedure (SOPs), *playbooks* and *runbooks,* that define actions that can be undertaken during an attack (Onwubiko & Ouazzane, 2019b). Playbooks and runbooks often outline defined action for known attacks. Most SOCs maintain some sort of a knowledge database for known and common attacks allowing analysts to rapidly respond to these attacks (Sundaramurthy et al., 2016). The processes in a SOC must be consistent with the organisational business objectives and must be implemented in collaboration with the related department. Processes must be repeatable, refined and optimised after any incidents, as SOC analysts depend on them (János & Dai, 2018). Research shows that SOC processes and their workflows are built around incident management systems and are often documented (Sundaramurthy et al., 2014). An effective SOC must have a process in place to address or triage some of the most common incidents such as phishing, malware infections and denial of service attacks.

Both the National Institute of Standards and Technology (NIST) (2012) and the SysAdmin, Audit, Network and Security (SANS) Institute (2018) provide cyber incident handling guidance that can be adapted to formalise incident handling in a SOC. Broadly speaking, the sequence proposed by NIST and SANS are synthesised and described as follows: *Preparation* – The argument here is that failing to prepare for an incident would lead to failure. Preparation starts with an overarching security policy that has the support of management, along with a well-defined process on how to respond when there is an attack. *Detection and Analysis* – A SOC needs to have a clear strategy and tools for detecting any deviations from the norm within their environment. Once an incident is identified the SOC would need to have a *containment strategy*. A *containment strategy* must outline techniques for stopping the identified threat from getting to other systems on the network and damage limitation. Following containment, a SOC can initiate an *Eradication and Recovery* plan to remove any artefacts left behind by the attacker. Information obtained from the identification and the containment phase will be used in determining the causes of the incident. Recovery may also entail putting any impacted system back onto the network. The final step of the incident handling process is the post-incident activity, also known as *Lesson Learnt*. Learning from the past and documenting the lesson learnt from an incident is an integral part of incident management and all good engineering practices (Lee, 2012). Lesson learnt documents could be used by analysts and engineers to improve their working practices. Figure 2 below shows the incident response process proposed by NIST (Souppaya & Scarfone, 2013).

Technologies

A SOC must be equipped with a range of security tools and software applications to have adequate visibility of the environment they are protecting (Kokulu et al., 2019). SOCs need software and hardware tools to respond to cyber threats. With the right tools and technology, the SOC can proactively hunt for signs of compromise in addition to detecting cyber threats. SOCs need use tools to identify security vulnerabilities and weaknesses in an organisations network. A SOC is unique to the organisation it belongs to, which means no two organisations are likely to have the same toolset (Schinagl et al., 2015). Some of the commonly used SOC toolings are described below:

Figure 2. NIST Incident Response Process (Souppaya & Scarfone, 2013)

- **Intrusion Detection System and Intrusion Prevention System (IDS/IPS)** - IDS/IPS are among the most widely used tools in most SOCs (Kwon et al., 2018). Both tools are designed to detect intrusions but work in a slightly different approach. An IDS detects an intrusion and sends a notification of it to a management console for an analyst to check whether this is a genuine alarm or a false positive (Chamiekara et al., 2017). In contrast, IPSs are designed to detect an alert and respond to an alert if it is deemed malicious, or if it poses threats. Despite their usefulness for detecting intrusion, Kwon et al. (2018) point out that they generate a large number of alerts, many of which are false positives. False positive involves reporting an alert as an attack, while in reality it poses no threat.
- **Firewalls** - Firewalls are often used to segment/separate a trusted network from an untrusted one, using a filtering mechanism, usually through an access control list (ACL). Firewall forms a key part of many network topologies and generates useful logs on network devices and user behavioral activities for the SOCs (Aijaz et al., 2015). Logs from firewalls can be fed into a central repository allowing correlation of events across the network.
- **Anti-viruses and Malware detection tools** - Anti-virus and malware detection tools are useful for detecting and preventing Trojans, Spyware and malicious code from running on an organisation's IT systems network. Again, logs from antivirus and malware detection tools can also be fed into SIEM, allowing an analyst to have visibility of what would otherwise be disparate data sources.
- **Security Information and Event Management (SIEM)** – SIEM is the evolution and integration of two technologies: Security Event Manager (SEM) and Security Information Manager (SIM). Whereas SEM focuses on log data collection and aggregation, SIM deals with correlation and normalisation of logs. Bringing these two technologies together allows a SIEM to perform log retention, aggregation, correlation and normalisation (Onwubiko & Ouazzane, 2019a). A SIEM allows for a centralised storage location where logs from multiple devices can be collated and analysed by a security analyst to determine whether any of those events pose threats (Chamiekara et al., 2017).
- **Ticketing and Messaging Systems** - Ticketing systems are used in SOCs for raising an incident, tracking the incident and managing the incident (Sundaramurthy et al., 2014). Ticketing systems are also used as a method of communicating and engaging with users on the network. In addition to a ticketing system, there should be dedicated telephone lines and email systems to aid with communication between teams and communication from users.

- **Specialist tools** - A SOC needs a range of specialist tools, like packet analysis tools and forensic tools to aid detailed investigation when analysing an incident. Tools such as Wireshark, Tripwire, DarkTrace and Encase Enterprise are among tools usually used by an analyst (Thomas, 2016). Tools must be used to assist and improve SOC operations such as audits, scans and responding to incidents (János & Dai, 2018). Tools must be tuned, patched and maintained. Deploying technology for the sake of technology is a pointless and costly exercise (Ernest and Young, 2014). Tools should be deployed only if it enhances the capability of the SOC and allows them to yield a better result.

EVOLUTION OF SOCs

SOCs have evolved over the years to adapt to changes to technologies and the trend in cyberattacks. Figure 3 depicts the evolution of SOCs. A business whitepaper published by Hewlett-Packard (HP) in 2013, suggests SOCs first emerged back in 1975 and existed mainly in the military and governmental organisations (Hewlett-Packard, 2013). According to HP, the first generation SOCs were often understaffed and relied on emerging technologies such as firewalls and antivirus to fend off would-be attackers. Zhong et al., (2016) mentioned that these SOCs were primarily used for intelligence gathering and managing IT security risk They also tended to be reactive and relied on signature-based solutions to detect signs of malicious activity against the organisations (Zhong et al., 2016). In essence, first-generation SOCs were set up to provide a formalised approach to monitoring and managing governmental and enterprise business IT assets. This initial concept of monitoring the network remains, to date, looking at extant literature.

Advances in technology and the sophisticated nature of cyberattacks in the mid-1990s resulted in the birth of the second-generation (2G) SOCs. This period was also marked by the introduction of vulnerability tracking systems and formalised system patching (Hewlett-Packard, 2013). Commercial companies began to offer security-monitoring solutions to paying customers in what is known as a Managed Security Service Provider (MSSP). In comparison to the first generation SOCs, the second generation SOCs saw a surge in the number of defensive security tools. Furthermore, tools such as vulnerability scanners, Intrusion Detection System (IDS) and Security Incident and Event Management (SIEM) became widely available (Hewlett-Packard, 2013). The introduction of SIEM also marked the beginning of using a central repository for correlating different security events into a single system, allowing SOC analysts to monitor from a single pane rather than the monitoring of multiple devices (Hámornik & Krasznay, 2017).

According to HP, financially driven attacks between 2002 and 2006 led to the development of the third-generation (3G) SOCs. 3G SOCs focused on three key areas: security monitoring, response and threat intelligence. This era saw the maturity of SOC services and the birth of the United States - Computer Emergency Response Team (US-CERT) and the Payment Card Industry (PCI). PCI mandated vendors to keep security and data protection standards. Also, regulatory requirements caused many organisations to take security and the protection of their network much more seriously. HP posit that between the years 2007 and 2012, businesses realised that intrusion into organisation networks was often inevitable, even with preventative measures and there was a need for improving existing SOCs' capabilities, resulting in the birth of the fourth-generation (4G) SOCs. Fourth-generation SOCs existed in an era characterised by hacktivism and Advanced Persistent Threats (APT) (Hewlett-Packard, 2013). Under 4G SOCs, businesses began to shift their attention from detection and prevention to Data Loss Prevention (DLP) and containment strategies.

HP suggests that the industry has now entered into a new phase with the introduction of the fifth-generation (5G) SOCs. However, they argue that 5G SOCs are still evolving. Under 5G SOCs, organisations rely on big data analysis and intelligence-driven methodologies, along with information sharing to find previously unknown attacks. 5G SOCs are more efficient, adaptive and automate many of the manual activities carried out by SOC analysts. Despite this automation, HP and many writers concede that without the human behind the technology, even the best technology will fail (Paul, 2014; Schinagl et al., 2015).

Figure 3. SOC Generations

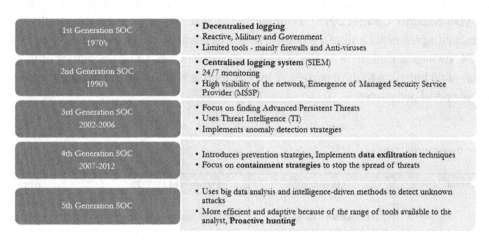

TYPES OF SOC IMPLEMENTATIONS

SOCs can be implemented using three main approaches: in-house SOC, outsourced SOC and a hybrid SOC (Falk et al., 2017). Organisations need to review these three options before deciding on which method suits their needs. The properties of these types of implementations are summarised in Table 1. With an in-house SOC, an organisation maintains the SOC from their premises. An organisation opting for an in-house SOC must be able to recruit and retain several SOC experts to run the operation of the SOC. In-house SOC experts, as explained by Miloslavkaya (2016), are often better placed to understand the overall architecture of a company's network than an outsourced SOC (also known as Managed Security Service Provider), who may have limited knowledge of the network. Such knowledge is essential during a detailed investigation into an incident. An in-house SOC can also be tailored to the precise business requirements and is expected to be more efficient and effective than an MSSP (Miloslavskaya, 2016).

However, an in-house SOC requires an initial cost outlay to building the SOC, which can be expensive to build and maintain for most small to medium-sized organisations (Shah, Ganesan, & Jajodia, 2018). Another downside is that an in-house SOC comes with the financial burden of having to train SOC analysts to the levels of expertise required to work in a SOC. SOC analysts working under an in-house SOC implementation need to demonstrate a high level of competence and effectiveness quickly, to justify the training investment. There is also the need for a periodic refreshing of hardware and technology to keep up with emerging threats. Jacobs et al. (Jacobs et al., 2013) suggest that there is no guarantee on a return on investment (ROI) for an in-house SOC.

An organisation may opt to outsource the monitoring of its network to a private third-party SOC provider, also known as MSSP (National Cyber Security Centre, 2018 ; Shah, Ganesan, & Jajodia, 2018). Outsourcing a SOC means that the MSSP handles the monitoring and responding to cyber incidents. Organisations using an MSSP will have a Service Level Agreement (SLA) on what is expected from the SOC (Shah, Ganesan, Jajodia, et al., 2018). MSSPs are generally cheaper than setting up an in-house SOC (Miloslavskaya, 2016). Miloslavskaya (2016) explains that MSSPs may be unbiased as they are not part of the organisational structure. However, there is some inherent risk when using an MSSP, which is mainly around employing the services of an MSSP, which means allowing external/third party entities to handle the organisation's data. MSSPs are often multi-tenanted, which can also mean that the intelligence gathered from one organisation may be used to improve services for other customers (National Cyber Security Centre, 2018). Data handed over to MSSPs can be mishandled or mismanaged. Contractual agreements will often outline the consequences of issues such as data mishandling. A hybrid SOC owns and runs an in-house SOC, but also outsources some operations of its monitoring and detection of an intrusion to third parties. A hybrid approach draws on the strengths and weaknesses of both in-house and outsourced.

Table 1. The three main types of SOC

Criteria	In-house	Outsourced (MSSP)	Hybrid
People(Skills Availability)	The organisation needs to recruit and maintain a team of skilled staff to run the SOC. A limited number of skilled professionals.	MSSP will have a pool of staff and resources to address the needs of their clients. They still have the challenge of maintaining skilled staff.	Hybrid SOC offers the middle ground. An organisation can maintain a relatively small number of staffs knowing that they can rely on the expertise from the outside to assist when needed.
Security Processes	Businesses can design and tailor their internal processes.	Processes and techniques used for one client may be used to solve a problem for another client.	Businesses design their in-house processes but have the flexibility of drawing on the tactics and processes of a third party.
Technology	The organisation owns the infrastructure and any associated software and licenses. This leads to high cost of investment. Hardware also needs a periodic refresh. Need to train staff to run the tools.	The cost of buying expensive assets will be offset by a number of clients.	Businesses can reduce the cost of having to invest in expensive tools. Businesses can draw on the tools and techniques of the MSSP.
Financial cost	High initial cost to set up and there are no guarantees on Return on Investment (ROI). There is also the cost associated with staffing.	Cost is typically low because the MSSP can leverage existing infrastructure for multiple clients.	Organisations can reduce initial investment, as they will outsource aspects of their operations to third parties.

THE MAIN FUNCTIONS OF A SOC

As mentioned earlier, a SOC offers several functions and not just the monitoring of an organisation's network with the purpose of detecting cyberattacks. The functions discussed below represent the key functions and services that can be offered by a SOC. These functions are based on in-depth analysis of existing literature (Jacobs et al., 2013; Majid & Ariffi, 2019; Onwubiko, 2015; Schinagl et al., 2015):

- **Monitoring and Detection** – The monitoring and detection function is at the heart of the SOC operation. To detect unusual activity on an organisation's network, such as business data exfiltration, unauthorised or attempted access to restricted information, a SOC collects and monitors security events from a wide range of sources such as servers, routers, end-point devices and associated peripherals. The monitoring function is performed by analysts, as they monitor computer network systems, devices and applications running on those devices on a 24/7/365 basis. The key objective is to identify changes in baseline, or for the observation of unusual activity. Onwubiko (2015) asserts that the monitoring function enables a SOC to identify, protect, detect, analyse and respond to threats.

- **Analysis Function** - This function involves an in-depth investigation into observed abnormal/ unusual activities seen across an organisational network. A SOC supports businesses to identify threats through a deep inspection of logs to see if there is any malicious activity (Botta et al., 2008). Analysis can be conducted using automated processes, customised script or carried out manually, albeit the manual process is highly ineffective and laborious (Onwubiko, 2015). Onwubiko (2015) explains how manual analysis can be done using improvised tools such as Microsoft Excel spreadsheet to analyse logs. Manual processes, however, as expected, are highly inefficient. The application of a Security Orchestration, Automation and Response (SOAR) solution can facilitate and automate the analysis process for SOCs (Mcevatt, 2019).

- **Response and Reporting Function** - Once an intrusion or a suspicious event/ activity is detected, a SOC needs to enact existing defined processes to react in a manner that will reduce any damage. A SOC can provide organisations with a properly defined response to an incident (Onwubiko, 2015). The response function also involves generating and providing reports regarding observed anomalies on the network (Botta et al., 2008).

- **Incident Management Function** - Incident management activity is at the heart of SOC operations. It encompasses the above three functions: monitoring and detection, analysis, responding and reporting of an incident. Incident handling evolves drawing on a pre-planned defined incident response process (SANS Institute, 2018). SOCs support business to handle cyberattacks in a way that would reduce disruption to services while ensuring continuity of the business operation. Jacobs et al. (2013) state that incident management is the ability to prepare, identify and escalate an incident.

- **Baseline and Vulnerability Function** - A SOC can help an organisation to identify vulnerabilities in their enterprise network by periodically running vulnerability scans (Farris et al., 2018). Having identified vulnerabilities, a SOC will then initiate patching of the devices with the vulnerabilities. Not patching systems leaves the organisation at the risk of that vulnerability being exploited by an adversary. A SOC may offer a baseline security function such as hardening of systems to remove unnecessary services or unused services across an organisation.

- **Intelligence Function** - The intelligence function is a continuous process that seeks to leverage indicators of compromise to discover previously unknown attacks (Miloslavskaya, 2018). Proactive intelligence gathering from open sources and security solutions vendor is an important activity for SOCs. Intelligence gleaned from a range of sources can be used by a SOC to develop effective use cases that can be used to detect cyberattacks. Miloslavskaya (2018) states that intelligence data can be used to better protect an organisation. The intelligence gathered through this analysis can also provide guidance for other analysts on the risk that the organisation faces. The intelligence function may entail implementing new rules, and use cases gathered from publicly available sources, such as CERTS and incorporating these into SOC systems, such as SIEMs to detect attacks. Intelligence function requires analysts to maintain situational awareness to understand emerging threats to introduce countermeasures. Intelligence function also involves sharing of indicators of compromise (IOC) within the team to help with the detection of attacks.

- **Forensic and Malware Analysis Function** – A SOC can offer forensic and malware analysis function to support an organisation to identify, preserve, recover, analyse and present digital evidence to establish digital crime (Schinagl et al., 2015). A skilled forensic investigator may be required to perform this function (Mcclain et al., 2015). It is important this work is done by a qualified skilled professional to ensure that forensic evidence is collected and analysed in a manner that would be admissible to a court of law (Zimmerman, 2014). This also includes how malware is analysed and reverse engineered (Zimmerman, 2014).

- **Penetration Testing Function** - To assess how effective and secure an organisation's defences are, a SOC may offer penetration-testing services to simulate an attack on the organisation's network. The objective of simulating such an attack is to identify which systems or devices can be breached (Schinagl et al., 2015). A SOC offering a penetration testing function can also help businesses to identify what information can be obtained by an attacker, if their systems are breached, allowing them to put in mitigation strategy. Also, penetration testing function can enable an organisation to appreciate how their systems would react when they are under attack.

- **Policies and Signatures Management Function** - A SOC can support businesses to maintain their use cases in their SIEM or signatures in their IDS. A SOC needs to maintain up-to-date use cases. Without this function, the number of false positives generated by these systems would be overwhelming for an analyst doing the monitoring and detection function. Effective policies and signature management also ensure that tools are configured with the correct policies capable of detecting known cyberattacks.

- **Compliance and Risk Management Function** – Many organisations have to deal with industrial and regulatory requirements, along with data protection and privacy laws. For example, an organisation may be required to keep logs over some time to allow auditors to review these logs if required, to trace security breaches. Often, there are penalties for non-compliance to these laws and regulations. One function of a SOC is to support businesses to realise this objective by offering services that handle issues around compliance. Similarly, a SOC can support organisations to carry out risk management activities, which may entail potential risk faced by the business and recommending mitigation strategies.

- **Engineering and Log Collection Function** - Log collection and retention of these logs is an important function for many SOCs. Besides collecting logs to fulfil, in some instances, regulatory requirements, Onwubiko (2015) states that without logs, it would be difficult to established whether there has been an intrusion. This position is supported by Mutewa et al. (2019) who posit that without log collection it would be impossible for any SOC to get visibility of what is happening on an organisation's network. Log collection can also be used to assist other teams, for example, Network Operations teams who deal with performance issues on a network to identify unusual activities across an organisation's network.

SOC CHALLENGES

Despite the many benefits offered by a SOC, there are several challenges faced by SOCs, which impact on their overall effectiveness and efficiency (Agyepong et al., 2019). Below are some of the main challenges faced by SOCs:

- **Large Number of Devices** - Most organisations own many computing assets and devices. Devices such as firewalls, servers, routers, switches and mobile devices such as laptops are usually operated by most organisations. These devices are log sources and are continuously generating logs whenever an event occurs (Onwubiko, 2015). The problem here is that it becomes difficult for a SOC to know which logs should be turned on and those that should be turned off for these devices. Feeding all these logs into SIEM without intelligent tuning of the logs will result in overwhelming analysts with too many false positive alerts (Onwubiko & Ouazzane, 2019a). Another challenge associated with the large number of end point devices is that most SOCs, as explained by Kokuklu et al. (2019), struggle to maintain effective visibility of all monitored devices. Many SOCs also struggle to comprehend the topology of the network under their management, which impedes analysts ability to maintain effective cyber situational awareness (Kokulu et al., 2019).

- **Amount of Logs** - Cybersecurity researchers usually point out that the number of alerts generated and received by SOC toolings, such as Security Information and Event Management, is more than any SOC can have the capacity to deal with. This is directly linked to the number of devices being monitored. Feng et al. (2017), for example, point out that a single firewall can generate gigabytes of data daily. Similarly, an IPS can generate thousands of events within the same time period. However, the majority of these alerts are classed as false alarms (false positives) (János & Dai, 2018). An efficient SOC needs to filter out false positives to reduce the workload on analysts. Tadda (2008) suggests the use of correlation systems such as SIEMs to reduce the number of false alerts. Sifting through a large volume of data can also result in alert fatigue in the analyst (Thomas, 2016). One of the contributing factors to burnout amongst analysts is the large number of false positives presented to them (Sundaramurthy et al., 2015). Analysts are also likely to miss malicious activity because finding what is true becomes like finding a needle in a haystack (Feng et al., 2017).

- **Sophisticated Attacks** - Criminals are increasingly using various sophisticated techniques to avoid detection. Detecting of stealthy and sophisticated attacks remains a major challenge for many SOCs. Detecting stealthy attacks such as Advanced Persistent Threats (APTs) cannot be done by simply using collecting the logs generated by different endpoints devices (János & Dai, 2018). For example, the level of skills required for detecting lateral movement of APTs is often beyond many analysts. With the skills shortage in the cyber industry, sophisticated attacks pose a major challenge for inexperienced or junior analysts (Agyepong et al., 2019). Dealing with sophisticated attacks requires in-depth knowledge and skills on the part of the analysts, which most SOCs do not have (Schinagl et al., 2015).

- **Regulatory and Compliance Requirements** - Regulatory and industry compliance can mandate a SOC to retain logs over a period of time. Given that most organisations would not like to take the risk of being fined for non-compliance, it places the onus on the business to provide the SOC with sufficient hardware for log collection. Hardware is expensive, placing an additional financial burden on the SOC. Also, the data collected by SOCs may be subject to privacy regulations.

CONCLUSION

SOCs are increasingly being used by organisations as part of their cybersecurity strategy. While SOCs help businesses to protect their network against cyberattacks it is important to note that SOCs offer several other functions to help improve the overall security posture of an organisation. This chapter presents basic concepts of a SOC and highlights that a SOC operates through the harmonisation of three components: *people*, *processes* and *technology*. A SOC needs to have people with the right skill set, a well-defined process and effective technology in order to detect and respond to threats. In terms of implementing a SOC, three main implementation strategies were presented: in-house SOC, outsourced SOC and a hybrid SOC. The main function of a SOC was presented before presenting some of the challenges that are faced by modern-day SOCs.

REFERENCES

Agyepong, E., Cherdantseva, Y., Reinecke, P., & Burnap, P. (2019). Challenges and performance metrics for security operations center analysts: a systematic review. *Journal of Cyber Security Technology*, 1–28. Retrieved from https://www.tandfonline.com/doi/full/10.1080/23742917.2019.1698178

Aijaz, L., Aslam, B., & Umar, K. (2015). Security operations center — A need for an academic environment. In *World Symposium on Computer Networks and Information Security (WSCNIS)* (pp. 1–7). 10.1109/WSCNIS.2015.7368297

Beek, C., Frosst, D., Greve, P., Kay, B., Lenaerts-Bergmans, B., & McFarland, C. ... Sun, B. (2016). *McAfee Labs Quarterly Threat Report December 2016*. Retrieved from www.mcafee.com/us/mcafee-labs.aspx

Botta, D., Werlinger, R., Gagné, A., Beznosov, K., Iverson, L., Fels, S., & Fisher, B. (2008). Towards understanding IT security professionals and their tools. In *Proceedings of the 3rd symposium on Usable privacy and security* (p. 100). ACM.

Brown, J. M., Greenspan, S., & Biddle, R. (2016). Incident response teams in IT operations centers: The T-TOCs model of team functionality. *Cognition Technology and Work*, *18*(4), 695–716. doi:10.100710111-016-0374-2

Chamiekara, G. W. P., Cooray, M. I. M., Wickramasinghe, L. S. A. M., Koshila, Y. M. S., Abeywardhana, K. Y., & Senarathna, A. N. (2017). AutoSOC: A low budget flexible security operations platform for enterprises and organizations. In *2017 National Information Technology Conference, NITC 2017* (pp. 100–105). 10.1109/NITC.2017.8285644

Chuan, B. L. J., Singh, M. M., & Shariff, A. R. M. (2019). APTGuard: Advanced persistent threat (APT) detections and predictions using android smartphone. In *Computational Science and Technology* (Vol. 481, pp. 545–555). Singapore: Springer Verlag. doi:10.1007/978-981-13-2622-6_53

Cichonski, P., Millar, T., Grance, T., & Scarfone, K. (2012). *Computer Security Incident Handling Guide Recommendations of the National Institute of Standards and Technology*. doi:10.6028/NIST.SP.800-61r2

Ernest and Young (EY). (2014). *Security Operations Centers — helping you get ahead of cybercrime*. Retrieved from www.ey.com/GISS2014

Falk, E., Repcek, S., Fiz, B., Hommes, S., State, R., & Sasnauskas, R. (2017). VSOC - A Virtual Security Operating Center. *2017 IEEE Global Communications Conference, GLOBECOM 2017 - Proceedings, 8*, 1–6.

Farris, K. A., Cybenko, G., College, D., Ganesan, R., & Jajodia, S. (2018). VULCON: A System for Vulnerability Prioritization, Mitigation, and Management. *ACM Trans. Priv. Secur, 21*(4), 28. doi:10.1145/3196884

Feng, C., Wu, S., & Liu, N. (2017). A user-centric machine learning framework for cyber security operations center. In *2017 IEEE International Conference on Intelligence and Security Informatics (ISI)* (pp. 173–175). Beijing, China: IEEE. 10.1109/ISI.2017.8004902

Hámornik, P. B., & Krasznay, C. (2017). *A Team-Level Perspective of Human Factors in Cyber Security: Security Operations Centers* (pp. 224–236). Cham: Springer. Retrieved from https://link.springer.com/content/pdf/10.1007%2F978-3-319-60585-2_21.pdf

Hewlett-Packard. (2013). *5G/SOC: SOC Generations -HP ESP Security Intelligence and Operations Consulting Services - Business white paper*. Retrieved from http://www.cnmeonline.com/myresources/hpe/docs/HP_ArcSight_WhitePapers_5GSOC_SOC_Generations.PDF

Jacobs, P., Arnab, A., & Irwin, B. (2013). *Classification of Security Operation Centers. In 2013 Information Security for South Africa* (pp. 1–7). IEEE. Retrieved from https://ieeexplore.ieee.org/document/6641054/

János, F. D., & Dai, P. H. N. (2018). Security concerns towards Security Operations centers. *2018 IEEE 12th International Symposium on Applied Computational Intelligence and Informatics (SACI)*, 273–278.

Kokulu, F. B., Bao, T., Doupé, A., Shoshitaishvili, Y., Ahn, G.-J., & Zhao, Z. (2019). *Matched and Mismatched SOCs : A Qualitative Study on Security Operations Center Issues. Association of Computing Machinery*. ACM. doi:10.1145/3319535.3354239

Kwon, T., Song, J., Choi, S., Lee, Y., & Park, J. (2018). VISNU: A Novel Visualization Methodology of Security Events Optimized for a Centralized SOC. *2018 13th Asia Joint Conference on Information Security (AsiaJCIS)*, 1–7. Retrieved from https://ieeexplore.ieee.org/document/8453754/

Lee, M. G. (2012). *Securing the human to protect the system: human factors in cyber security. In 7th IET International Conference on System Safety, incorporating the Cyber Security Conference 2012* (pp. 41–41). IET. Retrieved from https://digital-library.theiet.org/content/conferences/10.1049/cp.2012.1519

Majid, M. A., & Ariffi, K. A. Z. (2019). Success Factors for Cyber Security Operation Center (SOC) Establishment. In *International Conference on Informatics, Engineering, Science and Technology.* Bandung: European Alliance for Innovation (EAI). 10.4108/eai.18-7-2019.2287841

Mcclain, J., Silva, A., Emmanuel, G., Anderson, B., Nauer, K., Abbott, R., & Forsythe, C. (2015). Human Performance Factors in Cyber Security Forensic Analysis. *Procedia Manufacturing, 3*, 5301–5307. doi:10.1016/j.promfg.2015.07.621

Mcevatt, P. (2019). Advanced Threat Centre and Future of Security Monitoring. *Fujitsu Scientific and Technical Journal, 55*(5), 16–22.

Medeiros, F. A., & Bygrave, L. A. (2015). Brazil's Marco Civil da Internet: Does it live up to the hype? *Computer Law & Security Review, 31*(1), 120–130. doi:10.1016/j.clsr.2014.12.001

Miloslavskaya, N. (2016). Security operations centers for information security incident management. In *Proceedings - 2016 IEEE 4th International Conference on Future Internet of Things and Cloud, FiCloud 2016* (pp. 131–138). 10.1109/FiCloud.2016.26

Miloslavskaya, N. (2018). Information security management in SOCs and SICs. *Journal of Intelligent & Fuzzy Systems, 35*(3), 2637–2647. doi:10.3233/JIFS-169615

Mutemwa, M., Mtsweni, J., & Zimba, L. (2019). Integrating a security operations centre with an organization's existing procedures, policies and information technology systems. In *2018 International Conference on Intelligent and Innovative Computing Applications, ICONIC 2018* (pp. 1–6). IEEE.

National Cyber Security Centre. (2018). *The cyber threat to UK business*. Retrieved from https://www.nationalcrimeagency.gov.uk/publications/785-the-cyber-threat-to-uk-business/file

Onwubiko, C. (2015). *Cyber security operations centre: Security monitoring for protecting business and supporting cyber defense strategy. In 2015 International Conference on Cyber Situational Awareness, Data Analytics and Assessment (CyberSA)* (pp. 1–10). London, UK: IEEE. Retrieved from https://ieeexplore.ieee.org/document/7166125/

Onwubiko, C., & Onwubiko, A. (2019). Cyber KPI for Return on Security Investment. In *2019 International Conference on Cyber Situational Awareness, Data Analytics And Assessment (Cyber SA)* (pp. 1–8). Oxford, UK: IEEE. 10.1109/CyberSA.2019.8899375

Onwubiko, C., & Ouazzane, K. (2019a). Cyber onboarding is "broken." In *2019 International Conference on Cyber Security and Protection of Digital Services (Cyber Security 2019)* (pp. 1–13). Oxford, UK: Institute of Electrical and Electronics Engineers Inc.

Onwubiko, C., & Ouazzane, K. (2019b). SOTER : A Playbook for Cyber Security Incident Management. *IEEE Transactions on Engineering Management*, 1–22.

Paul, C. C. L. (2014). Human-Centered Study of a Network Operations Center: Experience Report and Lessons Learned. In *Proceedings of the ACM Workshop on Security Information Workers* (pp. 39–42). Retrieved from https://dl.acm.org/citation.cfm?id=2663899

Research and Markets. (2019, May 22). *SOC as a Service Market - Global Forecast to 2024*. Retrieved March 25, 2020, from https://www.globenewswire.com/news-release/2019/05/22/1840685/0/en/SOC-as-a-Service-Market-Global-Forecast-to-2024.html

SANS Institute. (2018). *SEC504: Hacker Techniques, Exploits, and Incident Handling*. Boston: The SANS Institute.

Schinagl, S., Schoon, K., & Paans, R. (2015). A framework for designing a security operations centre (SOC). In *2015 48th Hawaii International Conference on System Sciences* (Vol. 2015-March, pp. 2253–2262). IEEE.

Shah, A., Ganesan, R., & Jajodia, S. (2018). A methodology for ensuring fair allocation of CSOC effort for alert investigation. *International Journal of Information Security, 18*, 1–20. doi:10.100710207-018-0407-3

Shah, A., Ganesan, R., Jajodia, S., & Cam, H. (2018). Adaptive reallocation of cybersecurity analysts to sensors for balancing risk between sensors. *Service Oriented Computing and Applications, 12*(2), 123–135. doi:10.100711761-018-0235-3

Souppaya, M., & Scarfone, K. (2013). NIST Special Publication 800-83 Revision 1 Guide to Malware Incident Prevention and Handling for Desktops and Laptops. *NIST Special Publication, 800*, 83. doi:10.6028/NIST.SP.800-83r1

Sundaramurthy, S., Ou, X., Bardas, A. G., Case, J., Wesch, M., … Rajagopalan, S. R. (2015). A Human Capital Model for Mitigating Security Analyst Burnout. In *Symposium on Usable Privacy and Security* (pp. 347–359). Academic Press.

Sundaramurthy, S. C., Case, J., Truong, T., Zomlot, L., & Hoffmann, M. (2014). A Tale of Three Security Operation Centers. In *Proceedings of the 2014 ACM Workshop on Security Information Workers - SIW '14* (pp. 43–50). Scottdale, AZ: ACM. doi:10.1145/2663887.2663904

Sundaramurthy, S. C., Florida, S., Mchugh, J., Ou, X., Florida, S., Wesch, M., … Bardas, A. G. (2016). Turning Contradictions into Innovations or : How We Learned to Stop Whining and Improve Security Operations In *Proceedings of the Turning Contradictions into Innovations or : How We Learned to Stop Whining and Improve* (pp. 237–251). USENIX.

Tadda, G. P. (2008). *Measuring Performance of Cyber Situation Awareness Systems. In 2008 11th International Conference on Information Fusion* (pp. 1–8). IEEE. Retrieved from https://ieeexplore.ieee.org/stamp/stamp.jsp?tp=&arnumber=4632229

Thomas, A. E. (2016). *Security operations center : analyst guide*. London: CreateSpace.

Tuglular, T., & Belli, F. (2008). Model-Based Mutation Testing of Firewalls. *Fast Abstracts of TAIC-PART Conference*.

Xia, H., & Xu, Y. (2017). Design and Research of Safety Test Model Based on Advanced Evasion Techniques. In *Global Conference on Mechanics and Civil Engineering (GCMCE 2017)* (Vol. 132, pp. 92–96). Atlantis Press. 10.2991/gcmce-17.2017.18

Zhong, C., Yen, J., Liu, P., & Erbacher, R. F. (2016). Automate Cybersecurity Data Triage by Leveraging Human Analysts' Cognitive Process. In *Proceedings - 2nd IEEE International Conference on Big Data Security on Cloud, IEEE BigDataSecurity 2016, 2nd IEEE International Conference on High Performance and Smart Computing, IEEE HPSC 2016 and IEEE International Conference on Intelligent Data and S* (pp. 357–363). New York: IEEE.

Zimmerman, C. (2014). *Cybersecurity Operations Center*. The MITRE Corporation.

KEY TERMS AND DEFINITIONS

APT (Advanced Persistent Threat): A type of a cyberattack in which an attacker gains unauthorised access to a network and its resources and remains undetected for over a long period of time.

False-Positive: Denotes a non-malicious security event or an alert that is reported as malicious by a security reporting tool.

MSSP (Managed Security Service Provider): An organisation that provides outsourcing security operations centre services to multiple clients.

Penetration Testing: A systematic process of simulating a cyberattack against an organisation to identify vulnerabilities in their networks and applications.

SIEM (Security Information and Event Management): A security solutions that collects, aggregates and analyse security events and logs from multiple IT infrastructures and security devices.

SOC (Security Operations Centre): A centralised location inside or outside an organisation that supports an organisation to defend their network against cyberattacks.

Trojan: A type of malicious software that is designed to look legitimate.

Chapter 7
Students' Intentions on Cyber Ethics Issues

Isaac Wiafe

 https://orcid.org/0000-0003-1149-3309
University of Ghana, Ghana

Winfred Yaokumah

 https://orcid.org/0000-0001-7756-1832
University of Ghana, Ghana

Felicia Amanfo Kissi

Ghana Institute of Management and Public Administration, Ghana

ABSTRACT

Cyber ethical decisions have grave moral, legal, and social consequences on individuals, organizations, and societies at large. This chapter examines the extent of cyber unethical intentions among students on cyber piracy, cyber plagiarism, computer crime and abuses, and cyber privacy infringement. Using frequency analysis and the t-test of independent samples, the results showed that almost 24% of the respondents have intentions to engage in cyber piracy and about 13% would infringe on others privacy in cyberspace. More respondents have intentions to commit cyber piracy as compared to other cyber ethic issues, while cyber privacy infringement was the least observed. Almost 30% of respondents had intentions to commit software piracy, and 18.6% would engage in hacking activities. Also, cybercrime and computer abuse were more common among males than females. Cyber plagiarism was significantly higher among foreign students when compared to local students. Cyber piracy, cyber plagiarism, computer crime, and cyber privacy infringement were significantly higher in public universities.

DOI: 10.4018/978-1-7998-3149-5.ch007

INTRODUCTION

Along with the benefits of the cyberspace comes ethical, legal, and moral challenges (Jamal, Ferdoos, Zaman, & Hussain, 2015). Individuals face multiple decisions in the cyberspace daily and resolve ethical dilemmas with or without conscious consideration of ethics. Ethics in the cyberspace (cyber ethics), examines the moral, legal, and social issues relating to the development and use of cybertechnology. While society is increasingly becoming concerned with ethical problems of the use of computers and the Internet (Onyancha, 2015), questions on "what is" or "what is not" ethical within the cyberspace is a dilemma. Ethical standards seek to guide or govern proper behaviours of employees in organizations or for professionals belonging to professional associations. Though the importance of professional ethics is acknowledged by researchers and practitioner (Bustard, 2018), the universal application of ethical codes is impracticable. What is ethical, legal and moral, varies among different cultures, organizations and countries (Tilley, Fredricks, & Hornett, 2012; Weaver, 2016).

Within the cyberspace, ethics deal with how individuals use the space in the context of their attitude's assumptions, beliefs, values, and knowledge (Da Veiga, 2016). This may be intentional or unintentional. While knowledge in ethics may enhance attitudes for dealing with ethical issues (Monteverde, 2014), and ethical culture is well appreciated (Gcaza, Von Solms, & Van Vuuren, 2015), research focusing on cyber ethics is limited. Thus, more studies are needed to explore ethical behaviour intentions and perceptions among cyber users. This will provide guidelines for encouraging appropriate ethical behaviour within the cyberspace (Burmeister, 2013). This chapter, therefore, seeks to (a) ascertain students' intentions on cyber ethical choices with regard to cyber piracy, plagiarism, computer crime and abuse, and cyberprivacy infringement and to (b) determine the different levels of such intentions between genders, nationalities, and universities. The remainder of the chapter is presented as follows; the next section presents a discussion on existing ethical guidelines, this is followed by the methods used for the study, then the findings, discussions, recommendations and conclusions are drawn.

BACKGROUND

Theories of Ethical Guidelines

Ethics seek to address questions on how humankind must live. Its guidelines are derived from theories including Deontology, Consequentialism, and Virtue ethics. Ethical theories provide perspectives for assessing and resolving ethical situations (Yaokumah, 2020). Deontology argues that to act ethically, one ought to follow the appropriate rules needed to perform his or her duty (Kant, 1998). This suggests that right actions are those that are performed out of duty, or in reverence to moral laws.

Consequentialism is the rightness or wrongness of actions, and it depends on an action's consequence (Scheffler, 1988; Sinnott-Armstrong, 2003; Stocker, 1969). Character ethics, also referred to as virtue ethics seek to answer, "what kind of person ought I to be". It focuses on character, with the underlying belief that a person of good character will take actions that are considered to morally best. Thus, a person with good character would not want to do things that might hurt others. Right actions are those that are performed by virtuous persons. In other words, character ethics is the moral character and habits of the person acting it.

Intellectual Property Rights

Intellectual property is an intangible property of any kind created by individuals or corporation. Intellectual property rights, therefore, relate to laws on copyright, patents, trademarks and designs. There are three main methods for protecting intellectual properties and these are (i) trade secrets, (ii) copyright and (iii) patents. Trade secrets are intellectual works or products belonging to businesses, which are not in the public domain. Copyrights are statutory grants that protect intellectual property from being copied for the life of the author plus 70 years while patents are grants for a creator of an invention to have an exclusive monopoly on ideas behind the invention for 20 years.

The reverse of intellectual property right is piracy. It is the unauthorized use or reproduction of work whose characteristics are protected by intellectual property rights. It can also be the attempt to use or reproduce other's work. The Internet facilitates piracy of digital goods (i.e. digital piracy). Digital or cyber piracy includes downloading or uploading digital goods such as software, documents, movies, and music by individual end-users from illegal sources without permission from the copyright holder. Downloading copyrighted materials without paying is currently the highest practice of piracy (Tomczyk, 2019). Such actions bring financial benefits to perpetrators by downloading copyrighted materials for free (Taylor, 2012) and causes financial loss to the owners (Hill, 2007). Digital piracy or cyber piracy has intellectual and monetary impacts. It decreases creativity amongst inventors (Hampton-Sosa, 2017) and it has been estimated that 42% of all software in use has been pirated. This brings a revenue loss of almost US$60 billion (Business Software Alliance, 2012).

Considering that some firms rely on the Internet for majority of their business transactions and operations, it is inevitable to avoid digital plagiarism. Additionally, social behaviour and existing ethical challenges have been transferred to the cyberspace (Smith & Rupp, 2002) and this makes it a challenge to curtail digital plagiarism. It has been argued that the high availability of pirated software and low censure of buying it, is a major contributing factor to the increase in pirated software (Moores & Dhillon, 2000). Perceived likelihood of prosecution has been found to impact piracy intentions (Akbulut & Dönmez, 2018). This is because, cyber piracy can emerge from any part of the Globe, thus the ability to track all perpetuators and prosecute them is almost impossible. Considering all this, some researchers have explained that piracy is justified and thus must not be criminalized (Mančić, 2010).

Cyber Privacy

Privacy is a claim by individuals preferring to be not observed or disturbed others. At such a state, they prefer to be left alone: free from surveillance or interference from other individuals, organizations, or states. Individuals within the cyberspace prefer to be able to control their information (Pluijmers & Weiss, 2002). As such, advancement in information systems and technology makes privacy issues a challenge. This is because current information systems are characterized by ubiquitous properties and thus can collect a larger amount of data from users. Particularly, within academic social networking sites users tend to trust each other and thus share information to promote knowledge sharing (Koranteng & Wiafe, 2018) without the considering privacy implications of the information they share. However, theories of privacy requires that processes used in gathering and disseminating information are (a) appropriate to a particular context, and (b) comply with norms that govern the flow of personal information in a given context (Moor, 1997; Posner, 1978; Tene & Polonetsky, 2013). Although some researchers have demonstrated that systems can be designed to ensure protection of personal data (Kuada, Wiafe, Addo, & Djaba, 2017), privacy challenges within the cyberspace continues to evolve.

Current research (Janssen & van den Hoven, 2015) have argued that protection of personal data and provision of controls over access to data by others can be ensured by preventing harm,: Information injustice and discrimination, and encroachment on moral autonomy and human dignity. Badu-Marfo, Farooq, & Patterson, (2019) argued that the challenge of privacy protection in big data in the face of personally identifiable information is the most relevant issue in modern technology advancement. This notion is supported by other researchers (Tene & Polonetsky, 2013). Considering the vast amount of data and detailed information about people in the cyberspace, methods are needed to protect these data. However, open data policies are becoming more common, and by their nature, impose much less controls on "who" and the number of people "who" could have access to potentially identifiable information (Badu-Marfo et al., 2019). Thus, there is a need to design privacy-friendly information technology (IT) systems (Janssen & van den Hoven, 2015). Yet, current literature on users' intentions of cyberspaces that will guide the design of privacy-friendly IT systems is limited.

Computer Ethics

Computer ethics focus on addressing computer crime and computer resource abuses. Computer crime entails the commission of illegal acts in which the computer may be the object or instrument of the crime, while computer abuse is an unethical act aimed at wasting computer resources. Computer ethics is the code of conduct that protects IT professionals and individual employees in organizations. State laws play a key role in computer ethics. They provide legislation that has a direct impact on information and communications technology (ICT) use. This includes data protection acts, contract laws and various regulatory frameworks. Ethics protect individuals from predation, breach of privacy, identity theft, and unlawful use of proprietary software. Although legal compliance is fundamentals for professionals, legalistic approaches to ethical issues have limitations. One of such limitations is the diversity of legal systems internationally. The jurisdiction of some laws results in a lack of uniformity in enforcement and applicability of laws in other environments.

Academic Integrity

Cyber plagiarism is copying, downloading or use in part, or all ideas from the Internet without proper attribution (Ercegovac, 2006). It is an act of forgery, piracy, and fraud which is criminal. It has devastating consequences aside its being criminal, because those who obtain qualifications through plagiarism may work in various sectors as professionals without the proper knowledge. Although, the use of the Internet and social networking sites in particular promote academic research and scholarship (Koranteng, Wiafe, Katsriku, & Apau, 2019), it has also facilitates plagiarism and academic theft (Akbulut et al., 2008).

Plagiarism can be detected either manually or with the aid of specialized software. Rogerson, (2017) noted that discovering irrelevant materials and irregularities in references can be a clue to the detection of plagiarism in people's work. Digital detection, on the other hand, involves sophisticated and are relatively accurate software that retrieves and presents the evidence so that it is easy to identify (Rodafinos, 2018). Although a number of studies have raised concerns about levels of plagiarism (Ercegovac, 2006; Granitz & Loewy, 2007; Lathrop & Foss, 2000; Mahmood, 2009; Rodafinos, 2018; Rogerson, 2017;

Tang, Chung, & Chen, 2018), studies that seek to measure intention levels among tertiary students, especially in developing countries is limited.

METHOD

A cyber ethic instrument was used to collect and analyse the data. The analyses sought to evaluate whether respondents have intentions to commit any of the discussed unethical behaviours. Eight hundred (800) questionnaires were sent to graduate and undergraduate students in eight (8) private and public universities in Ghana. A convenient sampling method was used for distributing the questionnaire. Five hundred and three (503) responses were received: this gives a response rate of 62.9%. Two hundred and sixty-two (262) of the respondents were males and the rest were females. This provided a near-balance in gender distribution (i.e. 52% of males and 48% of females). Students from other countries (i.e. international students) formed 8% of the responses and the rest were Ghanaians.

Undergraduate students were 70% and graduate students including those doing research were 30%. Forty per cent were from private universities and the rest were from public universities. Table 1 presents a summary of respondents' description. The data was analysed by (a) ascertaining the intention of participants' cyber ethics behaviour (i.e. cyber piracy, cyber plagiarism, computer crime and abuse, and cyberprivacy violation) and (b) determining the differences in intentions on cyber piracy, cyber plagiarism, computer crime and abuse, and cyberprivacy violation among genders, nationalities and university types. The first part of data analysis uses descriptive statistics (mean and percentages) and the second part used the t-test of independent samples.

Table 1. Description of Respondents (n=503)

			Freq	%
Gender				
	Male		262	52
	Female		241	48
Nationality				
	Ghanaians		463	92
	Foreigners		40	8
Level				
	Undergraduate		352	70
	Graduate		151	30
Institution				
	Private		201	40
	Public		302	60

FINDINGS

Respondents' Cyber ethics Behaviour Intention

The findings demonstrated that almost 24% of the respondents have an intention to be involved in cyber piracy, 14% have an intention to plagiarize or commit computer crime, and 13% would infringe on others privacy within cyberspaces (see Figure 1). Accordingly, respondents are more likely to commit cyber ethic violations in cyber piracy as compare to cyberprivacy. Table 2 shows the means and standard deviations of each factor relating to cyber ethics behaviour intentions.

Among all, the most predominant ethical intentions of respondents were (a) Not spreading wrong information about others (about 91%), (b) Not violating the privacy and confidentiality of information (such as trade secret and password) (about 90%); (c) Not disclosing confidential institutional information (89.8%), (d) Not taking credit for someone else's work (89.6%), and (e) Not stealing funds by the use of the Internet (89.4%).

Figure 1. Participants Intention on Cyber ethics behaviour

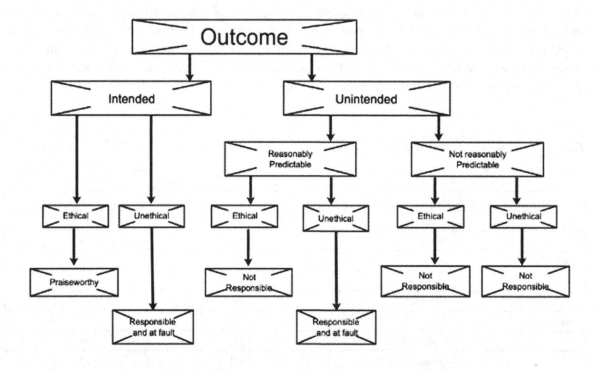

Regarding cyber piracy, 29.6% of the respondents reported an intention to buy software with a single-user license and installing it on multiple computers, and 26.6% would download or distribute copyrighted materials illegally (see Figure 2). The study also found that 17.4% of respondents have an intention to hire someone on the Internet to write their term paper, project, or research paper for them. Almost sixteen per cent (15.6%) confirmed that they will add names of non-contributing persons to a research paper for publication, whereas 15.4% would purchase or download a research paper from the Internet and submit it as their own (see Figure 3). About nineteen per cent (18.6%) of the respondents confirmed that they have intentions to engage in black hat hacking and 17% would perform cyber fraud.

Moreover, 11% indicated that they have intentions to send virus-infected files over the Internet. With respect to cyberprivacy infringement, 20.2% have intentions to read other's private messages without their consents, 15.2% would obtain other's private file, and 8.8% would spread inaccurate information about other people. Figures 1 – 5 are diagrammatic summaries of the findings from the study.

Table 2. Descriptive Statistics (n=503)

Ethics	No	Items	Mean	Std. Dev	%
Cyber Piracy	1	Not downloading or distributing copyrighted materials.	3.67	1.381	73.4
	2	Not copying articles from the Internet and turning it to one's own.	4.22	1.112	84.4
	3	Buying software with a single user license and then install it on multiple computers.	3.52	1.440	70.4
		Total			76.1
Cyber Plagiarism	4	Not taking credit for someone else's work.	4.48	0.846	89.6
	5	Not hiring someone to write a term paper, project, or a research paper.	4.13	1.218	82.6
	6	Not purchasing and submitting a research or term paper from the Internet to a class as one's own work.	4.23	1.101	84.6
	7	Not cheating on a graded assignment or examination.	4.32	1.015	86.4
	8	Not plagiarizing other people's work without citing.	4.40	.919	88
	9	Not adding the name of a non-contributing person as an author in a project.	4.22	1.107	84.4
	10	Not coping and pasting materials found on the Internet for an assignment without acknowledgment.	4.37	0.917	87.4
	11	Not deliberately providing inaccurate references for a project.	4.43	0.916	88.6
		Total			86.5
Computer Ethics	12	Not hacking into a computer system.	4.07	1.236	81.4
	13	Not performing cyber fraud.	4.15	1.222	83
	14	Not involving in cyber bullying.	4.40	0.974	88
	15	Not sending files infected with viruses over the Internet	4.45	0.928	89
	16	Not stealing funds by the use of Internet	4.47	0.971	89.4
		Total			86.2
Cyber Privacy	17	Not disclosing confidential institutional information.	4.49	0.858	89.8
	18	Not spreading wrong information about other people.	4.56	0.763	91.2
	19	Not violating the privacy and confidentiality of information (e.g. trade secret, password).	4.51	0.830	90.2
	20	Not obtaining another person's private files.	4.24	1.093	84.8
	21	Not reading someone else's email or WhatsApp messages.	3.99	1.228	79.8
	22	Not using technology to infringe on other people privacy rights.	4.34	0.987	86.8
	23	Not collecting and sharing information about other people.	4.34	.978	86.8
		Total			87.1

Figure 2. Percentage of respondents with cyber piracy intention

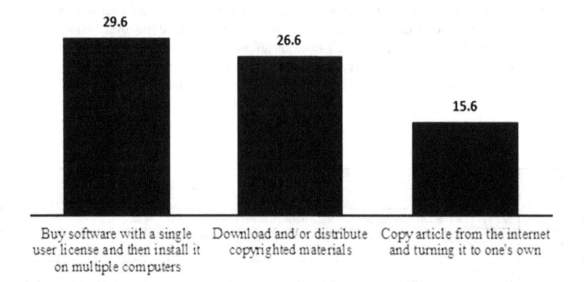

Respondents' Characteristics and Cyber Ethics Behaviours Intentions

Gender Differences in Cyber ethics Behaviour Intention

An independent-samples t-test was conducted to compare computer ethics behaviour intentions of male and female students (see Table 3 and Table 4). There was a significant difference in the scores for female (M=4.49, SD= 0.811) and male (M=4.25, SD= 0.935) in computer ethics; t (501) = -2.557, p = .011. These results suggest that male students are more likely to engage in computer crime and abuse as compared to female students. There was no significant difference in intellectual property rights (t (501) = 0.761, p = 0.447) for female (M=3.74, SD=1.089) and male (M=3.82, SD=1.115).

Also, there was no significant difference in academic integrity (t (501) = -1.460, p = 0.145) for female (M=4.49, SD=.743) and male (M=4.38, SD= 0.802) and there was no significant difference in cyberprivacy scores (t (501) = -1.114, p = 0.266) for female (M=4.44, SD=0.790) and male (M=4.35, SD=0.781).

Nationality Differences in Cyber ethics Behaviour Intention

A significant difference was observed between local (M=4.44, SD=.742) and foreign (M=4.08, SD=1.079) students with respect to academic integrity; t (496) = -2.670, p = 0.008. The result suggested that foreign students are more likely be involved in academic dishonesty (plagiarism) as compared to local students. However, there was no significant difference in the scores of intellectual property rights (t (496) = 0.962, p = 0.336) for local (M=3.79, SD=1.105) and foreign students (M=3.97, SD=1.134).

Figure 3. Percentage respondents with intention to plagiarize

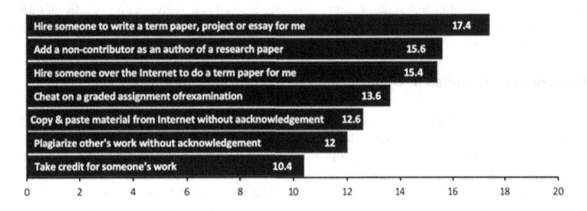

Figure 4. Percentage of respondents with cybercrime and computer abuse intention

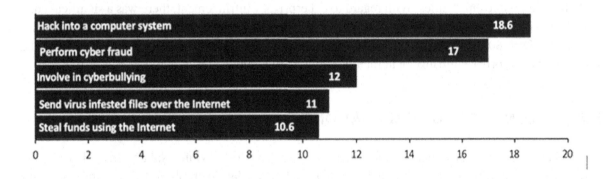

Figure 5. Percentage of respondents with intention to violate cyberprivacy

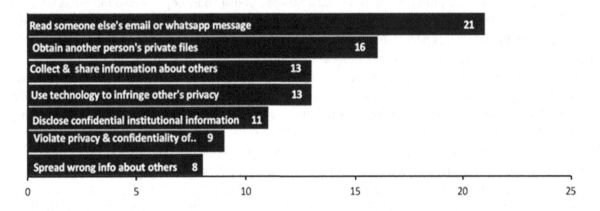

There was also no significant difference in computer ethics scores (t (496) = -2.670, p = 0.398) for local (M=4.33, SD=.886) and foreign students (M=4.19, SD=1.117). There was no significant difference in cyberprivacy scores (t (496) = -.386, p = 0.699) for local (M=4.39, SD= 0.759) and foreign students (M=4.33, SD=0.986).

University Differences in Cyber Ethics Behaviour Intention

The study found a significant difference in intellectual property rights scores (t (498) = 8.143, p < 0.001) for private (M=4.27, SD=4.27) and public (M=3.50, SD=0.750) universities. The finding suggests that students in public universities are more likely to be involved in cyber piracy than those in private universities. Again, there was a significant difference in academic integrity scores (t (498) = 3.714, p = 0.447) for private (M=4.57, SD=0.750) and public (M=4.30, SD=0.797) universities. Similarly, this result means that students in public universities are more likely to be engaged in plagiarism than those in private universities. Moreover, there was a significant difference in the scores for private (M=4.60, SD=0.726) and public (M=4.14, SD=0.962) universities in computer ethics; t (498) = 5.779, p = 0.011. Thus, again, students in public universities would be more likely to commit computer crime as compared with those in private universities. With regard to cyberprivacy infringement, there was a significant difference in the scores (t (498) = 5.351, p = 0.266) for private (M=4.60, SD=0.689) and public universities (M=4.23, SD=0.805). This finding suggests that students in public universities would more likely be involved in cyberprivacy infringement than those in private universities.

DISCUSSION AND RECOMMENDATIONS

It is a challenge to change human attitude, intention and behaviour (Wiafe, Nakata, & Gulliver, 2014) and therefore, there is the need for studies to that seek to explain patterns in behavioural intentions in various domains. Accordingly, this study sought to investigate the intentions of students regarding cyber ethics behaviour. The results from the investigations have shown that intention to commit cyber piracy dominates cyber ethics breach issues. This is because 29.6% of the respondents had intentions to be involved in software piracy and 26% would download or distribute copyrighted materials without permission. The findings support studies that argued that students perceive copying of commercial software from the Internet as acceptable (Siegfried, 2004). Globally, there has been increase in the incidence of intellectual property rights violations as the amount of illegal downloads and software privacy continues to increase (Benfratello & Di Francesco, 2019; Gallegos & Cook, 2000; Moores & Dhillon, 2000; Tomczyk, 2019). Some researchers have argued that perceived subjective norms, the proximity of offenders, attitude towards piracy and availability of capable guardians impact online piracy intentions (Petrescu, Gironda, & Korgaonkar, 2018). Other have argued that it is influenced by poverty, as many individuals and small businesses particularly in developing countries could not afford commercial software (Charoensukmongkol, Daniel, Sexton, & Kock, 2012). Thus, they advocate for the need for improvement in the economic wealth of pirates.

Contrarily to existing studies that argue that males indulge more in cyber piracy (Moores & Dhillon, 2000; Sulphey & Jnaneswar, 2013), this study did not observe a significant difference between males and females This therefore suggests that intentions of cyber piracy violation cannot be considered on gender

Table 3. Differences in cyber ethics

Control Group	Cyber Ethics	Group	N	Mean	SD	Std. Error Mean	Differences in Cyber Ethics	Comment
Gender	Intellectual Property	Male	369	3.82	1.115	.058	Not significant	
		Female	134	3.74	1.089	.094		
	Academic Integrity	Male	369	4.38	.802	.042	Not significant	
		Female	134	4.49	.743	.064		
	Computer Ethics	Male	369	4.25	.935	.047	Significant	Males are more likely to perform computer crime and computer abuses as compared with females.
		Female	134	4.49	.811	.070		
	Cyber Privacy	Male	369	4.35	.781	.041	Not significant	
		Female	134	4.44	.790	.068		
Nationality	Intellectual Property	International	36	3.97	1.134	.189	Not significant	
		Local	462	3.79	1.105	.051		
	Academic Integrity	International	36	4.08	1.079	.180	Significant	Foreign students are more like to engage in academic dishonest (plagiarism) as compared with local students.
		Local	462	4.44	.742	.035		
	Computer Ethics	International	36	4.19	1.117	.186	Not significant	
		Local	462	4.33	.886	.041		
	Cyber Privacy	International	36	4.33	.986	.164	Not significant	
		Local	462	4.39	.759	.035		
University	Intellectual Property	Private	197	4.27	4.27	.059	Significant	Students in public universities would more likely be involved in piracy than those in private universities.
		Public	303	3.50	1.151	.066		
	Academic Integrity	Private	197	4.57	.750	.053	Significant	Students in public universities would more likely be involved in plagiarism than those in private universities.
		Public	303	4.30	.797	.046		
	Computer Ethics	Private	197	4.60	.726	.052	Significant	Students in public universities would more likely be involved in computer crime than those in private universities.
		Public	303	4.14	.962	.055		
	Cyber Privacy	Private	197	4.60	.689	.049	Significant	Students in public universities would more likely be involved in privacy infringement in the cyberspace as compared with those in private universities.
		Public	303	4.23	.805	.046		

basis in recent times. However, considering that some researchers have demonstrated that information security issues are gender related (Yaokumah, 2016), there is the need for further investigations to explain the gender relationship in terms of cyber ethics and information security. This is because cyber ethics impacts cyber security and it is therefore expected that issues of gender would be similar in both domains.

The number of respondents (18.6%) that declared an intention to engage in black hat hacking or perform cyber fraud (17%) supports existing arguments that cyber fraud is rising (Kemp, Miró-Llinares, & Moneva, 2020). Besides, male students were found to be more likely to be engaged in computer crime and computer abuses than female students. It has however been argued that even though more males are involved in cyber fraud as compared to females, females mostly play professionally and unique roles in cyber fraud (Jegede, Elegbeleye, Olowookere, & Olorunyomi, 2016). They provide effective deceptive techniques that facilitate the process. There is, therefore, the need for strong moral and ethics awareness. This cannot be overemphasized. Particularly, considering that cyber fraud awareness is biased towards males (Cassiman, 2019). Perhaps academic curriculums need to be redesigned to emphasised cyber

Table 4. Differences in cyber ethics, intellectual property, academic integrity, and cyber privacy

Control Group	Cyber Ethics	Equal Variances	Levene's Test for Equality of Variances		t-test for Equality of Means					95% Confidence Interval of the Diff	
			F	Sig.	t	df	Sig. (2-tailed)	Mean Diff	Std. Error Diff	Lower	Upper
Gender	Intellectual Property	Assumed	0.370	.543	.761	501	.447	.085	.112	-.134	.305
		Not assumed			.769	240.840	.443	.085	.111	-.133	.303
	Academic Integrity	Assumed	1.409	.236	-1.460	501	.145	-.116	.079	-.272	.040
		Not assumed			-1.512	252.843	.132	-.116	.077	-.267	.035
	Computer Ethics	Assumed	4.897	.027	-2.557	501	.011	-.2336	.091	-.412	-.054
		Not assumed			-2.732	269.619	.007	-.2336	.085	-.401	-.065
	Cyber Privacy	Assumed	.136	.713	-1.114	501	.266	-.088	.079	-.243	.067
		Not assumed			-1.108	233.388	.269	-.088	.079	-.244	.069
Nationality	Intellectual Property	Assumed	.016	.898	.962	496	.336	.185	.192	-.192	.561
		Not assumed			.942	40.362	.352	.185	.196	-.211	.580
	Academic Integrity	Assumed	16.823	.000	-2.670	496	.008	-.356	.133	-.618	-.094
		Not assumed			-1.944	37.623	.059	-.356	.183	-.727	.015
	Computer Ethics	Assumed	5.554	.019	-.846	496	.398	-.132	.156	-.440	.175
		Not assumed			-.695	38.509	.491	-.132	.191	-.518	.253
	Cyber Privacy	Assumed	3.226	.073	-.386	496	.699	-.052	.134	-.316	.212
		Not assumed			-.309	38.301	.759	-.052	.168	-.392	.288
University	Intellectual Property	Assumed	42.918	.000	8.143	498	.000	.772	.095	.586	.959
		Not assumed			8.707	492.561	.000	.772	.089	.598	.947
	Academic Integrity	Assumed	2.609	.107	3.714	498	.000	.265	.071	.125	.405
		Not assumed			3.763	436.764	.000	.265	.070	.127	.403
	Computer Ethics	Assumed	22.858	.000	5.779	498	.000	.464	.080	.306	.621
		Not assumed			6.126	486.997	.000	.464	.076	.315	.612
	Cyber Privacy	Assumed	10.157	.002	5.351	498	.000	.373	.070	.236	.510
		Not assumed			5.529	462.059	.000	.373	.067	.240	.506

ethics, since this will enhance the knowledge, skills, and attitudes for dealing with such issues (Monteverde, 2014). Educators should also be provided with the requisite skills, knowledge and understanding of cyber ethics, cyber safety, and cyber security issues(Pusey & Sadera, 2011). Additionally, methods must be put in place to ensure that users of cyberspaces comply with existing ethical policies, since it has been demonstrated that the provision of policies promotes proper operational activities (Yaokumah, Brown, & Dawson, 2016).

Respondents' intention on cyber plagiarism also raises critical concerns. As mentioned, 17.4% of the respondents would hire someone to write a research paper for them using the Internet, whiles 15.6% would add names of non-contributing persons to a research article for publication, and 15.4% would purchase or download a research paper from the Internet and submit it as theirs. These trends support existing findings (Granitz & Loewy, 2007; Mahmood, 2009). Some studies have argued that the increase in academic dishonesty and plagiarism is due to current improvement in accessing cyberspace contents (Sulphey & Jnaneswar, 2013). As much as one third of undergraduate students have plagiarized (Novotney, Academy, & Diego, 2011). To address this issue, it is suggested that members of the academic community should cultivate trust, fairness, respect and responsibility as part of their work ethics (Swartz & Cole, 2013). Also, the use of plagiarism software has been observed to be effective for tracking and controlling of plagiarism (Tang et al., 2018).

The results found that foreign students would more likely be engaged in academic dishonestly as compared with local students. Although some studies have acknowledge this (Amsberry, 2009), there is the need for further investigations to explain the phenomenon. This is because some studies have explained that this phenomenon is mostly unintentional and they require a cultural reorientation (Bamford & Sergiou, 2005). However, this is arguable since the laws of plagiarism are universal.

CONCLUSION

The chapter addressed moral, legal, and social issues of cyber ethics among students in a developing country. It discussed the extent of cyber piracy, cyber plagiarism, computer crime and abuses, and cyberprivacy infringement. Largely, software piracy intentions were observed to account for the biggest proportion of all the cyber ethics violations. Also, the level of students' intention to commit computer crime and computer abuses was high. This raises concerns. It was suggested that educators need to pay attention to cyber ethical training as part of the curriculum. More importantly, the study provides further insights into cyber ethics intentions among genders and nationalities, and the findings refuted some existing studies. Thus, there is a need for future studies to be conducted to focus on cross-cultural relationship and intentions of cyber ethical issues.

REFERENCES

Akbulut, Y., Şendağ, S., Birinci, G., Kılıçer, K., Şahin, M. C., & Odabaşı, H. F. (2008). Exploring the types and reasons of Internet-triggered academic dishonesty among Turkish undergraduate students: Development of Internet-Triggered Academic Dishonesty Scale. *Computers & Education*, *51*(1), 463–473. doi:10.1016/j.compedu.2007.06.003

Amsberry, D. (2009). Deconstructing plagiarism: International students and textual borrowing practices. *The Reference Librarian*, *51*(1), 31–44. doi:10.1080/02763870903362183

Badu-Marfo, G., Farooq, B., & Patterson, Z. (2019). A perspective on the challenges and opportunities for privacy-aware big transportation data. *Journal of Big Data Analytics in Transportation*, *1*(1), 1–23. doi:10.100742421-019-00001-z

Bamford, J., & Sergiou, K. (2005). International students and plagiarism: An analysis of the reasons for plagiarism among international foundation students. *Investigations in University Teaching and Learning*, *2*(2), 17–22.

Benfratello, L., & Di Francesco, F. (2019). *Software License Compliance A quantitative study on software piracy in Italy*. Academic Press.

Burmeister, O. K. (2013). Achieving the goal of a global computing code of ethics through an international-localisation. *Ethical Space: The International Journal of Communication Ethics*, *10*(4), 25–32.

Business Software Alliance. (2012). *Shadow market 2011*. Retrieved from https://globalstudy.bsa.org/2011/downloads/study_pdf/2011_BSA_Piracy_Study-Standard.pdf

Bustard, J. D. (2018). Improving Student Engagement in the Study of Professional Ethics: Concepts and an Example in Cyber Security. *Science and Engineering Ethics*, *24*(2), 683–698. PMID:28401507

Cassiman, A. (2019). Spiders on the World Wide Web: Cyber trickery and gender fraud among youth in an Accra zongo. *Social Anthropology*, *27*(3), 486–500. doi:10.1111/1469-8676.12678

Charoensukmongkol, P., Daniel, J. L., Sexton, S., & Kock, N. (2012). Analyzing software piracy from supply and demand factors the competing roles of corruption and economic wealth. *International Journal of Technoethics*, *3*(1), 28–42. doi:10.4018/jte.2012010103

Da Veiga, A. (2016). A cybersecurity culture research philosophy and approach to develop a valid and reliable measuring instrument. *Proceedings of 2016 SAI Computing Conference, SAI 2016*, 1006–1015. 10.1109/SAI.2016.7556102

Ercegovac, Z. (2006). What students say they know, feel, and do about cyber-plagiarism and academic dishonesty? A case study. *Proceedings of the American Society for Information Science and Technology*, *42*(1). doi:10.1002/meet.1450420142

Gallegos, F., & Cook, C. (2000). Software piracy: Some facts, figures, and issues. *Information Systems Security*, *8*(4), 1–23. doi:10.1201/1086/43307.8.4.20000101/31078.5

Gcaza, N., Von Solms, R., & Van Vuuren, J. (2015). An ontology for a national cyber-security culture environment. *Proceedings of the 9th International Symposium on Human Aspects of Information Security and Assurance, HAISA 2015*, 1–10.

Granitz, N., & Loewy, D. (2007). Applying ethical theories: Interpreting and responding to student plagiarism. *Journal of Business Ethics*, *72*(3), 293–306. doi:10.100710551-006-9171-9

Hampton-Sosa, W. (2017). The impact of creativity and community facilitation on music streaming adoption and digital piracy. *Computers in Human Behavior*, *69*, 444–453. doi:10.1016/j.chb.2016.11.055

Hill, C. W. L. (2007). Digital piracy: Causes, consequences, and strategic responses. *Asia Pacific Journal of Management*, *24*(1), 9–25. doi:10.100710490-006-9025-0

Jamal, A., Ferdoos, A., Zaman, M., & Hussain, M. (2015). Cyber-ethics and the perceptions of internet users: A case study of university students of Islamabad. *Pakistan Journal of Information Management and Libraries*, *16*, 8–20.

Janssen, M., & van den Hoven, J. (2015). *Big and Open Linked Data (BOLD) in government: A challenge to transparency and privacy?* Elsevier.

Jegede, A. E., Elegbeleye, A. O., Olowookere, E. I., & Olorunyomi, B. R. (2016). Gendered alternative to cyber fraud participation: An assessment of technological driven crime in Lagos State, Nigeria. *Gender & Behaviour, 14*(3), 7672–7692.

Kant, I. (1998). Critique of Pure Reason (P. Guyer & A. Wood, Trans. & Eds.). Cambridge University Press.

Kemp, S., Miró-Llinares, F., & Moneva, A. (2020). The Dark Figure and the Cyber Fraud Rise in Europe: Evidence from Spain. *European Journal on Criminal Policy and Research*, 1–20. doi:10.100710610-020-09439-2

Koranteng, F. N., & Wiafe, I. (2018). Factors that Promote Knowledge Sharing on Academic Social Networking Sites: An Empirical Study. *Education and Information Technologies*, 1–26. doi:10.100710639-018-9825-0

Koranteng, F. N., Wiafe, I., Katsriku, F. A., & Apau, R. (2019). *Understanding trust on social networking sites among tertiary students: An empirical study in Ghana.* Applied Computing and Informatics; doi:10.1016/j.aci.2019.07.003

Kuada, E., Wiafe, I., Addo, D., & Djaba, E. (2017). *Privacy enhancing national identification card system. In 2017 IEEE AFRICON: Science, Technology and Innovation for Africa.* AFRICON. doi:10.1109/AFRCON.2017.8095596

Kumah, P., Yaokumah, W., & Buabeng-Andoh, C. (2018). Identifying HRM Practices for Improving Information Security Performance: An Importance-Performance Map Analysis. *International Journal of Human Capital and Information Technology Professionals, 9*(4), 23–43. doi:10.4018/IJHCITP.2018100102

Lathrop, A., & Foss, K. (2000). Student cheating and plagiarism in the Internet era. *A Wake-up Call.*

Mahmood, Z. (2009). Contract cheating: A new phenomenon in cyber-plagiarism. *Communications of the IBIMA, 10*(12), 93–97.

Mančić, Ž. (2010). Cyber piracy and morality: Some utilitarian and deontological challenges. *Filozofija i Drustvo, 21*(3), 103–117. doi:10.2298/FID1003103M

Monteverde, S. (2014). Undergraduate healthcare ethics education, moral resilience, and the role of ethical theories. *Nursing Ethics, 21*(4), 385–401. doi:10.1177/0969733013505308 PMID:24311237

Moor, J. H. (1997). Towards a theory of privacy in the information age. *ACM Sigcas Computers and Society, 27*(3), 27–32. doi:10.1145/270858.270866

Moores, T., & Dhillon, G. (2000). Software piracy: A view from Hong Kong. *Communications of the ACM, 43*(12), 88–93. doi:10.1145/355112.355129

Novotney, B. A., Academy, U. S. N., & Diego, S. (2011). *Beat the cheat Beat the cheat.* Academic Press.

Onyancha, O. B. (2015). An informetrics view of the relationship between internet ethics, computer ethics and cyberethics. *Library Hi Tech, 33*(3), 387–408. doi:10.1108/LHT-04-2015-0033

Petrescu, M., Gironda, J. T., & Korgaonkar, P. K. (2018). Online piracy in the context of routine activities and subjective norms. *Journal of Marketing Management, 34*(3–4), 314–346. doi:10.1080/026725 7X.2018.1452278

Pluijmers, Y., & Weiss, P. (2002). *Borders in cyberspace: Conflicting public sector information policies and their economic impacts.* Citeseer.

Posner, R. A. (1978). Economic theory of privacy. *Regulation, 2,* 19.

Pusey, P., & Sadera, W. A. (2011). Cyberethics, Cybersafety, and Cybersecurity: Preservice Teacher Knowledge, Preparedness, and the Need for Teacher Education to Make a Difference. *Journal of Digital Learning in Teacher Education, 28*(2), 82–85. doi:10.1080/21532974.2011.10784684

Rodafinos, A. (2018). Plagiarism Management: Challenges, Procedure, and Workflow Automation. *Interdisciplinary Journal of E-Skills and Lifelong Learning, 14,* 159–175. doi:10.28945/4147

Rogerson, A. M. (2017). Detecting contract cheating in essay and report submissions: Process, patterns, clues and conversations. *International Journal for Educational Integrity, 13*(1), 10. doi:10.100740979-017-0021-6

Scheffler, S. (1988). *Consequentialism and its Critics.* Oxford University Press on Demand.

Siegfried, R. M. (2004). Student Attitudes on Software Piracy and Related Issues of Computer Ethics. *Ethics and Information Technology, 11530*(516), 215–222. doi:10.100710676-004-3391-4

Sinnott-Armstrong, W. (2003). *Consequentialism.* Academic Press.

Smith, A. D., & Rupp, W. T. (2002). Issues in cybersecurity; understanding the potential risks associated with hackers/crackers. *Information Management & Computer Security, 10*(4), 178–183. doi:10.1108/09685220210436976

Stocker, M. (1969). Consequentialism and its complexities. *American Philosophical Quarterly, 6*(4), 276–289.

Sulphey, M. M., & Jnaneswar, K. (2013). A study on the academic dishonesty, anomia and unethical behaviour among business graduates. *The Journal of Contemporary Management Research, 8*(2), 57–72.

Swartz, L. B., & Cole, M. T. (2013). Students' perception of Academic Integrity in Online Business Education Courses. *Journal of Business and Educational Leadership, 4*(1), 102.

Tang, J.-H., Chung, T.-Y., & Chen, M.-C. (2018). Plagiarism Cognition, Attitude and Behavioral Intention: A Trade-Off Analysis. *International Conference on Information and Knowledge Engineering,* (1), 149–144. Retrieved from https://csce.ucmss.com/cr/books/2018/LFS/CSREA2018/IKE9002.pdf

Taylor, S. A. (2012). Evaluating digital piracy intentions on behaviors. *Journal of Services Marketing, 26*(7), 472–483. doi:10.1108/08876041211266404

Tene, O., & Polonetsky, J. (2013). A theory of creepy: Technology, privacy and shifting social norms. *Yale JL & Tech., 16,* 59.

Tilley, E. N., Fredricks, S. M., & Hornett, A. (2012). Kinship, culture and ethics in organisations: Exploring implications for internal communication. *Journal of Communication Management (London)*, *16*(2), 162–184. doi:10.1108/13632541211217588

Tomczyk, Ł. (2019). The Practice of Downloading copyrighted files among adolescents in Poland: Correlations between piracy and other risky and protective behaviours online and offline. *Technology in Society*, *58*, 101137. doi:10.1016/j.techsoc.2019.05.001

Weaver, G. R. (2016). Businesses : Culture ' s Role Ethics Programs in Global in Managing Ethics Gary R. Weaver. *Journal of Business Ethics*, *30*(1), 3–15. doi:10.1023/A:1006475223493

Wiafe, I., Nakata, K., & Gulliver, S. (2014). Categorizing users in behavior change support systems based on cognitive dissonance. *Personal and Ubiquitous Computing*, *18*(7), 1677–1687. doi:10.100700779-014-0782-3

Yaokumah, W. (2016). The influence of students' characteristics on mobile device security measures. *International Journal of Information Systems and Social Change*, *7*(3), 44–66. doi:10.4018/IJISSC.2016070104

Yaokumah, W. (2020). Predicting and Explaining Cyber Ethics with Ethical Theories. *International Journal of Cyber Warfare & Terrorism*, *10*(2), 46–63. doi:10.4018/IJCWT.2020040103

Yaokumah, W., Brown, S., & Dawson, A. A. (2016). Towards modelling the impact of security policy on compliance. *Journal of Information Technology Research*, *9*(2), 1–16. doi:10.4018/JITR.2016040101

KEY TERMS AND DEFINITIONS

Academic Integrity: It is the commitment to and demonstration of honest and moral behaviour in an academic setting.

Computer Abuse: The incident caused by intentional acts from which a perpetrator could have realized a gain and a victim could have suffered a loss.

Computer Crime: The use of computer as an instrument to further illegal ends.

Cyber Ethics: The study of moral, legal, and social issues involving cyber technology. It examines the impact that cyber technology has on social, legal and moral systems.

Cyber Piracy: Using the internet to illegally copy and /or distribute software or intellectual property protected under copy right law.

Cyber Plagiarism: Copying or downloading in part or in their entirety articles or research papers found on the internet and not giving proper attribution or acknowledgement.

Cyberprivacy: The individual right to control the distribution or dissemination of information about himself when using the internet. This involves using right techniques and technologies to protect an individual sensitive data online.

Ethics: Moral principles that govern a person's behaviour or in conducting of an activity.

Intellectual Property: Intellectual property is an intangible property used by individuals or corporations. Three different legal traditions protect intellectual property, trade secrets, copyrights, and patent.

Chapter 8

Taxonomy of Login Attacks in Web Applications and Their Security Techniques Using Behavioral Biometrics

Rizwan Ur Rahman

Maulana Azad National Institute of Technology, Bhopal, India

Deepak Singh Tomar

Maulana Azad National Institute of Technology, Bhopal, India

ABSTRACT

Research into web application security is still in its initial phase. In spite of enhancements in web application development, large numbers of security issues remain unresolved. Login attacks are the most malevolent threats to the web application. Authentication is the method of confirming the stated identity of a user. Conventional authentication systems suffer from a weakness that can compromise the defense of the system. An example of such vulnerabilities is login attack. An attacker may exploit a pre-saved password or an authentication credential to log into web applications. An added problem with current authentication systems is that the authentication process is done only at the start of a session. Once the user is authenticated in the web application, the user's identity is assumed to remain the same during the lifetime of the session. This chapter examines the level login attacks that could be a threat to websites. The chapter provides a review of vulnerabilities, threats of login attacks associated with websites, and effective measures to counter them.

INTRODUCTION AND OVERVIEW OF CYBER SECURITY

Cyber security is the security of web associated frameworks, including equipment, programming and information, from digital assaults. In a registering setting, security includes cyber security and physical security - both are utilized by ventures to ensure against unapproved access to server farms and other

DOI: 10.4018/978-1-7998-3149-5.ch008

electronic frameworks. Data security, which is intended to keep up the privacy, uprightness and accessibility of information, is a subset of cyber security (Solms & Niekerk, 2013). Suppliers of personal computer (PC) administrations (like managing an account, email, or online networking) have the obligation of keeping programmers out of individuals' frameworks. As a PC client, you can do your part by being watchful about who you converse with over the Internet, what data you share, and by picking and utilizing solid passwords. PC passwords are amongst the most imperative apparatuses used to ensure data on PC frameworks. Similarly, as you do not need anybody taking your secret word and picking up control of your Instagram account, banks need to avoid potential risk to shield offenders from taking cash. Since passwords are so imperative, it is a wrongdoing to take passwords and to deliberately get into other individuals' PCs.

You utilize PC passwords consistently, regardless of whether to get to your email account, person to person communication locales, or even to do web-based saving of money. One of the difficulties you may have when picking a secret word is making it simple for you to recollect, however hard for other individuals to figure out. It may not be a smart thought, for instance, to utilize your puppy's name, your road address, or any data that is by one way or another associated with your username. For example, if Sue Jones utilizes the login "SJones" to get to her email and lives at 314 Apple Pie Road, the secret word "pie314" probably won't be a decent decision. Do you see why? In spite of the fact that it may be simple for her to recall, it is short and contains her street address. A more grounded secret key may be "9J8LZcWAMzjJQUnD"...if she could recall it. That is surely any longer, it is anything but a word, and it doesn't have any recognizable data. Be that as it may, who can recall that? What's more, in the event that you record it and lose the bit of paper, that isn't generally more secure.

A solid secret key is one that you can recall effectively, yet that is really long. It is comprised of two or three words, numbers and accentuation, however doesn't have anything in it that somebody would figure out. There is a great deal of systems for making solid passwords. The precedent is from an online absolutely irregular secret word generator. It basically picked 16 characters indiscriminately.

- Another technique is to begin by thinking about a passphrase, which is an expression you like or a statement from a motion picture. At that point utilize the primary letter of every one of the words and put in a number or accentuation (Keith et al., 2009).
- Another normal methodology is to utilize two totally disconnected words and separate them by numbers or characters; is "deaf+anteater" simple to recollect? Is it still simple to recollect whether you sprinkle in a few numbers, as maybe the telephone number where you used to live; "deaf555+4715anteater" may be harder for somebody to figure?
- Or consider a hogwash word that doesn't mean anything, yet you can even now articulate it, as "USiFiPiZOG" is a case of a pronounceable irregular secret word. Contrast that with the one beginning with "9J8" in the passage. Is it simpler or harder to recollect? Memory traps that assist us recollect things are called mental aides.

What cyber security can anticipate? The utilization of cyber security can help counteract cyber-attacks, information ruptures and data fraud. At the point when an organization has a solid feeling of system security and a viable episode reaction plan, it is better ready to anticipate and moderate these assaults.

The main objective of this chapter is to study defence mechanism in cyber security needed in today's world, its importance and why it has become such a big topic for discussion. The chapter aims at understanding the potential risks and threats present along with it and why ensuring security of user is of primary concern. Specifically, the chapter is to study the various attacks and potential defense mechanisms available for security provision and also finding the most suitable and effective combination for the same. The emphasis is on finding the theoretical concepts and research work implications of the results proposed and not only focusing on the practical concepts. Thus, we aim at drawing out results which could be used in future real-time studies by means of collective learning, problem solving and collaborative research work through proper coordination and cooperation.

The first section introduces the overview of login attacks, including brute force attack and dictionary attack, key logger attack and phishing attack. The next section presents the vulnerabilities in web applications, their types and vulnerability scanners. The last section presents the taxonomy of detection and prevention methods against login attacks. This second section also presents developed attack scenario and methodology using behavioural biometrics.

TAXONOMY OF LOGIN ATTACKS IN WEB APPLICATION

A prominent amongst the most hazardous components of web application security is always advancing nature of security hazards. The traditional methodology has been to concentrate resources on urgent framework segments and secure against the maximum known dangers, which implied leaving parts undefended and not ensuring frameworks against less unsafe dangers.

To manage the current situations, warning associations are advancing a more proactive and versatile methodology. The National Institute of Standards and Technology also referred as NIST, for example, as of late issued refreshed rules in its hazard evaluation structure that prescribe a move toward consistent observing and continuous appraisals. Because of security dangers, interests in cyber security advancements and administrations are expanding. In 2017, Gartner anticipated that overall spending on data security items and administrations would reach $83.4 billion - a 7% expansion from 2016 - and that it would keep on developing to $93 billion by 2018 (Van et al., 2013).

The way toward staying aware of new advancements, security patterns and risk insight is a testing assignment. Nonetheless, it's important with the end goal to shield data and different resources from login threats, which take numerous forms. Figure 1 shows the taxonomy of login attacks.

Figure 1. Taxonomy of Login Attacks

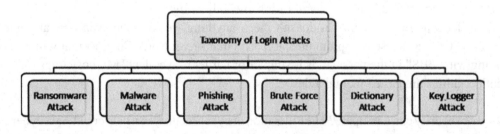

Ransomware

It is a sort of malware that includes an aggressor bolting the injured individual's PC framework records - normally through encryption - and requesting an instalment to unscramble and open them (Gazet, 2010).

Malware

It is any document or program used to hurt a PC client, for example, worms, PC infections, Trojan ponies and spyware (Willems et al., 2007).

Phishing

It is a type of extortion where false messages are sent that look like messages from respectable sources; nonetheless, the aim of these messages is to take delicate information, for example, charge card or login data (Ho et al., 2019).

Brute Force Attack

A programmer utilizes a PC program or content to attempt to sign in with conceivable secret word mixes, normally beginning with the least demanding to-figure passwords. So simply think: if a programmer has an organization rundown, one can without much stretch figure usernames. In the event that one client has a "Password123", he will rapidly have the capacity to get in (Sadasivam et al., 2018).

Dictionary Attack

A programmer utilizes a program or content to attempt to login by pushing through mixes of normal words. Conversely with an animal power assault, where a substantial extent key space is sought efficiently, a lexicon assault attempts just those conceivable outcomes which are well on the way to succeed, ordinarily got from a rundown of words for instance a lexicon (subsequently the expression word reference assault). By and large, lexicon assaults succeed on the grounds that numerous individuals tend to pick passwords which are short (7 characters or less, for example, single words found in word references or straightforward, effortlessly anticipated minor departure from words, for example, adding a digit (Singh & Pandey, 2015).

Key Logger Attack

A programmer utilizes a program to follow the majority of a client's keystrokes. So, by the day's end, everything the client has composed—including their login IDs and passwords—have been recorded. A key lumberjack assault is not the same as a savage power or word reference assault from numerous points of view. Not the slightest of which, the key logging program utilized is malware (or an all-out infection) that must initially make it onto the client's gadget (regularly the client is deceived to download it just by tapping on a connection in an email). Key lumberjack assaults are likewise unique in light of the fact that more grounded passwords don't give much security against them, which is one reason that multifaceted verification (MFA) is turning into an absolute necessity have for all organizations and associations.

With two-factor verification (additionally called multifaceted confirmation, 2FA, and propelled validation), a client is required to not just give a secret key to access the framework, yet in addition an another security "factor," like a one of a kind one-time get to code created from a token gadget or secure portable application on their cell phone. A system ensured by MFA is about invulnerable to an outside assault; regardless of whether a programmer can achieve a framework secret key, he won't have the capacity to give the required second security factor.

Distributed Brute-Force Attacks

A distributed brute force attack in which a hacker exploits a huge number of computers spread around the globe on Internet to obtain credential in order to evade any security mechanisms you have in implemented.

VULNERABILITIES IN WEB APPLICATION

Definition of Vulnerability in context to Web Application

Vulnerability in web application is a term which can be defined as a deficiency, imperfection, limitation, or insufficiency of a web application that could leave the application open to assaults. Such deficiency or defects leaves the web application exposed to threats. Due to advancement in web application development and digitization it has fundamental need to stop the information from exploitation and advance attacks. Vulnerabilities in web application make it probable for the hackers to target web application to execute their code on the in web application to exploit data (Ten et al., 2008).

VULNERABILITY TYPES IN WEB APPLICATION

User Enumeration

User Enumeration is a general kind of web application vulnerability. This sort of vulnerability takes place wherever there is login webpage and forgot password facility. This is executed by a hacker by the exploitation of brute force attacks to estimate or verify the valid user (Rahman & Tomar, 2018).

In a login web form if application user enters incorrect user-name then web application returns a message showing that the wrong user-name and likewise if the password is mistaken web application return a message showing password wrong and if both are erroneous then a different message pops up. The malicious hacker is searching for such actions and replies by the web application and the legitimacy of user name and password so that the malicious hacker could exploit brute force attack to break the web application (Shah & Mehtre, 2015).

Security Configuration

Security configuration consists of every one of the features which exploits security configuration. These security configurations if altered unconstructively have an effect on the web applications. The security configurations suggest to the security features that are taken care whilst the setting up and building of web applications and network equipment are done so to diminish the vulnerabilities (Scarfone & Mell, 2010).

Evaluation of Remote Code

Evaluation of remote code typically happens in web sites so to get advantage from others effort and study. In this attack a remote-code is inserted in the computer file or string and it get executed by the application parser. This activity is not designed by the programmer of that web application.

Invalidated Forwards and Redirects

Invalidated forwards and redirects occur whilst a number of web applications are in agreement for il-legal or un-trusted inputs that could lead to forward the web application to the URL address which is contained in the illegal or un-trusted input. By this URL address redirect the hacker which could cause troubles by scamming and then thieving credentials of application users. As the customized links is as analogous to the original website as a result, it is trouble-free for the hackers to make modification and blocked the user (Rafique et al., 2015).

Insufficient Web Application Layer Protection

The data in application which is there could be a fragile link in your web application which may be bro-ken and can cause problem in the security of web applications. If the hacker got the fault or limitation of the web application then he or she is able to introduce modification in web sites and could commit the cyber-crime. A number of basic web sites vulnerability exploits are Cross Site Scripting (XSS), SQL Injection, Cross Site Request Forgery (CSRF) and etc.

Vulnerability Scanner

It is a category of web-code or script that executes analytic phase of vulnerability evaluation. It is exploited for examination of impending threats at the points in the web applications to identify loop holes. It sets up, gives details, and arranges the security loop-holes in a web application. There are many kinds of vulnerability scanners and one of the most common vulnerability scanners is Nessus. This vulnerability scanner exploits regular vulnerabilities and several exposed architectures with the intention that simple cross-linking may be done between security tools. Nessus exploits its own attack programming language to found threats and possible attacks. Vulnerability scanners are consequently helpful since they found the weakness of web applications at the security loop-holes and work according to that (Kals et al., 2006).

There are varieties of vulnerability scanner tools:

WPScan

WPScan is a kind of vulnerability scanner for non-profitable websites used by blog maintaining engi-neers and security experts. WPScan can be exploited on web platforms such as Joomla and WordPress. It is a black-box vulnerability scanner exploited in Joomla and WordPress. This is used by both security experts and application developers. WPScan is a web platform that protects the websites and maintains its safety, but some troubles may be resolved by just updating it. The WPscan characteristics comprises of directory indexing on exposed plug ins, susceptible data discovery by means of bared log files. The vulnerability recognition to evaluate the websites with known vulnerable websites, plug-ins and themes details to spot which plug-ins are installed and turned on, user-name finding using user-name enumeration and many others (Sinha, 2018).

Sucuri

Sucuri is made by Daniel in the year 2000 (Daniel et al., 2010). Sucuri is very famous tool in context to security of web application particularly for WordPress. This tool is complimentary for all WordPress web platform users. It works easily and directly with the additional existing security software. It offers a number of security features to its potential application users. Sucuri scanner identifies warnings, security matters and malwares presence in the web application source code. It assists the security administrator to make sure the security of the web application. Its main characteristic is obtaining email notifications for security matters, set-up scans as a planned task, set-up scans as an agenda task, spot application malware viruses, examine application security facts, information and scrutinize blacklist status.

Pentest Scanning Tools

Pentest is Scanning tool that facilitates the application developer to discover flaws in web applications. This is a web platform to discover or distinguish unidentified vulnerabilities in the web applications that could cause security break. The pentest tool assault the web application from within in the identical way the hacker can carry out that from outside the web application. There are special kinds of pentest tools one of most common is Netsparker. Netsparker by design distinguish XSS, CSRF and SQL Injection a in the web applications. Its attributes are minimum configuration necessitates, complete scalable solution and many other. Apart from that there are numerous new pentest tools that are exploited for security of web application for instance Zap, superscan, scappy, sqlmap, probe.ly, wireshark, Kali, samauri framework, aircrack, dradis, rapid, hping, Ettercap, sqlninja, BeEF etc.

WEB APPLICATION THREATS

Definition of Threat

As defined in Oxford Dictionary web application threat is "the possibility of malicious attempt to damage or disrupt a computer or system". This definition is not absolute because it does not consist of the effort to lift the data or access computer files or penetrate data. So, this explanation describes the threat as an opportunity but in terms of web application security, the threat is characterized more strongly to an attacker or an adversary who is attempting to gain access to a web application and have sufficient potential to carry out any harm to it.

So, in broad terms finishing the definition of threats in terms of web application and network security, threat is the potential that could cause damage relatively serious damage to the web application. As a result, in formal terms threat is the potential for the weaknesses to turn to the severe attack, which is adequate to cause any harm to the web application and are competent adequate to the web application and network security to danger and therefore could be a cause of far above the ground application damage.

Threats may consist of various forms of viruses, Trojans and Back-door so as to outright attacks from the attackers. Since the preponderance threats consists of numerous exploits thus the expression "blended threat" is further precise when we talk about such attacks.

Threats Types in Web Applications

In the year 2012, Roger Grimes a writer listed these five as widespread web application threats: Advanced Persistent Threats (APT), Phishing, Social Engineered Attacks, Un-patched applications, Network worms.

However, with the progression in web technology and the heavy use of the Internet in each and all domains results further threats and in the year 2016, Bob Gourley released a video film which is having commentary on the web security and privacy technologies concerning the up-and-coming threats to web application security and their inferences. That filmed explained about two key features that were rising at that particular time first was Internet of Things (IoT) and second was Big Data. At the moment, the list of web application threats may be seen in further way (Rizwan, 2014).

Web Application Injection Attacks

Web Application Injection attacks comes into the group of those attacks which makes the attack competent of injecting un-trusted input into the URL or web code. All of these inputs subsequently get executed by the parser or interpreter as a script or command during the rendering phase. All of these attacks are the treacherous attacks for web application security. They could lead to loss of data, data stealing, DoS (Denial of Service) and numerous other harms.

These Web Application injection attacks are key fears in web application security. It permits the hacker to hack the application from within system rather than from external system. CSRF (Cross Site Request Forgery), SQL Injection, XSS (Cross Site Scripting) these types of attacks come into the class of web application injection attacks. These are not only unsafe however they are common in the majority of the authorized web applications. Although for these injection attacks a lot of applications are available to avert the web application from damage.

SQL Injection

SQL Injection is the most widespread category of attacking method whereby the hacker inserts the query code into the URL or web form, query onto a web application to carry out remote command. This assault possibly will demolish web application database. In this SQL injection placement of malevolent script is done between the web codes. The major reason of this SQL injection is to maneuver the DBMS or to take out the data. This is exploited to assault the data driven web applications. As a result, this attack could cause unfavorable effect on business application as well. By exploiting an SQL Injection attack, in excellent situations, an attacker may use it to assault the application. It may influence verification and authorization methods and attacker may recover the contents of a complete database. This may also be exploited to insert, alter, and remove records in a database. And provide chance to the hacker to illegal access to susceptible data which could consists of information regarding clients, personal identifiable numbers, property data, and much more susceptible information (Halfond et al., 2006).

Code Injection

Code injection is the malicious introduction of code into a system. The code injected in the application is capable of intruding database integrity. It can also create privacy, security issues. It can also change data and because of this even data correctness comes into picture. It is also done with the intention to steal data. It also can take control over the bypass access and authentication control. Code injection attacks can multitude applications that are based on user input for execution. Even the SQL injection also falls into the category of code injection. Other types of code injection are script injection, shell injection and dynamic evaluation. It is used to alter the data to give false data. Code injection attacks are not easy to find. There are many solutions that have been developed to find these for both architecture and application. Some of the examples are parameterization, input validation, addition of extra layer of protection, privilege setting for different actions, and many more (Vogt et al., 2007).

Cross Site Scripting

Cross site scripting is also an injection attack. In this type of attack the attacker adds malicious data into the content from other trusted sites. Cross-site scripting attacks takes place when an unreliable source is licensed to inject its own code into an application or web application. The malicious code is added with dynamic content sent to end browser. There are three different types of XSS stored, reflected and DOM based XSS. Different methods are present to prevent this attack one of the methods is escaping user input, sanitizing user input, input validation (Moore & Clayton, 2007).

Phishing Attack

A Phishing attack is a security attack that tries to gain delicate, private information. Such kinds of attacks are basically done where authentication is needed such as credit card information, user-name, and password credentials. Cyber attackers also use social engineering to influence end users for performing certain action such as clicking on a malicious link or file or some site or attackers tends to extract personal information from user's data. This may cause risk to both individuals and organizations. Any kind of data is useful and sensitive; rather it is organizational data or personal data. In addition, some phishing attacks can manipulate organizations data to trick the targets into revealing sensitive information. Attackers mostly targets information regarding user's bank details, card details, company data and any sensitive information that can be important for others (Owens & Matthews, 2008).

Brute Force Attack

Brute force attack is a most general method to go into to a website or web application which is confined by user-name and password. It is a technique that works in a repetitive method until the hacker obtains the legitimate combination of user-name and password. As a result, brute force assault is a recurring attack state of art. This is a computational technique which is not exploited by ordinary users. These techniques are exploited by intruders and assailants to get legitimate combination. The key reason of hacker is to get illegitimate access and to embezzle valuable data. There are a number of defensive measures that could be taken to avoid these attacks. These actions are complexity of passwords and its length, limiting login attempt, by means of CAPTCHA, two-way authentication and many more (Han et al., 2002).

Back-Door Attack

A back-door is type of a bug that annuls standard authentication technical steps to enter into web application. It results in remote access to the application resources inside a web application for instance, files, and database. This enables attacker's accomplishment of remotely executing application commands and update malware. Backdoor fixing is possible by taking guide with the assistance of vulnerable elements of a web application. If set up, it becomes very tricky to spot as files tend to assemble them in a messy method. All of these malicious back-doors are exploited for various malicious behaviors such as Data stealing, session hijacking, APT physical attacks, launch of Distributed Denial of Service (DDoS), Man in the Middle Attack, Scarping attacks.

Man-in-the-Middle Attack

Man-in-the-middle attack also represented as MITM is a class of eavesdropping action and it is also known as a fire brigade attack. In this attack, communiqué between two clients is hijacked and altered by an uncertified attacker. Typically, the hacker tends to snoop and spy by obstructing the ordinary key communication exchange and resend the message. In this method, the communiqué between two clients tends to be regular. This typical scenario did not baffle the sender as the message transferred is altered or not and if it is transferred to the recipient or to the assailant. As a result, the assailant controls the entire communiqué (Callegati et al., 2009).

NoSQL Injection Attack

NoSQL Injection is security threat on NoSQL databases that let hackers take access of NoSQL database queries through the insecure use of user input. It is exploited by a hacker to reveal unauthorized data, alter data, enhance privileges and take control of whole application.

PROPOSED METHODOLOGY USING BEHAVIORAL BIOMETRICS

Risk Assessment of a Biometric Continuous Authentication Protocol for Internet Services - Amongst the numerous security necessities that must be ensured, secure client verification is a standout amongst the most key. Confirmation is customarily executed just at login stage, in view of username and secret word. Be that as it may, a solitary verification point may not generally ensure an adequate level of security, particularly with regards to basic frameworks. Nonstop confirmation is the convention that applies different biometric attributes to persistently figure its trust in the client.

Continuous Authentication

This step involves the development of a suitable combination of passwords (dictionary and brute force attack) that best serves our purpose. The combination can be then tested on various parameters such as typing speed, throughput etc.

Application Design

We then create a client-server user application which can be used as a framework for testing the attack. For this purpose, the application has to be deployed on database.

A single time authentication is a secret phrase that is substantial for just a one login session or swap, on a framework or other computerized gadget. OTPs keep a planned distance from various insufficiency that are related with customary static clandestine word based verification; a variety of executions additionally join two factor validation by guaranteeing that the one-time secret phrase expects access to something a man has .The most critical favourable position that is implies that a potential interloper who figures out how to record an One Time Password that was at that point used to sign into an administration or to direct an exchange won't have the capacity to manhandle it, because it will never again be legitimate

Integration of Security in Defence Mechanism

In this step we add the various security features in our application such as keystroke dynamics and mouse dynamics for user authentication and encryption of data that would be stored in a database.

Deployment

In this step we finally deploy our test application with database. The application can then be tested with its various features.

Testing

In this phase we finally test our application with various forms of login attacks and record the results in order to ensure whether our application is working the way it is expected to.

System Development

In the ongoing Continuous Authentication examine work, confront and delicate biometric was utilized for confirmation. For sure, the uniqueness of finger impression is high when contrasted and confront and delicate biometrics. In light of this, unique mark acknowledgment is considered as the underlying methodology. Another model of Continuous Authentication System has been proposed. The modalities incorporate both hard and delicate biometrics.

Figure 2 shows the architecture of continuous authentication system.

Keystroke Dynamics

There are two phases to recognize certifiable and impostor client.

- Enrolment Stage
- Authentication Stage

Figure 2. Architecture of Continuous Authentication System

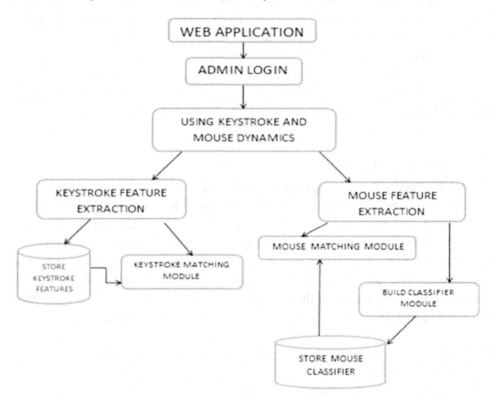

At the enlistment arrange client join their login points of interest, for example, client name and secret phrase which is retyped for a few times. Keystroke term is the interim of time that a key is squeezed and freed. Keystroke dormancy is the interim of time the squeezed of between two back to back keys interim of time to free a key and press the key successor, which is known as flight time, stay time (Young et al., 2019).

- Flight time-The time take between discharging the key and squeezing the following key.
- Dwell time-The time taken to press a single key.

Mouse Dynamics

In the proposed framework, the mouse elements are utilized as an elective technique for confirmation. Following are the manners in which we changed over the crude mouse occasions into four distinct activities.

1. Mouse Single Click: The element is like a Single Key Action, i.e. the time length between mouse catch press and discharge.
2. Mouse Double Click: The highlights are equivalent to those of a Key Digraph Action. Two successive mouse clicks are viewed as a double tap when add up to time duration, (say) < 1000.
3. Mouse Move: This activity was framed by the arrangement of mouse move occasions.

Mouse Drag Drop: This activity is fundamentally the same as the Mouse Move Action, yet for this activity first here must be a mouse click down occasion pursued by mouse move successions and after that mouse click up occasion (Antal & Egyed, 2019).

Calculation USED

1. Dwell Time
2. Flight Time Latency
3. Words Total Time Duration.

Stage 1: Begin with the unfilled set.
Stage 2: Calculate weights of all highlights utilizing paradigm work.
Stage 3: Pick the most excellent component and put in it to the generated pool of hopeful element subset.
Stage 4: Repeat stages two to three till a pre-defined number of highlights are chosen or until the point that no conceivable single component expansion would cause an expansion in a higher assessment of the foundation work. Information parameters incorporate abide time, flight time inactivity and words add up to time span. Abide time is the time the key is squeezed in. Flight time inactivity is the time take between discharging the key and squeezing the following key. Words add up to time length is the aggregate time determined from the press time to discharge time.

The aggregate time estimation is put away in the database in millisecond (ms) design.

Words add up to time term (WT) = endTime – startTime
Where, endTime = key discharge time, startTime = key press time

New keystroke information portrayal demonstrates dependent on potential capacities is proposed to permit maintaining data about control, times and key estimations of keystroke activities. The proposed model dependent on "official statement" times for each key can store data about keystrokes.

The framework is lightweight as it is actualized for the head. Future work would incorporate producing keystroke models for different clients too alongside other conceivable conduct highlights like face acknowledgement, step examination and different highlights.

In the process of developing the system we go through various steps shown in figure 3 which are as follows: -

1) The raw data has been derived which is login into the system through log data.
2) That log data entered is pre-processing i.e. data is prepared and iterated until it is ready to process further.

Then features are selected depending on the research as follow:

Features of Keystroke and Mouse Dynamics Are Discussed As

Dwell time- Dwell *time* (information retrieval), a relevance indicator measuring the *time* the user remains at a search result after a click i.e. the time duration that a key is pressed.
Flight time - It is the time duration in between releasing a key and pressing the next key

Figure 3. Process of Developing a System

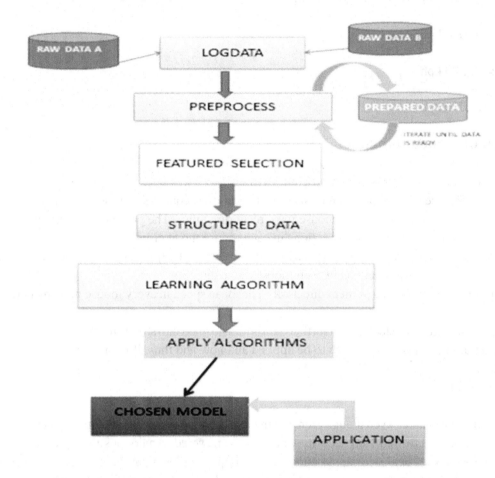

Features of Keystroke Dynamics

- Average of dwell-time-The average dwell time of a series of keystrokes.
- Average of flight-time - The mean flight time of a sequence of keystrokes.
- Standard deviation of dwell-time - The standard deviation of dwell time of a sequence of keystrokes.
- Standard deviation of flight time - The standard deviation of flight time of a sequence of keystrokes.
- Mean of flight times per type of user behaviour - The mean of flight time for each type of user keystroke behaviour.
- Average Typing Speed The average typing speed of a sequence of keystrokes.
- WPM – the rate of identified present typing words per minute

A mean number of characters in typed keystrokes apparently set to five a fifty-minute hour since it is the expected minutes an entry operative will be submitting data in a usual work-day hour

The resultant formula:

(wpm*5) *50 = kph

General calculations based on this formula:

40 wpm = 10,000 kph

50 wpm = 12,500 kph

60 wpm = 15,000 kph

Features of Mouse Dynamics

a) Mean click time - The mean of mouse clicks times.
b) Ratio of Silence - The proportion of silence amount of a sequence of mouse actions.
c) Percentage of mouse action per mouse movement direction - The percentage of mouse action occurrence of a sequence of mouse actions in each mouse move direction.
d) Proportion of displacement per mouse movement direction - The proportion of mouse move distance of a sequence of mouse actions in each mouse move direction
e) Mean speed per mouse movement direction - The mean speed in every mouse movement direction.

4) After the features are selected then further data is transformed into structured data as per requirement.
5) Further algorithm is found which to be applied and how and thus, it is implemented.

CONCLUSION

As explained in the chapter, even though there are many advantages of web applications, there are various realistic issues related to web sites security wants to be answered. Analogous to any web application, various security issues deal with applications which require authentication. In this chapter, security methods of such detective methods and preventive methods of web applications from login attacks are surveyed, and the most important features and elements of login attacks are also scrutinized. It is exposed that all of these attacks have a ruthless impact on websites and the attacks could lead to serious problems for end users. Nearly all key attacks on authentication along with the possible impacts and the available countermeasures have been described.

REFERENCES

Antal, M., & Egyed-Zsigmond, E. (2019). *Intrusion detection using mouse dynamics*. IET Biometrics. doi:10.1049/iet-bmt.2018.5126

Callegati, F., Cerroni, W., & Ramilli, M. (2009). Man-in-the-Middle Attack to the HTTPS Protocol. *IEEE Security and Privacy, 7*(1), 78–81. doi:10.1109/MSP.2009.12

Gazet, A. (2010). Comparative analysis of various ransomware virii. *Journal in Computer Virology, 6*(1), 77-90.

Halfond, W. G., Viegas, J., & Orso, A. (2006, March). A classification of SQL-injection attacks and countermeasures. In *Proceedings of the IEEE International Symposium on Secure Software Engineering* (Vol. 1, pp. 13-15). IEEE.

Han, H., Lu, X. L., Lu, J., Bo, C., & Yong, R. L. (2002). Data mining aided signature discovery in network-based intrusion detection system. *Operating Systems Review*, *36*(4), 7–13. doi:10.1145/583800.583801

Ho, G., Cidon, A., Gavish, L., Schweighauser, M., Paxson, V., Savage, S., . . . Wagner, D. (2019). Detecting and characterizing lateral phishing at scale. In *28th {USENIX} Security Symposium ({USENIX} Security 19* (pp. 1273-1290). USENIX.

Islam, M. R. U., Islam, M. S., Ahmed, Z., Iqbal, A., & Shahriyar, R. (2019, July). Automatic Detection of NoSQL Injection Using Supervised Learning. In *2019 IEEE 43rd Annual Computer Software and Applications Conference (COMPSAC)* (Vol. 1, pp. 760-769). IEEE. 10.1109/COMPSAC.2019.00113

Kals, S., Kirda, E., Kruegel, C., & Jovanovic, N. (2006, May). Secubat: a web vulnerability scanner. In *Proceedings of the 15th international conference on World Wide Web* (pp. 247-256). ACM. 10.1145/1135777.1135817

Kc, G. S., Keromytis, A. D., & Prevelakis, V. (2003, October). Countering code-injection attacks with instruction-set randomization. In *Proceedings of the 10th ACM conference on Computer and communications security* (pp. 272-280). ACM.

Keith, M., Shao, B., & Steinbart, P. (2009). A behavioral analysis of passphrase design and effectiveness. *Journal of the Association for Information Systems*, *10*(2), 2. doi:10.17705/1jais.00184

Moore, T., & Clayton, R. (2007, June). An Empirical Analysis of the Current State of Phishing Attack and Defence. WEIS.

Owens, J., & Matthews, J. (2008, March). A study of passwords and methods used in brute-force SSH attacks. *USENIX Workshop on Large-Scale Exploits and Emergent Threats (LEET)*.

Rafique, S., Humayun, M., Hamid, B., Abbas, A., Akhtar, M., & Iqbal, K. (2015, June). Web application security vulnerabilities detection approaches: A systematic mapping study. In *Software Engineering, Artificial Intelligence, Networking and Parallel/Distributed Computing (SNPD), 2015 16th IEEE/ACIS International Conference on* (pp. 1-6). IEEE. 10.1109/SNPD.2015.7176244

Rahman, R. U., & Tomar, D. S. (2018). Botnet Threats to E-Commerce Web Applications and Their Detection. In Improving E-Commerce Web Applications Through Business Intelligence Techniques (pp. 48-81). IGI Global.

Rahman, R. U., & Tomar, D. S. (2018). Security Attacks on Wireless Networks and Their Detection Techniques. In *Emerging Wireless Communication and Network Technologies* (pp. 241–270). Singapore: Springer. doi:10.1007/978-981-13-0396-8_13

Rahman, R. U., Verma, R., Bansal, H., & Tomar, D. S. (2020). Classification of Spamming Attacks to Blogging Websites and Their Security Techniques. In *Encyclopedia of Criminal Activities and the Deep Web* (pp. 864–880). IGI Global. doi:10.4018/978-1-5225-9715-5.ch058

Rahman, R. U., Wadhwa, D., Bali, A., & Tomar, D. S. (2020). The Emerging Threats of Web Scrapping to Web Applications Security and Their Defense Mechanism. In Encyclopedia of Criminal Activities and the Deep Web (pp. 788-809). IGI Global. doi:10.4018/978-1-5225-9715-5.ch053

Sadasivam, G. K., Hota, C., & Anand, B. (2018). Honeynet Data Analysis and Distributed SSH Brute-Force Attacks. In *Towards Extensible and Adaptable Methods in Computing* (pp. 107–118). Singapore: Springer. doi:10.1007/978-981-13-2348-5_9

Sadasivam, G. K., Hota, C., & Anand, B. (2018). Honeynet Data Analysis and Distributed SSH Brute-Force Attacks. In *Towards Extensible and Adaptable Methods in Computing* (pp. 107–118). Singapore: Springer. doi:10.1007/978-981-13-2348-5_9

Scarfone, K., & Mell, P. (2010). *The common configuration scoring system (ccss): Metrics for software security configuration vulnerabilities*. NIST interagency report, 7502.

Shah, S., & Mehtre, B. M. (2015). An overview of vulnerability assessment and penetration testing techniques. *Journal of Computer Virology and Hacking Techniques, 11*(1), 27–49. doi:10.100711416-014-0231-x

Singh, V., & Pandey, S. K. (2019). *Revisiting Cloud Security Threat: Dictionary Attack*. Available at SSRN 3444792.

Ten, C. W., Liu, C. C., & Manimaran, G. (2008). Vulnerability assessment of cybersecurity for SCADA systems. *IEEE Transactions on Power Systems, 23*(4), 1836–1846. doi:10.1109/TPWRS.2008.2002298

ur Rahman, R., Tomar, D. S., & Das, S. (2012, May). Dynamic image based captcha. In *2012 International Conference on Communication Systems and Network Technologies* (pp. 90-94). IEEE.

Ur Rizwan, R. (2012). Survey on captcha systems. *Journal of Global Research in Computer Science, 3*(6), 54–58.

Van der Meulen, R., & Rivera, J. (2013). *Gartner predicts by 2017, half of employers will require employees to supply their own device for work purposes*. Gartner.com.

Vogt, P., Nentwich, F., Jovanovic, N., Kirda, E., Kruegel, C., & Vigna, G. (2007, February). Cross Site Scripting Prevention with Dynamic Data Tainting and Static Analysis. *NDSS, 2007*, 12.

Von Solms, R., & Van Niekerk, J. (2013). From information security to cyber security. *Computers & Security, 38*, 97-102.

Willems, C., Holz, T., & Freiling, F. (2007). Toward automated dynamic malware analysis using cwsandbox. *IEEE Security and Privacy, 5*(2), 32–39. doi:10.1109/MSP.2007.45

Young, J. R., Davies, R. S., Jenkins, J. L., & Pfleger, I. (2019). Keystroke Dynamics: Establishing Keyprints to Verify Users in Online Courses. *Computers in the Schools, 36*(1), 48–68. doi:10.1080/07380569.2019.1565905

KEY TERMS AND DEFINITIONS

Cyber Security: It is the security of web associated frameworks, including equipment, programming, and information from digital assaults.

Malware: It is program used to hurt a PC client.

Phishing: It is a type of extortion where false messages are sent that look like messages from respectable sources.

Ransomware: It is a sort of malware that includes an aggressor attacking individual's PC framework.

Threat: The likelihood of malevolent attempt to injure or interrupt a web application.

Vulnerability: It is defined as a flaw, fault, or insufficiency of a system.

Chapter 9
Evaluating the Effectiveness of Deterrence Theory in Information Security Compliance:
New Insights From a Developing Country.

Felix Nti Koranteng
University of Education, Winneba, Kumasi Campus, Ghana

Richard Apau
ⓘ https://orcid.org/0000-0002-5621-1435
Kwame Nkrumah University of Science and Technology, Ghana

Jones Opoku-Ware
ⓘ https://orcid.org/0000-0002-7828-1725
Kwame Nkrumah University of Science and Technology, Ghana

Akon Obu Ekpezu
ⓘ https://orcid.org/0000-0002-9502-1052
Cross River University of Technology, Cross River, Nigeria

ABSTRACT

There is a long-held belief that deterrence mechanisms are more useful in developing countries. Evidence on this belief is anecdotal rather than empirical. In this chapter, individual compliance to information system security policy (ISSP) is examined through the lenses of deterrence theory. The effects of certainty of detection and severity of punishment on attitude towards compliance and also ISSP compliance behaviour are investigated. A survey questionnaire was distributed to gather responses from 432 individuals who are staff of a public university in Ghana. The data was analysed using partial least square structural equation modelling (PLS-SEM). The results indicate that severity of punishment has a positive effect on attitude towards compliance and ISSP compliance behaviour. However, certainty of detection neither affected attitude towards compliance nor ISSP compliance behaviour. It is recommended that organizations enhance the severity of sanctions imposed on those who violate ISSPs. Future studies should explore how users apply neutralization techniques to evade sanctions.

DOI: 10.4018/978-1-7998-3149-5.ch009

INTRODUCTION

Globally, businesses rely heavily on Information Systems (IS) to function efficiently. Therefore, the security of these systems remains crucial (Chen, Wu, Chen, & Teng, 2018). Despite increasing investments in intrusion detection and prevention tools, incidences of Information System (IS) breaches continue to rise. This is because intrusion sources and vulnerabilities often originate from individual's activities within the organization. Thus, unacceptable end-user behavior accounts for many security issues in organizations (Safa et al., 2019). Consequently, many organizations employ guidelines and requirements laid out in their IS Security Policy (ISSP) to influence end-user behavior. Nonetheless, users rarely comply with these rules (Willison & Warkentin, 2013). This makes the individual users in organizations the weakest link in information security assurance (Tsohou & Holtkamp, 2018; Yoo, Sanders, & Cerveny, 2018).

Several studies have investigated information security compliance. Whilst some studies acknowledge deterrence mechanisms as effective means of ISSP compliance in organizations (Herath & Rao, 2009a; Safa et al., 2019), other studies contradict this assertion (Chen et al., 2018; Siponen & Vance, 2010; Rajab & Eydgahi, 2019). Therefore, there is dissonance on the effectiveness of deterrence mechanisms in ensuring ISSP compliance. In most instances, the disagreement has been attributed to the differences in geographical boundaries within which prior studies were conducted (D'arcy & Herath, 2011). To explain further, deterrence mechanisms seem to have been less effective in individualist societies than in collectivist (Hofstede, 1983). Therefore, it is anticipated that deterrence mechanisms for encouraging ISSP compliance will likely be more effective in collectivist societies than in individualist ones. Collectivist societies emphasize on cohesiveness among individuals and thus seek to prioritize the interest of the society over the individual good or welfare (Tan, Nainee, & Tan, 2016). On the other hand, individualistic societies tend to produce individuals with self-concepts who are focused on independence rather than interdependence. Therefore, people in individualist societies tend to prioritize the individual good over that of the group or society (Lapidot-Lefler & Hosri, 2016). Afukaar (2003), for instance, has indicated that deterrence mechanisms are effective in influencing ISSP compliance in developing countries since many of these countries are collectivist. This assertion is based on purely anecdotal evidences rather than empirical.

In this regard, this chapter examines ISSP compliance in a developing country through the lens of the classical Deterrence Theory (Higgins, Wilson, & Fell, 2005). It investigates the direct effects of Severity of Punishments and Certainty of Detection on ISSP Compliance Intention and also how Attitude Toward Compliance mediate these relationships. As a first step, relevant literature and theoretical frameworks are presented in the following section. This is followed by an analysis and discussion of the findings based on which conclusions and recommendations are drawn.

LITERATURE REVIEW

In recent years, approaches for ensuring information security have shifted focus from technology to the human perspective. Literature suggests that insiders through their ignorance, negligence or deliberate acts subject organizations' IS to various threats (Safa et al., 2019). Indeed, many security issues are as a result of the actions or inactions of end-users (Cheng, Li, Li, Holm, & Zhai, 2013). Despite the provision of ISSPs which stipulates desired security behavior, end-users mostly choose to engage in abusive behavior. Therefore, many scholars recommend deterrent and preventive approaches (e.g. sanctions) to influence end-user compliance to information security. For instance, Johnston and Warkentin (2010) point out that fear of sanctions is a significant predictor of intention to comply with ISSP. In a similar investigations into factors that affect security behavior, scholars have discovered that formal sanctions, threat appraisals, detection certainty, punishment certainty, and severity play a crucial role in ISSP compliance intention (Cheng et al., 2013; Herath & Rao, 2009a; Ifinedo, 2012; Li, Zhang, & Sarathy, 2010; Safa et al., 2019).

Contrary to the assertions that deterrence mechanisms influence compliance intentions, many other studies have refuted these claims (Chen et al., 2018; Rajab & Eydgahi, 2019; Siponen & Vance, 2010). Having assessed the use of neutralization mechanisms, Siponen and Vance (2010) concluded that formal sanctions are less effective in ensuring security policy compliance. Relatedly, other studies have also found that severe punishment does not affect compliance intentions (Chen et al., 2018; Rajab & Eydgahi, 2019). This suggests incoherencies in the findings of prior studies. As earlier indicated, such contradictions have been attributed to the differences in the geographic locations within which these studies were conducted. For example, whereas Cheng et al., (2013) conducted their study in China, Ifinedo (2012)'s findings were constraint within the borders of Canada. According to Hofstede's insights, Canada is a more individualist country as compared to China which more or less could be conveniently classified as a collectivist society. Consequently, many scholars posit that deterrent mechanisms are more effective in collectivist areas (such as Africa) than individualists (Afukaar, 2003; Hovav & D'Arcy, 2012). This is because the cultural features of collectivist societies manifest in social harmony, relational hierarchy, reverence for authority and face-saving (Karlin & Weil, 2019). Hence, individuals behave appropriately towards the ethical standards to avoid reprehension. However, these assertions are mostly conceptual and lack empirical backing. In this chapter, the validity of these claims is tested through the lenses of the Deterrence Theory (Higgins et al., 2005).

Theoretical Background and Hypotheses

Due to the increased relevance of people in information security, research focusing on security behavior has surged considerably. As indicated in the literature review, factors of the deterrent theory have been prominent in examining ISSP compliance. As proposed by Higgins et al. (2005), the deterrence theory assumes that people's behavior and decisions towards crime is influenced by the maximization of benefits and minimization of cost. According to the theory, people will not abuse ISSPs when they believe the cost of non-compliance outweighs the benefits. It posits that deterrent approaches such as disincentives and sanctions guide security policy compliance behavior. However, the effectiveness of these disincentives is only manifested through certainty of detection and severity of punishment (Safa et al., 2019). Thus, if end users believe that their abuse of IS resources will be detected (certainty of detection) and will attract harsh punishments such as fines and imprisonment (severity of punishment), they will adhere to ISSPs.

Although attitude is not included in the main theoretical model, some scholars have shown that punishment severity influences people's attitudes towards behavior (Pahnila, Siponen, & Mahmood, 2007). Attitude is a person's judgment towards a particular behavior or concept (Safa et al., 2019). It is a consequence of the person's previous experiences and surrounding environments. Given that loyalty is paramount in collectivist societies and people behave in a way that benefits the entire group. It is important to identify if users in such societies possess favorable judgments towards ISSPs and how these feelings influence their intention to comply with ISSPs. Consequently, Attitude towards Compliance is integrated into the deterrence model. This chapter, therefore, presents a model that investigates the direct effect of Certainty of Detection and Severity of Punishment on Compliance Intention and how Attitude towards ISSPs mediate these relationships. Table 1 summarizes the definitions of the constructs and their sources from literature.

Table 1. Construct definition and sources

Construct	Definition	Source
Certainty of Detection (CD)	The belief that abuse of IS resources will be detected.	(Herath & Rao, 2009b)
Severity of Punishment (SP)	The believe that abuse of IS resources will attract harsh punishment.	(Safa et al., 2015)
Attitude Towards Compliance (ATT)	A person's positive and negative feelings toward compliance behavior.	(Safa et al., 2019)
Compliance Intention (CI)	It is the possibility that users will comply with ISSPs in the near future.	(Cheng et al., 2013)

Certainty of Detection

Certainty of detection has been identified to influence security behavior of users. It posits that crime is less likely to occur in areas with high detection probability. For example, criminals are less likely to rob buildings with security equipment such as cameras and alarm systems. Therefore, people will abandon unacceptable behavior if there is a high probability of capture. In other words, users will be motivated to follow ISSPs when they perceive that the possibility of been caught when they violate security policies is high. Indeed, findings from Herath and Rao (2009a), Herath and Rao (2009b) and Rajab and Eydgahi (2019) confirm that detection certainty affects people's feelings and intention to comply with ISSPs. To confirm this relationship in developing countries, it is hypothesized that:

H_{1a}: Certainty of Detection positively affects Compliance Intention.
H_{1b}: Certainty of Detection positively affects Attitudes towards Compliance.

Severity of Punishment

Severity of Punishment describes the degree of severity of sanctions that are imposed on people for deviant behavior. It is the harshness of punishment that are executed on users who violate the security policy. In ensuring ISSP compliance, it is believed that when the severity of punishment increases, users will be more inclined to follow accepted guidelines. This assertion is confirmed by Safa et al. (2019). Meanwhile, Herath and Rao (2009a) found that sanction severity has a negative influence on compliance intention. Thus, the higher the severity of punishment, the lesser users follow ISSPs. On the other hand, Chen et al., (2018) found no direct effect of sanction severity on compliance intention. The inconsistencies in the studies mentioned above suggest a lack of clarity on the influence of severity of punishment on ISSP compliance intention. Therefore, to eliminate any doubts on the influence of severity of punishment on compliance, it is postulated that:

H_{2a}: Severity of Punishment positively affects Attitudes towards Compliance

H_{2b}: Severity of Punishment positively affects Compliance Intention.

Attitude Towards Compliance and Compliance Intention

Attitude denotes a person's judgment of a phenomenon. Attitude towards ISSP, however, refers to a person's overall affective feeling towards ISSP compliance (Safa et al., 2019). This may be informed by a person's prior experiences (Ajzen, 1991). Consequently, Ajzen (1991) argues that attitude is a strong antecedent of behavioral intention. Studies have confirmed that users will readily comply when they possess favorable judgment towards ISSPs (Ifinedo, 2014; Safa, Von Solms, & Furnell, 2016). However, Wiafe, Nakata, and Gulliver (2014) have provided evidence that attitude does not always predict behavior. Therefore, to confirm the relationship between attitude and compliance intention in developing countries, it is hypothesized that:

H_3: Attitude Towards Compliance positively affects Compliance Intention.

Based on the stated hypothesis, a model is therefore postulated to show the hypotheses that have been formulated. Figure 1 demonstrates the hypothesized model for the study.

Figure 1.

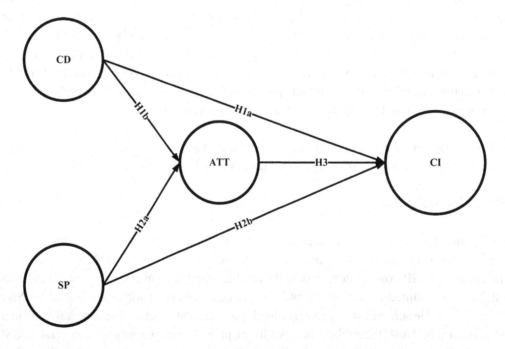

Research Methodology

Since this study seeks to test hypotheses related to the effectiveness of deterrence mechanisms on ISSP compliance, the deductive approach was suitable (Saunders, Lewis, Thornhill, & Wilson, 2009). Consequently, links to an English based survey questionnaire designed using GoogleForms was sent to respondents via email. Individual respondents were conveniently sampled. To ensure confidentiality and anonymity, the questionnaire gathered data on only relevant demographics aside from their opinions on Certainty of Detection, Severity of Punishment, Attitude Towards Compliance and ISSP Compliance Intention. However, the data collected was analyzed using Partial Least Square Structural Equation Modelling (PLS-SEM). This data analysis approach is appropriate because it is robust to multivariate distribution errors. Moreover, it is efficient for estimating the relationships between latent variables (Hair, Risher, Sarstedt, & Ringle, 2019). All question items recorded favorably above the 0.7 Cronbach's alpha reliability threshold required by Bagozzi, Yi and Phillips (1991).

DATA ANALYSIS

Respondents' Demographics

A total of 432 responses were compiled after the data collection period which lasted for a month. All responses were valid because all fields were designated to be mandatory. A male majority (74%) along with a female minority of (26%) was recorded. In addition, the majority (90%) of the respondents were below 30 years while only 10% were above. With regard to educational background, 78% of the respondents were undergraduates while 22% were postgraduate students.

Table 2. Respondents' demographics

Demographics	Value	Frequency	Percentage
Sex			
	Male	318	74%
	Female	114	26%
Age			
	Below 30	387	90%
	30 and Above	48	10%
Education Level			
	Undergraduate	336	78%
	Postgraduate	99	22%

Reliability and Validity Tests

The constructs were evaluated for internal consistency, convergent and discriminant validity as well as multicollinearity. Internal consistency was measured with Cronbach Alpha and composite reliability. The results shown in Table 3 show that all constructs were reliable since they met the 0.7 requirement proposed by Bagozzi et al., (1991). On the other hand, convergent validity was measured using Average Variance Extracted (AVE) as recommended by Wixom and Watson (2001). The results confirmed that all constructs met the 0.5 required threshold by Wixom and Watson (2001) (see table 3). Furthermore, Fornell and Larcker (1981)'s criteria were adopted to assessed discriminant validity. The square roots of the AVEs of the latent variables were juxtaposed with correlations among the other variables. As the authors prefer, all the square roots of AVEs were higher than the other correlations. The highlighted diagonal values in Table 3 represents discriminant validity. Finally, the possibility of collinearity was evaluated using Variance Inflation Factor (VIF) (see Table 3). VIF lower than 3 meets the acceptable tolerance level required by Hair et al., (2019).

Table 3. Construct reliability and validity

	CA	CR	AVE	VIF	ATT	CD	CI	SP
ATT	0.814	0.890	0.730	1.102	0.855			
CD	0.796	0.880	0.710	1.221	0.220	0.842		
CI	0.851	0.910	0.771		0.610	0.316	0.878	
SP	0.725	0.844	0.644	1.2-63	0.283	0.411	0.368	0.803

NB: CA, Cronbach's Alpha; CR, Composite Reliability; AVE, Average Variance Extracted; VIF, Variance Inflation Factor.

Structural Model

The proposed model was estimated using the bootstrap technique in PLS-SEM. This approach was preferred since the sample size is larger than 100. Path coefficients were significant when p-values were less than 0.05. The analysis revealed that while some of the proposed relationships were significant, others were insignificant. Specifically, Severity of Punishment influenced Attitude Towards Compliance ($\beta = 0.231$, $p < 0.01$) and ISSP Compliance Intention ($\beta = 0.162$, $p < 0.02$). On the contrary, Certainty of Detection failed to affect either Attitude Towards Compliance ($\beta = 0.125$, $p > 0.08$) or Compliance Intention ($\beta = 0.132$, $p > 0.08$). However, Attitude Towards Compliance had a significant effect on Compliance Intention ($\beta = 0.535$, $p < 0.001$). The summary is shown in Figure 2 and Table 4. The effect of the exogenous variables was also assessed. According to Cohen (1988), effect sizes are irrelevant if $f^2 < 0.02$, small when $f^2 > 0.02$, medium when $f^2 > 0.15$ and large if $f^2 > 0.35$. From the results in Table 4, Attitude Towards Compliance had the largest effect on ISSP Compliance Intention (0.453). Severity of Punishment (0.37) and Certainty of Detection (0.25) had small effects on ISSP Compliance Intention. However, while Severity of Punishment (0.49) had a medium effect, the effect of Certainty of Detection (0.014) on Attitude Towards Compliance was irrelevant.

Figure 2.

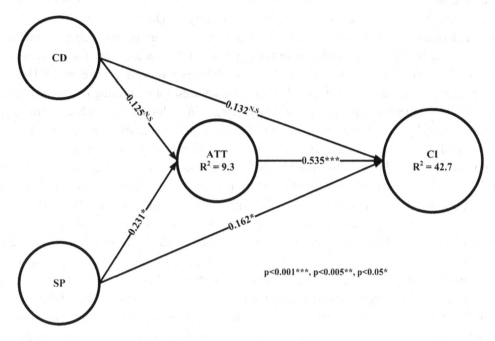

Table 4. Significance of path coefficients

	Original Sample (O)	Sample Mean (M)	Standard Deviation (STDEV)	T Statistics (|O/ STDEV|)	P Values	Results	f^2
ATT -> CI	0.535	0.527	0.066	8.099	0.000	Supported	0.453
CD -> ATT	0.125	0.131	0.089	1.399	0.081	Not Supported	0.014
CD -> CI	0.132	0.143	0.095	1.383	0.084	Not Supported	0.025
SP -> ATT	0.231	0.239	0.094	2.461	0.007	Supported	0.049
SP -> CI	0.162	0.165	0.077	2.115	0.017	Supported	0.037

DISCUSSION

The research model presented in this chapter investigated the effectiveness of deterrent approaches in ensuring ISSP compliance in developing countries. Specifically, the model examined the influence of Certainty of Detection and Severity of Punishment on Attitude Towards Compliance and Compliance Intention. It also investigated the effect of Attitude Towards Compliance on Compliance Intention.

Findings from the study indicate that a considerable amount of the variance in Compliance Intention (52.7%) is explained by the exogenous variables (Certainty of Detection, Severity of Punishment and Attitude Towards Compliance). From this result, the potency of the deterrence model in explaining compliance behavior is confirmed. Furthermore, contrary to earlier assertions by Rajab and Eydgahi

(2019), the findings suggest that the effectiveness of deterrent approaches in ensuring ISSP compliance is manifested through Severity of Punishment than Certainty of Detection. Specifically, Severity of Punishment had a significant effect on Attitude Towards Compliance and Compliance Intention. In other words, users are likely to positively respond and comply with ISSPs when there are harsh punishments for violations. This is consistent with D'Arcy et al. (2009) but deviates from Chen et al. (2018). Nonetheless, this is reasonable given that many people who are punished for exhibiting delinquent behavior in developing countries are often stigmatized. Similarly, offense in such societies leads to shame and loss of face. Therefore, users by way of avoiding reprehension, shame and sanctions adhere to ISSPs. As a result, management is advised to lay out harsh punishments for information system security policy violations.

Certainty of Detection did not significantly predict Attitude Towards Compliance and Compliance Intention. Though this is consistent with D'Arcy et al. (2009), it is surprising that the attitudes and intentions of users are not influenced by the probability of being caught for violations. Perhaps, this is because people in developing countries lack requisite computer skills, therefore their mistakes lead to IS security violations which they may not be aware of. However, given the educational background of the respondents in this study, it is also possible that users adopt neutralization techniques such as denial of responsibility to justify computer abuse (Siponen & Vance, 2010). For instance, users may argue that they were unaware their actions would lead to a violation, the situation was beyond their control or perhaps, the ISSP policy was unclear (Puhakainen, 2006). Though security training may be ineffective in such instances, management through effective employee relations can mitigate these excuses and improve security behavior (Yaokumah, Walker, & Kumah, 2019). Finally, contrary to claims by Wiafe et al. (2014), Attitude Towards Compliance predicted Compliance Intention. Thus, if users have favorable judgments towards ISSPs, they will be motivated to comply with ISSPs.

FUTURE RESEARCH DIRECTIONS

The chapter acknowledges certain limitations in terms of the sampling criteria and size which constraint its findings. Future works are encouraged to use different sampling techniques as well as a larger sample size to determine the viability of these findings. Further, how users use neutralization techniques to circumvent sanctions as well as ways as to how it can be minimized can be explored by future studies.

CONCLUSION

The significance of the security of an organization's Information System (IS) is undoubted. Secured systems do not only reduce an organization's financial loses but increases its integrity and reputation. However, end-user behavior is a dominant factor in ensuring IS security. This study makes significant progress towards explaining the effectiveness of deterrent mechanisms in ensuring ISSP compliance in developing countries. Responses from 432 participants were rigorously analyzed using Partial Least Square Structural Equation Modelling. The outcome of the study suggests that the efficacy of the deterrent theory is manifested in Severity of Punishment than Certainty of Detection. This implies that management should exert harsh punishment for ISSP violations. It is believed that such punishment will encourage compliance behavior. Although this study is constraint in terms of sample size and methods, future studies should investigate how end-users use neutralization techniques to circumvent sanctions as well as how it can be minimized.

REFERENCES

Afukaar, F. K. (2003). Speed control in developing countries: Issues, challenges and opportunities in reducing road traffic injuries. *Injury Control and Safety Promotion*, *10*(1–2), 77–81. doi:10.1076/icsp.10.1.77.14113 PMID:12772489

Ajzen, I. (1991). The theory of planned behavior. *Organizational Behavior and Human Decision Processes*, *50*(2), 179–211. doi:10.1016/0749-5978(91)90020-T

Bagozzi, R. P., Yi, Y., & Phillips, L. W. (1991). Assessing construct validity in organizational research. *Administrative Science Quarterly*, *36*(3), 421–458. doi:10.2307/2393203

Chen, X., Wu, D., Chen, L., & Teng, J. K. L. (2018). Sanction severity and employees' information security policy compliance: Investigating mediating, moderating, and control variables. *Information & Management*, *55*(8), 1049–1060. doi:10.1016/j.im.2018.05.011

Cheng, L., Li, Y., Li, W., Holm, E., & Zhai, Q. (2013). Understanding the violation of IS security policy in organizations: An integrated model based on social control and deterrence theory. *Computers & Security*, *39*, 447–459. doi:10.1016/j.cose.2013.09.009

Cohen, J. (2013). *Statistical power analysis for the behavioral sciences*. Routledge. doi:10.4324/9780203771587

D'arcy, J., & Herath, T. (2011). A review and analysis of deterrence theory in the IS security literature: Making sense of the disparate findings. *European Journal of Information Systems*, *20*(6), 643–658. doi:10.1057/ejis.2011.23

D'Arcy, J., Hovav, A., & Galletta, D. (2009). User awareness of security countermeasures and its impact on information systems misuse: A deterrence approach. *Information Systems Research*, *20*(1), 79–98. doi:10.1287/isre.1070.0160

Fornell, C., & Larcker, D. F. (1981). Evaluating structural model with unobserved variables and measurement errors. *JMR, Journal of Marketing Research*, *18*(1), 39–50. doi:10.1177/002224378101800104

Hair, J. F., Risher, J. J., Sarstedt, M., & Ringle, C. M. (2019). When to use and how to report the results of PLS-SEM. *European Business Review*, *31*(1), 2–24. doi:10.1108/EBR-11-2018-0203

Herath, T., & Rao, H. R. (2009a). Encouraging information security behaviors in organizations: Role of penalties, pressures and perceived effectiveness. *Decision Support Systems*, *47*(2), 154–165. doi:10.1016/j.dss.2009.02.005

Herath, T., & Rao, H. R. (2009b). Protection motivation and deterrence: A framework for security policy compliance in organizations. *European Journal of Information Systems*, *18*(2), 106–125. doi:10.1057/ejis.2009.6

Higgins, G. E., Wilson, A. L., & Fell, B. D. (2005). An application of deterrence theory to software piracy. *The Journal of Criminal Justice and Popular Culture, 12*(3), 166–184.

Hofstede, G. (1983). National cultures in four dimensions: A research-based theory of cultural differences among nations. *International Studies of Management & Organization, 13*(1–2), 46–74. doi:10.1080/00208825.1983.11656358

Hovav, A., & D'Arcy, J. (2012). Applying an extended model of deterrence across cultures: An investigation of information systems misuse in the US and South Korea. *Information & Management, 49*(2), 99–110. doi:10.1016/j.im.2011.12.005

Ifinedo, P. (2012). Understanding information systems security policy compliance: An integration of the theory of planned behavior and the protection motivation theory. *Computers & Security, 31*(1), 83–95. doi:10.1016/j.cose.2011.10.007

Ifinedo, P. (2014). Information systems security policy compliance: An empirical study of the effects of socialization, influence, and cognition. *Information & Management, 51*(1), 69–79. doi:10.1016/j.im.2013.10.001

Johnston & Warkentin. (2010). Fear Appeals and Information Security Behaviors: An Empirical Study. *MIS Quarterly, 34*(3), 549. doi:10.2307/25750691

Karlin, N. J., & Weil, J. (2019). Exploring Cultural Similarity and Cultural Diversity: A Cross-National Study of Nine Countries. *Journal of Aging Science, 7*, 204. doi:10.35248/2329-8847.19.07.204

Li, H., Zhang, J., & Sarathy, R. (2010). Understanding compliance with internet use policy from the perspective of rational choice theory. *Decision Support Systems, 48*(4), 635–645. doi:10.1016/j.dss.2009.12.005

Pahnila, S., Siponen, M., & Mahmood, A. (2007). Employees' behavior towards IS security policy compliance. In *2007 40th Annual Hawaii International Conference on System Sciences (HICSS'07)* (p. 156b-156b). Academic Press.

Puhakainen, P. (2006). *A design theory for information security awareness*. Faculty of Science. University of Oulu. Retrieved from http://en.scientificcommons.org/13922630

Rajab, M., & Eydgahi, A. (2019). Evaluating the explanatory power of theoretical frameworks on intention to comply with information security policies in higher education. *Computers & Security, 80*, 211–223. doi:10.1016/j.cose.2018.09.016

Safa, N. S., Maple, C., Furnell, S., Azad, M. A., Perera, C., Dabbagh, M., & Sookhak, M. (2019). Deterrence and prevention-based model to mitigate information security insider threats in organizations. *Future Generation Computer Systems, 97*, 587–597. doi:10.1016/j.future.2019.03.024

Safa, N. S., Sookhak, M., Von Solms, R., Furnell, S., Ghani, N. A., & Herawan, T. (2015). Information security conscious care behavior formation in organizations. *Computers & Security, 53*, 65–78. doi:10.1016/j.cose.2015.05.012

Safa, N. S., Von Solms, R., & Furnell, S. (2016). Information security policy compliance model in organizations. *Computers & Security, 56*, 70–82. doi:10.1016/j.cose.2015.10.006

Saunders, M., Lewis, P., Thornhill, A., & Wilson, J. (2009). Business research methods. *Financial Times*.

Siponen & Vance. (2010). Neutralization: New Insights into the Problem of Employee Information Systems Security Policy Violations. *MIS Quarterly, 34*(3), 487. doi:10.2307/25750688

Tan, S. A., Nainee, S., & Tan, C. S. (2019). Filial Piety and Life Satisfaction Among Malaysian Adolescents in a Multi-Ethnic, Collectivist Society. In *2nd International Conference on Intervention and Applied Psychology (ICIAP 2018)* (pp. 1–5). Academic Press.

Tsohou, A., & Holtkamp, P. (2018). Are users competent to comply with information security policies? An analysis of professional competence models. *Information Technology & People, 31*(5), 1047–1068. doi:10.1108/ITP-02-2017-0052

Wiafe, I., Nakata, K., & Gulliver, S. (2014). Categorizing users in behavior change support systems based on cognitive dissonance. *Personal and Ubiquitous Computing, 18*(7), 1677–1687. doi:10.100700779-014-0782-3

Willison, R., & Warkentin, M. (2013). Beyond deterrence: An expanded view of employee computer abuse. *Management Information Systems Quarterly, 37*(1), 1–20. doi:10.25300/MISQ/2013/37.1.01

Wixom, B. H., & Watson, H. J. (2001). An empirical investigation of the factors affecting data warehousing success. *Management Information Systems Quarterly, 25*(1), 17–41. doi:10.2307/3250957

Yaokumah, W., Walker, D. O., & Kumah, P. (2019). SETA and Security Behavior: Mediating Role of Employee Relations, Monitoring, and Accountability. *Journal of Global Information Management, 27*(2), 102–121. doi:10.4018/JGIM.2019040106

Yoo, C. W., Sanders, G. L., & Cerveny, R. P. (2018). Exploring the influence of flow and psychological ownership on security education, training and awareness effectiveness and security compliance. *Decision Support Systems, 108*, 107–118. doi:10.1016/j.dss.2018.02.009

KEY TERMS AND DEFINITIONS

Attitude Towards Compliance (ATT): A person's positive and negative feelings toward information systems security policy compliance.

Certainty of Detection (CD): The believe that abuse of information systems resources will be detected.

Compliance Intention (CI): It is the possibility that users will comply with information systems security policy the near future.

Deterrence: An action of discouraging improper security behavior by instilling fear of punishment.

Information Systems (IS): An integrated set of digital products for collecting, processing and storing organizations' informational resources.

Information Systems Security Policies (ISSPs): They are guidelines that outlines acceptable behaviour for ensuring information security.

Severity of Punishment (SP): The believe that abuse of information systems resources will attract harsh punishment.

Chapter 10
Factors Influencing Information Security Policy Compliance Behavior

Kwame Simpe Ofori
iD https://orcid.org/0000-0001-7725-9756
School of Management and Economics,
University of Electronic Science and Technology
of China, China

Osaretin Kayode Omoregie
Department of Finance, Lagos Business School,
Pan-Atlantic University, Nigeria

Hod Anyigba
Nobel International Business School, Ghana

Makafui Nyamadi
Department of Operations and Information
Systems, Business School, University of Ghana,
Ghana

George Oppong Appiagyei Ampong
Department of Management, Ghana Technology
University College, Ghana

Eli Fianu
Ghana Technology University College, Ghana

ABSTRACT

One of the major concerns of organizations in today's networked world is to unravel how employees comply with information security policies (ISPs) since the internal employee has been identified as the weakest link in security policy breaches. A number of studies have examined ISP compliance from the perspective of deterrence; however, there have been mixed results. The study seeks to examine information security compliance from the perspective of the general deterrence theory (GDT) and information security climate (ISC). Data was collected from 329 employees drawn from the five top-performing banks in Ghana and analyzed with PLS-SEM. Results from the study show that security education training and awareness, top-management's commitment for information security, and peer non-compliance behavior affect the information security climate in an organization. Information security climate, punishment severity, and certainty of deterrent were also found to influence employees' intention to comply with ISP. The implications, limitations, and directions for future research are discussed.

DOI: 10.4018/978-1-7998-3149-5.ch010

INTRODUCTION

"Data breaches keep happening. So why don't you do something? – The New York Times"

Worldwide IT security spending was poised to increase to $124 billion dollars in 2019 from $71.1 billion in 2017 (Gartner, 2018; Hwang et al., 2017). Big ticket cases of data breaches in 2017 and 2018 more than ever, highlighted the need for better systems and controls to curtail and contain data protection contraventions. Both small and large companies like Yahoo, AT&T Citi Bank, JP Morgan, and Equifax have all fallen prey to data protection problems, internally (New York Times, 2018). Data compliance has become a key competitive resource employed by firms to outpace their competitors – typically involving the adoption and use of security policy initiatives (Kim & Kim, 2017). It is therefore by no means an understatement when reiterated that information security and its application is pivotal to the firms growth and success (Doherty et al. 2009). Furthermore, clarity has been established that the human element is major cause of information security breachesin organizations. In other words information security policy behavior is key to improving information security levels in organizations (Balozian & Leidner, 2017).

Prior research has attempted to explain information security policy breaches through the General Deterrence Theory (Chan et al., 2005; Donalds & Osei-Bryson, 2020; C. Lee et al., 2016; S. M. Lee et al., 2004), Theory of Planned Behavior, Protection Motivation Theory and Organizational Theory (Rajab & Eydgahi, 2019). While organizational theory focuses on the effect of security climate on security policy compliance (Chan et al., 2005), deterrence theory highlights the effect of user awareness of IS security countermeasures on perceived certainty and severity of organizational sanctions (D'Arcy et al., 2009). According to the literature, one key way to encourage and motivate employees to comply with Information Security Policy (ISP) is the enforcement of sanctions under the general deterrence theory framework (GDT) (Aurigemma & Mattson, 2017). The GDT framework embraces disinsentives that match appropriate sanctions to violators of the ISP (Wall et al., 2013). In other words, if employees perceive that there are harsh penalties once they are caught violating information systems security policy; they are less likely to violate information systems security policy (Cheng et al., 2013). Further, Diver (2007) opines that understanding and interpreting the effects of sanctions are critical because employee non-compliance is typically the mainspring of all ISPs. This therefore almost certainly addresses the relevance of the GDT in enforcing ISP. As maintained by the literature, another major compliance attribute – information security climate – has been found to have significant impact on compliance because workplace quality devoid of anti-compliance behavior is driven by the nature of peer socialization in the organization (Yazdanmehr & Wang, 2016). Although studies on GDT and security climate have laid solid foundation in the field, they have largely been inconclusive with respect to compliance (Chen et al., 2018; D'Arcy et al., 2009; Herath et al., 2018; Herath & Rao, 2009; Safa et al., 2019).

Clearly, there is a lack of coherence on the integration of general deterrence theory (GDT) – a theory that speaks to compliance bahavior and organizational Information Security Climate (ISC). In this study, we use the GDT as a foundation to build an integrated information security policy compliance behavior model that incorporates critical turnaround factors: Information Security Climate (ISC), Intention to Comply (INT) and GDT constructs. This research attempts to provide a systematic insight of the factors affecting information security policy compliance. In particular, an attempt to highlight key antecedent factors affecting policy compliance behavior in order to enhance organizational capabilities of safeguarding systems to enhance productivity and security. Specifically, these factors can contribute to enhanced employee awareness creation, creating a conducive environment for security alertness and adoption and increasing employees' ability to comply with policies.

First, the research approaches security compliance behavior with a new approach. Although the GDT has been previously used to understand the reasons why employees will or will not comply with policy instruments in a given situation, it has yet to be used to interpret the security climate of organizations in management information systems (MIS) research. Second, components of information security policy compliance behavior perceived under the GDT is integrated with security climate to understand antecedent factors affecting policy compliance. It is expected that this study will provide a comprehensive understanding of how organizations need to effectively implement security compliance policies in today's dynamic business environment.

BACKGROUND

Background on Information Security Compliance

The ever-increasing use of information systems (IS) and its tools, the affordability of computers coupled with the level of dependency of today's world on information creates the need to secure data and enhance IS security at all times. The security of organizations IS largely depends on the type of IS policies in place as well as the degree to which these policies are implemented within the organization (Aurigemma & Panko, 2011; Hina & Dominic, 2018; Hu et al., 2012; Kolkowska et al., 2017; Sohrabi Safa et al., 2016). The extent to which IS policies support IS security have been proved to rely on the extent to which employees within the firm comply with these policies (Cram et al., 2017; D'Arcy & Herath, 2011). This need has raised concerns for research in the area of IS compliance by stakeholders in organizations; thus, the focus for this study.

The main aim for IS security in firms is to protect them from hackers and other external threats to getting the information from the client and from firms that can use this piece of stolen information unethically (Hina & Dominic, 2018; Kim & Kim, 2017; Nasir et al., 2018; Von Solms, 2005). To avoid the threats posed by these hackers, firms try to empower their employees through training provided by security experts in their information technology (IT) department to help them form an unbreakable link in their security chain (Alshare et al., 2018; Bansal et al., 2016; C. Lee et al., 2016). These security trainings take varied forms as individual employees have different levels of knowledge and understanding of IS security issues, thus, specified comprehensive guidelines are provided. These guidelines are referred to as IS security policies. It is always expected that all employees comply with these IS security policy guidelines at all times to foster strength in the firm's IS structure. Once any of these policies are broken or compromised, the firm becomes vulnerable to IS breaches and attacks from outside or from within, leading to 'insider threat' to IS security (Hina & Dominic, 2018; Siponen et al., 2014; Sommestad et al., 2014; Van Niekerk & Von Solms, 2010). Increasingly, apart from the usual external threats, internal threats are have seen sharp increases – growing in appetite.

For a completely assured IS security, there is the need for individuals to practise all the guidelines spelt out in the IS policy. Some of these policies may be seen as negligible to others but this may be very costly, considering the labor and logistics involved in undertaking them. This is termed as 'willful noncompliance' in the IT industry which comes with diverse repercussions (Aurigemma & Panko, 2011; Hardy, 2006; Hina & Dominic, 2018; Kolkowska et al., 2017; Sohrabi Safa et al., 2016; Vroom & Von

Solms, 2004). To avert these repercussions, it is prudent that firms enforce security compliance in all cases and at all times. These ISPs help firms lower and effectively manage IS risks, foster good corporate governance and information technology (IT) through security compliance (Da Veiga & Eloff, 2007; Moulton & Coles, 2003; Rocha Flores et al., 2014; Thomson & Von Solms, 2005; Von Solms, 2005).

Organizational Information Security Climate

Studies have revealed that firm's information security climate develops in a similar way just as organizational culture (Alhogail, 2015; Alnatheer, 2015; Lacey, 2010; Van Niekerk & Von Solms, 2010). This usually starts with the firm's board approving the firms IS strategy for effective management of the firm's IS and its tools in the short to long term. The board is also responsible for the provision of the intent and direction for the utmost protection of its database and information through established IS policies in place. A case in point is that, the board can state in its IS security policy the value it places on its information as an asset to the business, thus the need for its confidentiality, integrity and preservation throughout its information lifecycle (Dhillon et al., 2016). In this regard, employees are expected to comply with the set of IS security policy of the firm at all times as influenced by intrinsic and extrinsic factors. This implies that the type of information security climate that materializes in firms is prudent to foster or hamper IS protection within firms. This need has caused firms to assess the information security climate at play in respective firms to determine whether this climate falls in line with the firm's strategy and vision in maintaining information security in the short to long term (D'Arcy & Greene, 2014; Da Veiga & Martins, 2015; Hina & Dominic, 2018).

Some studies have revealed that the presence and type of security culture in firms are crucial in individual employees' compliance with information security policies (Da Veiga & Eloff, 2010; Da Veiga, 2016; Hina & Dominic, 2018; Karlsson et al., 2018). Another study also posits that the establishment of an information security climate in firms has a positive impact on the way employees perceive and behave towards information security issues to guard against information breaches and other unethical security issues from internal or external sources (Parsons et al., 2010). Some critical success factors to information security climate in firms include: the support received from top management on information security, the establishment of an effective information security policy and its awareness creation, the training of staff on compliance with this information security policy, the assessment and analysis of risks of information security, the firm's organizational culture, and compliance with information security policy with ethical conducts (Alshare et al., 2018; Parsons et al., 2010). Among these factors, top management support stands out as a noteworthy predictor of firms' information security climate.

Employees are largely influenced by their peers based on the organizational norms they follow. To buttress this point, Venkatesh et al. (2003) find a significant relationship between social influence and intention to use information systems. Similarly, employees tend to copy the behavior of their peers and grow confident over their actions with time. Thompson et al. (1994, p. 173) also reiterates that "individuals with little experience will have their beliefs about job fit influenced by advertising, opinions expressed by peers, and current practices in the organization". An inexperienced employee may hold unrealistic beliefs about how senior colleagues may perceive their actions or inactions which makes them susceptible to social pressure. In practice, employees accomplish task and routines based on peer practices in order to minimize the fear of non-compliance. A non-compliance behavior in the context of information security refers to some degree of belief or ideas that peers are not rule following (Hwang et al., 2017). For example, Lee & Lee (2002) found that enhanced occupational subjective norms and the willingness to comply will decrease the misuse of secutity systems.This directly implies that employee's security compliance are predetermined by peers (Padayachee, 2012).

Studies have revealed that for top management to provide significant support in the establishment of good information security climate, there is the need for them to be educated and trained on information security issues (Chan et al., 2005; Goo et al., 2014; Shih, 2015; Yazdanmehr & Wang, 2016). The education and training of top management translate into a positive influence on building the right information security climate to help guard against insider and outsider security threats that arise in the course of business operations. From the above arguments, we propose that:

H_1: *Security Education, Training and Awareness has a significant positive influence on Information Security Climate.*

H_2: *Top-Management Commitment to Information Security positively affects Information Security Climate.*

H_3: *Information Security Climate positively affects employees' intention to comply with information security policy*

H_4: *Peer Non-Compliance Behavior has a negative effect Information Security Climate.*

General Deterrence Theory

This study employs the General Deterrence Theory (GDT) in explaining the factors influencing information security policy compliance behavior. According to the GDT, people will generally weigh the pros and cons before they engage in any act of crime (Cameron, 1988; Stafford, 2015). They will only choose crime when they perceive the benefits associated with it pays. If the individuals come to the conclusion that there is a great chance of them being caught and a severe punishment meted-out accordingly, there is a higher chance that such individuals will not engage in these acts. Based on this theory, Herath & Rao (2009) posit that as the certainty and severity of punishment increases, the rate of unacceptable behavior in society or in firms will decrease. Thus, the severity and certainty of punishment will lead to a positive effect on the intent of individuals to engage in security compliance with information security policies of organizations (Siponen et al., 2014). Their study further revealed that the certainty to detect unacceptable behavior in firms has a positive impact on employees' intentions to comply with IS security policies at all times (Siponen et al., 2014).

Once the crime detection system of firms breaks down the intentions not to comply with IS security policy will increase (Milgrom & Roberts, 1982; Quackenbush, 2011; Sitren & Applegate, 2012; Stafford, 2015; Watling et al., 2010). Their study also revealed that deterrent severity had a greater impact on compliance than deterrent certainty (Stafford, 2015). Another study also revealed that sanctions which consisted severity, of social pressure from direct supervisors, colleagues and expert IS security staff, detection probability, social pressure and swiftness of legal sanctions have impact on the likelihood of compliance with IS policies (Cheng et al., 2014; D'Arcy et al., 2009; Johnson et al., 2015; Paternoster & Piquero, 1995; Williams & Hawkins, 1986; Zagare & Kilgour, 2000). These stands as countermeasures and strong disincentives that dissuade people from committing antisocial acts. In line with the arguments above, we therefore hypothesize that:

H_5: *Punishment Severity has a positive effect on employees' intention to comply with information security policy.*

H$_6$: *Deterrent Certainty has a positive effect on employees' intention to comply with information security policy.*

H$_7$: *Employees' intention to comply with the information security policy has a positive effect on employees' actual compliance behavior.*

Figure 1. Hypothesized model

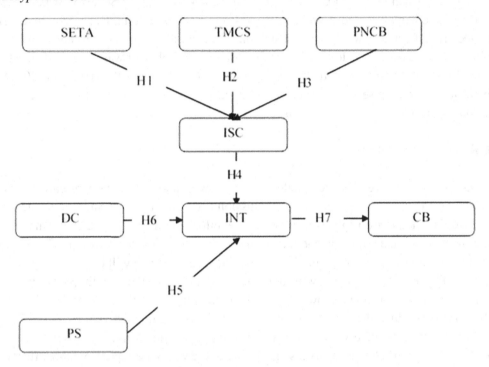

METHODOLOGY

Instrument Development

The measurement items for the latent variables in the current study were adopted from previous studies to improve content validity (Straub et al., 2004). In all, there were eight constructs, each of which were measured with multiple items. The items were, however, re-worded to reflect the context of the study environment. The resulting questionnaire was pretested with 25 experienced MIS professionals in the banking industry and senior researchers with expertise on the subject matter to review, give comments and make suggestions to improve the questions. Their comments were incorporated to make the questionnaire more comprehensible. Further, a pilot study was conducted with 85 employees to validate the instruments. Results from an exploratory factor analysis showed that the instrument had good validity.

Measurement Instrument

Security Education, Training and Awareness was measured with five items adopted from D'Arcy, Hovav, and Galletta (2009). The three items used to measure Top management commitment to security (TMCS) was adopted from D'Arcy and Greene (2014). Peer Non-Compliance Behavior was measured with three items adopted from Hwang et al. (2017) while Information Security Climate was measured with five items adopted from Chan et al. (2005) and Goo et al. (2014). Perceived Severity of punishment was measured with three items adopted from Herath and Rao (2009) and Son (2011). The three items used to measure Deterrent Certainty was adopted from Son (2011) while Compliance Intention was measured with four items derived from Ifinedo (2012). Lastly, Compliance behavior was measured with four items derived from Siponen, Mahmood, and Pahnila (2014) and Humaidi and Balakrishnan (2017). All the measurement items were presented in English and measured using a five-point Likert scale anchored between strongly disagree (1) and strongly agree (5).

Sample And Data Collection

In order to test the hypothesized research model, the researchers adopted a survey research methodology to collect data. Due to the nature of the study, permission had to be sought from top management of the banks considered in the survey. High level and mid-level information systems managers in the 5 topmost performing banks in Ghana were considered for the study. The researchers explained the importance of the research to the managers and assured them that the data collected will be treated with the utmost confidentiality. The researchers also promised to share a summary of their findings with the managers. Having convinced the managers to allow us to perform our study with their banks, we shared a link to our web-based survey which they in turn sent to their employee mailing list. A total of 1235 employees at various levels were contacted via email to fill the web-based questionnaire. After two weeks, 213 employees had responded. The managers resent the link to the web-based questionnaire after two weeks and reminded employees who had not previously completed the questionnaire to do so in the next two weeks of grace period. In the next two weeks, 116 more employees responded. Since the web-based questionnaire was configured to force respondents to answer all questions, none of the responses were discarded. A total of 329 respondents participated in the survey. Of this number, 172 were males and 157 were females.

Common Method Bias

Common method bias could pose a threat to the conclusions drawn from the hypothesized relationships since the study adopts a cross-sectional design and also because both dependent and independent variables are collected from the same respondents (Podsakoff, Mackenzie, and Podsakoff, 2003). Suggestions by Mackenzie and Podsakoff (2012) were followed to address any issues of common method bias. First of all, some items were reversed to guarantee that all responses do not correspond to a larger effect. Secondly, items were randomly arranged in the questionnaire in order to reduce floor effect that may force respondents to provide monotonous responses from participants. Finally, the Harman's one factor test was employed to check the potential existence of common method bias. The first factor accounts for only 25.23%, which shows that common method bias is not likely to pose a significant problem in this study.

RESULTS AND ANALYSIS

Data collected from the survey was analysed using the Partial Least Square approach to Structural Equation Modeling (PLS-SEM) on SmartPLS Version 3. Structural Equation Modeling (SEM) allowed the researchers to test causal relationships between latent variables in the proposed research model. There are two approaches to SEM (Hair et al., 2014); the covariance-based SEM that requires the data to exhibit multivariate normality and the variance-based approach PLS-SEM which does not require multivariate normality. A preliminary study of the data collected showed that the data was non-normal, hence our choice of PLS-SEM. In line with the two-step approach to evaluating Structural Equation Models recommended by Chin (1998) the reliability and validity of the measurement model was first tested and then the significance of structural paths between the latent constructs in the hypothesized model were also assessed.

Measurement Model Assessment

The measurement model was assessed based on reliability, convergent validity and discriminant validity. The reliability of the constructs was assessed with Cronbach's alpha and composite reliability. From Table 1 it can be seen that both Cronbach's alpha and Composite reliability values for all constructs are compellingly higher than 0.7 threshold recommended by Henseler, Hubona, and Ray (2016). Convergent validity of the measurement model was assessed using the Average Variance Extracted. Hair et al. (2014) recommend that AVE should be greater than 0.5 for convergent validity to be assured. From Table 1 it can be seen that AVE values for all constructs are greater than the 0.5 threshold, indicative of good convergent validity.

Discriminant validity is assured when the following three conditions are met: (a) the loadings of each construct is greater than the cross loadings with other constructs (Chin, 1998); (b) the square root of the AVE for each construct is greater than the correlation between that construct and any other construct (Fornell & Larcker, 1981); (c) the heterotrait-monotrait ratio of correlations (HTMT) values are less than 0.85. From Table 2 it can be seen that the loadings of each construct are greater than the cross-loadings. The results in Table 2 shows that the square root of the AVE for each construct is greater than the cross correlation with other constructs. Finally, results of the more recent $HTMT_{0.85}$ criterion presented in Table 3 also proves discriminant validity has been achieved. In all, the results showed that the psychometric properties of the measures used in the study were adequate.

Structural Model Assessment

Having verified the measurements model, the structural model was assessed to determined whether the structural relations in the model being tested are meaningful. A bootstrap resampling procedure (with an iteration of 5000 sub-samples drawn with replacements from the initial sample of 329) was used to determine the significance of the path coefficients in the structural model. The explanatory power of the structural model was assessed by its ability to predict endogenous construct using the coefficient of determination R^2. Results for the assessment of the structural model are presented in Table 4 and Figure 2.

Table 1. Factor loadings and reliability statistics

	CB	INT	DC	ISC	PNCB	PS	SETA	TMCS	α	C.R	A.V.E
CB1	**0.856**	0.584	0.390	0.368	-0.155	0.308	0.387	0.285	0.857	0.902	0.700
CB2	**0.847**	0.555	0.461	0.386	-0.220	0.347	0.346	0.254			
CB3	**0.887**	0.537	0.400	0.288	-0.180	0.317	0.238	0.244			
CB4	**0.750**	0.428	0.218	0.288	-0.162	0.274	0.250	0.252			
INT1	0.482	**0.838**	0.533	0.301	-0.197	0.519	0.275	0.224	0.887	0.922	0.747
INT2	0.538	**0.886**	0.574	0.372	-0.165	0.538	0.367	0.260			
INT3	0.550	**0.882**	0.581	0.364	-0.166	0.487	0.233	0.203			
INT4	0.616	**0.851**	0.524	0.387	-0.219	0.482	0.356	0.285			
DC1	0.437	0.594	**0.889**	0.309	-0.197	0.502	0.361	0.226	0.848	0.908	0.768
DC2	0.415	0.561	**0.901**	0.307	-0.194	0.496	0.403	0.274			
DC3	0.319	0.524	**0.837**	0.241	-0.153	0.421	0.250	0.135			
ISC1	0.371	0.349	0.313	**0.842**	-0.412	0.242	0.390	0.520	0.865	0.908	0.712
ISC2	0.336	0.390	0.291	**0.845**	-0.385	0.177	0.332	0.439			
ISC3	0.364	0.354	0.259	**0.873**	-0.372	0.162	0.420	0.461			
ISC4	0.269	0.298	0.236	**0.813**	-0.333	0.163	0.368	0.414			
PNCB1	-0.173	-0.193	-0.204	-0.466	**0.936**	-0.123	-0.229	-0.160	0.913	0.945	0.851
PNCB2	-0.203	-0.178	-0.163	-0.370	**0.918**	-0.099	-0.216	-0.090			
PNCB3	-0.223	-0.227	-0.206	-0.390	**0.914**	-0.106	-0.240	-0.076			
PS1	0.285	0.539	0.494	0.215	-0.146	**0.880**	0.245	0.129	0.847	0.907	0.765
PS2	0.320	0.471	0.419	0.118	-0.042	**0.862**	0.189	0.137			
PS3	0.376	0.522	0.501	0.243	-0.117	**0.881**	0.321	0.168			
SETA1	0.293	0.252	0.306	0.394	-0.262	0.177	**0.801**	0.291	0.846	0.889	0.617
SETA2	0.319	0.274	0.308	0.358	-0.174	0.233	**0.760**	0.269			
SETA3	0.317	0.322	0.326	0.358	-0.189	0.268	**0.813**	0.342			
SETA4	0.308	0.298	0.289	0.254	-0.090	0.278	**0.774**	0.230			
SETA5	0.222	0.267	0.293	0.363	-0.221	0.205	**0.777**	0.201			
TMCS1	0.260	0.220	0.154	0.381	-0.036	0.119	0.244	**0.809**	0.821	0.893	0.735
TMCS2	0.238	0.220	0.194	0.476	-0.080	0.174	0.287	**0.874**			
TMCS3	0.295	0.281	0.264	0.529	-0.176	0.131	0.338	**0.888**			

Note: CB – Cmpliance Behavior, INT – Compliance Intention, DC – Deterent Certainty, ISC – Information Security Climate, PNCB – Peer Non-Compliance Behavior, PS – Punishment Severity, SETA – Security Education, Training and Awareness, TMSC – Top Management Commitment for Information Security, α – Cronbach's alpha, C.R – Composite Reliability, AVE – Average Variance Extracted

In support of hypotheses H1, Security Education, Training and Awareness (SETA) was found to have a significant positive effect on Information Security Climate ($\beta = 0.216$, $p = 0.000$). Top Management Commitment to Information Security (TMCS) was found to have the most significant effect on Information Security Climate ($\beta = 0.430$, $p = 0.000$). Peer Non-Compliance Behavior (PNCB) was also found to have a significant negative effect on Information Security Climate ($\beta = -0.341$, $p = 0.000$), providing support for H3. This result implies that as Peer Non-Compliance behavior increase it is expected that a non-favorable information security climate would be formed. As expected, Information Security Climate was found to have a significant positive impact on employee' Intention to comply with information security policy ($\beta = 0.212$, $p = 0.000$). Deterrent Certainty was found to have the most significant effect on employees Intention to comply with Information Security Policy ($\beta = 0.395$, $p = 0.000$). Punishment Severity was also found to have a significant effect on employees Intention to comply with information security policy ($\beta = 0.324$, $p = 0.000$), providing support for H6. As expected employees' Intention to comply with information security policy was found to have a significant positive effect on Actual Compliance Behavior ($\beta = 0.634$, $p = 0.000$). In all 40.2% of the variance in Compliance behavior was explained by the model. The overall fitness of the model was assessed using the SRMR composite factor model. The composite model SRMR value for the model was 0.055, below the 0.08 threshold recommended by Hu and Bentler (1999). This is an indication that the proposed model presents a good model fit.

Table 2. Testing discriminant validity using Fornell-Larcker criterion

	CB	INT	DC	ISC	PNCB	PS	SETA	TMCS
CB	**0.837**							
INT	0.634	**0.864**						
DC	0.448	0.640	**0.876**					
ISC	0.400	0.413	0.327	**0.844**				
PNCB	-0.214	-0.216	-0.208	-0.447	**0.923**			
PS	0.373	0.585	0.541	0.222	-0.119	**0.875**		
SETA	0.370	0.357	0.388	0.448	-0.247	0.290	**0.785**	
TMCS	0.309	0.282	0.243	0.546	-0.121	0.166	0.342	**0.857**
Note: Square root of the AVEs are shown in bold on the diagonal								

Table 3. Testing discriminant validity using the HTMT ratio

	CB	INT	DC	ISC	PNCB	PS	SETA	TMCS
CB								
INT	0.720							
DC	0.512	0.736						
ISC	0.459	0.469	0.378					
PNCB	0.245	0.240	0.234	0.496				
PS	0.438	0.674	0.634	0.254	0.131			
SETA	0.431	0.413	0.454	0.513	0.271	0.346		
TMCS	0.368	0.327	0.282	0.636	0.127	0.198	0.401	

Table 4. Hypotheses testing

Hypotheses	Path	Path Coefficient	T Statistics	P Values	Result	
H1	SETA →ISC	0.216	4.189	0.000	Supported	
H2	TMCS →ISC	0.430	8.332	0.000	Supported	
H3	PNCB→ ISC	-0.341	7.687	0.000	Supported	
H4	ISC →INT	0.212	4.565	0.000	Supported	
H5	PS → INT	0.324	4.950	0.000	Supported	
H6	DC →INT	0.395	5.545	0.000	Supported	
H7	INT → CB	0.634	12.617	0.000	Supported	
Model Fit						
SRMR	0.055					

Figure 2. Estimated structural model

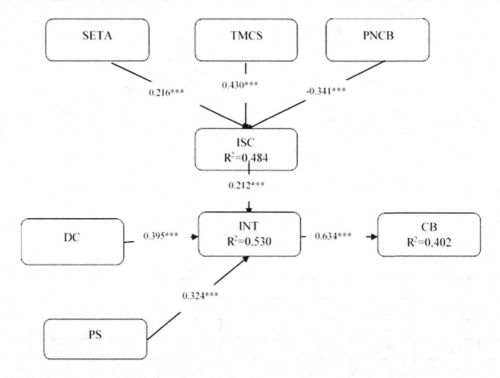

SOLUTIONS AND RECOMMENDATIONS

Following the model of this study based on integrated Information Security Climate and the General Deterrence Theory, seven hypotheses were stated to be tested. Findings from the analysis using the Partial Least Square approach to Structural Equation Modeling (PLS-SEM) suggest that all the relationships stated are all supported empirically. This suggests that all the constructs of information security climate and general deterrence theory are significant in explaining information security compliance behavior of employees in Ghana. By implication, security climate and deterrence influence information security policy compliance behavior.

Findings from our analysis confirmed the positive influence of security education, training and awareness on information security climate as did the hypothesis that stated that security education, training and awareness have a significant positive influence on information security climate. This suggests that security education, training and awareness inherent in an organization would improve the security climate of the organization. Also, the management of information systems must invest in education, training and awareness programmes for employees over time. The practice will become institutionalized over time as everyone in the organization will become conscious of information security and as a result most employees will be willing to follow the rules guiding the use of the information system. This finding is evident in studies such as (D'Arcy et al. 2009; Thomson & van Niekerk, 2012; Hwang et al. 2017; D'Arcy & Greene, 2014), who submitted that efforts by organizations that improve the awareness, training and education of employees have significant influence on information security climate.

In the same vein, the statement that top-management commitment for information security positively affects information security climate is upheld. The implication of this is that favorable behavior of top managers toward information security policy (in terms of compliance, supervision, education, training, procedures, regulations and awareness, behavior, and investment in security system) improves employees' perception of information security climate towards compliance behavior. In other words, when employees observe commitment to information security by top managers, their perception of information security climate improve and are motivated to comply with information security policies. Findings from Chan et al (2005); Hu et al. (2012), D'Arcy & Greene (2014) support this finding as they share the opinion that top-managers behavior toward information security policy influence information security climate.

Similarly, the third hypothesis of this study stating that peer non-compliance behavior has a negative effect on information security climate was supported statistically (t=7.69, $p<0.05$) with a path coefficient of -0.341. This suggests that observed non-compliance behavior of fellow workers in an organization will negatively impact the perception of the information security climate which might influence other employees in the organization to behave in an illicit manner. This finding is as well supported by existing literature (see Chan et al. 2005; Goo et al. 2013; Cheng et al. 2013; Hwang et al. 2017)

Security education, training and awareness, top-management commitment and peer behavior was found to impact information security climate significantly. It is further revealed that information security climate significantly affect intentions to comply with information security policy (t=4.57, $p<0.05$) as presented in the fourth hypothesis of this study with a path coefficient of 0.212. The result suggests that favorable perception of the information security climate of an organization positively influence employees' intention to comply with information security policy. The implication here is that, when an employee develops a security climate with compliance behavior, the intention to follow information security guidelines is motivated within him/her. This finding also follows from existing literature such as Goo et al. (2014), Chan et al. (2005) and D'Arcy and Greene (2014) who report findings that suggest the positive influence of information security climate on the compliance behavior of employees towards information security policies.

In terms of deterrence, the hypothesis that "punishment severity has a positive effect employees' intention to comply with information security policy" is statistically supported. This finding suggests that the perception of severity of punishment positively influences information security system compliance intention which implies that as the perception of severity and cruelty of punishment for committing illicit act with the information system increases there is increased intention to follow security rules of the organization. Likewise, this finding is consistent with the those of Hareth & Rao (2009), Cheng et al. (2013), D'Arcy et al. (2009), Ifinedo (2012, 2016) and Siponen et al (2014).

Moreover, findings on the deterrent certainty confirm the argument that certainty of sanction will motivate employees' compliance intention. Finding from the analysis support our argument as stated in the fifth hypothesis. This finding as against the submissions of most studies in the literature (for example see Cheng et al. (2013), Hareth & Rao (2009), Klien & Luciano (2016) and Ifinedo (2016)) suggest insignificance of certainty of punishment to compliance behavior shows that deterrence certainty is even important that severity of deterrence as the observed coefficient is greater than that of severity. By implication, when the perception of certainty of being caught or detected is high, employees are demotivated to violate security system instructions and thereby motivate the intentions to comply with security policy. This is also corroborated by D'Arcy et al. (2009) who found positive effect of certainty of sanction on compliance behavior towards information security policy.

All the factors of interest of this study that influence compliance intention have been upheld by the analysis. The result from the analysis further supports the positive influence of intentions to comply with information security policy on actual information security policy compliance behavior. It suggests that information security policy compliance intention strongly and positively affects actual information security compliance behavior. This finding is also evident in the works of Sponen et al. (2014), Siponen et al (2010) and Sommestad et al. (2015).

FUTURE RESEARCH DIRECTIONS

As evidenced by most research, our own research has some limitations. First of all, the study was based on data collected from employees of only the five top-performing banks in Ghana. Care should be taken when generalizing the findings to the whole banking sector of the financial services sector in Ghana or elsewhere. In the future, researchers could replicate the study to cover other sectors of the economy or other financial institutions outside the banking sector. Even though a number of precautionary measures, such as safeguarding the anonymity of the participants and use of hypothetical scenarios of the company were taken to prevent the possibility of evaluation apprehension bias, some participants in our survey may still have provided responses that are socially desirable instead of how they actually feel. The study was also based on the general deterrence theory, which deals more with coercive controls. In future studies, it would be interesting to explore remunerative factors too.

CONCLUSION

Though recent studies are emphasizing the adoption factors that are intrinsic to employees in order to encourage compliance behavior, this study presents some fundamental findings that may benefit information system managers. Organizations are established to achieve preconceived goals and as such are unwilling to allow some callous behavior from deviant employees to truncate the successful achievement of these set goals. Findings from this study revealed that contextual variables are important to motivating compliance with information security policy. Therefore, information system managers are adviced to ensure that top managers lead by example in following information security policy. Top managers also ought to put in place measures that will encourage compliance behavior in their organizations – in this context, banks. More so, continual awareness and training should be initiated to better acquaint employees of the dangers of non-compliance and the existence of punishment for violation of laid down security policies.

In addition, the study presented findings concerning deterrence. Severity and certainty of sactions are revealed to significantly influence compliance behavior. Additionaly, this study places more importance on certainty than severity of sanctions. Therefore, information system managers are advised to implement a deterrent framework that will be swift and certain to detect non-compliance with information security policy. More so, the punishment to such act should be severe enough to serve as example and deterrent for other employees.

Some studies have downplayed the importance of General Deterrence theory based on the some intrinsic arguments. However, this study has come to uphold the importance of the deterrence construct on information security compliance. Moreover, contrary to studies that have upheld only the severity of punishment and suggested that certainty of punishment is not important, this study has posited that certainty of deterrence is more important. This finding cannot be adjudged to be erroneous. Logically, a very severe punishment can only be implemented when the certainty of deterrent is high. It becomes useless when the certainty of the punishment or deterrent is low. This study further justifies the use of environmental or contextual factors as important factors in explaining information security policy compliance behavior as all the considered constructs are revealed to be influential on compliance. Therefore, this study provides an empirical validation of the General Deterrence theory and the Security Climate framework of information security compliance behavior.

REFERENCES

Alhogail, A. (2015). Design and validation of information security culture framework. *Computers in Human Behavior*, *49*(1), 567–575. doi:10.1016/j.chb.2015.03.054

Alnatheer, M. A. (2015). Information Security Culture Critical Success Factors. 12th International Conference on Information Technology - New Generations, 37–86. 10.1109/ITNG.2015.124

Alshare, K. A., Lane, P. L., & Lane, M. R. (2018). Information security policy compliance: A higher education case study. *Information and Computer Security*, *26*(1), 91–108. doi:10.1108/ICS-09-2016-0073

Aurigemma, S., & Mattson, T. (2017). Deterrence and punishment experience impacts on ISP compliance attitudes. *Information and Computer Security*, *25*(4), 421–436. doi:10.1108/ICS-11-2016-0089

Aurigemma, S., & Panko, R. (2011). A composite framework for behavioral compliance with information security policies. *Proceedings of the Annual Hawaii International Conference on System Sciences*, 3248–3257. 10.1109/HICSS.2012.49

Balozian, P., & Leidner, D. (2017). Review of IS Security Policy Compliance. *ACM SIGMIS Database: The DATABASE for Advances in Information Systems*, *48*(3), 11–43. doi:10.1145/3130515.3130518

Bansal, G., Green, W., Hodorff, K., & Marshall, K. (2016). *Moral Beliefs and Organizational Information Security Policy Compliance : The Role of Gender*. Academic Press.

Cameron, S. (1988). The Economics of Crime Deterrence: A Survey of Theory and Evidence. *Kyklos*, *41*(2), 301–323. doi:10.1111/j.1467-6435.1988.tb02311.x

Chan, M., Woon, I., & Kankanhalli, A. (2005). Perceptions of information security at the workplace : Linking information security climate to compliant behavior. *Journal of Information Privacy and Security*, *1*(3), 18–41. doi:10.1080/15536548.2005.10855772

Chen, X., Wu, D., Chen, L., & Teng, J. K. L. (2018). Sanction severity and employees' information security policy compliance: Investigating mediating, moderating, and control variables. *Information & Management*, *55*(8), 1049–1060. doi:10.1016/j.im.2018.05.011

Cheng, L., Li, W., Zhai, Q., & Smyth, R. (2014). Understanding personal use of the Internet at work: An integrated model of neutralization techniques and general deterrence theory. *Computers in Human Behavior*, *38*, 220–228. doi:10.1016/j.chb.2014.05.043

Cheng, L., Li, Y., Li, W., Holm, E., & Zhai, Q. (2013). Understanding the violation of IS security policy in organizations: An integrated model based on social control and deterrence theory. *Computers & Security*, *39*, 447–459. doi:10.1016/j.cose.2013.09.009

Chin, W. W. (1998). The partial least squares approach to structural equation modeling. In G. A. Marcoulides (Ed.), *Modern Methods for Business Research* (Vol. 295, pp. 295–336). Lawrence Erlbaum Associates, Publisher; doi:10.1016/j.aap.2008.12.010

Cram, W. A., Proudfoot, J. G., & D'Arcy, J. (2017). Organizational information security policies: A review and research framework. *European Journal of Information Systems*, *26*(6), 605–641. doi:10.105741303-017-0059-9

D'Arcy, J., & Greene, G. (2014). Security culture and the employment relationship as drivers of employees' security compliance. *Information Management & Computer Security*, *22*(5), 474–489. doi:10.1108/IMCS-08-2013-0057

D'Arcy, J., & Herath, T. (2011). A review and analysis of deterrence theory in the IS security literature: Making sense of the disparate findings. *European Journal of Information Systems*, *20*(6), 643–658. doi:10.1057/ejis.2011.23

D'Arcy, J., Hovav, A., & Galletta, D. (2009). User awareness of security countermeasures and its impact on information systems misuse: A deterrence approach. *Information Systems Research*, *20*(1), 79–98. doi:10.1287/isre.1070.0160

Da Veiga, A. (2007). An information security governance framework. *Information Systems Management*, *24*(4), 361–372. doi:10.1080/10580530701586136

Da Veiga, A. (2016). Comparing the information security culture of employees who had read the information security policy and those who had not Illustrated through an empirical study. *Information and Computer Security*, *24*(2), 139–151. doi:10.1108/ICS-12-2015-0048

Da Veiga, A., & Eloff, J. H. P. (2010). A framework and assessment instrument for information security culture. *Computers & Security*, *29*(2), 196–207. doi:10.1016/j.cose.2009.09.002

Da Veiga, A., & Martins, N. (2015). Information security culture and information protection culture: A validated assessment instrument. *Computer Law & Security Review, 31*(2), 243–256. doi:10.1016/j.clsr.2015.01.005

Dhillon, G., Syed, R., & Pedron, C. (2016). Interpreting information security culture: An organizational transformation case study. *Computers & Security, 56*, 63–69. doi:10.1016/j.cose.2015.10.001

Diver, S. (2007). Information security policy –adevelopment guide for large and small companies, Sans Institute.

Doherty, N., Anastasakis, L., & Fulford, H. (2009). Institutional repository the information security policy unpacked : A critical study of the content of university policies. *International Journal of Information Management, 29*(6), 449–457. doi:10.1016/j.ijinfomgt.2009.05.003

Donalds, C., & Osei-Bryson, K. M. (2020). Cybersecurity compliance behavior: Exploring the influences of individual decision style and other antecedents. *International Journal of Information Management, 51*, 102056. doi:10.1016/j.ijinfomgt.2019.102056

Fornell, C., & Larcker, D. F. (1981). Evaluating structural equation models with unobservable variables and measurements error. *JMR, Journal of Marketing Research, 18*(1), 39–50. doi:10.1177/002224378101800104

Gartner. (2018, August). Gartner forecasts worldwide information security spending to exceed $124 billion in 2019. *Gartner Newsroom.*

Goo, J., Yim, M. S., & Kim, D. J. (2014). A path to successful management of employee security compliance: An empirical study of information security climate. *IEEE Transactions on Professional Communication, 57*(4), 286–308. doi:10.1109/TPC.2014.2374011

Hair, J. F., Hult, T. M., Ringle, C., & Sarstedt, M. (2014). *A Primer on Partial Least Squares Structural Equation Modeling (PLS-SEM)*. Sage Publications. doi:10.1016/j.lrp.2013.01.002

Hardy, G. (2006). Using IT governance and COBIT to deliver value with IT and respond to legal, regulatory and compliance challenges. *Information Security Technical Report, 11*(1), 55–61. doi:10.1016/j.istr.2005.12.004

Henseler, J., Hubona, G., & Ray, P. A. (2016). Using PLS path modeling in new technology research : Updated guidelines. *Industrial Management & Data Systems, 116*(1), 2–20. doi:10.1108/IMDS-09-2015-0382

Herath, T., & Rao, R. H. (2009). Protection motivation and deterrence: A framework for security policy compliance in organisations. *European Journal of Information Systems, 18*(2), 106–125. doi:10.1057/ejis.2009.6

Herath, T., Yim, M. S., D'Arcy, J., Nam, K., & Rao, H. R. (2018). Examining employee security violations: Moral disengagement and its environmental influences. *Information Technology & People, 31*(6), 1135–1162. doi:10.1108/ITP-10-2017-0322

Hina, S., & Dominic, P. D. D. (2018). Information security policies ' compliance : A perspective for higher education institutions. *Journal of Computer Information Systems*, 1–11. doi:10.1080/08874417.2018.1432996

Hu, L., & Bentler, P. M. (1999). Cutoff criteria for fit indexes in covariance structure analysis: Conventional criteria versus new alternatives. *Structural Equation Modeling*, *6*(1), 1–55. doi:10.1080/10705519909540118

Hu, Q., Dinev, T., Hart, P., & Cooke, D. (2012). Managing Employee Compliance with Information Security Policies: The Critical Role of Top Management and Organizational Culture. *Decision Sciences*, *43*(4), 615–660. doi:10.1111/j.1540-5915.2012.00361.x

Humaidi, N., & Balakrishnan, V. (2017). Indirect effect of management support on users' compliance behaviour towards information security policies. *The HIM Journal*, *47*(1), 17–27. doi:10.1177/1833358317700255 PMID:28537207

Hwang, I., Kim, D., Kim, T., & Kim, S. (2017). Why not comply with information security? An empirical approach for the causes of non-compliance. *Online Information Review*, *41*(1), 2–18. doi:10.1108/OIR-11-2015-0358

Ifinedo, P. (2012). Understanding information systems security policy compliance: An integration of the theory of planned behavior and the protection motivation theory. *Computers & Security*, *31*(1), 83–95. doi:10.1016/j.cose.2011.10.007

Johnson, J. C., Leeds, B. A., & Wu, A. (2015). Capability, Credibility, and Extended General Deterrence. *International Interactions*, *41*(2), 309–336. doi:10.1080/03050629.2015.982115

Karlsson, M., Denk, T., & Åström, J. (2018). Perceptions of organizational culture and value conflicts in information security management. *Information and Computer Security*, *26*(2), 213–229. doi:10.1108/ICS-08-2017-0058

Kim, S. S., & Kim, Y. J. (2017). The effect of compliance knowledge and compliance support systems on information security compliance behavior. *Journal of Knowledge Management*, *21*(4), 986–1010. doi:10.1108/JKM-08-2016-0353

Kolkowska, E., Karlsson, F., & Hedström, K. (2017). Journal of Strategic Information Systems Towards analysing the rationale of information security non-compliance : Devising a Value-Based Compliance analysis method. *The Journal of Strategic Information Systems*, *26*(1), 39–57. doi:10.1016/j.jsis.2016.08.005

Lacey, D. (2010). Understanding and transforming organizational security culture. *Information Management & Computer Security*, *18*(1), 4–13. doi:10.1108/09685221011035223

Lee, C., Lee, C. C., & Kim, S. (2016). Understanding information security stress: Focusing on the type of information security compliance activity. *Computers & Security*, *59*, 60–70. doi:10.1016/j.cose.2016.02.004

Lee, J., & Lee, Y. (2002). A holistic model of computer abuse within organizations. *Information Management & Computer Security*, *10*(2), 57–63. doi:10.1108/09685220210424104

Lee, S. M., Lee, S. G., & Yoo, S. (2004). An integrative model of computer abuse based on social control and general deterrence theories. *Information & Management*, *41*(6), 707–718. doi:10.1016/j.im.2003.08.008

Mackenzie, S. B., & Podsakoff, P. M. (2012). Common method bias in marketing : Causes, mechanisms, and procedural Remedies. *Journal of Retailing*, *88*(4), 542–555. doi:10.1016/j.jretai.2012.08.001

Milgrom, P., & Roberts, J. (1982). Predation, reputation, and entry deterrence. *Journal of Economic Theory*, *27*(2), 280–312. doi:10.1016/0022-0531(82)90031-X

Moulton, R., & Coles, R. S. (2003). Applying information security governance. *Computers & Security*, *22*(7), 580–584. doi:10.1016/S0167-4048(03)00705-3

Nasir, A., Arshah, R. A., & Hamid, M. R. A. (2018). The Significance of Main Constructs of Theory of Planned Behavior in Recent Information Security Policy Compliance Behavior Study : A Comparison among Top Three Behavioral Theories. *IACSIT International Journal of Engineering and Technology*, *7*(29), 737–741. doi:10.14419/ijet.v7i2.29.14008

Padayachee, K. (2012). Taxonomy of compliant information security behavior. *Computers & Security*, *31*(5), 673–680. doi:10.1016/j.cose.2012.04.004

Parsons, K., Mccormac, A., Butavicius, M., & Ferguson, L. (2010). *Human factors and information security : Individual, culture and security environment*. Science And Technology. doi:10.14722/ndss.2014.23268

Paternoster, R., & Piquero, A. (1995). Reconceptualizing deterrence: An empirical test of personal and vicarious experiences. *Journal of Research in Crime and Delinquency*, *32*(3), 251–286. doi:10.1177/0022427895032003001

Podsakoff, P. M., Mackenzie, S. B., & Podsakoff, N. P. (2003). Common method biases in behavioral research: A critical review of the literature. *The Journal of Applied Psychology*, *88*(5), 879–903. doi:10.1037/0021-9010.88.5.879 PMID:14516251

Quackenbush, S. L. (2011). Deterrence theory: Where do we stand? *Review of International Studies*, *37*(2), 741–762. doi:10.1017/S0260210510000896

Rajab, M., & Eydgahi, A. (2019). Evaluating the explanatory power of theoretical frameworks on intention to comply with information security policies in higher education. *Computers & Security*, *80*, 211–223. doi:10.1016/j.cose.2018.09.016

Rocha Flores, W., Antonsen, E., & Ekstedt, M. (2014). Information security knowledge sharing in organizations: Investigating the effect of behavioral information security governance and national culture. *Computers & Security*, *43*(1), 90–110. doi:10.1016/j.cose.2014.03.004

Safa, N. S., Maple, C., Furnell, S., Azad, M. A., Perera, C., Dabbagh, M., & Sookhak, M. (2019). Deterrence and prevention-based model to mitigate information security insider threats in organisations. *Future Generation Computer Systems*, *97*, 587–597. doi:10.1016/j.future.2019.03.024

Shih, S. P., & Liou, J. Y. (2015). Investigate the Effects of Information Security Climate and Psychological Ownership on Information Security Policy Compliance. In PACIS (p. 28).

Siponen, M., Adam Mahmood, M., & Pahnila, S. (2014). Employees' adherence to information security policies: An exploratory field study. *Information & Management*, *51*(2), 217–224. doi:10.1016/j.im.2013.08.006

Sitren, A. H., & Applegate, B. K. (2012). Testing Deterrence Theory with Offenders: The Empirical Validity of Stafford and Warr's Model. *Deviant Behavior*, *33*(6), 492–506. doi:10.1080/01639625.2011.636685

Sohrabi Safa, N., Von Solms, R., & Furnell, S. (2016). Information security policy compliance model in organizations. *Computers & Security, 56,* 1–13. doi:10.1016/j.cose.2015.10.006

Sommestad, T., Hallberg, J., Lundholm, K., & Bengtsson, J. (2014). Variables influencing information security policy compliance. *Information Management & Computer Security, 22*(1), 42–75. doi:10.1108/IMCS-08-2012-0045

Son, J. Y. (2011). Out of fear or desire? Toward a better understanding of employees' motivation to follow IS security policies. *Information & Management, 48*(7), 296–302. doi:10.1016/j.im.2011.07.002

Stafford, M. C. (2015). Deterrence Theory: Crime. In International Encyclopedia of the Social & Behavioral Sciences: Second Edition (pp. 18–168). doi:10.1016/B978-0-08-097086-8.45005-1

Straub, D., Boudreau, M.-C., & Gefen, D. (2004). Validation guidelines for IS positivistic research. *Communications of the Association for Information Systems, 13*(1), 380–427.

Thompson, R. L., Higgins, C. A., & Howell, J. M. (1994). Influence of experience on personal computer utilization: Testing a conceptual model. *Journal of Management Information Systems, 11*(1), 167–187. doi:10.1080/07421222.1994.11518035

Thomson, K. L., & Von Solms, R. (2005). Information security obedience: A definition. *Computers & Security, 24*(1), 69–75. doi:10.1016/j.cose.2004.10.005

Van Niekerk, J. F., & Von Solms, R. (2010). Information security culture: A management perspective. *Computers & Security, 29*(4), 476–486. doi:10.1016/j.cose.2009.10.005

Venkatesh, V., Morris, M. G., Davis, G. B., & Davis, F. D. (2003). User acceptance of information technology: Toward a unified view. *Management Information Systems Quarterly, 27*(3), 425–478. doi:10.2307/30036540

Von Solms, S. H. (2005). Information Security Governance - Compliance management vs operational management. *Computers & Security, 24*(6), 443–447. doi:10.1016/j.cose.2005.07.003

Vroom, C., & von Solms, R. (2004). Towards information security behavioural compliance. *Computers & Security, 23*(3), 191–198. doi:10.1016/j.cose.2004.01.012

Wall, J. D., Palvia, P., & Lowry, P. B. (2013). Control-Related Motivations and Information Security Policy Compliance: The Role of Autonomy and Efficacy. *Journal of Information Privacy and Security, 9*(4), 52–79. doi:10.1080/15536548.2013.10845690

Watling, C. N., Palk, G. R., Freeman, J. E., & Davey, J. D. (2010). Applying Stafford and Warr's reconceptualization of deterrence theory to drug driving: Can it predict those likely to offend? *Accident; Analysis and Prevention, 42*(2), 452–458. https://www.ncbi.nlm.nih.gov/entrez/query.fcgi?cmd=Retrieve&db=PubMed&list_uids=20159066&dopt=Abstract doi:10.1016/j.aap.2009.09.007 PMID:20159066

Williams, K. R., & Hawkins, R. (1986). Perceptual research on general deterrence: A critical review. *Law & Society Review, 20*(4), 545–572. doi:10.2307/3053466

Yazdanmehr, A., & Wang, J. (2016). Employees' information security policy compliance: A norm activation perspective. *Decision Support Systems, 92,* 36–46. doi:10.1016/j.dss.2016.09.009

Zagare, F. C., & Kilgour, D. M. (2000). Perfect deterrence. *Cambridge Studies in International Relations*, *24*(1), 15–25.

KEY TERMS AND DEFINITIONS

Compliant Information Security Behavior: Refers to the set of core information security activities that need to be carried out by individuals to maintain information security as defined by information security policies.

Deterrence: Is defined as the preventative effect that actual or threatened punishment has on potential offenders.

General Deterrence Theory (GDT): Originates from criminology. It proposes that severe, swift, and certain sanctions result in deterring individuals from engaging in particular behaviours.

Information Security Climate: Is defined as the employee's perception of the current organizational state in terms of information security as evidenced through dealings with internal and external stakeholders.

Information Security Culture: Is defined as a natural aspect in the daily activities of every employee.

Information Security Education: Refers to a program or efforts to make employees aware of the environment, policy and manual of an organization's security.

Perceived Severity of Punishment: Is defined as actor's subjective judgment of how costly to himself the penalty he expects would be.

Chapter 11
Biometric Authentication Schemes and Methods on Mobile Devices:
A Systematic Review

Akon Obu Ekpezu

iD https://orcid.org/0000-0002-9502-1052

Cross River University of Technology, Cross River, Nigeria

Enoima Essien Umoh

Cross River University of Technology, Nigeria

Felix Nti Koranteng

University of Education, Winneba, Kumasi Campus, Ghana

Joseph Ahor Abandoh-Sam

iD https://orcid.org/0000-0002-8815-0913

Valley View University, Ghana

ABSTRACT

Due to the sensitivity and amount of information stored on mobile devices, the need to protect these devices from unauthorized access has become imperative. Among the various mechanisms to manage access on mobile devices, this chapter focused on identifying research trends on biometric authentication schemes. The systematic literature review approach was adopted to guide future researches in the subject area. Consequently, seventeen selected articles from journals in three databases (IEEE, ACM digital library, and SpringerLink) were reviewed. Findings from the reviewed articles indicated that touch gestures are the predominant authentication technique used in mobile devices, particularly in android devices. Furthermore, mimic attacks were identified as the commonest attacks on biometric authentic schemes. While, robust authentication techniques such as dental occlusion, ECG (electrocardiogram), palmprints and knuckles were identified as newly implemented authentication techniques in mobile devices.

DOI: 10.4018/978-1-7998-3149-5.ch011

INTRODUCTION

In recent times mobile devices have gained popularity and have become an integral part of our daily lives. This popularity and rise is a result of the mobility and portability of computing devices in addition to its ability to store personal information that allows users to perform relevant tasks as and when required (Lee et al., 2016). However, the sensitivity and amount of information stored on mobile devices make it susceptible to vulnerabilities. Notably, there is a higher risk of breach in privacy due to ease of losing the device (Abdulaziz and Jugal, 2016). This has called for an increased need for improved authentication mechanisms in mobile devices. Mobile user authentication is the process of verifying and ensuring that only authentic and authorized users are granted access to the mobile device. It is achieved through assessing something the user knows (knowledge factor), something the user has (possession factor) and something the user is (biometric factor). Although the first two approaches contribute a great deal, they are faced with drawbacks that make them vulnerable to both internal and external attacks. Hence, it is an inefficient method for authentication (Shankar et al., 2016). The third has gained popularity as an authentic alternative to the first two categories (Tao and Veldhuis, 2010).

Biometrics authentication (i.e. "something the user is") is a unique, non-duplicable, non-transferable and automated recognition of individuals based on their physiological or behavioural characteristics (Saevanee et al., 2012). The use of biometrics as a means of authentication is convenient as users carry their biometrics identity always. Also, biometrics are reliable since they ensure the physical presence of users (Tao and Veldhuis, 2010). Furthermore, in mobile devices, it has an added advantage because no external hardware device or sensors are required for authentication. Modern mobile devices are developed and equipped with inbuilt sensors which can be used to achieve this task. Data extracted with these sensors are used for implicit user authentication as well as protection against unauthorized access to sensitive information (Crawford and Renaud, 2014). Despite the current increase in mobile biometric authentication research, literature on its progress, patterns and trends of implementation is lacking.

Accordingly, this chapter presents a systematic review of biometric authentication techniques used in mobile devices. It seeks to provide researchers and practitioners summaries of related issues on biometric authentications on mobile devices. The paper is presented as follows: firstly, literature on existing related systematic review studies is presented, this is followed by the motivation for the study, a list of review questions and the methodology used for conducting the review. The findings and results from the selected articles are summarized before discussions and conclusions are drawn.

RELATED STUDIES

To justify the need for this review, a search for existing systematic reviews on the subject area was conducted. The aim of this was to establish the current status of research summaries done in the subject area.

Guliani et al., (2018), Jagadeesh and Patil (2017) as well as Patil and Gudasalamani (2016) surveyed iris recognition system. In their review, they provided various methods and algorithms used by different researchers and their effect on the performance of iris recognition systems. They explained the evolution of various parameters to enhance the recognition ability of a biometric method and identified the drawbacks and future works. As a tool for electronic transaction authentication and electronic assessment Ojo et al., (2016) and Shunmugam & Selvakumar (2015) discussed uni-modal biometrics and its limitations, they pointed out the need for Multimodal biometrics and also identified Multimodal methods adopted in recent works.

On keystroke dynamics as a behavioral biometric technique, (Ali et al., 2015; Bhatt & Santhanam, 2013; Pahuja & Nagabhushan, 2015; Pisani & Lorena, 2013) presented a detailed survey on the most recent research in the area of authentication, they evaluated the research by the conditions under which data was collected, classification algorithms used and the performance of the system. They also identified some drawbacks in the current system and made some recommendations for future research. A comprehensive survey on the deployment of Electrocardiogram (ECG) as a behavioral biometric authentication system was done by Ojo et al., (2016) and Tantawi et al., (2012). They gave an overview of the ECG stating some of the features extracted for authentication purposes. Some caveats of the ECG based approach were discussed and recommendations for future works were made.

Agarwal et al., (2014) provided a detailed description of vein recognition technology, the arrangements, infrared imaging and pattern extraction strategies. They also presented pointers to vein biometrics as a new research area in biometric authentication.

Some researchers (Dharavath, Talukdar, & Laskar, 2013; Kataria, Adhyaru, Sharma, & Zaveri, 2013; Meng, Wong, Furnell, & Zhou, 2015; Roger, Begonya, & Roman, 2017; Sudhamani, Venkatesha, & Radhika, 2012) have summarized the various authentication techniques into three categories namely; currently in use, still in limited use, and underdevelopment or still in the research realm concerning modalities, fusion functions and challenges. Key challenges such as creation of Multimodal databases, lack of reusable biometrics module and the unified framework and improvement of usability and authentication systems were identified by these researchers. They also identified the strengths and limitations of the various techniques and highlighted various future works.

Alzubaidi & Kalita, (2016) narrowed their scope of Multimodal biometrics to behavioral biometrics authentication on smartphones. The concept of continuous authentication, current approaches and mechanisms of behavioral biometrics concerning methodologies, associated datasets and evaluation techniques were discussed.

In summary, it was observed that only two studies (Pisani & Lorena, 2013 and Alzubaidi & Kalita, 2016) discussed the methods adopted for their systematic review, the processes involved and the results obtained. Meng et al., (2015) and Alzubaidi & Kalita, (2016) specified mobile devices as the application domain for biometrics authentication, while the other two (Ojo et al., 2016; Shunmugam and Selvakumar, 2015) discussed authentication schemes in electronic transactions.

Considering that summaries concerning biometric authentication have focused on specific authentication techniques and approaches, with little emphasis on mobile devices, some questions on biometric authentications on mobile device research remains unanswered. Hence, the need for a systematic review with specific focus on biometric authentication in mobile devices.

Review Questions

This study seeks to answer pertinent questions (see table 1) that will facilitate research in biometric authentication with emphasis on mobile devices. Presently, due to rapid advancement in artificial intelligence, computational power and speed, newer verification and authentication methods are introduced. Yet, information regarding the efficacy and efficiency of these emerging methods are limited. Mostly, researchers who introduce such methods fail to provide reasonable comparison with existing systems. Predominantly, they compare their systems with other systems they consider to be effective. However, due to the lack of comprehensive summaries in biometric authentication on mobile devices, their selection of existing effective methods is arbitrary, ill-defined and thus not based on empirical evidence. Again, questions regarding attacks that existing authentication schemes seek to address, the types of dataset used for evaluation, evaluation methods and performance continues to be unanswered. Table 1 is a list of review question for the study and their respective motivations.

Table 1. Review Questions and Corresponding Motivation

	Question	Motivation
RQ1	What are the existing biometric authentication techniques for mobile devices?	This review question seeks to identify dominant user authentication techniques used in mobile devices. This questions also seeks to identify newer methods of authentications and patterns of adoption over the years.
RQ2	What attacks are the different techniques resilient to?	This review question seeks to identify security attacks that have been circumvented by these biometric techniques.
RQ3	What mobile sensors were used?	This is to identify sensors in mobile devices that are dominantly used for biometric authentications.
RQ4	What features were extracted for authentication?	This review question is to identify the various features that are extracted from users for biometric authentication purposes on mobile devices.
RQ5	What classification algorithms were used (classifiers)?	This review question is to identify the dominantly used classifiers and how they perform.
RQ6	What measures are used to evaluate the performance of these biometric techniques?	This review question is to identify the various metrics used for performance evaluation.
RQ7	What application domain is mobile device biometric authentications dominating?	This review question is to identify mobile devices that are dominantly used for the experiments.
RQ8	What is the signal authentication time?	To identify techniques with the minimum and maximum authentication time.
RQ9	What datasets are used to evaluate the performance classifiers (private, public, or unknown)? - How many users/records are used to test the proposed authentication technique?	This review question is to identify experiments with re-usable or reachable datasets. Also, it will provide information on the performance of the various techniques on a particular dataset.
RQ10	What is the direction of future work	This review question is to identify current challenges and future research directions in the area of biometric authentication on mobile devices.

REVIEW METHODOLOGY

Search Protocol

To ensure a comprehensive and unbiased systematic review, the SPIDER (Sample, Phenomenon of Interest, Design, Evaluation, and Research Type) approach to systematic review was adopted for the study. This approach was adopted because it allows the selection of qualitative, quantitative and mixed research (Cooke, Smith, & Booth, 2012). A search protocol was developed to guide the process in other to reduce researchers' biasness in study selection. A list of related keywords was identified to guide the search. Each member in the research team made a list of keywords and the team discussed and selected the most appropriate. The final list of keywords used was divided into two categories, those relating to biometrics (biometrics authentication, behavioural biometrics, physiological biometrics and biometrics authentication systems) and those relating to mobile devices. The keywords were combined to form four search phrases; biometrics authentication and mobile devices, behavioural biometrics and mobile devices, physiological biometrics and mobile devices, and mobile biometrics authentication systems.

Resources For Performing The Systematic Literature Review

To identify existing trends in mobile biometric authentication research, literature on its progress, patterns and trends of implementation, a set of criteria was defined to guide study selection:

C1. Studies between January 2008 and August 2018 were selected. The academic databases used were; IEEE, ACM digital library and Springer link.

C2. Studies whose title included keywords from both categories of keywords were selected. Studies in which the title included terms such as; recognition, verification, identification, validation, adoption and mobile sensors, were excluded.

C3. Studies in which the abstract did not mention either the classifiers or evaluation metrics were excluded. This criterion was used because the classifier is the core functional unit of any biometric system, responsible for classification (Richiardi & Kryszczuk, 2011).

C4. All selected studies were primary studies: systematic reviews and surveys were excluded.

Application of the Search Expressions

The different databases were searched using the search expressions, the first set of exclusions performed were based on criteria one (C1) and results were exported to Microsoft excel. Conditional formatting was used to exclude studies based on criterion two. Abstracts of the resulting studies were accessed based on C3, C4 and C5. Table 2 shows the number of studies used for the review.

Table 2. Number of Returned References

Database	Observations	C1	C2	C3	C4	C5
IEEE Xplore	251	69	24	8	8	6
ACM digital library	14,801	91	26	14	13	10
Springer Link	222	65	11	9	5	1
Total	15,274	225	61	31	26	17

REVIEW RESULTS

The focus in this section is on the seventeen (17) selected publications. For ease of use, they are labelled A1 to A17 (see appendix A). The following subsections are organized to answer the research questions (table 1): biometric authentication techniques, extracted features, classification algorithms, performance evaluation, and future work.

Figure 1 shows the growth trend in primary studies used. No study was recorded between 2008 and 2009, however, a rapid growth rate of 12% was observed between the years 2010 and 2013. Though there was a fall between 2014 and 2015, between 2016 and 2017 the publication trend increased by over 50% but in 2018 it dropped to 2.

Figure 1. Publications by year of Biometric Authentication in Mobile Devices

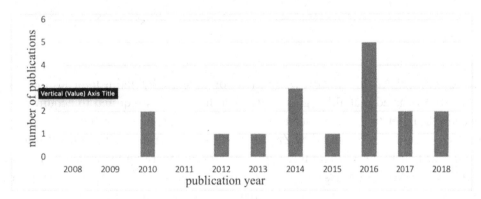

Biometric Techniques (RQ1)

Biometrics is broadly classified into two categories: physiological and behavioral biometrics. Physiological biometrics is based on the physical traits of the individual, they include; face, iris, retina, ear, fingerprint, palm print, finger/hand geometry, vein. While behavioral biometric is based on the inherent behavioral traits of the individual, they include; hand waving, keystroke dynamics, touchscreen, gait, signature, voice, behavior profiling, ECG, DNA (Kim et al., 2010).

Figure 2 shows the distribution of different techniques used in by the various studies.

It was observed that, although both behavioral and physiological techniques were used; touch gesture (a behavioral biometric technique), was the dominant authentication technique. It was used by Ahmed et al., (2017), Bo et al., (2013), Buriro et al., (2018), Frank and Berkeley (2016), Gong et al., (2016), Park and Kim (2016) and Vasiete et al., (2014).

Touch gestures entail authenticating a user based on his behavioural patterns; the differences in the tap-timings, touch screen actions, keystrokes, and applications used (Buriro et al., 2018). Vasiete et al., (2014) adds that it can be further enhanced by combining it (i.e. touch gestures) with facial recognition to produce a non-intrusive authentication system that runs continuously in the background while users perform their various operations.

Figure 2. Chart showing the distribution of biometric authentication techniques used

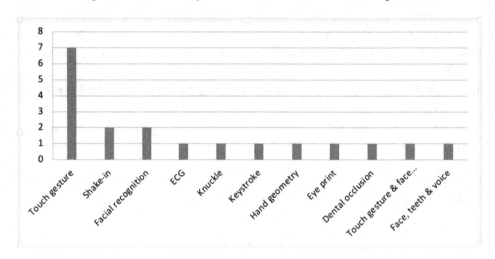

Furthermore, some researchers justified their choice of technique by stating their advantages. Arteaga-Falconi et al., (2016) stated that although sophisticated hardware is required to acquire signals using ECG, it conceals the biometric features of the user during authentication, as well as protect the user from passive attacks. Shake-in was proposed by Zhu et al., (2017) because it is flexible, reliable and easy to deploy. The use of knuckles according to Kozik (2012) is an emerging technique that could enhance hand-based biometric systems because it is easily accessible, invariant to emotions such as tiredness and rich in distinctive texture features. As a way of circumventing voice printing schemes, dental occlusion which involves sounds generated from the click of the teeth was proposed due to its robustness to noise and security against replay and observation attacks (Zou et al., 2018).

Resilient Biometric Attacks (RQ2)

One of the security concerns of biometrics is that it is publicly available hence, it is vulnerable to security attacks which are explicit to specific or generic techniques (Galbally et al., 2014). Consequently, authentication techniques have been developed to circumvent these attacks. Figure 3 categorizes the attacks for the techniques that are resilient.

With touch gesture as the dominant authentication technique, figure 3 shows that it is also the technique with the highest number of attacks that it is resilient to (forgery, spoofing, shoulder surfing, random attacks). On the other hand, it can be observed that out of the ten techniques, mimic attacks are common to five of them.

Figure 3. Distribution of circumvented attacks

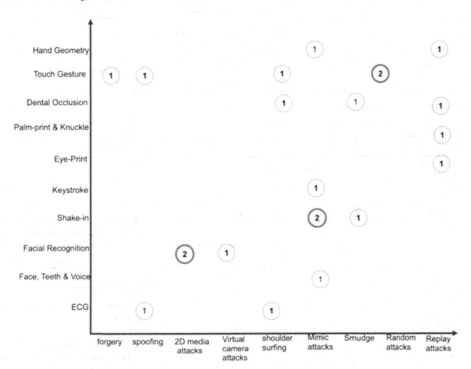

Sensors, Extracted Features and Classification Algorithms/Techniques (RQ3,4&5)

According to Chen et al., (2014), biometric authentication in mobile devices is possible because of the availability of inbuilt sensors: light sensors, sound sensors, motion sensors, cameras, etc. Based on data extracted from the reviewed articles, table 3 highlights the various sensors that enable authentication in mobile devices, the features extracted from these sensors to define users and the algorithms or classifiers used for experiments.

Table 3. Sensors used and extracted features

Ref.	Technique	Sensors used	Extracted features	Algorithms/Classifiers
A1.	ECG	Lead 1	RLP RP, RQ, RS, RT, RTP, RQA$_A$, and RSA	Hierarchical-scheme algorithms
A2.	Face, teeth & voice	Camera and microphone	2D-DCT, Pitch and MFCC	Weighted-summation rule (WSR), k-Nearest Neighbor (kNN), Fisher and Gaussian classifiers.
A3.	Facial recognition	Low end camera	Facial features: eyebrow, eyes, nose & mouth	Viola-jones face (VJF) detection algorithm
A4.	Shake-in	Motion sensors	Finger velocity, device acceleration & stroke time	Support vector machine (SVM)
A5.	Keystroke	Motion sensors	Digraph (2G) & trigraph (3D) keystroke, hold time, typing completion time and accelerometer biometrics	Decision tree, J48, Naïve Bayes, Neural networks
A6.	Eye print	Light camera	LL, LR, RL, RR	Viola-jones eye (VJE) detection algorithm
A7.	Palm print and knuckle	Camera	Wrinkles, valley, lifeline	Euclidean distance, k-Nearest Neighbor (k-NN)
A8.	Facial recognition	Light and motion sensors	Face images	Motion-vector correlation algorithm
A9.	Bilock: Dental occlusion	Microphones	13-order Mel frequency cepstral coefficients (MFCC)	Support Vector Machine (SVM)
A10.	Shake-in	Motion sensors	Acceleration and rotation	Sequential minimal optimization (SMO), logistic regression, random forest, J48, multi-layer perceptron (MLP)
A11.	Touch gesture	Motion sensors	-	k-NN
A12.	Touch gesture and facial recognition	Light and motion sensors	-	Gaussian model, k-Nearest Neighbor (kNN)
A13.	Touch gesture	Touch screen and motion sensors	-	Naïve Bayes, logistic, multilayer perception (MLP), simple logistic, SMO, decision tree, Random forest
A14.	Hand geometry	Camera	-	Manhattan distance (MD)
A15.	Touch gesture	Motion sensors	Dwell time and flight time	Bayesian, Random forest, kNN, MLP
A16.	Touch gesture	Motion sensors	Coordinate, duration, pressure, vibration and rotation	Support vector machine (SVM)
A17.	Touch gesture	Motion sensors	End-to-end lines, average velocity, start locations, end locations of a stroke, etc.	Support vector machine (SVM)

From table 3, ensuing sensors were used: lead I, camera, motion sensors, and microphone. Although motion sensors were predominantly used, it can be observed that different sets of features were extracted from it. The motion sensors included gyroscopes and accelerometers while cameras used were front camera of mobile devices. All sensors except the lead I sensor were inbuilt sensors. The ECG lead I sensor is a heart monitor for mobile phones that produces unique signal from users. The lead I sensor (left arm-right arm) allows users to input their biometric data by touching two electrodes with their fingers

(Arteaga-Falconi et al., 2016). These extracted features from the heartbeat were selected because they tend to remain identifiable in the presence of noise. The extracted features of eye-prints, denoted as LL, LR, RL, RR represent; left eye looking left, left eye looking right, right eye looking left and right eye looking right respectively.

Studies in which the extracted features were not clearly stated are indicated with "dash" in table 3. Arteaga-Falconi et al., (2016) proposed an ECG authentication approach that is exclusive to mobile phones and thus developed a hierarchical scheme algorithm. The advantage of the developed algorithm is its ability to reduce signal acquisition time to 4s. Additionally, a linear normalization process of the signal based on a unitary system was applied to match the ECG of the subject irrespective of any changes in the heartbeat rate (Arteaga-Falconi et al., 2016).

The proposed Multimodal approach by Kim, et al., (2010) entailed using fusion techniques such as weighted summation rule, K-NN, fisher and Gaussian classifiers to integrate the proposed teeth, voice and face modalities. Additionally, an AdaBoost algorithm was used to detect the teeth region, while the embedded hidden Markov model (EHMM) algorithm with the two-dimensional discrete cosine transform (2D-DCT) was used for teeth authentication. Pitch frequency and the Mel-frequency Cepstral coefficients (MFCC) was used for voice authentication, while the Gaussian mixture model (GMM) algorithm was applied to represent the voice signal.

The Viola-Jones face detector was used by both Chen et al., (2014) and Tao and Veldhuis (2010). Tao and Veldhuis (2010) used a combination of local structures as templates to enable efficient detection of face patterns that have similar structures. Their algorithms were written in C++ and the Intel OpenCV library was used to facilitate the implementation. Chen et al., (2014) used Haar-like features for real-time detection of face and facial regions such as eyes or nose. It was implemented in tools such as Haar Cascades in OpenCV and, JavaC.

Conversely, Gottemukkula et al., (2015) used the Viola Jones-based eye detection to find the ocular region along with three interest point finder algorithms namely Harris-Stephens (HS), features from accelerated segment test (FAST) and speeded up robust features (SURF).

A one-class SVM classifier was trained with pattern-based features and experimental results showed that even with a rough configuration, SVM can easily detect shakes from impostors (Zhu et al., 2017). On the other hand, Zou et al., (2018) used a two-class SVM classifier with radical basis function (RBF kernel). They extracted 13-order MFCC from each signal segment with a Hamming window and trained the classifiers on a desktop with four-core Intel ® Xeon (R) E3-1231 CPU and 16G RAM running Windows * with MatLab R2015b software.

Corpus et al., (2016) used RapidMiner data mining tools to develop models by training decision tree, J48, naïve bayes, and neural network classifiers. The classifiers were trained using three features; keystroke dynamic features, accelerometer biometrics and the combination of both accelerometer and keystroke dynamic features. It was observed that the models generated with neural networks performed better and that the models worked best when both keystroke and accelerometer were combined.

Kozik (2012) used texture feature extraction methods such as probabilistic Hough Transform (PHT) and Speeded UP Robust Feature (SURF). The k-NN set yielding the lowest score from the selected images was chosen as the input for SURF-based classifier.

Some researchers used more than one classifier for the experiment. However, based on the results from the performance metrics and authentication time they were able to identify the best amongst the group of classifiers they selected (see figure 5 for the best classifiers). Figure 4 shows the frequency

Figure 4. Chart showing frequency of classifiers

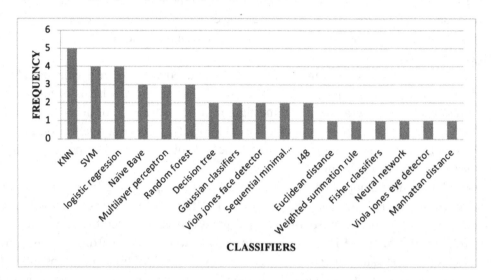

distribution of algorithms used in the selected articles, while figure 5 shows the best classifiers as identified by the researchers.

To classify the feature data of a user, several tools and algorithms were used in the various authentication experiments (see table 3). Machine learning techniques were predominantly used. Amongst the various machine learning techniques used, k-nearest neighbour (k-NN) a supervised machine learning algorithm was the most used.

Yet it was observed (see figure 5) that SVM had the highest number of studies classified as the best classification algorithm. This is based on a count of classifiers that were identified as best based on an acceptable performance rate and classification modelling time in the reviewed articles.

Figure 5. Chart showing frequency of best classifiers

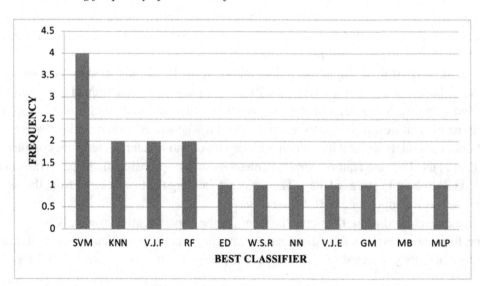

Performance Evaluation and Application Domain (RQ6 &7).

The aim of evaluating an authentication system includes providing a balance between strong protection and correctness of the authentication process, achieving an almost accurate estimate of user authenticity and providing minimal execution time as well as power consumption on mobile devices (Abdulaziz & Jugal, 2016).

Various metrics have been used for evaluating each of the proposed authentication techniques. As shown in table 4, the following metrics were used: false acceptance rate (FAR), false rejection rate (FRR), equal error rate (ERR) and accuracy rate (AR – some studies record it as prediction accuracy or recognition accuracy). Also, the application domain of mobile devices used for the test was grouped into three categories; android devices, iOS, and others.

Table 4. Application domain, Authentication Techniques, Classifiers, and Performance Evaluation Results

Device type	Techniques	Classifiers	FAR%	FRR%	EER%	AR%	TIME (s)	Test users
Android devices: tablets, smart phones, & smart watches								
HP iPAQ rw6100	Face, Teeth and Voice	Weight summation	-	-	1.7	-	4	50
Google Nexus 4	Shake-In	SVM	-	-	1.2	-	0.7	20
Any android mobile device	Keystroke dynamics	ANN	7	-	-	70	30	30
Canon, HTC & Motorola phones	Palm-print and Knuckle	KNN	-	-	1.0	-	-	84
Galaxy nexus phone	Facial Recognition	Viola jones face detector	2	-	-	97	3	9
Samsung Galaxy tab and Huawei watch 2	Dental Occlusion	SVM	0.8	4.3	-	-	-	50
Samsung Galaxy note 4	Shake-In	Random forest	-	-	0.1	-	5	30
Nexus 5 device	Touch Gesture	k-NN	-	-	0.1	-	-	52
Nexus 4 phone	Facial Recognition and Touch Gesture	Gaussian model	-	-	-	98	-	30
Google Nexus 5	Touch Gesture	Random forest	-	-	0.7	92.8	3.9	94
Huawei, Samsung and LG-Flex 2	Hand Geometry	MLP	-	-	-	85.8	-	97
Any android phone	Touch Gesture	SVM	-	-	0.00	99	-	100
Htc one smartphone	Touch Gesture	SVM	-	-	0.2	-	120	25
Ios devices								
iPhone 5	Eye-print	Viola-jones eye detector	-	-	0.04	-	30	226
iPad 2	Touch-gesture	Manhattan distance	-	-	-	97	3.3	44
Other devices								
Windows phone	Facial recognition	Viola-jones face detector	-	-	2	-	30	20
Any mobile phone case	ECG	Euclidean distance	-	-	-	84.9	4	73

FAR, FRR, EER, and AR: In terms of accuracy rate (AR) and false acceptance rate (FAR), Neural Networks recorded the lowest accuracy rate (AR) of 70% and FAR of 7.0%. Although Corpus et al., (2016) recorded a low FAR, it indicates that the model is good at blocking illegal access, they also acknowledged the low AR as being a little above average and concluded that the model cannot accurately identify mobile users.

Considering the performance of all the classifiers used in the 17 studies reviewed, SVM (Bo et al., 2013) had the highest accuracy rate of 99% and the highest false reject rate (FRR) of 0.00%.

Additionally, to further evaluate the performance of the proposed system, Buriro et al., (2018) used System Usability Scale (SUS), a 10-questions based questionnaire to evaluate the usability of the system. While Zou et al., (2018) did a post user survey in terms of overall rating and willingness to use the proposed method in public with questionnaires consisting of three questions.

Application domain: As shown in table 4, the techniques were dominantly tested and implemented on android devices. Sixteen studies used inbuilt sensors. Arteaga-Falconi et al., (2016) used a heart monitor sensor that can be embedded in the casing of any mobile device. They also compared their results with three existing algorithms on authentication time, FAR and TAR. The results showed that their algorithm had a shorter acquisition time of four (4) seconds.

Authentication Time: Shake-in/SVM (Zhu et al., 2017) and Touch gesture/SVM (Gong, et al., 2016) had the lowest (0.7seconds) and highest (120seconds) authentication time respectively. According to Gong, et al., (2016), the authentication time was set to 120seconds to evaluate the effectiveness of their model in circumventing mimic attacks.

Number of Users and Datasets (RQ8 & 9)

To identify experiments with re-usable or reachable datasets, the datasets, as well as the number of users used for the authentication experiment, was also considered.

With the number of test users ranging from nine (9) to two hundred and twenty-six (226), Gottemukkula et al., (2015) had the highest number of users extracted from a public database while Chen, (2014) had the least number of users using a private database. It is therefore argued that the low accuracy rate obtained by neural networks was as a result of the small number of test users. Furthermore, the source of datasets was analysed as shown in figure 6. Majority of the researchers stated insufficient readily

Figure 6. distribution of datasetsa

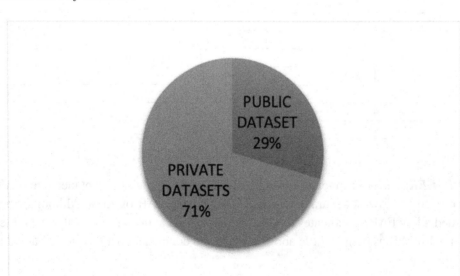

available datasets as a limitation to study. Therefore, they used privately generated data from volunteers, friends, and colleagues.

The downside to the use of private datasets is that it is limited to members of the research team that collected the data: hence such experiments are irreproducible and unable to be analysed further by other interested researchers. Public databases included Physionet, the BioID, the FERET, the YaleB, and the FRGC. The chart shows that 71% of the dataset was privately generated, while 29% were from publicly available datasets.

Future Studies in Biometric authentication (RQ10)

Future works identified in the reviewed articles were categorized as follows:

1. The use of advanced machine learning techniques (Arteaga-Falconi et al., 2016; Zhu et al., 2017; Zou et al., 2018)
2. Developing and adding more sophisticated features and modalities for feature extraction and selection (Corpus et al., 2016; Gottemukkula et al., 2015; Mahfouz et al., 2017), (Park and Kim, 2016), Buriro et al., (2018), Buriro et al., (2018), Sae-bae and Jakobsson (2014).
3. Investigating more screen settings that will disable attacks to touch-based authentication systems Gong et al., (2016).

DISCUSSIONS AND LIMITATIONS

Discussions

This review covered both behavioral and physiological biometric authentication techniques. However, we observed from the review that researchers were more interested in behavioral biometric techniques mainly because it enables continuous and non-intrusive authentication mechanisms, compared to physiological techniques.

Most of the experiments were done in a controlled environment; devoid of typical environmental situations and variables like nervousness, fear or anxiety, or activities like walking or running on the part of the user, the limitation with this is that results obtained from these experiments do not reflect what could happen in reality.

On the classification algorithms used, most of the researchers used machine learning algorithms. According to Abdulaziz and Jugal, (2016), machine learning algorithms are more appropriate for continuous non-intrusive authentication as they are well suited to generalize from the past user behavior as well as make future predictions. Considering the popularity and efficacy of neural networks (deep learning techniques) in accurately identifying patterns, very few researchers used this technique. We envisage that more researchers will explore this technique in future works.

A major research challenge recorded by the researchers was the unavailability of biometric datasets. This is understandable considering the sensitivity of biometric information. However, it is important to note that, in the instance of readily available datasets, research time will be saved, and it will allow researchers to focus more on the development of the classification algorithms.

Choras and Kozik (2012), proposed the use of palmprints and knuckles as an authentication technique because it is invariant to emotions. However, considering the sensitivity of information stored in mobile devices and the robustness of biometric authentication techniques in circumventing attacks, a user may be under physical threat by an attacker to allow access to the device. Accordingly, the authors propose that future works should consider authentication approaches that can sense user emotions like fear and anxiety. Additionally, while considering better authentication techniques, the authors opine that; developers should put into consideration the size of the mobile device, as well as the cost and implementation, there should strike a balance between the authentication process and the authentication time, and finally, there should be a balance between high-security mechanisms and usability.

LIMITATIONS AND CONCLUSIONS

The validity of this review may be affected by missing relevant studies for the following reasons. Firstly, the selected database does not represent an exhaustive list of publications in the subject area. Secondly, some studies fitting the scope of this review were not retrieved during the automated search process. Thirdly, some studies may have also been missed due to technical issues of the automated search engines or during the conditional formatting process. Also, not all publications clearly described the details of certain information that were needed to answer the research questions. Hence, the authors had to infer certain pieces of information.

The primary focus of this review was on identifying biometric security measures that exist in literature. Particularly, we focused on biometric features that are used to verify that a person trying to access a particular device (mobile device) is authentically authorized to do so.

Accordingly, we sought to identify research trends in the subject area. To perform this task, this review identified dominant authentication techniques and attacks that there are resilient to, sensors in mobile devices that enable authentication, features extracted from the user, classification algorithms, performance metrics, datasets and application domains.

Based on data extracted from the reviewed articles, a popular application domain in biometric authentication on mobile devices is its use in android based touch screen devices (see table 4). The dominant technique used was touch gestures and the techniques with unique characteristics were Bilock (dental occlusion) and electrocardiogram (ECG). Mimic attacks which according to Vasiete, (2014) and Zou et al., (2018) is the most difficult attack to circumvent in a biometric system was also identified as the dominant attack that the different techniques were resilient to. In addition to summarizing key information in the subject area, this work also detailed the process involved in the systematic review process.

Mobile devices undoubtedly represent a unique environment that requires a secured, reliable and robust authentication mechanism. Although many authentication approaches have been implemented by researchers, numerous problems in security and privacy constantly abound.

Therefore, new methods must be explored; methods that integrate multiple characteristics and vast security against both internal and external attacks. In touch screens, for instance, both behavioral and physiological characteristics of the user can be integrated for multimodal authentication.

Designing a reliable authentication system for mobile devices is not a walk in the park, while more research is done into developing a more robust and secure authentication system, we opine that researchers should explore the use of more advanced classifiers. Also considering the limitation of inadequate datasets, options like cross-validation, transfer learning, and ensemble learning techniques should be considered.

REFERENCES

Abdulaziz, A., & Jugal, K. (2016). Authentication of Smartphone Users Using Behavioral Biometrics. *IEEE Communications Surveys and Tutorials*, *18*(3), 1998–2026. doi:10.1109/COMST.2016.2537748

Agarwal, A., Maheshwari, S., & Yadav, G. (2014). A review on vein biometric recognition using geometric pattern matching techniques. *Proceedings of the 2014 Conference on IT in Business, Industry and Government: An International Conference by CSI on Big Data, CSIBIG 2014*, 1. 10.1109/CSIBIG.2014.7056935

Ali, M. L., Tappert, C. C., Qiu, M., & Monaco, J. V. (2015). Authentication and identification methods used in keystroke biometric systems. *Proceedings - 2015 IEEE 17th International Conference on High Performance Computing and Communications, 2015 IEEE 7th International Symposium on Cyberspace Safety and Security and 2015 IEEE 12th International Conference on Embedded Software and Systems, H*, 1424–1429. 10.1109/HPCC-CSS-ICESS.2015.66

Arteaga-Falconi, J. S., Al Osman, H., & El Saddik, A. (2016). ECG Authentication for Mobile Devices. *IEEE Transactions on Instrumentation and Measurement*, *65*(3), 591–600. doi:10.1109/TIM.2015.2503863

Bhatt, S., & Santhanam, T. (2013). Keystroke dynamics for biometric authentication-A survey. *Proceedings of the 2013 International Conference on Pattern Recognition, Informatics and Mobile Engineering, PRIME 2013*, 17–23. 10.1109/ICPRIME.2013.6496441

Bo, C., Zhang, L., Li, X.-Y., Huang, Q., & Wang, Y. (2013). SilentSense : Silent User Identi fi cation Via Touch and Movement Behavioral Biometrics. *MobiCom'13*, 187–189.

Buriro, A., Gupta, S., Crispo, B., & Frari, F. D. (2018). Dialerauth: A motion-assisted touch-based smartphone user authentication scheme. CODASPY 2018 - Proceedings of the 8th ACM Conference on Data and Application Security and Privacy, 2018-Janua, 267–276. 10.1145/3176258.3176318

Chen, S., Pande, A., & Mohapatra, P. (2014). *Sensor-Assisted Facial Recognition : An Enhanced Biometric Authentication System for Smartphones*. Academic Press.

Choras, M., & Kozik, R. (2012). Contactless palmprint and knuckle biometrics for mobile devices. Pattern Anal Applic, (123), 73–85. doi:10.100710044-011-0248-4

Cooke, A., Smith, D., & Booth, A. (2012). Beyond PICO: The SPIDER tool for qualitative evidence synthesis. *Qualitative Health Research*, *22*(10), 1435–1443. doi:10.1177/1049732312452938 PMID:22829486

Corpus, K. R., Gonzales, R. J. D., Morada, A. S., & Vea, L. A. (2016). Mobile user identification through authentication using keystroke dynamics and accelerometer biometrics. *Proceedings of the International Workshop on Mobile Software Engineering and Systems - MOBILESoft '16*, 11–12. 10.1145/2897073.2897111

Crawford, H., & Renaud, K. (2014). Understanding user perceptions of transparent authentication on a mobile device. *Journal of Trust Management*, *1*(1), 7. doi:10.1186/2196-064X-1-7

Dharavath, K., Talukdar, F. A., & Laskar, R. H. (2013). Study on Biometric Authentication Systems, Challenges and Future Trends. *RE:view*. doi:10.1109/ICCIC.2013.6724278

Galbally, J., Marcel, S., & Fierrez, J. (2014). Biometric antispoofing methods: A survey in face recognition. *IEEE Access: Practical Innovations, Open Solutions, 2*, 1530–1552. doi:10.1109/ACCESS.2014.2381273

Gong, N. Z., Moazzezi, R., Payer, M., & Frank, M. (2016). Forgery-Resistant Touch-based Authentication on Mobile Devices. ASIA CCS '16, 499–510.

Gottemukkula, V., Saripalle, S., Tankasala, S. P., & Derakhshani, R. (2015). *Method for using visible ocular vasculature for mobile biometrics*. doi:10.1049/iet-bmt.2014.0059

Guliani, N., Shukla, M. K., Dubey, A. K., & Jaffery, Z. A. (2018). Analysis of multimodal biometrie recognition using Iris and sclera. *2017 6th International Conference on Reliability, Infocom Technologies and Optimization: Trends and Future Directions*, 472–475. 10.1109/ICRITO.2017.8342473

Jagadeesh, N., & Patil, C. (2017). A B rief R eview of the I ris R ecognition S ystems for D eveloping a U ser- F riendly B iometric A pplication. *International Conference on Energy, Communication, Data Analytics and Soft Computing (ICECDS-2017) A*, 3309–3312.

Kataria, A. N., Adhyaru, D. M., Sharma, A. K., & Zaveri, T. H. (2013). A survey of automated biometric authentication techniques. *2013 Nirma University International Conference on Engineering, NUiCONE 2013*, 1–6. 10.1109/NUiCONE.2013.6780190

Kim, D. J., Chung, K. W., & Hong, K. S. (2010). Person authentication using face, teeth and voice modalities for mobile device security. *IEEE Transactions on Consumer Electronics, 56*(4), 2678–2685. doi:10.1109/TCE.2010.5681156

Lee, T. K., Kim, T. G., & Im, E. G. (2016). User Authentication Method using Shaking Actions in Mobile Devices. *Proceedings of the International Conference on Research in Adaptive and Convergent Systems - RACS '16*, 142–147. 10.1145/2987386.2987411

Mahfouz, A., Mahmoud, T., & Eldin, A. (2017). Poster: A Behavioural Biometric Authentication framework on Smartphones. *ASIA CCS '17 April 02-06, 2017*, 923–925. 10.1074/jbc.272.22.14115

Meng, W., Wong, D. S., Furnell, S., & Zhou, J. (2015). Surveying the development of biometric user authentication on mobile phones. *IEEE Communications Surveys and Tutorials, 17*(3), 1268–1293. doi:10.1109/COMST.2014.2386915

Ojo, S. O., Zuva, T., & Ngwira, S. M. (2016). Survey of biometric authentication for e-Assessment. *2015 International Conference on Computing, Communication and Security, ICCCS 2015*. 10.1109/CCCS.2015.7374150

Pahuja, G., & Nagabhushan, T. N. (2015). Biometric authentication & identification through behavioral biometrics: A survey. *Proceedings - 2015 International Conference on Cognitive Computing and Information Processing, CCIP 2015*. 10.1109/CCIP.2015.7100681

Park, J., Kim, T., & Im, E. G. (2016). Touch Gesture Data based Authentication Method for Smartphone Users. RACS'16, 136–141.

Patil & Gudasalamani. (2015). *A Survey on Iris Recognition Systems*. Academic Press.

Pisani, P. H., & Lorena, A. C. (2013). A systematic review on keystroke dynamics. *Journal of the Brazilian Computer Society*, *19*(4), 573–587. doi:10.100713173-013-0117-7

Richiardi, J., & Kryszczuk, K. (2011). *Biometric Systems Evaluation*. Academic Press.

Roger, O., Begonya, G.-Z., & Roman, Y. (2017). *Multimodal Biometric Systems : a systematic review*. Academic Press.

Sae-bae, N., & Jakobsson, M. (2014). *Hand Authentication on Multi-Touch Tablets*. Academic Press.

Saevanee, H., Clarke, N. L., & Furnell, S. M. (2012). Multi-modal behavioural biometric authentication for mobile devices. *IFIP Advances in Information and Communication Technology*, *376*, 465–474. doi:10.1007/978-3-642-30436-1_38

Shankar, V., Singh, K., & Kumar, A. (2016). IPCT : A scheme for mobile authentication &. *Perspectives on Science*, *8*, 522–524. doi:10.1016/j.pisc.2016.06.009

Shunmugam, S., & Selvakumar, R. K. (2015). Electronic transaction authentication - A survey on multimodal biometrics. *2014 IEEE International Conference on Computational Intelligence and Computing Research, IEEE ICCIC 2014*, 1–4. 10.1109/ICCIC.2014.7238509

Sudhamani, M. J., Venkatesha, M. K., & Radhika, K. R. (2012). Revisiting feature level and score level fusion techniques in multimodal biometrics system. *Proceedings of 2012 International Conference on Multimedia Computing and Systems, ICMCS 2012*, 881–885. 10.1109/ICMCS.2012.6320155

Tantawi, M. M., Revett, K., Tolba, M. F., & Salem, A. (2012). On the use of the electrocardiogram for biometrie authentication. *2012 8th International Conference on Informatics and Systems (INFOS)*.

Tao, Q., & Veldhuis, R. (2010). Biometric authentication system on mobile personal devices. *IEEE Transactions on Instrumentation and Measurement*, *59*(4), 763–773. doi:10.1109/TIM.2009.2037873

Vasiete, E., Chen, Y., Ian, C., Yeh, T., Patel, V., Davis, L., & Chellappa, R. (2014). Toward a Non-Intrusive, Physio- Behavioral Biometric for Smartphones. *MobileHCI*, 501–506.

Zhu, H., Hu, J., Chang, S., & Lu, L. (2017). ShakeIn: Secure User Authentication of Smartphones with Single-Handed Shakes. *IEEE Transactions on Mobile Computing*, *16*(10), 2901–2912. doi:10.1109/TMC.2017.2651820

Zou, Y., Zhao, M., Zhou, Z., Lin, J., Li, M., & Wu, K. (2018). *BiLock : User Authentication via Dental Occlusion Biometrics*. Academic Press.

KEY TERMS AND DEFINITIONS

Behavioural Biometrics: Is a method for uniquely recognizing an individual using measurable patterns in human activities or actions.

Biometrics Authentication: A unique, non-duplicable, non-transferable, and automated system that authorizes an individual to access a particular device based on his/her physiological or behavioural characteristics.

Equal Error Rate: Is an algorithm used to predetermine the threshold values for false acceptance rate and false rejection rate in a biometric security system.

False Acceptance Rate: Is the measure of the rate at which a biometric security system will incorrectly accept an access attempt by an unauthorized user.

False Reject Rate: Is the measure of the rate at which a biometric security system will incorrectly reject an access attempt by an authorized user.

Multimodal Biometrics: Is a biometric identification system that uses two or more biometric modalities to uniquely identify an individual.

Physiological Biometrics: Is a method for uniquely recognizing an individual using his or her intrinsic physical traits.

Unimodal Biometrics: Is a biometric identification system that uses a single biometric attribute to uniquely identify an individual.

APPENDIX

Selected Studies

Arteaga-Falconi, J. S., Al Osman, H., & El Saddik, A. (2016). ECG Authentication for Mobile Devices. *IEEE Transactions on Instrumentation and Measurement*, 65(3), 591–600. https://doi.org/10.1109/ TIM.2015.2503863

Bo, C., Zhang, L., Li, X.-Y., Huang, Q., & Wang, Y. (2013). SilentSense : Silent User Identi fi cation Via Touch and Movement Behavioral Biometrics. *MobiCom'13, September 30–October 4, 2013, Miami, FL, USA. ACM 978-1-4503-1999-7/13/09*, 187–189. Retrieved from doi:10.1145/2500423.2504572

Buriro, A., Gupta, S., Crispo, B., & Frari, F. D. (2018). Dialerauth: A motion-assisted touch-based smartphone user authentication scheme. *CODASPY 2018 - Proceedings of the 8th ACM Conference on Data and Application Security and Privacy*, 267–276. doi:10.1145/3176258.3176318

Chen, S., Pande, A., & Mohapatra, P. (2014). Sensor-Assisted Facial Recognition : An Enhanced Biometric Authentication System for Smartphones. MobiSys'14, June 16 – 19, 2014 (pp. 109–122). Bretton Woods, NH, USA: Retrieved from; https://dx.doi.org/10.1145/2594368.2594373.

Choras, M., & Kozik, R. (2012). Contactless palmprint and knuckle biometrics for mobile devices. *Pattern Anal Applic*, (123), 73–85. doi:10.100710044-011-0248-4

Corpus, K. R., Gonzales, R. J. D., Morada, A. S., & Vea, L. A. (2016). Mobile user identification through authentication using keystroke dynamics and accelerometer biometrics. *Proceedings of the International Workshop on Mobile Software Engineering and Systems - MOBILESoft '16*, 11–12. doi:10.1145/2897073.2897111

Gong, N. Z., Moazzezi, R., Payer, M., & Frank, M. (2016). Forgery-Resistant Touch-based Authentication on Mobile Devices. *ASIA CCS '16, Xi'an, China*, 499–510. Retrieved from doi:10.1145/2897845.2897908

Gottemukkula, V., Saripalle, S., Tankasala, S. P., & Derakhshani, R. (2015). Method for using visible ocular vasculature for mobile biometrics. *IET Journals*, 3–12. doi:10.1049/iet-bmt.2014.0059

Kim, D. J., Chung, K. W., & Hong, K. S. (2010). Person authentication using face, teeth and voice modalities for mobile device security. *IEEE Transactions on Consumer Electronics*, 56(4), 2678–2685. https://doi.org/10.1109/TCE.2010.5681156

Lee, T. K., Kim, T. G., & Im, E. G. (2016). User Authentication Method using Shaking Actions in Mobile Devices. *Proceedings of the International Conference on Research in Adaptive and Convergent Systems - RACS '16*, 142–147. doi:10.1145/2987386.2987411

Mahfouz, A., Mahmoud, T., & Eldin, A. (2017). Poster: A Behavioural Biometric Authentication framework on Smartphones. *ASIA CCS '17 April 02-06, 2017, Abu Dhabi, United Arab Emirates*, 923–925. doi:10.1074/jbc.272.22.14115

Park, J., Kim, T., & Im, E. G. (2016). Touch Gesture Data based Authentication Method for Smartphone Users. *RACS'16. Odense, Denmark*, 136–141. Retrieved from doi:10.1145/2987386.2987410

Sae-bae, N., & Jakobsson, M. (2014). *Hand Authentication on Multi-Touch Tablets. ACM HotMobile '14* (pp. 1–6). CA, USA: Sannta Barbara.

Tao, Q., & Veldhuis, R. (2010). Biometric authentication system on mobile personal devices. *IEEE Transactions on Instrumentation and Measurement, 59*(4), 763–773. https://doi.org/10.1109/TIM.2009.2037873

Vasiete, E., Chen, Y., Ian, C., Yeh, T., Patel, V., Davis, L., & Chellappa, R. (2014). Toward a Non-Intrusive, Physio- Behavioral Biometric for Smartphones. *MobileHCI*, 501–506. Retrieved from doi:10.1145/2628363.2634223

Zhu, H., Hu, J., Chang, S., & Lu, L. (2017). ShakeIn: Secure User Authentication of Smartphones with Single-Handed Shakes. *IEEE Transactions on Mobile Computing, 16*(10), 2901–2912. https://doi.org/10.1109/TMC.2017.2651820

Zou, Y., Zhao, M., Zhou, Z., Lin, J., Li, M., & Wu, K. (2018). BiLock : User Authentication via Dental Occlusion Biometrics. *Proc. ACM Interact. Mob. Wearable Ubiquitous Technology, 2*(3), 29. Retrieved from doi:10.1145/3264962

Chapter 12
Security and Ethical Concerns of Affective Algorithmic Music Composition in Smart Spaces

Abigail Wiafe
ⓘD https://orcid.org/0000-0001-6019-6074
University of Eastern Finland, Finland

Pasi Fränti
ⓘD https://orcid.org/0000-0002-9554-2827
University of Eastern Finland, Finland

ABSTRACT

Affective algorithmic composition systems are emotionally intelligent automatic music generation systems that explore the current emotions or mood of a listener and compose an affective music to alter the person's mood to a predetermined one. The fusion of affective algorithmic composition systems and smart spaces have been identified to be beneficial. For instance, studies have shown that they can be used for therapeutic purposes. Amidst these benefits, research on its related security and ethical issues is lacking. This chapter therefore seeks to provoke discussion on security and ethical implications of using affective algorithmic compositions systems in smart spaces. It presents issues such as impersonation, eavesdropping, data tempering, malicious codes, and denial-of-service attacks associated with affective algorithmic composition systems. It also discusses some ethical implications relating to intensions, harm, and possible conflicts that users of such systems may experience.

INTRODUCTION

Development of computer or algorithmic music is one of the different technologies and techniques that aid music composition. Many artists attempt to compose music, however, some of these music lack the needed aesthetic and creativity. For instance, it is often difficult to meet the timing of instruments as well as adhere to well-defined musical keys in various octaves. Music composition requires in-depth

DOI: 10.4018/978-1-7998-3149-5.ch012

knowledge on processes and techniques which mostly overwhelm human cognition. Hence, the introduction of automated music composition processes has presented benefits. For example, it enables novice musicians to compose music. Studies have argued that algorithmic composition reduces the amount of time "spent" due to failed efforts and ideas in composing music (Lopez-Rincon, Starostenko, & Ayala-San Martin, 2018). The use of computers for automatic composition presents an opportunity in which computer aided composition and emotional assessment is combined to produce *affective algorithmic composition (AAC)*.

AACs are emotionally intelligent automatic music generation systems that explores the current emotions or mood of a listener to compose an affective music that aims at altering his or her mood to a predetermined one (Kirke et al., 2013, Williams et al., 2017). Specifically, it seeks to target an individual's affective descriptor (emotional response) in other to alter his or her mood (Williams et al., 2015). Considering the capabilities of AACs as affective systems, and its incorporation into smart spaces make it possible to use music to intentionally control a listener's mood within a defined space. A *smart space* is a space that uses networked sensors and other communication methods to facilitate device to device communication to improve user interactions and experiences within their immediate environment.

However, AACs are faced with security challenges: especially in cases where they are implemented in smart spaces. This is because smart spaces are networked, hence, they can be targeted by intruders. Once compromised, attackers can gain control and carry out malicious activities including changing contents of composed music, manipulating sensitive data, controlling moods of listeners and detecting user-influence profiles. More importantly, the lack of confidentiality, integrity and availability of music composed automatically, may potentially disrupt its widespread adoption. Therefore, mechanisms that seek the prevention and protection of unauthorized access, use or destruction of related user information is imperative. Yet, relevant studies that examine the possible security challenges and implications of AACs are lacking.

In response, this chapter discusses security challenges and threats associated with the fusion of AAC and smart spaces. It is motivated by the suspicion that formalized music and AAC has not explicitly confronted issues in cybersecurity. Hence, the chapter seeks to provoke thinking in research and practice in the use of AACs in smart spaces. The discussion is structured as follows: Section 2 provides an overview of affective algorithms composition of music, an exploration of related literature about security issues in Internet of Things (IoT) and a formal definition for a "secured AAC". Section 3 describes possible security threats associated with AAC, whereas section 4 is on related ethical issues. Lastly, section 5 proposes future work and conclusion.

RELATED LITERATURE

Affective Algorithmic Music Composition

Over the years, different algorithmic music composition models and applications have been developed based on artificial intelligent (AI) techniques including neural networks, deep learning, stochastic and heuristic composition models. Examples of algorithmic music compositions include works done by Scirea, Barros, Shaker, & Togelius (2015). They developed a Scientific Music Generator (SMUG) that is capable of producing lyrics and melodies from real-world data such as academic papers. Papadopoulos, Roy, & Pachet (2016) developed a web-based application (FlowComposer) for musical lead sheets that is able to generate melodies by itself. In other studies, techniques have been employed to enhances voice and word representation in music composition (Makris et al., 2015; Shin et al., 2017). Although, algorithmic music composition is not new, Lopez-Rincon et al., (2018) acknowledges that recent advancements have improved the automation of algorithmic music composition.

The use of algorithms in music composition dates back to the era of the Pythagoras, who discovered that numbers and mathematical equations can be used for music composition. Mathematical modelling is perhaps one of the earliest formulations of automatic music composition. Developing mathematical models and implementing it effectively and efficiently enhances algorithmic composed music. Methods including stochastic processes (Jones, 1981) and Markov Chains (Ramanto et al., 2017) have been demonstrated to be effective. Other researchers and practitioners have adopted different approaches including grammars which have been identified to be effective in the analysis and composition of music. In particular, studies have identified six types of grammars used for music composition (Roads & Wieneke, 1979). In recent times, newer methods such as knowledge-based systems (Delgado et al., 2009), evolutionary methods (Matić, 2010), learning systems (Rodrigues et al., 2016) and hybrids of these methods (Fox & Crawford, 2016) have been used to compose music.

Williams et al., (2015) explained that AAC presents a number of opportunities and benefits to almost all aspects of human wellbeing. Especially in healthcare it can be used for therapeutic purposes. For example, AAC is used to compose music that reduces the emotional distress of a patient based on his or her mood (Kemper & Danhauer, 2005). Again, it has the ability to produce larger music samples within a short time: a feature that provides a lager sample of music that can be selected by users for reducing stress levels. Aside from this, it allows novice musicians to compose music with little or no assistance.

AAC presents a future where users can compose personalized music that is tailored for their needs base on context and their immediate environment. Specifically, considering that recent advancement in intelligent and smart spaces are capable of sensing occupant's mood, the fusion of AAC and smart space technologies is inevitable. This notion is supported by recent arguments by Stibe & Wiafe, (2018) who advocated for spaces that seeks to intentionally alter human behaviour. Thus, there is the need for researchers to consider the security and ethical issues of AACs in smart spaces. This is because, considering the permeating effective of music in a smart space and its ability to alter mood suggests that there can be devasting implications if they are not secured. Yet, research on security challenges and threats associated in the domain is lacking.

Security Issues in IOTs

Currently, adoption of intelligent techniques for automating and supporting communications between gargets is increasing in our immediate environments (Balandin & Waris, 2009). This includes spaces such as homes, offices and motor vehicles. Yet, the incorporation of intelligence and automation into such spaces expose it to security and ethical issues (Khatoun & Zeadally, 2017), especially when these systems are interconnected. Boyes (2013), argued that malware attacks on smart spaces continue to increase, whilst others (Koscher et al., 2010; Valasek & Miller, 2013) have also demonstrated that the use of malicious code for manipulating autonomous vehicle components, such as disabling brakes and locking doors have increased. Consequently, a number of studies have investigated these issues and have provided suggestions, methods and frameworks for combatting the security threats and challenges these systems present (Altawy & Youssef, 2016; Taghavi et al., 2017). Amidst these existing studies, there is lack of investigations on AAC specific issues. However, as explained earlier, there is the need for discussions on security issues in the domain.

Defining Security in Automatic Affective Composition

It is imperative to contextualize cybersecurity issues in AAC and also acknowledge that it extends beyond protection of physical infrastructure. Accordingly, in this study, a "secured Affective Automatic Composition system is defined as:

a set of hardware and software designed for automatic composition of affective music that is ethically validated and also capable of preventing unauthorized access, loss, interception and corruption of data.

This definition is inspired by existing studies (Schatz & Wall, 2017) that argues that organizational security issues should seek to ensure confidentiality, integrity and availability through the use of policies, tools, technology, concepts, process, actions and guidelines. Although one may argue that security issues within the organization are generic and thus similar principles can be applied, it is worth noting that affective properties of AAC present additional challenges that may not be considered as core when discussing an organization's information system. In other words, existing studies and conceptualizations of cybersecurity pay more attention to the organization and user asset, whiles less emphasis is given to situations in which a system has an intent to alter a user's mood.

Threats and Security Challenges to Affective Automatic Composition

Similar to arguments made by Boyes, (2003) security threats in AAC can be categorized into four main types. These are threats from malicious outsiders; malicious insiders; non-malicious insiders; and nature. These threats may come in different forms including, impersonation and identity spoofing, eavesdropping, user profiled tampering, malicious codes and denial-of-service. Next is a discussion on possible security threats and challenges of AAC systems.

Impersonation

Impersonation is the act of pretending to be another person for the purpose of fraud or entertainment. Although issues on impersonation and identity spoofing have been largely explored in different domains (Wu et al., 2015), its effects in AAC in relation to smart spaces is yet to be discussed. The security impact of impersonation in this context may lead to two major issues: such as data theft and unauthorized composition or unauthentic (i.e. non-affective music) music for legitimate users.

As in most information systems, an unauthorized user can gain access to relevant information through impersonation. Similarly, in AAC within an enabled smart space, the impersonator may have access to sensitive data about a user and use it for malicious purposes. Particularly, the impersonator can compose music. In such instances, the authenticity of the composed music becomes questionable. This is because, during composition, listener modelling and profiling is crucial for a successful effect (the composed music ability to alter mood). Hence, music composed by an impersonator cannot be considered to be authentic.

This further leads to the second possible effect: the affective impact of music composed by an illegitimate user for a legitimate one. This may have a devasting effect. For instance, an impersonator can manipulate the emotions of a legitimate user by impersonating and suggesting profiles that deliberately alters the legitimate user's mood to the preference of the impersonator. Subsequently, there is a need to ensure that protocols are implemented to authenticate the identity of users (composers). AAC can adopt or adapt existing parameters that are used to validate a user's identity. Perhaps, the most common of all is the use of passwords. Researchers have advised that it is proper to create complex passwords by combining upper- and lower-case letters, numbers and symbols. Nonetheless, studies indicate that passwords are less effective as compared to other parameters such as biometric information (O'Gorman, 2003). Considering the possible impact of impersonation, it is recommended that biometric authentications are used in these systems. Authentication systems such as fingerprints, facial, iris recognition and voice texture are preferred. They provide enhanced security and a better user experience considering the domain of use.

Eavesdropping

Eavesdropping is a common network attack that needs to be considered in AAC systems. It is an unethical act in which an individual illegitimately intercept a private conversation, communication, digital transmission or activities of others without their consent. Through this process, attackers can have access to relevant information such as passwords, biodata and profile data. It poses privacy issues in AAC because it may lead to the disclosure of listeners profiles which can later be used for impersonating. There is no ambiguity about the emotional contagion ability of music (Egermann & McAdams, 2013). It can also alter cognition. Emotions are short-lived episodes that are evoked by triggering identifiable event. A user's emotional profile contains information that can be used to manipulate that individual. Again, since AAC seeks to create affect (a state that is longer than emotion) and alter mood (a longer-lived state that direct cognitive task), eavesdropping can provide information on a user's affect compositions. Information can be generated from the generic profile of a user to be altered.

It is imperative to implement mechanisms that seek to protects AAC from eavesdropping. The use of data encryption algorithms during data transmissions and transits must be implemented. All data in the AAC system including emotional targets, musical data, algorithm composition rules and the affective output must be encrypted. This will ensure that communication intercepted during transfer is secured.

Data Tampering

When unauthorized users gain access either through impersonation or eavesdropping, they may tamper with data. Data tampering is the act of using unauthorized means to deliberately manipulate or modify data. Although this concept has been largely explored in other domains, discussions on data tempering in AAC is limited. AAC uses music composition which depends heavily on data and thus ensuring that this data remains safe, authentication and security is a challenge. Music files, emotional targets files, musical data representations and algorithmic composition rules can be edited, fabricated or falsified by hackers. This can affect the quality, verifiability and validity of the composed music. More importantly, distortions in the algorithmic composition rules will greatly affect the music output. Hence, data tampering poses a security threat to AAC.

To curtail this phenomenon, firewalls and stronger access control measures must be implemented on AAC systems. Firewalls provide controls for incoming and outgoing data traffic in a system. Also, hardware or software can use pre-set criteria or rules to filter the sensitive files and applications that need to be protected.

Malicious Codes and Denial-of-Service Attacks

Threats from malicious users in AAC might be minimal, yet software for music generation may be unnecessarily compromised. Malicious codes are codes in software systems designed to create vulnerabilities that may lead to undesirable effects, data theft, damages or other security breach. Emotions and moods are delicate and thus extra care and measures must be put in place to ensure that systems do not contain malicious codes that may have devastating effects on users. Although it is a challenge to prevent malicious codes and attacks, timely detection, system's alerts and flags can be used to prevent it from spreading rapidly. In AAC systems, the spread of malicious codes may distort the composition of music tempo, rhythm, lyrics and pitch. This will lead to composition of unauthentic music with either less or no affect.

Similarly, denial-of-service (DoS) attack that seeks to make computers or network resources unavailable for its intended may affect the availability of music. In most cases, DoS attacks either flood target systems with traffic or heavy information with the intention of triggering a system crash. In AAC systems, although such attacks may not directly inflict financial cost on its victims (relative to enterprise and e-commerce systems), the indirect cost can be colossal. The deprivation of affective music to users may be life threatening especially if the systems designed for therapeutic purposes. Attacks on AAC can be addressed by adopting methods proposed by Carl, Kesidis, Brooks, & Rai (2006). This includes activity profiling, change-point detection and wavelet-based signal analysis. With regard to the issue of malicious codes, similar methods are effective (Lyons-Burke, 2013).

Ethical Issues in AAC

Ethical considerations are vital in all systems that seek to alter cognition, emotions or mood. This is because, any alteration on cognition, emotions or mood is difficult to reverse or may be irreversible. AAC systems have functionalities that include compositional processes and affective performance structures. They use generative or transformative algorithms to induced or perceived to induce affective states of users (Williams et al., 2015). They adopted emotional models (i.e. categorical or dimensional models) to profile it users. Since users interact with systems that have intentions, any unethical practice may result in an unwanted effect. Below is a discussion on some ethical considerations of AAC systems in smart spaces.

Intended and Unintended Effects

Similar to systems that are designed to intentionally alter human behaviour (Oinas-Kukkonen & Harjumaa, 2009; Wiafe & Nakata, 2012), AAC systems may result in either an intended or unintended effect. Accordingly, design ethics as proposed by Berdichevsky & Neuenschwander, (1999) is useful in this context. Designers use information about users to compose music that is capable of inducing affects. Consequently, this provides designers and systems administrators information about users, which they (users) themselves may not know. In some cases, the system collects information from other sources and analyse them to enhance user profile modelling. This activity, therefore, makes users vulnerable since their profile information becomes public when outsourcing from other sources.

The affective output (the generated music) may also be intended or unintended. Intend AAC outputs can further be classified as either ethical or unethical. Similar to Berdichevsky & Neuenschwander's, (1999) argument, designers of AAC systems must account for unethical intended outcomes. With regard to affective outputs that are unintended, designers must ensure that they eliminate unethical outputs that are reasonably predictable. Figure 1 is a diagrammatic representation of designers output as agued by Berdichevsky & Neuenschwander, (1999).

Figure 1. Ethical responsibilities of AAC adopted from (Berdichevsky & Neuenschwander, 1999)

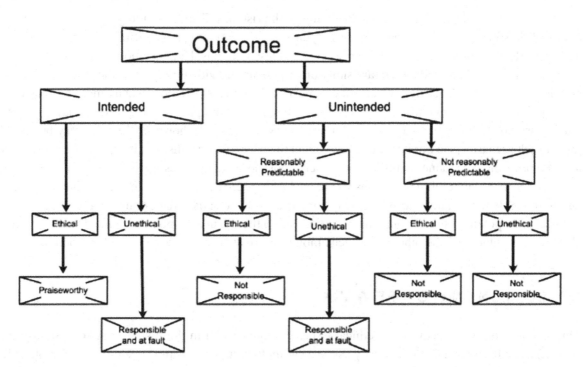

Using AAC to Cause Harm

Affective outputs that are intended or unintended can result in either a physical or psychological harm, if proper measures are not put in place. Considering the functionalities of AAC as discussed earlier, there are possibilities that it can compose music that a listener does not wish to hear. In some cases, the impact on hearing such music especially those with lyrics (i.e. songs) that seek to weaken moral values may result in psychological harm. Also, exposure to tunes that represent frustrations and sorrow over prolong periods also raises ethical concerns. This is because music therapy studies have demonstrated that individuals experience desired activation patterns when they listen to their preferred music and vice versa when music generates dissonance (Moore, 2013).

There may be situations where users prefer to restrain their emotions because they fear that a hidden feeling or emotion can be inferred by others through AAC systems. AAC systems target specific emotions of listeners and compose suggested music based on their emotions. Issues regarding, the possibility of leaked emotions, or revelations of depressed users who wish to conceal their status must be of paramount interest to designers. Similar concerns have been raised by other researchers in affective and emotion designers (Anna et al., 2018). There is the potential that individuals or group of individuals may control other's emotions and moods. For instance, owners of smarts spaces may restrict or trigger particular emotions of occupants within the space. As owners of such spaces they may have access or rights to alter composition algorithms to ensure that particular emotions are exhibited by occupants.

Dual Emotions and Conflicts

An issue that presents diverging ethical challenge is the risk of misunderstanding of a user's emotion. Although existing systems are capable of classifying human emotions using multimodal approaches with higher levels of accuracy, they are still constrained in classifications. Human emotions are complex and multi-dimensional. Especially, there are situations where an individual may be in the state of multiple emotions, yet existing algorithms can compose music only for a single emotion at a time. This may lead to the possibility of misclassification and unseen biases. For example, an AAC system may compose music based on exhibits that suggests that a user is crying (i.e. sad), however the tears may be out of joy. In such scenarios, the implications of AAC and the psychological distress it exposes the user to, in its attempt to alleviate sadness (although the user is not) needs to be investigated.

User conflicts can result in situations where an AAC system detects multiple users within a particular space. In such situations the system may compose music to satisfy the dominating user. However, considering a potential situation in which a composition that induces happiness in the dominant user's also induces sadness for the other user. Such ambiguities may have devasting impacts on both users.

CONCLUSION AND FUTURE WORK

This chapter discussed security and ethical issues that are crucial in the fusion of AAC systems into smart spaces. It established that security assessment in domain requires the development of applicable methodologies to curb possible threats. Considering that cyberattack poses threat to AAC systems, it is argued that attention must be given to security issues that may impact the successful adoption of AAC systems in smart spaces. Attacks ranging from music datasets captured and manipulated to generate unauthentic affective music needs further investigations. The present definition for secure affective algorithmic composition proposed in this chapter is relevant as it provides a thinking framework for both designers and practitioners in this domain. It is however acknowledged that the study failed to address all security and ethical challenges of AAC systems, as such future studies should consider other possible security issues associated with AAC systems.

REFERENCES

Altawy, R., & Youssef, A. M. (2016). Security, privacy, and safety aspects of civilian drones: A survey. *ACM Transactions on Cyber-Physical Systems, 1*(2), 1–25. doi:10.1145/3001836

Anna, P. S., Cooney, M., Pashami, S., Anna, A. S., Fan, Y., & Nowaczyk, S. (2018). Pitfalls of Affective Computing: How can the automatic visual communication of emotions lead to harm, and what can be done to mitigate such risks? *WWW'18 Companion: The 2018 Web Conference, 2018*, 1563–1566.

Balandin, S., & Waris, H. (2009). Key properties in the development of smart spaces. *Lecture Notes in Computer Science, 5615*(2), 3–12. doi:10.1007/978-3-642-02710-9_1

Berdichevsky, D., & Neuenschwander, E. (1999). *Toward an Ethics of Persuasive Technology*. Academic Press.

Boyes, H. (2003). *Resilience and cyber security of technology in the built environment*. Institute of Engineering and Technology.

Boyes, H. A. (2013). Cyber security of intelligent buildings: a review. *8th IET International System Safety Conference Incorporating the Cyber Security Conference 2013*, 1.1-1.1. 10.1049/cp.2013.1698

Carl, G., Kesidis, G., Brooks, R. R., & Rai, S. (2006). Denial-of-service attack-detection techniques. *IEEE Internet Computing, 10*(1), 82–89. doi:10.1109/MIC.2006.5

Delgado, M., Fajardo, W., & Molina-Solana, M. (2009). Inmamusys: Intelligent multiagent music system. *Expert Systems with Applications, 36*(3), 4574–4580. doi:10.1016/j.eswa.2008.05.028

Egermann, H., & McAdams, S. (2013). Empathy and Emotional Contagion as a Link Between Recognized and Felt Emotions in Music Listening. *Music Perception, 31*(2), 139–156. doi:10.1525/mp.2013.31.2.139

Fox, R., & Crawford, R. (2016). A hybrid approach to automated music composition. *Advances in Intelligent Systems and Computing, 464*, 213–223. doi:10.1007/978-3-319-33625-1_20

Jones, K. (1981). Compositional Applications of Stochastic Processes. *Computer Music Journal, 5*(2), 45. doi:10.2307/3679879

Kemper, K. J., & Danhauer, S. C. (2005). Music as therapy. *Southern Medical Journal, 98*(3), 282–288. doi:10.1097/01.SMJ.0000154773.11986.39 PMID:15813154

Khatoun, R., & Zeadally, S. (2017). Cybersecurity and privacy solutions in smart cities. *IEEE Communications Magazine, 55*(3), 51–59. doi:10.1109/MCOM.2017.1600297CM

Koscher, K., Czeskis, A., Roesner, F., Patel, S., Kohno, T., Checkoway, S., & ... . (2010). Experimental security analysis of a modern automobile. *2010 IEEE Symposium on Security and Privacy*, 447–462. 10.1109/SP.2010.34

Lopez-Rincon, O., & Starostenko, O., & Ayala-San Martin, G. (2018). Algoritmic music composition based on artificial intelligence: A survey. *2018 International Conference on Electronics, Communications and Computers (CONIELECOMP)*, 187–193. 10.1109/CONIELECOMP.2018.8327197

Lyons-Burke, K. (2013). *Office Instruction Title: Malicious Code Protection Guidance Revision Number: 1.0*. Academic Press.

Makris, D., Kaliakatsos-Papakostas, M. A., & Cambouropoulos, E. (2015). Probabilistic Modular Bass Voice Leading in Melodic Harmonisation. *ISMIR*, 323–329.

Matić, D. (2010). A genetic algorithm for composing music. *Yugoslav Journal of Operations Research*, *20*(1), 157–177. doi:10.2298/YJOR1001157M

Moore, K. S. (2013). A systematic review on the neural effects of music on emotion regulation: Implications for music therapy practice. *Journal of Music Therapy*, *50*(3), 198–242. doi:10.1093/jmt/50.3.198 PMID:24568004

O'Gorman, L. (2003). Comparing passwords, tokens, and biometrics for user authentication. *Proceedings of the IEEE*, *91*(12), 2021–2040. doi:10.1109/JPROC.2003.819611

Oinas-Kukkonen, H., & Harjumaa, M. (2009). Persuasive systems design: Key issues, process model, and system features. *Communications of the Association for Information Systems*, *24*(1), 28. doi:10.17705/1CAIS.02428

Papadopoulos, A., Roy, P., & Pachet, F. (2016). Assisted lead sheet composition using flowcomposer. *International Conference on Principles and Practice of Constraint Programming*, 769–785. 10.1007/978-3-319-44953-1_48

Ramanto, A. S., Nur, U., & Maulidevi, S. T. (2017). *Markov Chain Based Procedural Music Generator with User Chosen Mood Compatibility*. Academic Press.

Roads, C., & Wieneke, P. (1979). Grammars as Representations for Music. *Computer Music Journal*, *3*(1), 48. doi:10.2307/3679756

Rodrigues, A., Costa, E., & Cardoso, A. (2016). *Evolving l-systems with musical notes*. Springer. https://link.springer.com/chapter/10.1007/978-3-319-31008-4_13

Schatz, D., & Wall, J. (2017). Towards a More Representative Definition of Cyber Security. *Journal of Digital Forensics, Security and Law, 12*(2).

Scirea, M., Barros, G. A. B., Shaker, N., & Togelius, J. (2015). SMUG. *Scientific Music Generator*, *299*, 204–211.

Shin, A., Crestel, L., Kato, H., Saito, K., Ohnishi, K., Yamaguchi, M., . . . Harada, T. (2017). *Melody generation for pop music via word representation of musical properties*. ArXiv Preprint ArXiv:1710.11549

Stibe, A., & Wiafe, I. (2018). *Beyond Persuasive Cities: Spaces that Transform Human Behavior and Attitude*. Persuasive Technology.

Taghavi, M., Bentahar, J., Bakhtiyari, K., & Hanachi, C. (2017). New insights towards developing recommender systems. *The Computer Journal*, *61*(3), 319–348. doi:10.1093/comjnl/bxx056

Valasek, C., & Miller, C. (2013). *Adventures in Automotive Networks and Control Units*. Technical White Paper.

Wiafe, I., & Nakata, K. (2012). *A semiotic analysis of persuasive technology : An application to obesity management. International Conference on Informatics and Semiotics in Organisations.*

Williams, D., Kirke, A., Miranda, E., Daly, I., Hwang, F., Weaver, J., & Nasuto, S. (2017). Affective Calibration of Musical Feature Sets in an Emotionally Intelligent Music Composition System. *ACM Transactions on Applied Perception, 14*(3), 1–13. doi:10.1145/3059005

Williams, D., Kirke, A., Miranda, E. R., Roesch, E., Daly, I., & Nasuto, S. (2015). Investigating affect in algorithmic composition systems. *Psychology of Music, 43*(6), 831–854. doi:10.1177/0305735614543282

Wu, Z., Evans, N., Kinnunen, T., Yamagishi, J., Alegre, F., & Li, H. (2015). Spoofing and countermeasures for speaker verification: A survey. In *Speech Communication* (Vol. 66, pp. 130–153). Elsevier. doi:10.1016/j.specom.2014.10.005

KEY TERMS AND DEFINITIONS

Affective Algorithmic Composition (AAC): A computer-aided system that generate new music with particular emotional qualities or affective intentions.

Data Tampering: The act of using authorized means to deliberately manipulate or modify data.

Eavesdropping: It is an unethical act in which an individual illegitimately intercept a private conversation, communication, digital transmission, or activities of others without their consent.

Impersonation: The act of pretending to be another person for the purpose of fraud or entertainment.

Malicious Codes: Are codes in software systems designed to create vulnerabilities that may lead to undesirable effects, data theft, damages or other security breach.

Secured Affective Automatic Composition System: A set of hardware and software designed for automatic composition of affective music that is ethically validated and also capable of preventing unauthorized access, loss, interception and corruption of data.

Smart Space: A smart space is a space that uses networked sensors and other communication methods to facilitate device to device communication to improve user interactions and experiences within their immediate environment.

Chapter 13

Towards a Student Security Compliance Model (SSCM):
Factors Predicting Student Compliance Intention to Information Security Policy

Felix Nti Koranteng

University of Education, Winneba, Kumasi Campus, Ghana

ABSTRACT

Users are considered the weakest link in ensuring information security (InfoSec). As a result, users' security behaviour remains crucial in many organizations. In response, InfoSec research has produced many behavioural theories targeted at explaining information security policy (ISP) compliance. Meanwhile, these theories mostly draw samples from employees often in developing countries. Such theories are not applicable to students in educational institutions since their psychological orientation with regards to InfoSec is different when compared with employees. Based on this premise, the chapter presents arguments founded on synthesis from existing literature. It proposes a students' security compliance model (SSCM) that attempts to explain predictive factors of students' ISP compliance intentions. The study encourages further research to confirm the proposed relationships using qualitative and quantitative techniques.

INTRODUCTION

Secured management of Information Security (InfoSec) continues to be one of the most relevant issues within organizations. This is because they thrive on intense use of information, hence there is no ambiguity that InfoSec is core to its activities. Traditionally, InfoSec has focused mostly on technological solutions (Öugütçü, Testik, & Chouseinoglou, 2016). However, the need for end-user behaviour has gained attention in recent times (Safa, Von Solms, & Furnell, 2016). This is because of the inability to monitor user behaviour at all times regardless of the increased sophistication of Information and Technology infrastructure and software development. Practitioners and researchers in InfoSec have come to realize that there is a need for Information Systems security solutions to cover a wider range of activities and give

DOI: 10.4018/978-1-7998-3149-5.ch013

equal attention to all. This is because, technology alone cannot be effective for addressing information security issues (Herath & Rao, 2009). Accordingly, research in InfoSec now addresses issues in three main areas namely; people, process and technology. With regard to technology, research work targets the introduction of infrastructure and cryptographic algorithms that enhance methods for prevention, detection, and response to security breaches. Similarly, security processes within the organization have been improved to ensure minimal compromise on confidentiality, integrity, and availability of information. Research on the psychological aspect and behaviour of users has also explored users' compliance with Information Security Policies (ISPs). Consequently, a number of factors have been identified to impact security compliance.

Even though this approach has proven to be somehow effective, majority of the existing studies that have empirically evaluated factors that impact InfoSec behaviour tend to draw their samples from employees of various organizations with little attention to academic institutions. Yet, these factors cannot be generalized and thus it is expected that they may not impact especially students in the manner in which they impact employees. It is however imperative to turn attention to InfoSec issues within higher education institutions considering their high consumption, usage, and knowledge of technology (Öugütçü et al., 2016). This raises further concerns given the increased risk that is associated with cyberspaces. Worriedly, studies that analyze the factors that impact student's compliance with ISPs in developing communities such as Africa. There is enough evidence that students in such areas pay less attention to information security issues (Gross & Acquisti, 2005). Hence this study seeks to present a literature analysis on the factors that impact compliance to information security with a particular focus on African students. It is expected that the findings will provide meaningful information to researchers and practitioners on how to promote information security policy compliance among students. This study, therefore, seeks to provoke thinking and argue for the need for a tailor-made model specific to explaining students' ISP compliance.

LITERATURE REVIEW

The importance of organizations' information security cannot be overemphasized. Hence, technological as well as behavioural measures are often initiated to curb the adverse effects of improper use and policy non-conformity. However, behavioural issues top the approaches in safeguarding information (Safa et al., 2016). Therefore, scholars have explored various avenues in an attempt to explain information security behaviour. Considering that human behaviour is complex and difficult to understand (Wiafe, Nakata, Moran, & Gulliver, 2011). Mostly, the factors that determine adherence to policies meant to guide security behaviour has been explored. Extant studies agree that deterrent mechanisms such as fear appeal, threat, certainty of and severity of punishment are effective in guiding people to comply with security policies (Cheng, Li, Li, Holm, & Zhai, 2013; Herath & Rao, 2009; Safa et al., 2019). Other studies have argued that concepts such as habit strength, security support, prior experiences, self-efficacy, and perceived vulnerability are more effective in explaining information security compliance (Ifinedo, 2012; Johnston & Warkentin, 2010; Tsai et al., 2016).

As already mentioned, majority of these existing studies tend to focus on information security issues within organizations with less attention on higher education institutions. Yet, students of higher education do not have the same psychological contract as compared to employees in organizations. This is because as employees of an organization find the need to protect vital documents of their organization, students, on the other hand, may not see themselves to be obliged in doing so. Consider a situation within an academic institution and issues regarding the protection of students' grades. Both faculty and staff may deem it as a responsibility to ensure that these scores are kept safe and, in an event where they see loopholes that leads to the leakage of such information, they may take appropriate actions. However, a student in this circumstance will not consider the same. Relatedly, Yoon and Kim (2012) demonstrated that students do not have similar information risk perception when compared to employees. This is much evident in many educational institutions including African (Ngoqo & Flowerday, 2015). Ngoqo & Flowerday (2015) suggest that many African students lack requisite conscious care on information security. Hence, their actions intentionally or unintentional subject institutions' IS resources to various risks. This lack of concern can be attributed to a lack of adequate IT skills, awareness of security policy and experience in dealing with possible and imminent threats on IS resources (Chandarman & Van Niekerk, 2017; Ngoqo & Flowerday, 2014).

Amidst these, studies on the determinants of InfoSec compliance behavior among students is scarce. It has thus become imperative for investigations to be conducted to determine the factors that contribute to student's compliance with ISPs. Students are the largest users of information systems infrastructure in all higher education institutes (Rhode, Richter, Gowen, Miller, & Wills, 2017) and they also form the largest populations within these institutions. As such, they can serve as an asset when they are provided with the appropriate skills. The relevance of InfoSec activities within higher education cannot be under-estimated, especially considering that higher education encompasses a number of vital documents (transcripts, certificates, examinations papers, etc.). In addition, students are the next generation of hackers, employees, and employers, and their understanding of InfoSec activities and the ability to comply is key to a successful future organization. It is therefore imperative to understand students' InfoSec behavior within the perspective of existing behavioral theories

BEHAVIORAL THEORIES AND INFOSEC ACTIVITIES

Theory of Planned Behavioral and Security Compliance

The Theory of Planned Behaviour (TPB) (Ajzen, 1991) is a prominent framework for explaining technology use behaviour. The theory is an upgrade of the Theory of Reasoned Action (Fishbein & Ajzen, 1977). TPB argues that a person's behaviour is influenced by their behavioural Intentions (INT). However, these effects are not direct but rather moderated by Actual Behavioural Control. Although this moderation effect is existent, many scholars have sort to adopt Perceived Behavioural Control (PBC) due to the difficulty in measuring Actual Behavioural Control. Aside from this, PBC along with Attitude (ATT) and Subjective Norm (SN) have been identified to influence Intentions (Shin & Hancer, 2016). Attitude is an individual's positive or negative judgment about a behaviour whereas Subjective Norm is a person's perceived expectations of relevant others.

There is evidence that these constructs are relevant in explaining security compliance behaviour. For instance, Ifinedo (2012) adopted the TPB to investigate IS security compliance of a group of employees. The study found significant effects of Subjective Norm and Attitude on Compliance Intention. Similarly, using the theory as a foundation, Kim, Yang, & Park (2014) concluded that, the variables in TPB is effective in predicting compliance behaviour. Other literature reviews have also pointed out that TPB constructs are the most relevant in explaining compliance intention and behaviour (Nasir, Arshah, &

Ab Hamid, 2018; Sommestad & Hallberg, 2013). This suggests that the theory is adequate for assessing students' information security compliance behaviour. Nonetheless, it is imperative to extend existing models and methods to complement the rapid changes in information security landscape. This paper therefore argues for the modification of TPB. It argues that the introduction of deterrence, information security awareness and information security knowledge sharing into TPB will facilitate the understanding of ISP compliance intention within the context of students of higher education. This is because some studies have found significant relationships between these constructs and security behaviour (Bulgurcu, Cavusoglu, & Benbasat, 2010; Safa et al., 2016).

The original theory (TPB) does not highlight the ordering of constructs with regards to their importance. Conversely, some scholars believe that the potency of some of the constructs reduces in different scenarios and environments. For instance, in the case where technology behavior and use is completely voluntary, Perceived Behavioural Control is of lesser value (Sommestad & Hallberg, 2013). The activities of students in ensuring information security compliance may be largely voluntary, thus, Perceived Behavioural Control can be omitted from the model under such circumstance. Meanwhile, new concepts (Deterrence, Information Security Awareness, and Information Security Knowledge Sharing) have been integrated with Attitude and Subjective Norm to form Students' Security Compliance Model (SSCM). Consequently, this chapter argues that Deterrence, Information Security Awareness, and Information Security Knowledge Sharing are direct predictors of Attitude and Subjective Norm. In addition, Attitude and Subjective Norm predicts students' compliance Intentions to information security. Figure 1 is a diagrammatic representation of the conceptualization of factors that influence students' information security compliance in higher education.

Deterrence Theories and Policy Conformity

As inferred earlier, information security policies enlist acceptable guidelines for ensuring information security. They also contain repercussions for non-compliance. The concepts originate from the General Deterrence Theory (GDT) which posits that an individual's decision to commit or abstain from crime is rational (Higgins, Wilson, & Fell, 2005). Thus, people compare the benefits and costs before committing a crime. In other words, a person will perpetuate a crime when he/she perceives that the benefits outweigh the cost and vice. As a result, several studies have found a nexus between willingness to comply with ISPs and perceived benefit/cost.

For instance, according to Parsons et al., (2015) employees in organizations with severe sanctions for non-compliance possess favorable attitudes towards information security. Similarly, Rajab and Eydgahi, (2019) and Safa et al., (2019) confirm that when people are certain that their non-compliance behavior will be detected and will lead to severe punishments, they tend to positively relate to ISP. In a study by Shreeve et al., (2002), students confirmed that penalties are effective in guiding behavior and that schools with penalty systems record higher conformance behavior from students. Recently, Patchin and Hinduja (2018) also found that student is deterred by threats of punishment. That is, in the absence of clear and consistent consequences for unacceptable security behavior, deviant behavior will fester. Deterrent approaches thus provide an effective alternative for guiding students' Attitude and behavior towards ISP.

Figure 1. Students' Security Compliance Model

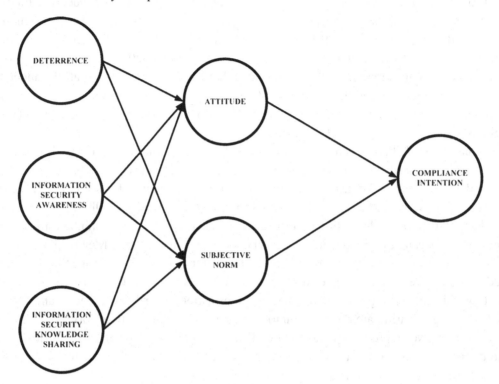

Information Security Awareness

Information Security Awareness is important in improving students' affect towards complying with ISP. For students' to appropriately handle data and interact with information systems, they must be equipped with the requisite skills. Indeed, proper knowledge and skills improve security behavior (Yaokumah, Walker, & Kumah, 2019). Badie and Lashkari (2012) contend that regardless of the sophisticated technologies and protection mechanisms, unaware users remain a viable vector for attacks. That is to say that, the lack of awareness and proper skills may lead individuals to commit intentional or unintentional errors that could be detrimental to information security. Jones, Chin, and Aiken (2014) assert that students lack proper education, training, and awareness and thus contributes to the growing security problems. Moreover, Farooq, Isoaho, Virtanen, and Isoaho (2015) found that more than 75% of students lack security training. Studies attribute this to the lack of comprehensive security programs available for students (Kim, 2014; Slusky & Partow-Navid, 2012). Meanwhile, institutions can provoke ISP compliance when programs aimed at training and increasing students' awareness of their roles and responsibilities with regards to InfoSec are implemented (Adams & Makramalla, 2015). This is because students who are better informed on information security will be better informed about the relevance of appropriate data handling techniques as well as the prevalence of imminent threats. Moreover, well-trained students exhibit a positive attitude toward information security policy (Parsons et al., 2015). Bulgurcu, Cavusoglu, and Benbasat (2010) provide empirical evidence for this assertion. Although their study sampled employees, it is possible similar results will be found among students.

Information Security Knowledge Sharing

Knowledge is a crucial asset in organizations. It provides the theoretical understanding, facts, and information for learning and experience (Safa et al., 2016). Knowledge sharing is the willingness of students to share the information they have acquired (Koranteng & Wiafe, 2019). Effective knowledge sharing has been established to help solve problems and enable the creation of new ideas. Knowledge, when shared evenly across the organizational structure improves efficiency, reduces cost and mitigates risks (Lee, Lee, & Sanford, 2011). Therefore, InfoSec knowledge sharing is an effective approach to mitigating the risks associated with information systems. For instance, if experts are challenged with a security problem, they could disseminate information on how it was solved and others could also implement proactive measures for similar future attacks. This reduces the time and money for developing duplicate solutions for similar attacks (Feledi, Fenz, & Lechner, 2013). Relevant studies have confirmed that InfoSec knowledge sharing thwarts security risks such as phishing (Arachchilage & Love, 2014; Tamjidyamcholo, Baba, Shuib, & Rohani, 2014). However, it continues to be one of the major challenges that hinder the progress of information security compliance among employees (Tamjidyamcholo et al., 2014). This situation may not be experienced among students because it has been demonstrated that students are motivated to share knowledge by taking advantage of advancement in modem technologies (Koranteng, Wiafe, & Kuada, 2019). Koranteng, Wiafe, Katsriku, and Apau (2019) posits that students have a high norm of reciprocity which positively affects their frequency of interactions. Due to the strong interaction ties among students, they willingly share knowledge and learn from each other (Eid & Al-Jabri, 2016). This is also corroborated by Aslam, Shahzad, Syed, and Ramish (2013). To this regard, students in higher education may share their knowledge on information security practices and this will impact the security behavior.

Attitude

As already indicated, Attitude refers to an individual's affect toward ISP (Ajzen, 1991). It describes a person's overall judgment on InfoSec and it is manifested in a person or entity. It originates from previous experiences, ideas or activities (Hepler, 2015). Extant studies have established a positive correlation between Attitude and compliance intention (Safa & Von Solms, 2016; Safa et al., 2016). In a related study, Safa et al., (2019) found that Attitude is a significant predictor of ISP compliance. That is, when users positively relate to ISPs, there is a high probability of compliance (Ifinedo, 2014). The new generation of students often referred to as Millennials are highly abreast of the issues surrounding InfoSec (Parker, Ophoff, Van Belle, & Karia, 2015). They experience or encounter multiple threats when using their personal devices such as mobile phones. Hence, many students understand the negative effects caused by such threats and are poised to have favorable opinions on InfoSec (Stanciu & Tinca, 2016). Yoon et al., (2012) contend that students exhibit a good InfoSec habit. Similarly, Hajli and Lin (2016) conclude that students possess a positive Attitude towards InfoSec. Likewise, Cordova, Eaton, Greer, and Smith (2017) also regard students' Attitude towards computer security threat as favourable. Although, Wiafe, Nakata, and Gulliver (2014) insists that Attitude do not always predict behavioural intentions, the authors also admit that there is relationship between. Indeed, Mayer, Kunz, and Volkamer (2017) confirms that Attitude remains a reliable factor for predicting compliance intention. Consequently, students' Attitude toward ISP compliance may predict compliance behavior.

Subjective Norm

Subjective Norm reflects the probability to perform a behavior due to the expectations of relevant others (Ajzen, 1991). An individual may perform a behavior because they perceived that people important to them deem it appropriate. Relevant research asserts that social pressure from significant others such as lecturers and supervisors may lead students to behave in a particular way (Safa et al., 2015). In other words, students occasionally want approval from respected colleagues and authorities, hence they seek to behave in ways they perceive to be in accordance with the expectations of these authorities. Some scholars assert that Subjective Norm is very influential in predicting technology behavior (Binyamin, Rutter, & Smith, 2018). For instance, Arpaci (2016) found that students accepted the use of mobile cloud storage services because of influences from significant others. Gong, Han, Li, Yu, and Reinhardt (2019) also concluded that students' behavioral intention to adopt online services is informed by perceptions of relevant others. Other scholars have also confirmed this relationship (Yeap, Ramayah, & Soto-Acosta, 2016). According to Halder, Pietarinen, Havu-Nuutinen, Pöllänen, and Pelkonen (2016), this relationship is stronger in developing countries. This is because, students in such countries tend to appreciate authorities and mostly conform to their expectations (Hofstede, 2001). As a result, findings from Buabeng-Andoh, Yaokumah, and Tarhini (2019) confirm that Subjective Norm is relevant in predicting students' behavioral intentions. Within the scope of ISP compliance, Cheng et al., (2013) have suggested that Subjective Norm influences ISP compliance. Similarly, findings from Foltz, Newkirk, and Schwager (2016) confirm that students' behavioral intentions on social networking sites security is impacted by Subjective Norm. Given these backgrounds, students may be likely to conform to security policy requirement due to the expectations of relevant other.

FUTURE RESEARCH DIRECTIONS

The chapter has reviewed extant empirical studies that provide a strong foundation on the factors that account for security compliance behavior among students. As earlier indicated, human elements in an organization remain key in ensuring the safety of information. People are considered the weakest link in InfoSec. Therefore, without a particular focus on how to improve information security behavior, institutions continue to be at risk. Eisenhardt, Gioia, and Langley (2016) believe that qualitative research is aimed at theory building since it aids researchers in defining the relationships between observed variables. To confirm or advance the proposed relationships in this chapter, future studies are encouraged to adopt different qualitative techniques to synthesize the relationships espoused. Based on the study's conceptual model and others derived from relevant qualitative reasoning, additional studies can focus on using quantitative techniques to empirically test the relationships proposed.

Moreover, the arguments in this chapter present a worrying trend that suggests a lack of educational programs and courses on information and computer security. While the focus of this chapter is not to assess the state of InfoSec education, it highlights the need for further investigations into the status of InfoSec related programs and training existent particularly in developing countries. This is because aside from the security of institutions' information, other studies have attributed the rapid rise in cybercrime incidents such as online fraud to the lack of relevant educational programs (Apau, Koranteng, & Adu, 2019). Finally, studies are also encouraged to examine the implications of the assertions delivered by this chapter and explore the possible and relevant policy directions that stakeholders could undertake to achieve desirable results.

CONCLUSION

Breaches in an organization's Information Systems (IS) security does not only cause financial losses but also loss of trust and reputation. Therefore, the protection of organizational information is very crucial. Institutions tend to channel huge investments into technology to safeguard ISs. However, this is inadequate, as attackers target people and not technology. However, to make users robust to techniques adopted by attackers, security policy compliance is key. Therefore, scholars have extensively explored the determinants of security policy compliance. This is aimed at developing frameworks that enhance users' compliance with information security. While these studies provide relevant recommendations, many of them draw samples from employees with very few focusing on students. Meanwhile, research has shown that the psychological disposition of students differs from employees as students readily disregard security policies. This chapter, therefore, performed a literature synthesis and developed a Students' Security Compliance Model (SSCM) aimed at explaining students' security policy compliance behavior. In SSCM, Attitude and Subjective Norm are dependent on Deterrence, Information Security Awareness, and Information Security Knowledge Sharing. In addition, Attitude and Subjective Norm predict students' compliance Intentions to information security. Future studies are encouraged to empirical test the proposed relationships in the model.

REFERENCES

Adams, M., & Makramalla, M. (2015). Cybersecurity skills training: an attacker-centric gamified approach. *Technology Innovation Management Review, 5*(1).

Ajzen, I. (1991). The theory of planned behavior. *Organizational Behavior and Human Decision Processes, 50*(2), 179–211. doi:10.1016/0749-5978(91)90020-T

Apau, R., Koranteng, F. N., & Adu, S. (2019). Cyber-crime and its effects on e-commerce technologies. *Journal of Information, 5*(1), 39–59. doi:10.18488/journal.104.2019.51.39.59

Arachchilage, N. A. G., & Love, S. (2014). Security awareness of computer users: A phishing threat avoidance perspective. *Computers in Human Behavior, 38*, 304–312. doi:10.1016/j.chb.2014.05.046

Arpaci, I. (2016). Understanding and predicting students' intention to use mobile cloud storage services. *Computers in Human Behavior, 58*, 150–157. doi:10.1016/j.chb.2015.12.067

Aslam, M. M. H., Shahzad, K., Syed, A. R., & Ramish, A. (2013). Social capital and knowledge sharing as determinants of academic performance. *Journal of Behavioral and Applied Management, 15*(1), 25–42.

Badie, N., & Lashkari, A. H. (2012). A new evaluation criteria for effective security awareness in computer risk management based on AHP. *Journal of Basic and Applied Scientific Research, 2*(9), 9331–9347.

Binyamin, S. S., Rutter, M. J., & Smith, S. (2018). The Influence of Computer Self-Efficacy and Subjective Norms on the Students' Use of Learning Management Systems at King Abdulaziz University. *International Journal of Information and Education Technology (IJIET)*, 8(10), 693–699. doi:10.18178/ijiet.2018.8.10.1124

Buabeng-Andoh, C., Yaokumah, W., & Tarhini, A. (2019). Investigating students' intentions to use ICT: A comparison of theoretical models. *Education and Information Technologies*, 24(1), 643–660. doi:10.100710639-018-9796-1

Bulgurcu, B., Cavusoglu, H., & Benbasat, I. (2010). Information security policy compliance: An empirical study of rationality-based beliefs and information security awareness. *Management Information Systems Quarterly*, 34(3), 523–548. doi:10.2307/25750690

Chandarman, R., & Van Niekerk, B. (2017). Students' cybersecurity awareness at a private tertiary educational institution. *African Journal of Information and Communication*, 20(20), 133–155. doi:10.23962/10539/23572

Cheng, L., Li, Y., Li, W., Holm, E., & Zhai, Q. (2013). Understanding the violation of IS security policy in organizations: An integrated model based on social control and deterrence theory. *Computers & Security*, 39, 447–459. doi:10.1016/j.cose.2013.09.009

Cordova, J., Eaton, V., Greer, T., & Smith, L. (2017). A comparison of CS majors and non-CS majors attitudes regarding computer security threats. *Journal of Computing Sciences in Colleges*, 33(2), 4–10.

Eid, M. I. M., & Al-Jabri, I. M. (2016). Social networking, knowledge sharing, and student learning: the case of university students. *Computers & Educationand Education, 99*, 14–27. Retrieved from http://ssrn.com/abstract=2780765

Eisenhardt, K. M., Gioia, D. A., & Langley, A. (2016). Theory-Method Packages: A Comparison of Three Qualitative Approaches to Theory Building. In Academy of Management Proceedings (Vol. 2016, p. 12424). Academic Press.

Farooq, A., Isoaho, J., Virtanen, S., & Isoaho, J. (2015). *Information security awareness in educational institution: An analysis of students' individual factors. In 2015 IEEE Trustcom/BigDataSE/ISPA* (Vol. 1, pp. 352–359). IEEE.

Feledi, D., Fenz, S., & Lechner, L. (2013). Toward web-based information security knowledge sharing. *Information Security Technical Report*, 17(4), 199–209. doi:10.1016/j.istr.2013.03.004

Fishbein, M., & Ajzen, I. (1977). *Belief, attitude, intention and behavior: An introduction to theory and research*. Reading, MA: Addison-Wesley.

Foltz, C. B., Newkirk, H. E., & Schwager, P. H. (2016). An empirical investigation of factors that influence individual behavior toward changing social networking security settings. *Journal of Theoretical and Applied Electronic Commerce Research*, 11(2), 1–15. doi:10.4067/S0718-18762016000200002

Gong, Z., Han, Z., Li, X., Yu, C., & Reinhardt, J. D. (2019). Factors influencing the adoption of online health consultation services: The role of subjective norm, trust, perceived benefit and offline habit. *Frontiers in Public Health*, 7, 286. doi:10.3389/fpubh.2019.00286 PMID:31637229

Gross, R., & Acquisti, A. (2005). Information revelation and privacy in online social networks. In Workshop On Privacy In The Electronic Society (pp. 71–80). doi:10.1145/1102199.1102214

Hajli, N., & Lin, X. (2016). Exploring the security of information sharing on social networking sites: The role of perceived control of information. *Journal of Business Ethics, 133*(1), 111–123. doi:10.100710551-014-2346-x

Halder, P., Pietarinen, J., Havu-Nuutinen, S., Pöllänen, S., & Pelkonen, P. (2016). The Theory of Planned Behavior model and students' intentions to use bioenergy: A cross-cultural perspective. *Renewable Energy, 89*, 627–635. doi:10.1016/j.renene.2015.12.023

Hepler, J. (2015). A good thing isn't always a good thing: Dispositional attitudes predict non-normative judgments. *Personality and Individual Differences, 75*, 59–63. doi:10.1016/j.paid.2014.11.016

Herath, T., & Rao, H. R. (2009). Encouraging information security behaviors in organizations: Role of penalties, pressures and perceived effectiveness. *Decision Support Systems, 47*(2), 154–165. doi:10.1016/j.dss.2009.02.005

Higgins, G. E., Wilson, A. L., & Fell, B. D. (2005). An application of deterrence theory to software piracy. *The Journal of Criminal Justice and Popular Culture, 12*(3), 166–184.

Hofstede, G. J. (2001). Adoption of communication technologies and national culture. *Information Systems Management, 6*(3), 55–74. doi:10.9876im.v6i3.107

Ifinedo, P. (2012). Understanding information systems security policy compliance: An integration of the theory of planned behavior and the protection motivation theory. *Computers & Security, 31*(1), 83–95. doi:10.1016/j.cose.2011.10.007

Ifinedo, P. (2014). Information systems security policy compliance: An empirical study of the effects of socialisation, influence, and cognition. *Information & Management, 51*(1), 69–79. doi:10.1016/j.im.2013.10.001

Johnston & Warkentin. (2010). Fear Appeals and Information Security Behaviors: An Empirical Study. *Management Information Systems Quarterly, 34*(3), 549. doi:10.2307/25750691

Jones, B. H., Chin, A. G., & Aiken, P. (2014). Risky business: Students and smartphones. *TechTrends, 58*(6), 73–83. doi:10.100711528-014-0806-x

Kim, E. B. (2014). Recommendations for information security awareness training for college students. *Information Management & Computer Security, 22*(1), 115–126. doi:10.1108/IMCS-01-2013-0005

Kim, S. H., Yang, K. H., & Park, S. (2014). An integrative behavioral model of information security policy compliance. *TheScientificWorldJournal, 2014*, 2014. doi:10.1155/2014/463870 PMID:24971373

Koranteng, F. N., & Wiafe, I. (2019). Factors that Promote Knowledge Sharing on Academic Social Networking Sites: An Empirical Study. *Education and Information Technologies, 24*(2), 1211–1236. doi:10.100710639-018-9825-0

Koranteng, F. N., Wiafe, I., Katsriku, F. A., & Apau, R. (2019). *Understanding trust on social networking sites among tertiary students: An empirical study in Ghana.* Applied Computing and Informatics. doi:10.1016/j.aci.2019.07.003

Koranteng, F. N., Wiafe, I., & Kuada, E. (2019). An Empirical Study of the Relationship Between Social Networking Sites and Students ' Engagement in Higher Education. *Journal of Educational Computing Research, 57*(5), 1131–1159. doi:10.1177/0735633118787528

Lee, G., Lee, W. J., & Sanford, C. (2011). A motivational approach to information providing: A resource exchange perspective. *Computers in Human Behavior, 27*(1), 440–448. doi:10.1016/j.chb.2010.09.006

Mayer, P., Kunz, A., & Volkamer, M. (2017). Reliable behavioural factors in the information security context. In *Proceedings of the 12th International Conference on Availability, Reliability and Security* (pp. 1–10). 10.1145/3098954.3098986

Nasir, A., Arshah, R. A., & Ab Hamid, M. R. (2018). The Significance of Main Constructs of Theory of Planned Behavior in Recent Information Security Policy Compliance Behavior Study: A Comparison among Top Three Behavioral Theories. *International Journal of Engineering & Technology, 7*(2.29), 737–741.

Ngoqo, B., & Flowerday, S. (2014). Linking student information security awareness and behavioural intent. In HAISA (pp. 162–173). Academic Press.

Ngoqo, B., & Flowerday, S. V. (2015). Exploring the relationship between student mobile information security awareness and behavioural intent. *Information & Computer Security, 23*(4), 406–420. doi:10.1108/ICS-10-2014-0072

Öugütçü, G., Testik, Ö. M., & Chouseinoglou, O. (2016). Analysis of personal information security behavior and awareness. *Computers & Security, 56*, 83–93.

Parker, F., Ophoff, J., Van Belle, J.-P., & Karia, R. (2015). Security awareness and adoption of security controls by smartphone users. In *2015 Second international conference on information security and cyber forensics (InfoSec)* (pp. 99–104). 10.1109/InfoSec.2015.7435513

Parsons, K. M., Young, E., Butavicius, M. A., McCormac, A., Pattinson, M. R., & Jerram, C. (2015). The influence of organizational information security culture on information security decision making. *Journal of Cognitive Engineering and Decision Making, 9*(2), 117–129. doi:10.1177/1555343415575152

Patchin, J. W., & Hinduja, S. (2018). Deterring teen bullying: Assessing the impact of perceived punishment from police, schools, and parents. *Youth Violence and Juvenile Justice, 16*(2), 190–207. doi:10.1177/1541204016681057

Rajab, M., & Eydgahi, A. (2019). Evaluating the explanatory power of theoretical frameworks on intention to comply with information security policies in higher education. *Computers & Security, 80*, 211–223. doi:10.1016/j.cose.2018.09.016

Rhode, J., Richter, S., Gowen, P., Miller, T., & Wills, C. (2017). Understanding Faculty Use of the Learning Management System. *Online Learning, 21*(3), 68–86. doi:10.24059/olj.v21i3.1217

Safa, N. S., Maple, C., Furnell, S., Azad, M. A., Perera, C., Dabbagh, M., & Sookhak, M. (2019). Deterrence and prevention-based model to mitigate information security insider threats in organisations. *Future Generation Computer Systems*, *97*, 587–597. doi:10.1016/j.future.2019.03.024

Safa, N. S., Sookhak, M., Von Solms, R., Furnell, S., Ghani, N. A., & Herawan, T. (2015). Information security conscious care behaviour formation in organizations. *Computers & Security*, *53*, 65–78. doi:10.1016/j.cose.2015.05.012

Safa, N. S., & Von Solms, R. (2016). An information security knowledge sharing model in organizations. *Computers in Human Behavior*, *57*, 442–451. doi:10.1016/j.chb.2015.12.037

Safa, N. S., Von Solms, R., & Furnell, S. (2016). Information security policy compliance model in organizations. *Computers & Security*, *56*, 70–82. doi:10.1016/j.cose.2015.10.006

Shin, Y. H., & Hancer, M. (2016). The role of attitude, subjective norm, perceived behavioral control, and moral norm in the intention to purchase local food products. *Journal of Foodservice Business Research*, *19*(4), 338–351. doi:10.1080/15378020.2016.1181506

Shreeve, A., Boddington, D., Bernard, B., Brown, K., Clarke, K., Dean, L., ... Shiret, D. (2002). Student perceptions of rewards and sanctions. *Pedagogy, Culture & Society*, *10*(2), 239–256. doi:10.1080/14681360200200142

Slusky, L., & Partow-Navid, P. (2012). Students information security practices and awareness. *Journal of Information Privacy and Security*, *8*(4), 3–26. doi:10.1080/15536548.2012.10845664

Sommestad, T., & Hallberg, J. (2013). A review of the theory of planned behaviour in the context of information security policy compliance. In *IFIP International Information Security Conference* (pp. 257–271). 10.1007/978-3-642-39218-4_20

Stanciu, V., & Tinca, A. (2016). Students' awareness on information security between own perception and reality--an empirical study. *Accounting and Management Information Systems*, *15*(1), 112–130.

Tamjidyamcholo, A., & Baba, M. S. (2014). Evaluation model for knowledge sharing in information security professional virtual community. *Computers & Security*, *43*, 19–34. doi:10.1016/j.cose.2014.02.010

Tsai, H. S., Jiang, M., Alhabash, S., LaRose, R., Rifon, N. J., & Cotten, S. R. (2016). Understanding online safety behaviors: A protection motivation theory perspective. *Computers & Security*, *59*, 138–150. doi:10.1016/j.cose.2016.02.009

Wiafe, I., Nakata, K., & Gulliver, S. (2014). Categorizing users in behavior change support systems based on cognitive dissonance. *Personal and Ubiquitous Computing*, *18*(7), 1677–1687. doi:10.100700779-014-0782-3

Wiafe, I., Nakata, K., Moran, S., & Gulliver, S. R. (2011). Considering user attitude and behaviour in persuasive systems design: the 3d-rab model. In ECIS (p. 186). Academic Press.

Yaokumah, W., Walker, D. O., & Kumah, P. (2019). SETA and Security Behavior: Mediating Role of Employee Relations, Monitoring, and Accountability. *Journal of Global Information Management*, *27*(2), 102–121. doi:10.4018/JGIM.2019040106

Yeap, J. A. L., Ramayah, T., & Soto-Acosta, P. (2016). Factors propelling the adoption of m-learning among students in higher education. *Electronic Markets*, *26*(4), 323–338. doi:10.100712525-015-0214-x

Yoon, C., Hwang, J.-W., & Kim, R. (2012). Exploring factors that influence students' behaviors in information security. *Journal of Information Systems Education*, *23*(4), 407–415.

KEY TERMS AND DEFINITIONS

Attitude: A student's positive or negative affect towards information security policy.

Deterrence: An action of discouraging improper security behavior by instilling fear of punishment.

Information Security Awareness: The degree to which students are conscious of acceptable security behavior.

Information Security Knowledge Sharing: The probability that students will willingly share the information security knowledge they have acquired.

Information Security Policies (ISPs): It denotes acceptable guidelines for ensuring institutions' information security.

Information Systems (IS): An integrated set of digital products for collecting, processing, and storing institutions' informational resources.

Subjective Norm: The likehood that a student will perform security behaviour because of the expectation of relevant others.

Chapter 14
IT Security Investment Decision by New Zealand Owner–Managers

Radiah Othman

(iD) https://orcid.org/0000-0002-9772-0439

School of Accountancy, Massey University, New Zealand

Sydney Kanda

7 Eyes Cyber Security Consultants, New Zealand

ABSTRACT

Small businesses employ 29% of New Zealand's private sector workforce and account for more than a quarter of its gross domestic product. Thus, a large-scale attack on small businesses could prove to be catastrophic to the economy. This chapter, which is framed by the protection motivation theory, explores 80 small business owners' IT security decision-making via an online survey. The findings revealed that 21% of small businesses were affected by ransomware. Fifty-one percent of the respondents did not have any anti-malware and none of the respondents used data classification, which means all information was regarded as the same. Since they managed to recover their backup information, they did not perceive the threat of ransomware as imminent. In terms of coping appraisal, it is assumed that if the business owner-managers believe that the capability of IT security investment averts threats in their organizations, they will be more inclined to develop an intention to invest in it.

INTRODUCTION

There is an abundance of studies on investment decision-making practices focusing on management accounting (MA) techniques and tools. In terms of investment decision-making behavior, previous research has largely focused on shareholders (e.g., Agyemang, 2019) rather than business owners, especially small-medium enterprises (SME). Lucas, Prowle, and Lowth (2013) surveyed SME business owners and indicated that less successful SMEs often did not use MA tecnhiques adequately. Research

DOI: 10.4018/978-1-7998-3149-5.ch014

has yet to cover New Zealand SME in this regard. With the exception of sustainability practices (Collins, Lawrence, Pavlovich, & Ryan 2007), MA research on SME in New Zealand is limited. In fact, little is known of the risk tolerance and uncertainty management behaviors associated with New Zealand (NZ) SME business decision-making and activities (Islam, Tedford, & Haemmerle, 2017).

Small businesses make the bulk of the business community in New Zealand. Currently, 97% of enterprises in New Zealand have fewer than 20 employees and are regarded as small enterprises (MBIE, 2015). Smaller businesses have higher failure costs, both at firm and personal levels (Islam et al., 2017). However, SMEs in New Zealand growth and development are influenced by attitudes of owner-managers (Islam et al., 2017; Lewis, 2008). Since they are constantly exposed to threats imposed by using information technology (IT) in their operation, the IT security investment they make could be critical to their survival. Collectively, they employ 29% of New Zealand's private sector workforce and account for more than a quarter of gross domestic product (NZentrepreneur, 2017). Thus, an attack on small business on a large scale could also be catastrophic to the economy. In addition, previous research on MA and IT security was conducted in isolation, focusing on ransomware threats. Thus, this study intends to address the knowledge gap by exploring New Zealand's small business owners' consideration of MA information in their IT security decision-making.

The main contribution of this chapter is twofold. First, the chapter extends studies on small businesses into MA decision-making studies and IT security literature framed by Protection Motivation Theory (PMT) (Menard, Bott, & Crossler, 2017; Rogers, 1983) from psychology. Second, it provides relevant insights on the current state of management accounting consideration in owner-managers' investment decisions. In terms of practical managerial significance, this study provides insight on the challenges and dilemmas faced by owner-managers in balancing the cost of investment required and the need to protect their businesses against security threats. Intuitively, it encourages managers to view IT security as a strategic resource rather than an outflow expenditure from their budget.

The conceptual framework proposed in this chapter aims to assist managers in redesigning IT strategy based on their assessment of vulnerability-threat analysis and realign them with required cyber essentials. This includes the flexibility to modify IT security policies, schedule periodic employee training, and to have an ongoing security audit. It will make managers more prepared to deal with constant and ever-evolving IT security threats and challenges.

The next section focuses on the background of ransomware threats and their impacts on New Zealand small businesses. The theoretical background is explained and then followed by research method and research findings. Then a conceptual framework of MA-driven IT security decision is proposed before the chapter concludes.

RELATED LITERATURE

Most businesses rely on computers and IT to the extent that it would be impossible to manage without them. Increasing investment in technological advances is necessary to increase presence, speed in responding to customers' needs, and leverage on competition in the targeted market. Information has become so prolific that companies have had to change their business models and processes to become more open by introducing multiple touch points for stakeholders and customers wanting to interact with them (Kwok, 2015). This also presents abundant opportunities for unauthorized access and data breaches (Watad, Washah, & Perez, 2018).

Ransomware is a digital blackmail in which a computer is taken hostage (Mansfield-Devine, 2016). It is a type of malware that extracts a ransom payment in exchange for unlocking access to an asset that belongs to the victim (Kaspersky, 2016). It is delivered through phishing emails, maltisements, and social engineering (Scott, 2016). The encrypted file uses strong cryptographic algorithms and it has replaced advanced persistent threat network attacks as the most problematic cyber threat (Kaspersky, 2016). While most ransomware attacks are concentrated in the US (43%), (United Nations, 2013), New Zealand has not been spared. Ransomware attacks in New Zealand have affected mobile users, Whanganui District Health Board, and small businesses (Cook, 2016; NZentrepreneur, 2017). Most large companies could pay the ransoms (Farlow, 2016), but not the small businesses.

IT security literature on New Zealand SMEs is under-researched. New Zealand SMEs have been the subjects of research in IT usage (Voges & Pulakanan, 2011) and outsourcing decisions (Su, Levina, & Ross, 2016), but the majority of the research concentrates on adoption (e.g., Kasanagottu & Bhattacharya, 2017) and eCommerce (Alley & Emery, 2017). Watad et al., (2017) suggest that any attack on small businesses may have severe consequences and it is critical that the businesses reduce the likelihood of potential threats to survive in the future.

THEORETICAL FRAMEWORK

Data and information protection are part of business strategy (Soomro, Shah, & Ahmed, 2016). The security of business information depends on the action of management and business (Soomro et al., 2016). A business' information, including details of the customers, is one of its important assets (Hedström, Kolkowsa, Karlsson, & Allen, 2011). Further, the nature of small businesses makes them particularly vulnerable to attacks. Security breaches can cause great financial losses and lack of proper security measures may lead to competitive disadvantage, yet smaller businesses place limited value on information and its security (Watad et al., 2018).

The action and decision on how to deal with potential losses hinge on various factors that individuals considered as risky (Hirsch, Reichert, & Sohn, 2017). In the case of IT security investment decisions, the perceived risks would depend on owner-managers' perceived vulnerability and perceived severity of investing (or not investing). Decision-makers are frequently blamed for making investment decisions that suit their interests and values (Ortner, Velthuis, & Wollscheid, 2017). In this regard, psychological theories are often used within contingency-based MA research by focusing on the influence of individuals' mental states and behaviors (Hall, 2016).

The Protection Motivation Theory

In terms of protecting businesses from exposure to IT security threats, specifically ransomware, this study adopts the Protection Motivation Theory (PMT) (Rogers, 1983) to examine, at the individual level, the influence of psychological reasoning (e.g., of motivation/emotion) on strategic investment decisions on IT security. PMT has been used in previous studies to predict individuals' behavior in relation to computer security (e.g., Westcott & Ronan, 2017; Barlette, Gundolf, & Jaouen, 2017)). This theory emanates from both threat appraisal and coping appraisal. Threat appraisal describes a business owner-manager's assessment of level of danger posed by a threatening event (Rogers, 1983; Ifinedo, 2012). It comprises the following: Perceived vulnerability and Perceived severity. Perceived vulnerability is an individual assessment of the probability of threatening events, such as ransom threats. Perceived severity is an individual judgement on how severe the consequential effect of an incident such as impending threats posed by ransomware to small businesses' IT. In MA terms, this could refer to the consideration of avoidable cost and opportunity cost in making IT security investment decisions.

The Protection Motivation Theory's coping appraisal refers to an individual coping ability with the consequential effects from the threat (Ifinedo, 2012). Coping appraisals include Self-efficacy, Response efficacy, and Response cost. Self-efficacy emphasizes the individual's ability or judgment regarding his or her capabilities to cope with or perform the recommended behavior (Menard et al., 2017; Ifinedo, 2012). Response efficacy is an individual perception on the benefits of actions taken (Rogers, 1983). In this study it is the owner-managers' belief in the benefit of the IT investment decisions made in mitigating IT threats such as ransomware. In MA terms, the coping investment decisions such as self-efficacy and response efficacy considers relevant data (Langfield-Smith, Thorne, Smith, & Hilton 2015). These data include the consideration of costs or benefits related to future, and those that differ between alternatives. Lastly, the response cost refers to the actual and perceived opportunity costs in adopting the recommended behavior such as time and effort. In this study it is making decisions to invest in IT security.

Research Methodology

An exploratory study using convenience sampling was conducted. Eighty small businesses were selected at random to participate in an online survey from July to August 2017. Table 1 shows the small businesses surveyed and their industrial categorizations. Thirty-nine out of 80 (49%) small business owner-managers agreed to participate in the study. Ten small businesses located in Wellington were also interviewed in person (hereafter, the interviewees) and the rest completed an online survey (hereafter, the respondents).

The next step was to assure the respondents that the online survey was genuine and that the findings were being collected for research purposes; therefore, a telephone follow-up was made. Most of the respondents requested further aggregate information to be reported and their demographic details not be identified in any way, which is therefore adhered to.

The same survey questions were used for Wellington respondents and the opportunity for onsite visits provided the opportunity for the field researcher to validate and corroborate physical evidence onsite. For example, the availability of the IT security measures such as server rooms. The interviewees were primarily the owners and, where possible, included IT managers or administrators. The interviews lasted from 30 to 90 minutes.

The data collected were analyzed using spreadsheets due to the small data sample while the interview data were coded based on thematic analysis guided by the theoretical framework variables: threat and coping appraisals. The threat appraisals were then further classified into perceived vulnerability and perceived severity. Coping appraisals were divided into self-efficacy and response cost categories. The coding was first done by the second researcher and later verified by the other researcher. Any discrepancies were revisited and resolved.

Table 2 shows that the majority of the small businesses who participated in the study were located in Wellington (25.6%), followed by Auckland (17.9%). The other businesses were from Rotorua, Christchurch, and Palmerston North (10.3%).

Table 1. Small businesses and industries surveyed

Industry	Number of Companies
Rental, Hiring, & Real Estate	10
Finance & Insurance	6
Agricultural, Forestry & Fishing	10
Construction	4
Professional & Technical Services	7
Information, Media & Communications	7
Administration & Support Services	6
Transport, Postal & Warehousing	4
Retail Trade	4
Wholesale Trade	4
Healthcare & Social Assistance	4
Accommodation & Food Services	3
Mining	3
Utilities	3
Manufacturing	2
Public Administration & Safety	2
Education & Training	1
Total	**80**

Table 2. Sampled small businesses in major cities and towns

City/Town	No. of small businesses
Auckland	7 (17.9%)
Christchurch	4 (10.3%)
Dunedin	2 (5.1%)
Napier	2 (5.1%)
Palmerston North	4 (10.3%)
Rotorua	4 (10.3%)
Taupo	3 (7.7%)
Tauranga	3 (7.7%)
Wellington	10 (25.6%)
Total	**39 (100%)**

Figure 1. Nature of small businesses participated in study

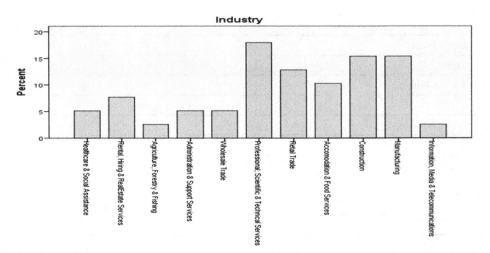

As shown in Figure 1, the top five businesses were in Professional, Scientific & Technical Services (17.9%), Construction (15.4%), Manufacturing (15.4%), Retail (12.8%), and Accommodation & Food Services (10.3%).

In regard to ransomware experience, only eight (21%) of small businesses were affected by ransomware: three in Wellington, two in Auckland, and one each in Taupo, Napier, and Christchurch. Of these eight, two affected businesses were from professional, scientific, and technical services and the other two were in the manufacturing industry. The other four businesses were from accommodation & support services, wholesale, retail, and construction.

FINDINGS

Threat Appraisal

Threat appraisal describes a business owner-manager's consideration of the severity posed by a threatening incident. Small business often devalue the importance of fundamental risk assessment that ultimately caused their failure (Islam et al., 2017, p.3)

Perceived Vulnerability

More than half of the respondents did not have any anti-malware and identity awareness. All the small businesses in the sample used the same Wi-Fi for staff and guests. They use the same cloud provider services and 29% share files from the same server, but ransomware attacks shared files and made them unusable by encrypting them. Eighteen percent of respondents gave information access to staff, depending on their roles. They did not perceive this as a security vulnerability. This is illustrated by one interviewee below:

…Information on the cloud is secure, right? The contractor who did the migration assured us it's the safest place to keep our files. And so far, so good! (R25 L9)

Within a small business context, information can be considered as the most valuable asset. Thus, classification is critical in ensuring all the information the business creates, gives out, and stores cannot not be taken away (Veltsos, 2016). Even though 90% of the business respondents had their financial-related information restricted in some other way, none of the respondents used classification, which means all information was regarded as the same. The most common reason was stated as below:

Everyone here looks at the same information when they want to make a decision. Classifying and restrictions might not work for us. It's a matter of trust. (R8 L14)

Since they did not perceive how vulnerable their business information was, the respondents were asked if they ever raised awareness about the dangers of ransomware, and if so, in what way. Thirteen percent of the respondents talked about it in day-to-day interactions in their offices, while 1% learnt about it from the news. Surprisingly, 85% of them never talked about it with their staff. Forty-four percent of the respondents allow staff to take their laptops home. In addition, nearly one-third of the respondents (26%) allow staff to share their login accounts. One respondent explained:

Sharing certain accounts simply makes life easier. If each person has their own account, it means one person will have to remember more passwords. (R10 L7)

Vance, Lowry, and Eggett (2013) warned that employees may steal information and have malicious intentions. In terms of IT security measure, a firewall is the first line of defense for every Internet connection (Meeuwisse, 2016). However, 23% of the respondents did not use a firewall, which meant they are directly connected to the Internet and, indeed, vulnerable to cyber attackers. Some did not even know if they were using a firewall. For instance:

I know of the internet router. I am not sure about the firewall. (R4 L29)

The respondents also admitted that they did not have any measures in place to protect their information on the cloud. Even though 39% did back up instantly as provided by the cloud services, the majority (64%) did not.

Perceived Severity

Perceived severity refers to the owner-managers' perception on how imminent the ransomware attack is to the security of his or her business information. Previous studies have shown that perceived severity tends to influence an individual's intention to follow protective actions (Menard et al., 2017; Barlette et al., 2017).

In the survey, even though 21% of the respondents reported to have been affected by ransomware at some point, none of them paid any ransom to retrieve their information. They managed to recover their information from backups from the cloud. This number could be higher, given that most businesses just pay the ransom secretly, fearing damage to their reputation and do not report being the victims. Since they managed to recover their backup information, they did not perceive the threat of ransomware as being imminent. In fact, 39% of the respondents disclosed that they did have a dedicated risk management position, but ransomware threat was not included. Those who experienced the attack were quite lax, as indicated below:

Which fool would target a small business like us and extort money? I am sure there are bigger fish to catch. (R11 L8)

The influence of perceived severity on protective action also depends on the attitude and concern levels of the individuals (Menard et al., 2017; Watad et al., 2018). The findings imply that the respondents did not perceive they were vulnerable and the threats to be imminent, and thus made the decision not to invest in IT security investment. There was no evidence of MA tools and information related to avoidable cost being considered when making a decision to (not) invest in IT security investment decisions.

Coping Appraisal

Based on our survey, 21% of the small businesses had been attacked by ransomware, but none of them paid any ransom to retrieve their information because they managed to recover their information from backups. Most of the backups used were from the cloud. This number could be higher, given that most businesses just pay the ransom secretly, fearing damage to their reputation.

Self-Efficacy

Previous studies have shown that if an individual is well-informed on how effective a coping mechanism is, that individual would be more adaptive towards the mechanism (Rogers, 1983). Similarly, out of 31 individuals who knew what ransomware was, only six depended on both the firewalls and anti-virus software. In general, this shows that if the business owner-managers believe that the capability of IT security investment averts threats in their organizations, they will more inclined to develop an intention to invest in it (Barlette et al., 2017; Watad et al., 2018). When asked about decisions in relation to protection strategies against malware and ransomware, the processes were not explicitly stated. For instance, one CEO responded:

...Dependent on IT devices and technical solutions like anti-virus, anti-malware. (R66 L5)

There is no evidence that before an IT security investment decision the business owner-managers would rely or consider costs and benefits in the future or comparison being made on alternatives with which to arrive at an investment decision. Typically, they are more interested in practical explanations, rather than those that are complex and hard to interpret.

Self-efficacy could be enhanced if the small businesses encourage sharing information about viruses or suspicious-looking emails to help raise awareness and foster a culture of being alert to cyber threats (Landers, 2016). In the survey, this mostly falls onto the IT managers' shoulders. None of the sampled small businesses had an IT security culture in their organization. In fact, even IT managers were not so keen on building a security culture, as one of them indicates below:

Awareness, yes. Culture? That is a stretch. (R28 L2)

In a Swedish study, Hedström et al., (2011) found that the management only saw information security as technology-based, not as manual administrative routines. Similarly, the owner-managers had never made an appraising of information security and cyber security needs.

Response Efficacy

Individuals' response to a threat depends on their perception of the threat riskiness and their willingness to accept the threat (Ifinedo, 2012). Thus, if a business owner-manager perceives ransomware is not a threat, he or she may be less concerned about investing in IT security. In the survey, 79% of the respondents were aware of the ransomware threat to their businesses. In terms of security measures, a big majority (82%) had an anti-virus program and 61% knew they had a firewall. It seems that viruses are the chief concerns as compared to other sources of security breach. However, much anti-virus software can only help prevent 40% or less of cyber-attacks (Meeuwisse, 2016). More than half (51%) used anti-malware software, which is a very encouraging result, especially when all of them used USBs. Unfortunately, none of the USBs were encrypted. When asked about this, one IT manager responded:

Having to encrypt data on USB's and on everyone's laptop hard drives is an overkill isn't it? We are only a small business... (R10 L17)

This type of response is quite worrying; the crippling of the small business sector would either mean a national crisis or 'business as usual' is no longer an option. This has ramifications for data theft as well, because someone could just plug an unencrypted USB into their computer and immediately upload data or, worse still, drop viruses.

The IT security in managing ransomware threat needs to be comprehensive and supported by top management (Watad et al., 2018). The majority in the sample (77%) of the study revealed that IT security issues were loosely spoken about. This is quite surprising, especially when information on security awareness was included as part of the recruitment process (21%). It is obvious that the communication of it was lacking, which would require more proactive action on the part of the management.

Table 3. Ransomware & Strategy

		Attacked		Total
		No	Yes	
Strategy	Not available	25	6	31
	Available	6	2	8
Total		31	8	39

Out of 39 small businesses, only eight (21%) had information security as part of their business strategy. It is interesting to note that only two out of eight small businesses that were attacked had an IT strategy in place. The majority, six out of eight, did not. When interviewed, there was no indication of MA tools being used in day-to-day decision-making, indicating a lack of strategic direction in preventing an attack and establishing a business recovery plan. Ownership over the organization's safety (Elbaz, 2016) would make individuals more receptive to information security precautions (Ifinedo, 2012). A budget or a provision should at least be prepared in anticipation of what could go wrong, but this was not the case in the sampled organizations in which the treatment was *business as usual*. In these organizations, information collected is often fragmented and private. Strategic information and budget preparation to cope or prepare for any adverse event were lacking.

Response Cost

Incurred expenses or adverse consequences resulting from the decisions made by the individuals are classified as response cost. As such, individuals such as the owner-managers are reticent to make the decision to invest in IT security if only a small amount is required, but they do not realize that the cost of not doing anything would far outweigh the cost of implementing security measures (Watad et al., 2018). Often, the action depends on the priorities set by the business (Lucas et al., 2013). This is similar to this study, as indicated below:

...There are far too many important work to be done than worry about IT security. IT security, it seems, is delegated to devices. (R15 L5)

Some businesses are failing to understand that information security involves not only technological tools but also people issues (Watad et al., 2018). In New Zealand, they often had to trade off some objectives (Lewis, 2008). In the UK, the owner-managers claimed they had no choice but to base on their experience (Lucas et al., 2013).

DISCUSSION

It can be observed that more than one-fifth of the respondents had been victims of ransomware attack, yet the same percentage revealed they did not use a firewall as the first line of defense. Particularly, some of them are not aware of whether they had a firewall or not. More than 82% did not restrict information access from their staff. Therefore, if any of the staff are vulnerable to security breach, directly or indirectly, the whole organization would be affected, which would be potentially a devastating outcome.

Some managers allowed their staff to take laptops home and share their accounts and unencrypted USBs 'to make life easier' and based on 'trust.' Most of them relied or expected the cloud service provider to protect their information without consideration of further back-up and were thinking that anti-virus software could solve the problems without having due regard that security breaches could have been more severe, especially when their financial information was not classified. They seemed to think that they were not vulnerable, and they were passing on the responsibilities to IT position to shoulder the burden. They also lacked effective and efficient assessment of risk, vulnerabilities of security breach threats, and awareness and training of their staff in this regard.

They did not seem to be aware that IT security investment should be part of their business strategy. Lack of a formal guide led them to perceive IT security as cost, a burden, and cash outflow rather than an investment. This misperception would require reconsideration of managerial accounting role in small businesses to guide the managers in making strategic decisions. Langfield-Smith et al., (2015) stress that MA focuses on the effective and efficient use of organizational resources to support managers in their routine and non-routine tasks. The available tools and techniques include a budgeting system, capital expenditure analysis, and costs and benefits analysis. If used appropriately, these tools and techniques can be fed into the appraisal processes, shaping the IT and business strategy. The outcome would be a dynamic process, not a static one.

Many large businesses have an established and dedicated system to approve, monitor, and control such expenditure, including the benefits derived from such investment, while in small businesses, such systems can be informal and the lack of guidance obvious. Regardless, not investing in the investment of strategic importance, such as IT security, can lead to serious consequences for the small businesses. As such, a framework that is MA driven to guide managers in making an informed IT security decision and business strategy is proposed below.

Proposed Framework: Management Accounting (MA) Driven IT Security Decision and Business Strategy

Technical competencies on IT security if complemented with a strategy would align the management of security with organizational strategies. It should synchronise to the change in business strategies in accordance to market position and uncertainties posed by the environment (Chen, Sun, Helms, & Jih, 2008). The management would be more alert of security threats and the adequacy of their response to such risks (Whitman, 2004)

UK Information Commissioner's Office (ICO) has recently released a document on a practical guide to IT security ideal for the small business, which highlights 10 important considerations, including assessing the threat and risks to your business and getting in line with cyber essentials. Figure 2 illustrates the proposed conceptual framework informed by Protection Motivation Theory and MA tools of relevant data consideration in making decisions, in line with the suggestions by ICO above.

In terms of applying the conceptual framework to their businesses, an owner-manager should *first* start by designing a clear IT strategy. An IT strategy should be comprehensive and focus on how technology is to be used to meet IT and business goals formulated in the business strategy. Both IT and business strategies are aligned by a strategic approach to managing and securing the information asset (Landers, 2016). *Secondly*, in order to keep the IT systems safe and secure, ICO (2016)'s first advice is to perform a threat appraisal by considering the vulnerabilities of all processes involved in collecting, storing, using, and disposal of personal and business information. The more valuable, sensitive, and confidential the information, the greater the threats imposed by the information. The owner-managers prefer to have the control and unrestricted access to sensitive information to have superior insights of their businesses (Lucas et al., 2013). By using information from the classification exercise, the small business can identify where the business-sensitive information is located (Menninger, 2016). MA analysis to quantify the benefits and the cost of the security would be useful.

Once the vulnerabilities and threats analysis is done, *thirdly*, the owner-manager can then get in line with cyber essentials such as firewalls and Internet gateways, secure configuration, and access controls, malware protection, and patch management and software updates (Veltsos, 2016). This is categorized as response and coping appraisals. In deciding which product would be suitable for the business, relevant cost information, including opportunity cost, must be considered, as there is no single product that would provide complete guarantee of security for the business (ICO, 2016). The *fourth* consideration would be in relation to the physical security of equipment that contains the personal and business information, including the data on devices being used away from the office. The right encryption to be used and security measures of the cloud provider must also be assessed. Frequent and scheduled backups are critical for fragile data to be recovered if lost (Kestle, 2013; Menninger, 2016). The *sixth* consideration is for the owner-managers to take some preventive actions such as identifying weak security points and develop procedures to continuously monitor them.

Figure 2. Conceptual Framework of MA-driven IT Security Investment Decision Strategy

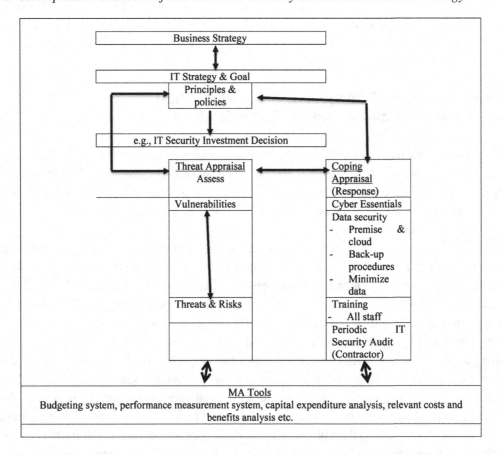

The *seventh* consideration is the assessment of the response and coping mechanism by reevaluating policies and procedures and become more effective in dealing with security threats (Watad et al., 2018). Information security should be treated as business security rather than a technical issue (Kwon, Ulmer, & Wang, 2012). Therefore, well-written policies should integrate well with business processes (ICO, 2016), simple and straightforward (Meeuwisse, 2016; Elbaz, 2016).

Employees should be trained in the security procedures of the company and security expectations upon hiring, as employees could potentially be the last line of defense when it comes to protecting sensitive information (Menninger, 2016; Soomro et al., 2016). This means all small businesses' employees, not only IT staff, need training periodically, including consequences of violating the security policies (Ifinedo, 2012; Drystek, 2016). The importance of the training should be given a priority in the budget.

ICO (2016)'s next advice is to keep an eye out for problems and know what should be done. Thus, threat appraisals should be made on an ongoing basis and addressed by the response/coping appraisals should the business suffer a data breach. A response plan should be established, and avoidable cost information should be quantified. ICO (2016) also suggests that data be minimized by excluding data that are out of date, inaccurate, and no longer useful. Security audit of the systems should be conducted, but one has to make sure than the contractor only acts on instructions and complies with certain obligations in the contract.

CONCLUSION

This chapter aims to explore owner-managers' investment decisions in relation to IT security in response to ransomware threats faced by small businesses in New Zealand. We use the Protection Motivation Theory of threats and coping appraisals in trying to understand the rationale behind their decision in investing (or not investing). The survey and interviews revealed that the owners-managers underrate the vulnerabilities and the severity of the IT security threats. This is compounded by the fact that most of the sampled small businesses lacked IT strategy and IT culture. It was obvious that the managers were constantly worried about the IT security threats and how best to protect the survival of their businesses. These worries, however, were not compensated by effectively assessing their vulnerabilities and threats to determine the relevant cyber essentials. Most importantly, they failed to view IT security investment as a strategic resource. Also, the surveyed managers did not use any MA tools in making a tactical decision in relation to IT security investment. Instead, their decisions were based on 'rule of thumb,' dictated by what was important at that time. As such, the conceptual framework proposed is aimed to assist managers facing similar issues in making an informed and structured decision in regard to their investment in IT security.

LIMITATIONS AND FUTURE RESEARCH

This study has two limitations. Firstly, the sample consists of a small number of small businesses in New Zealand, which might not be representative of small businesses experiences, awareness, and strategies adopted by other small businesses in New Zealand or other countries in other continents. Future studies might want to explore similar issues in their countries and continents. Secondly, in order to secure participation, the respondents were assured that demographic details would not be collected and analyzed. Therefore, other useful analyses, including their gender and qualifications, could not be inferred.

Future research could further test the applicability of the framework in small businesses in other countries using case study method by conducting interviews with the owner-managers, IT managers, or managers responsible for IT security in the organisations. The interview would provide valuable feedback for the refinement of the framework towards a better strategy in facilitating small business managers in protecting and coping with ever-challenging cyber threats. The findings could provide important insights into the development of survey instrument and hypotheses for large-scale and longitudinal survey research in the future.

A snapshot nature of the study could be replicated on a large-scale nationwide survey, which could be beneficial for the government and relevant for ministerial agencies in introducing specific practical policies in relation to IT security issues. Such efforts would increase awareness among the businesses and the public, especially on the consequences of the attacks on the society and economy of the country.

This research received no specific grant from any funding agency in the public, commercial, or not-for-profit sectors.

REFERENCES

Agyemang, O. S. (2019). Linking personal values to investment decisions among individual shareholders in a developing economy. In *Behavioral finance and decision-making models* (pp. 24–45). IGI Global. doi:10.4018/978-1-5225-7399-9.ch002

Alley, C., & Emery, J. (2017). Taxation of cross-border e-commerce: Response of New Zealand and other OECD countries to BEPS Action 1. *Journal of International Taxation*, *28*(9), 38–45.

Ban, L., & Heng, G. (1995). Computer security issues in small and medium-sized enterprises. *Singapore Management Review*, *17*(1), 15–30.

Barlette, Y., Gundolf, K., & Jaouen, A. (2017). CEOs' information security behavior in SMEs: Does ownership matter? *Systemes D'information Management*, *22*(3), 7–45.

Black, C. (2016). *Ransomware on the rise: An enterprise guide to preventing ransomware attacks*. New York: Carbon Black.

Brooks, W. J., Warren, M. J., & Hutchinson, W. (2002). A security evaluation criteria. *Logistics Information Management*, *15*(5/6), 377–384. doi:10.1108/09576050210447064

Chen, R., Sun, C., Helms, M. M., & Jih, W. (2008). Aligning information technology and business strategy with a dynamic capabilities perspective: A longitudinal study of a Taiwanese semiconductor company. *International Journal of Information Management*, *28*(5), 366–378. doi:10.1016/j.ijinfomgt.2008.01.015

Collins, E., Lawrence, S., Pavlovich, K., & Ryan, C. (2007). Business networks and the uptake of sustainability practices: The case of New Zealand. *Journal of Cleaner Production*, *15*(8–9), 729–740. doi:10.1016/j.jclepro.2006.06.020

Cook, F. (2016). *Ransomware holds world hostage*. Retrieved from https://www.nzherald.co.nz/business/news/article.cfm?c_id=3&objectid=11604911

Drystek, D. (2016). Security awareness: The "people part" of information systems. In M. Behan (Ed.), *Beginner's guide to information security*. San Francisco: Peerlyst.

Elbaz, L. (2016). *Essentials of cybersecurity*. San Francisco: Peerlyst.

Ernst & Young. (2012). *Fighting to close the gap*. Retrieved from https://www.ey.com/Publication/vwLUAssets/GISS2012/$FILE/EY_GISS_2012.pdf

Farlow, M. (2016). *Ransomware: Protect your network*. Graham, NC: Comtech Solution.

Hall, C., & Rusher, K. (2004). Risky lifestyles? Entrepreneurial characteristics of the New Zealand bed and breakfast sector. In R. Thomas (Ed.), *Small forms in tourisms: International perspective* (pp. 83–98). Amsterdam: Elsevier. doi:10.1016/B978-0-08-044132-0.50009-5

Hall, M. (2016). Realising the richness of psychology theory in contingency-based management accounting research. *Management Accounting Research*, *31*, 63–74. doi:10.1016/j.mar.2015.11.002

Han, J., & Tan, H. T. (2009). Investors' reactions to management earnings guidance: The joint effect of investment position, news valence, and guidance form. *Journal of Accounting Research*, *48*(1), 81–104. doi:10.1111/j.1475-679X.2009.00350.x

Harrison, D. A., Mykytyn, P. P. Jr, & Riemenschneider, C. K. (1997). Executive decisions about adoption of information technology in small business: Theory and empirical tests. *Information Systems Research*, *8*(2), 171–195. doi:10.1287/isre.8.2.171

Hedström, K., Kolkowsa, E., Karlsson, F., & Allen, J. P. (2011). Value conflicts for information security management. *The Journal of Strategic Information Systems*, *20*(4), 373–384. doi:10.1016/j.jsis.2011.06.001

Hirsch, B., Reichert, B. E., & Sohn, M. (2017). The impact of clawback provisions on information processing and investment behavior. *Management Accounting Research*, *37*, 1–11. doi:10.1016/j.mar.2016.12.001

Ifinedo, P. (2012). Understanding information systems security policy compliance: An integration of the theory of planned behavior and the protection motivation theory. *Computers & Security*, *31*(1), 83–95. doi:10.1016/j.cose.2011.10.007

Information Commissioner's Office (ICO). (2016). *A practical guide to IT security – ideal for the small business*. Retrieved from https://ico.org.uk/media/for-organisations/documents/1575/it_security_practical_guide.pdf

Islam, A., Tedford, D., & Haemmerle, E. (2017). *Risk determinants of small and medium sized manufacturing enterprises (SMEs) – an empirical investigation in New Zealand*. Retrieved from https://www.anzam.org/wp-content/uploads/pdf-manager/1874_ISLAMMD_235.PDF

Kasanagottu, S., & Bhattacharya, S. (2017). Significant IT adoption factors by small enterprises in the auto ancillary industry. *International Journal of Applied Business and Economic Research*, *15*, 367–379.

Kaspersky. (2016). *IT threat evolution in Q1 2016 report*. San Francisco: Kaspersky Labs.

Kestle, R. (2013). *The role of IS assurance & security management*. Derbyshire: University of Derby.

Kwok, E. (2015). *Understanding the new cyber reality: Information Security Study 2015*. London: Deloitte.

Kwon, J., Ulmer, J. R., & Wang, T. (2012). The association between top management involvement and compensation and information security breaches. *Journal of Information Systems*, *27*(1), 219–236. doi:10.2308/isys-50339

Landers, J. (2016). *Preventing ransomware: Enterprise malware defense – 39 technical and administrative best practices for 2016*. New York: Amazon Digital Services.

Langfield-Smith, K., Thorne, H., Smith, D., & Hilton, R. (2015). *Management accounting: Information for creating and managing value*. McGraw-Hill Education.

Lewis, K. (2008). Small firm owners in New Zealand: In it for the 'good life' or growth? *Small Enterprise Research, 16*(1), 61–69. doi:10.5172er.16.1.61

Lucas, M., Prowle, M., & Lowth, G. (2013). Management accounting practices of (UK) small-medium-sized enterprises (SMEs): Improving SME performance through management accounting education. *Chartered Institute of Management Accountant, 9*(4), 1–14.

Mansfield-Devine, S. (2016). Ransomware: Taking businesses hostage. *Network Security, 10*(10), 8–17. doi:10.1016/S1353-4858(16)30096-4

MBIE. (2015). *Small businesses in New Zealand. How do they compare with larger firms?* Wellington: MBIE.

Meeuwisse, R. (2016). *Cybersecurity: Home and small business.* Hythe: Cyber Simplicity Ltd.

Menard, P., Bott, G. J., & Crossler, R. E. (2017). User motivations in protecting information security: Protection motivation theory versus self-determination theory. *Journal of Management Information Systems, 34*(4), 1203–1230. doi:10.1080/07421222.2017.1394083

Menninger, M. (2016). *Information security for small businesses.* Chicago: Security Elements.

Miller, P., & Power, M. (2013). Accounting, organizing and economizing: Connecting accounting research and organization theory. *The Academy of Management Annals, 7*(1), 557–605. doi:10.5465/19416520.2013.783668

NZentrepreneur. (2017). *Kiwi small-and medium-sized businesses lucrative targets for cybercrime, ransomware.* Retrieved from https://nzentrepreneur.co.nz/kiwi-small-medium-sized-businesses-lucrative-targets-cybercrime-ransomware/

Ortner, J., Velthuis, L., & Wollscheid, D. (2017). Incentive systems for risky investment decisions under unknown preferences. *Management Accounting Research, 36*, 43–50. doi:10.1016/j.mar.2016.09.001

Parker, C., & Castleman, T. (2007). New directions for research on SME-eBusiness: Insights from an analysis of journal articles from 2003–2006. *Journal of Information Systems and Small Business, 1*(1), 21–40.

Pulakanam, V., & Suraweera, T. (2010). Implementing accounting software in small businesses in New Zealand: An exploratory investigation. *Accountancy Business and the Public Interest, 9*, 98–124.

Rogers, R. (1983). Cognitive and physiological processes in fear-based attitude change: A revised theory of protection motivation. In J. Cacioppo & R. Petty (Eds.), *Social psychophysiology: A sourcebook* (pp. 153–176). New York: Guilford Press.

Scott, J. (2016). *The ransomware report.* New York: ICIT.

Soomro, Z. A., Shah, M. H., & Ahmed, J. (2016). Information security management needs more holistic approach: A literature review. *International Journal of Information Management, 36*(2), 215–225. doi:10.1016/j.ijinfomgt.2015.11.009

Su, N., Levina, N., & Ross, J. W. (2016). The long-tail strategy of IT outsourcing. *MIT Sloan Management Review, 57*(2), 81.

United Nations. (2013). *Comprehensive study on cybercrime: Draft*. New York: United Nations.

Vance, A., Lowry, P. B., & Eggett, D. (2013). Using accountability to reduce access policy violations in information systems. *Journal of Management Information Systems*, *29*(4), 263–290. doi:10.2753/MIS0742-1222290410

Veltsos, C. (2016). *Small business cyber security quickstart guide*. New York: Infosec.

Voges, K. E., & Pulakanam, V. (2011). Enabling factors influencing internet adoption by New Zealand small and medium size retail enterprises. *International Review of Business Research Papers*, *7*(1), 106–117.

Watad, M., Washah, S., & Perez, C. (2018). IT security threats and challenges for small firms: Managers' perceptions. *International Journal of the Academic Business World*, *12*(1), 23–29.

Westcott, R., Ronan, K., Bambrick, H., & Taylor, M. (2017). Expanding protection motivation theory: Investigating an application to animal owners and emergency responders in bushfire emergencies. *BMC Psychology*, *5*(1), 13. doi:10.118640359-017-0182-3 PMID:28446229

Whitman, M. E. (2004). In defense of the realm: Understanding the threats to information security. *International Journal of Information Management*, *24*(1), 43–47. doi:10.1016/j.ijinfomgt.2003.12.003

Widener, S. (2006). Human capita, pay structure, and the use of performance measures in bonus compensation. *Management Accounting Research*, *17*(2), 198–221. doi:10.1016/j.mar.2005.06.001

KEY TERMS AND DEFINITIONS

Decision-Making: The process that a small business owner-manager undertakes in making the selection of a course of action available.

Encryption: The process of encoding business files and documents to allow only authorized parties to access.

Investment: The action of investing or allocating business funding.

IT Security: The practice of protecting and securing business information using hardware and software.

Malware: A type of software that can cause damage to business information.

Management Accounting: The process and analysis of information, such as cost, by the owner-manager in considering alternatives to achieve strategic goals.

Small Business: A business with fewer than 20 employees that operates in New Zealand.

Chapter 15
Threat Detection in Cyber Security Using Data Mining and Machine Learning Techniques

Daniel Kobla Gasu

ⓘ https://orcid.org/0000-0002-6208-6095

Department of Computer Science, University of Ghana, Ghana

ABSTRACT

The internet has become an indispensable resource for exchanging information among users, devices, and organizations. However, the use of the internet also exposes these entities to myriad cyber-attacks that may result in devastating outcomes if appropriate measures are not implemented to mitigate the risks. Currently, intrusion detection and threat detection schemes still face a number of challenges including low detection rates, high rates of false alarms, adversarial resilience, and big data issues. This chapter describes a focused literature survey of machine learning (ML) and data mining (DM) methods for cyber analytics in support of intrusion detection and cyber-attack detection. Key literature on ML and DM methods for intrusion detection is described. ML and DM methods and approaches such as support vector machine, random forest, and artificial neural networks, among others, with their variations, are surveyed, compared, and contrasted. Selected papers were indexed, read, and summarized in a tabular format.

INTRODUCTION

Cyber security requirements in organizations have evolved in the last several decades as a consequence of communication networks and information systems having become an essential factor in economic, social development and almost every facet of our daily lives (Singh & Nene, 2013). Security challenges such as intrusion, malware, phishing, misuse of the system, unauthorized modification of information (Vani & Krishnamurthy, 2018) and denial of service attacks pose threats to cyber infrastructure. Moreover, attackers constantly adapt to detection schemes and actively seek to exploit new vulnerabilities. Threats are becoming more advanced with the emergence of Advanced Persistent Threats (APTs), social engi-

DOI: 10.4018/978-1-7998-3149-5.ch015

neering, ransomware, and fraud committed through digital identity theft (Suraj, Kumar Singh, & Tomar, 2018). Hence, for detection schemes to remain relevant they must necessarily deal with the distribution of data changes over time (non-stationarity) (Verma, 2018).

This survey paper focuses on Machine Learning (ML) and Data Mining (DM) techniques for cyber security, particularly intrusion detection. Papers that had more citations were preferred because these described popular techniques. However, it was also recognized that this emphasis might overlook significant new and emerging techniques, so some of these papers were chosen also. Four research questions were posed. These questions were then used to collect the necessary information from papers in the review process. The section below enumerates the review questions.

SRQ1: Which journal is the dominant cyber threat detection journal?

SRQ2. What kind of data mining and machine learning algorithms were used in detecting threats in cyber space?

SRQ3. What kind of datasets were used for training algorithms to detect threats?

SRQ4. What methodology was adopted in conducting the research?

The aforementioned review questions were motivated by the following objectives. They are arranged in the order the review questions are stated.

1. To identify the most important cyber threat detection journal
2. To identify the effectiveness of using data mining and machine learning in cyber security analytics to detect threats to cyber infrastructure
3. To identify whether predictive models are repeatable or not by examining the usage of public datasets.
4. To identify the appropriateness of methodologies used.

This systematic literature review (SLR) is being undertaken to:

*   Systematically review literature on various data mining and machine learning techniques in support of cyber security analytics to detect threats and predict cyber-attacks.
*   Conduct an examination of papers in data mining and machine learning in relation to the various algorithms implemented.
*   Present a clear picture of the current state of research in the field of data mining and machine learning in support of threat detection and intrusion detection.
*   Present a summary of research results and provide pointers to areas and ideas that may be identified as candidates for future research.

This paper is divided into 6 sections. Section two describes the main steps in conducting this review. Background to study and overview of Data Mining and Machine Learning methods for attack/Intrusion detection is presented in Section three. Section four presents the results of the review. Sections 5 discusses the results and section six concludes the paper by providing an outlook on future research.

BACKGROUND

Cyber security are the techniques or processes used to protect networks, devices, programs, and data from attack, damage, or unauthorized accesses (Apurva, Ranakoti, Yadav, Tomer, & Roy, 2018). Cyber security systems are composed of network based defense systems and host based defense systems. Network-based defense systems control network flow by network firewall, spam filter, antivirus, and network intrusion detection system (IDS). Host-based defense systems control upcoming data in a workstation by firewall, antivirus, and intrusion detection system (IDS) installed in hosts (Buczak & Guven, 2016).

ML and DM techniques have aided in the development of predictive models that enable a real-time cyber response after a sequence of cyber security processes. This includes real-time data sampling, selection, analysis and query, and mining peta-scale data to classify and detect attacks and intrusions on a computer network (Dua & Xian, 2011). DM is the extraction, or "mining," of knowledge from a large amount of data.

ML involves the processes of building a scientific model after discovering knowledge from sample data set or data sets (Dua & Xian, 2011). ML/DM algorithms are broadly categorized as: supervised, and unsupervised, (Buczak & Guven, 2016).

In supervised ML, data sets containing a collection of data instances each of which can be described using a set of attributes (features) and the associated labels are given to train a function (Rokach & Maimon, 2010), and a learning model is trained such that the output of the function can be predicted. Supervised learning algorithms include artificial neural network (ANN), support vector machine (SVM), and decision trees (DT).

On the other hand, no target or label is given in sample data in unsupervised ML implementations (Dua & Xian, 2011). They are designed to summarize the key features of the data and to form the natural clusters of input patterns. Moreover unsupervised ML is difficult to evaluate, because it does not have an explicit teacher and, thus, does not have labeled data for testing. Examples of unsupervised ML methods include k-means clustering, hierarchical clustering, and self-organization map

Several reviews and surveys have been carried out in related domains, Buczak and Guven (2016), presented a focused review of ML and DM methods employed in cyber security for intrusion detection. The paper included a short tutorial and description of each ML and DM method. Salo, Injadat, Nassif, Shami, and Essex (2018) presented an analysis based on the strengths and weaknesses of 19 selected DM techniques for intrusion detection.

Ahmed, Naser Mahmood, and Hu (2016) on the other hand focused on an in-depth analysis of four major categories of anomaly detection techniques which include classification, statistical, information theory and clustering. Challenges with the datasets used for network intrusion detection was also discussed. Makani and Reddy (2018) also presents detailed taxonomy of machine-learning-based- anomaly detection methods and its suitability and applicability for application in Mobile Adhoc Networks (MANETS).

Aburomman and Reaz (2017) presented an overview of various ensemble and hybrid intrusion classification techniques considering both homogeneous and heterogeneous types of methods. It was noted that the generalization ability of a multi-classifier system is usually better than a single classifier. Folino and Sabatino (2016) focused on ensemble-based algorithms in support of data mining techniques that can be implemented in a parallel/distributed environments. A discussion on supervised data mining algorithms, anomaly detection and, in particular clustering for data streams in real-time was also presented.

Ariyaluran Habeeb et al (2019) focused on anomaly detection methods and real time big data processing technologies for intrusion detection for IoT domain. Moustafa, Hu, and Slay (2019) presented a description of various anomaly based Decision Engine (DE) approaches, including ensemble learning and deep learning methods.

Mahdavifar and Ghorbani (2019) discussed Deep Learning (DL) approaches for intrusion detection, malware detection, phishing/spam detection, and website defacement detection. An elaboration on four major modules including analysis, feature extraction, preprocessing, and DL-based classifiers was presented. It was noted that DL is highly recommended to use in domains where large quantities of raw data is generated, alleviating the burden of heavy pre-processing of the input data.

The purpose of this paper is to review literature for a comprehensive overview of current trends and state of the arts Machine Learning and Data Mining applications in Cyber security and in particular, threat/intrusion detection. Thus, emphasis is placed on description of the ML/DM methods of each paper included in this review and summarized in a table.

REVIEW PROCESS

The phases of the study adapted the guidelines of Kitchenham (Kitchenham, 2004). Firstly, the study was planned, thus, the need for the literature review was established as well as initial review protocol developed. Secondly, literature review was conducted. Finally, the results were summarized in a table and discussed in this paper. The following section presents the detail steps followed in conducting the review. Figure 1 shows the Preferred reporting items for systematic reviews and meta-analyses (PRISMA) flow diagram for this review (Moher, Liberati, Tetzlaff, & Altman, 2009).

ELIGIBILITY CRITERIA

Primary studies covering data mining and machine learning in cyber security in support of intrusion detection were identified. The primary studies were searched from three established databases containing scientific publications. Meta data of found papers were downloaded in a "comma separated value" files for filtering. In order to find relevant literature, we utilized the following inclusion and exclusion criteria in selecting primary studies

For inclusion, the accepted literature must meet the following requirements

- Publications that report on the use of Data Mining and Machine learning in cyber security to detect threats, intrusion or predict cyber-attack.
- Papers that cover the use of cyber analytics, machine learning and data mining in support of detecting threats or predicting cyber-attacks.
- Date of publication should be between January 2015 and September 2019 in order to be included.
- Should have been cited at least two times every year since the year of public, thus a minimum of 2 if published in 2019, 4 if published in 2018, 6 if published in 2017, 8 if published in 2016 and 10 if published in 2015.
- Papers should be published in English Language.

Figure 1. PRISMA flow diagram: adapted from PRISMA statement

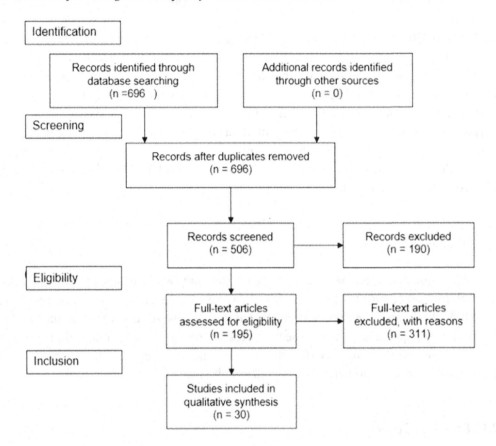

For exclusion, the following criteria will be used

- Publications will be excluded if their main focus is not on the use of Data Mining and Machine learning in cyber security to detect threats or predict cyber attack
- Papers that just propose an approach or describe the use of use of Data Mining and Machine learning in cyber security – (with no 'actual implementation' component) shall be excluded.
- Papers and reports will be excluded where only the abstract, but not the full text, is available.
- Letters, editorials and position papers will all be excluded.

The process of including and excluding papers is as follows. Firstly, inclusion and exclusion criteria were applied to papers based on their title and abstract. Thereafter, duplicates were removed with the aid of Mendely as well as manually. Selected papers were then downloaded and read, and the inclusion and exclusion criteria applied based on paper content (mainly introduction and conclusion).

IDENTIFICATION OF SEARCH

The literature search considered only journal articles. Although the discussed subject are studied in the field of cyber security, the topics are often addressed in journals on computer networks and communications. Due to the specific nature of this work, journals dedicated to formal methods in computer science, such as expert systems and their applications, were survey for this paper.

Table 1 identifies the number of results returned as well corresponding databases when the search string ("Intrusion detection" OR "cyber security") AND ("data mining" OR "Machine learning") was run on each of the databases.

Table 1. Databases

Database	Number of Articles
ACM Digital Library	86
IEEE Explore	16
Scopus	594

RESULTS

This section provides answers to research questions posed. Appendix 1 shows a summary of each paper used in this review. A total of 30 relevant journal articles were selected to become the primary reference in completing the Systematic Literature Review.

Articles used in this paper were published between the year 2015 and 2019. 91% were indexed in Scopus, 7% in ACMDL and 2% from IEEE. Figure 2 shows the distribution of papers from the 3 databases used. It is intuitive to note that Scopus indexes papers from the other data bases and hence it has the highest number of papers among the three data bases. Even though Scopus has the highest number of papers, most were actually published by IEEE and other data bases.

Data Mining and Machine Learning Algorithms Used in Detecting Threats in Cyber Space

Several ML and DM algorithms are popular in the research community and used extensively in the area of cyber security. These techniques have been applied to intrusion detection with the hope of improving detection rates and adaptability but most suffer a lot of setbacks including dependency on domain knowledge, insufficient learning capability with big data, and lack of modularity and transferability (Z. Wang, 2018). Figure 3 shows the distribution of implemented algorithms in primary sources reviewed in this paper.

Support Vector Machine algorithms constitutes the highest implementations with a value of 15%, it is then followed by random forest with a value of 11% of the distribution. Third highest algorithm implementation with a value of 8.3% is Extreme Learning Machine. 6.7% each was observed for K-Nearest Neighbor and Decision tree with 5.0% each for K-means clustering and Naïve Bayes. The rest of the algorithms had values less than 4%, thus, between 3.3% and 1.7%.

Figure 2. Number of papers per database

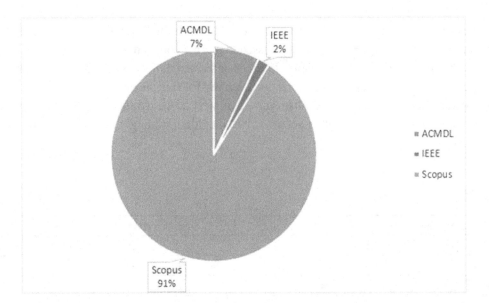

These algorithms are usually implemented together with one or two other algorithms in order to harness the combined advantages. Da Costa et al. (2019) noted, whereas some techniques can achieve high accuracy, in contrast, the training time and classification overhead increases. On the other hand, some techniques behave in the reverse, i.e., the accuracy is stabilized, but at the price of a high computational burden for training and testing.

SVM based classifier was implemented with a modified K-means clustering employed for feature reduction, (Al-Yaseen, Othman, & Nazri, 2017). Gauthama Raman, Somu, Kirthivasan, Liscano, and Shankar Sriram (2017) also implemented SVM based classifier, with Hypergraph based Genetic algorithm for feature selection. Ahmad, Basheri, Iqbal, and Rahim (2018) implemented all top 3 algorithms and compared them for performance of which ELM was found to be superior in accuracy. It was observed from the results that, SVM, RF and ELM techniques require data pre-processing and feature selection to improve the classification (Aloqaily et al., 2019).

On the other hand (J. Li, Zhao, & Li, 2018) implemented RF for feature selection with K-means and AdaBoost for classification. ELM's have also been implemented either alone for classification, in (Kozik, Choraś, Ficco, & Palmieri, 2018) or in conjunction with other techniques for feature selection, in (C. R. Wang, Xu, Lee, & Lee, 2018).

Distribution of Data Set

Figure 4 shows the distribution of data sets used in training algorithms. NSL KDD is the most used data set with of a percentage score 22.7%. This is then followed closely by KDDCup 99 data sets with a value of 20.5%. Unknown data set follows with a value of 15.9%. Kyoto 2006+ data set has usage percentage of 6.8%, UNB ISCX and UNSW NB15 with 4.5% each. The remaining public data sets have not seen much usage with their values at 2.3% each.

Figure 3. Distribution of ML/DM algorithms implemented

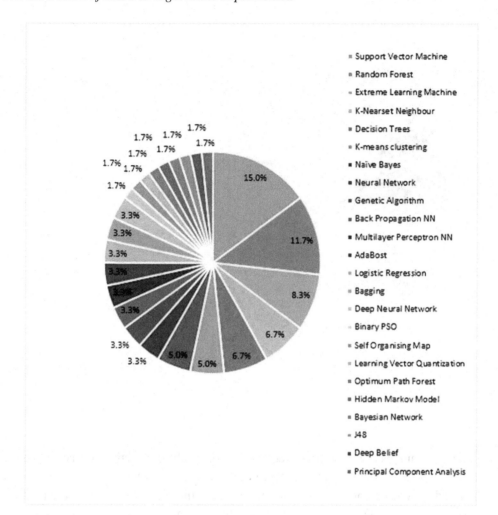

Methodology Used in Research

Research conducted to build efficient models for cyber threat and intrusion detection emphasizes two essential characteristics. The first is concerned with finding optimal feature subset and secondly employing robust classification schemes (Siddique, Akhtar, Lee, Kim, & Kim, 2017). Feature selection techniques are employed to reduce the data dimensionality, speed-up the classification process, reduce storage capacity, and improve data quality for classification (Aloqaily, Otoum, Ridhawi, & Jararweh, 2019).

Approaches adopted for feature selection include filter methods, wrapper methods, and embedded methods. In the filter based techniques, features are ranked based on how salient they are in helping the algorithm distinguish the normal traffic from the attack traffic (Zolanvari, Teixeira, Gupta, Khan, & Jain, 2019). Wrapper methods conduct a search for optimal subset of features using the learning algorithm itself as part of the evaluation function whereas embedded techniques perform feature selection as part of the learning process and are usually specific to given learning model (Cohen, Nissim, & Elovici, 2018)

Figure 4. Distribution of data set

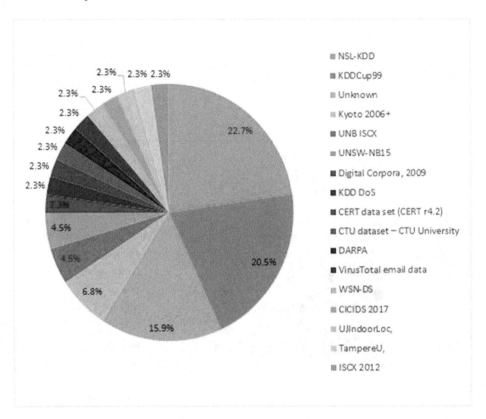

Classification techniques are then employed after feature subset selection to discriminate between the normal and malicious traffic patterns (Gauthama Raman et al., 2017). Learning models are validated using benchmark data sets. Performance metrics employed in the evaluation of learning models include optimal feature subset, classifier accuracy, detection rate, runtime analysis, and false alarm rate.

SOLUTIONS AND RECOMMENDATIONS

In the subsections above, results to review questions were presented as is. The goal in this section is to discuss the results in the context of RQ2, RQ3, and RQ4 posed. Results presented by figure 2 to RQ1 indicates that more relevant papers on machine learning and data mining applications in cyber security was found in Scopus database.

Figure 3 shows the distribution of implemented Machine leaning and Data Mining algorithms in the selected review papers. SVM has the highest implementations with a value of 15%. However, most of the selected papers implement SVM with one or two other algorithms depending on the objectives of the research. Thus there seem to be no single algorithmic solution to the application of machine learning and data mining to cyber security challenges.

In (Gauthama Raman, Somu, Kirthivasan, Liscano, & Shankar Sriram, 2017), Classifiers trained with feature subset obtained from feature selection technique show that HG –GA SVM perform better than the existing techniques with respect to various performance metrics (Classification accuracy, Detection rate, False alarm rate and Runtime analysis). It concluded that SVM technique achieves improved classification accuracy (approx. 2%).

Random Forest and Extreme Learning Machine follows SVM as the next most implemented ML/DM algorithms (11.7% and 8.3% respectively) in cyber security applications. In (Domb, Bonchek-Dokow, & Leshem, 2017), Excel with its machine learning add-on, was used as a platform for rule extraction and Random Forest Algorithm for rule execution. ELM outperforms other methods, such as ANN, in classifying attacks under the Probe category. However, its performance in terms of classifying attacks falling under other categories is poor. A combination of SVM and ELM can improve attack-detection performance(Al-Yaseen et al., 2017).

Closely following ELM is KNN and Decision Tree algorithms with values of 6.7% each. The KNN algorithm classifies objects based on the closest training examples in the feature space. That is, an object is classified in terms of its distances to the nearest cluster (W. Li, Meng, Kwok, & IP, 2017). Classification algorithms compared for performance; K- nearest neighbor (KNN), Back propagation neural networks (BPNN) and Decision tree (DT) revealed that KNN can achieve a better performance than the other two classifiers (i.e., higher accuracy and lower time consumption)(W. Li et al., 2017).

Decision Trees are rule-based learning methods that creates a classification model, to predict the value of a target variable by learning simple decision rules inferred from the data features (Zhang, Gardner, & Vukotic, 2019). In (Aloqaily et al., 2019), where Deep Believe Network was employed for feature selection and Decision Tree for classification, an overall accuracy of 99.43% with 99.92% detection rate were achieved. A false positive rate of 0.96% and a false negative rate of 1.53% were observed. This results shows the effectiveness of Decision Tree in real cyber-security attack scenarios.

The remaining algorithms surveyed in this paper had values between 5% and 1.5%, implying that these algorithms have not seen much implementations in the past 5 years. The reason for this is that, most systems built based on such techniques suffer from the dependency on domain knowledge, insufficient learning capability with big data, and lack of modularity and transferability (Z. Wang, 2018).

CONCLUSION AND FUTURE RESEARCH DIRECTION

This paper presented a literature review of Data Mining and Machine Learning methods for cyber threat detection and intrusion detection. The paper, which has mostly focused on the last five years, surveys the latest applications of ML and DL in the field of intrusion detection. Unfortunately, the most effective method of intrusion detection has not yet been established.

Each approach to implementing an intrusion detection system has its own advantages and disadvantages, a point apparent from the results of various algorithms implemented. Thus, it is difficult to choose a particular method to implement a cyber-attack prediction or intrusion detection system over the others. The particular method to choose largely depends on the nature of the environment and objectives to be achieved. Whereas some techniques can achieve high accuracy, in contrast, the training time and classification overhead increases. On the other hand, some techniques have the accuracy is stabilized, but at the price of a high computational burden for training and testing

Datasets for network intrusion detection are very important for training and testing modules. However, there are many problems with the existing public dataset, such as imbalanced data and outdated attack content. Tope benchmark data sets that are publicly available includes KDDCup99, NSL-KDD, Kyoto 2006+ and UND-ISCX

Network information update very fast, which brings to the DM and ML models training and use with difficulty. Models need to be retrained long-term and quickly, hence incremental learning and lifelong learning is a promising area in the study of this field in the future. Also Big data capabilities will be required in managing the exponential growth in data for cyber-attack prediction and intrusion detection. Thus, techniques that perform better with fast growing and large of data sets will be good candidate further research. Further, since research in the area of IDS has focused on improving accuracy and efficiency, finding the intrinsic characteristics that relates features and classification in order to determine the best combination of learning approaches is key.

REFERENCES

Aburomman, A. A., & Reaz, M. B. I. (2017). A survey of intrusion detection systems based on ensemble and hybrid classifiers. *Computers & Security*, *65*, 135–152. doi:10.1016/j.cose.2016.11.004

Ahmad, I., Basheri, M., Iqbal, M. J., & Rahim, A. (2018). Performance Comparison of Support Vector Machine, Random Forest, and Extreme Learning Machine for Intrusion Detection. *IEEE Access: Practical Innovations, Open Solutions*, *6*, 33789–33795. doi:10.1109/ACCESS.2018.2841987

Ahmed, M., Naser Mahmood, A., & Hu, J. (2016). A survey of network anomaly detection techniques. *Journal of Network and Computer Applications*, *60*, 19–31. doi:10.1016/j.jnca.2015.11.016

Al-Yaseen, W. L., Othman, Z. A., & Nazri, M. Z. A. (2017). Multi-level hybrid support vector machine and extreme learning machine based on modified K-means for intrusion detection system. *Expert Systems with Applications*, *67*, 296–303. doi:10.1016/j.eswa.2016.09.041

Aloqaily, M., Otoum, S., Al Ridhawi, I., & Jararweh, Y. (2019). An intrusion detection system for connected vehicles in smart cities. *Ad Hoc Networks*, *90*, 101842. doi:10.1016/j.adhoc.2019.02.001

Apurva, A., Ranakoti, P., Yadav, S., Tomer, S., & Roy, N. R. (2018). Redefining cyber security with big data analytics. *2017 International Conference on Computing and Communication Technologies for Smart Nation, IC3TSN 2017,* 199–203.

Ariyaluran Habeeb, R. A., Nasaruddin, F., Gani, A., Targio Hashem, I. A., Ahmed, E., & Imran, M. (2019). Real-time big data processing for anomaly detection: A Survey. *International Journal of Information Management*, *45*, 289–307.

Buczak, A. L., & Guven, E. (2016). A Survey of Data Mining and Machine Learning Methods for Cyber Security Intrusion Detection. *IEEE Communications Surveys and Tutorials*, *18*(2), 1153–1176. doi:10.1109/COMST.2015.2494502

Cohen, A., Nissim, N., & Elovici, Y. (2018). Novel set of general descriptive features for enhanced detection of malicious emails using machine learning methods. *Expert Systems with Applications*, *110*, 143–169. doi:10.1016/j.eswa.2018.05.031

da Costa, K. A. P., Papa, J. P., Lisboa, C. O., Munoz, R., & de Albuquerque, V. H. C. (2019). Internet of Things: A survey on machine learning-based intrusion detection approaches. *Computer Networks*, *151*, 147–157. doi:10.1016/j.comnet.2019.01.023

Domb, M., Bonchek-Dokow, E., & Leshem, G. (2017). Lightweight adaptive Random-Forest for IoT rule generation and execution. *Journal of Information Security and Applications*.

Dua, S., & Xian, D. (2011). Data Mining and Machine Learning in Cybersecurity. Auerbach Publications.

Folino, G., & Sabatino, P. (2016). Ensemble based collaborative and distributed intrusion detection systems: A survey. *Journal of Network and Computer Applications*, *66*, 1–16. doi:10.1016/j.jnca.2016.03.011

Gauthama Raman, M. R., Somu, N., Kirthivasan, K., Liscano, R., & Shankar Sriram, V. S. (2017). An efficient intrusion detection system based on hypergraph - Genetic algorithm for parameter optimization and feature selection in support vector machine. *Knowledge-Based Systems*, *134*, 1–12. doi:10.1016/j.knosys.2017.07.005

Kitchenham, B. (2004). *Procedures for performing systematic reviews.* Keele University, UK and National ICT Australia.

Kozik, R., Choraś, M., Ficco, M., & Palmieri, F. (2018). A scalable distributed machine learning approach for attack detection in edge computing environments. *Journal of Parallel and Distributed Computing*, *119*, 18–26. doi:10.1016/j.jpdc.2018.03.006

Li, J., Zhao, Z., & Li, R. (2018). Machine learning-based IDS for softwaredefined 5G network. *IET Networks*, *7*(2), 53–60. doi:10.1049/iet-net.2017.0212

Li, W., Meng, W., Kwok, L. F., & Ip, H. H. S. (2016, June). Enhancing collaborative intrusion detection networks against insider attacks using supervised intrusion sensitivity-based trust management model. *Journal of Network and Computer Applications*, *77*, 135–145. doi:10.1016/j.jnca.2016.09.014

Mahdavifar, S., & Ghorbani, A. A. (2019). Application of deep learning to cybersecurity: A survey. *Neurocomputing*, *347*, 149–176. doi:10.1016/j.neucom.2019.02.056

Makani, R., & Reddy, B. V. R. (2018). Taxonomy of Machine Leaning Based Anomaly Detection and its suitability. *Procedia Computer Science*, *132*, 1842–1849. doi:10.1016/j.procs.2018.05.133

Moher, D., Liberati, A., Tetzlaff, J., & Altman, D. G. (2009). Preferred reporting items for systematic reviews and meta-analyses: The PRISMA statement. *BMJ (Clinical Research Ed.)*, 339. PMID:19622551

Moustafa, N., Hu, J., & Slay, J. (2019). A holistic review of Network Anomaly Detection Systems: A comprehensive survey. *Journal of Network and Computer Applications, 128*, 33–55.

Rokach, L., & Maimon, O. (2010). *Data Mining and Knowledge Discovery Handbook*. Boston, MA: Springer.

Salo, F., Injadat, M., Nassif, A. B., Shami, A., & Essex, A. (2018). Data mining techniques in intrusion detection systems: A systematic literature review. *IEEE Access: Practical Innovations, Open Solutions*, *6*, 56046–56058. doi:10.1109/ACCESS.2018.2872784

Singh, J., & Nene, M. J. (2013). A Survey on Machine Learning Techniques for Intrusion Detection Systems. *International Journal of Advanced Research in Computer and Communication Engineering*, *2*(11), 4349–4355.

Suraj, M. V., Kumar Singh, N., & Tomar, D. S. (2018). Big data Analytics of cyber attacks: A review. *2018 IEEE International Conference on System, Computation, Automation and Networking, ICSCA 2018*, 1–7. 10.1109/ICSCAN.2018.8541263

Vani, Y. S. K., & Krishnamurthy. (2018). Survey: Anomaly detection in network using big data analytics. *2017 International Conference on Energy, Communication, Data Analytics and Soft Computing, ICECDS 2017*, 3366–3369.

Verma, R. (2018). Security analytics: Adapting data science for security challenges. *IWSPA 2018 - Proceedings of the 4th ACM International Workshop on Security and Privacy Analytics, Co-Located with CODASPY 2018*, 40–41.

Wang, C. R., Xu, R. F., Lee, S. J., & Lee, C. H. (2018). Network intrusion detection using equality constrained-optimization-based extreme learning machines. *Knowledge-Based Systems*, *147*, 68–80. doi:10.1016/j.knosys.2018.02.015

Wang, Z. (2018). Deep Learning-Based Intrusion Detection with Adversaries. *IEEE Access: Practical Innovations, Open Solutions*. doi:10.1109/ACCESS.2018.2854599

Zhang, J., Gardner, R., & Vukotic, I. (2019). Anomaly detection in wide area network meshes using two machine learning algorithms. *Future Generation Computer Systems*, *93*, 418–426. doi:10.1016/j.future.2018.07.023

Zolanvari, M., Teixeira, M. A., Gupta, L., Khan, K. M., & Jain, R. (2019). *Machine Learning-Based Network Vulnerability Analysis of Industrial Internet of Things. IEEE Internet of Things Journal.* doi:10.1109/JIOT.2019.2912022

KEY TERMS AND DEFINITIONS

Anomaly: An occurrence of a point in the feature space that is considered to be an outlier from the region of normal behaviour.

Classification: The process by which an algorithm/model segregates the feature space into different classes.

Cyber Security: The set of technologies, tools, and processes designed to preserve the integrity, confidentiality, and availability of the cyber infrastructure.

Data Mining: The application of specific algorithms for extracting useful patterns from data for insight.

Detection Accuracy: The exactness with which a detection model is able to detect malicious traffic.

False Alarm Rate: The rate at which normal traffic is misclassified as being malicious.

Feature Selection: The process of selecting feature set that will reduce dimensionality, speed up classification and improve detection rate.

Intrusion Detection: The classification and response to attacks or violations of the security policies automatically, at network and host levels, in cyber infrastructure in a manner to preserve the Integrity, Confidentiality and availability of the infrastructure.

Machine Learning: The field of study that is concerned with given computers the ability to learn from their experience and environment without being explicitly programmed.

Threat: Any entity that can exploit a vulnerability to cause harm to cyber infrastructure.

APPENDIX

Table 2. Summary of data extraction using review questions

No.	Authors	Topic Area/Theme/Sub Theme	Journal/ Algorithm/ Data set (RQ1/RQ2/RQ3)	RQ4 - Methodology Used	Findings/Recommendation
1	Malik A.J., Shahzad W., Khan F.A. (2015)	Network intrusion detection using hybrid binary PSO and random forests algorithm	John Wiley and Sons Inc. -Security and Communication Networks Binary PSO, random forests KDDCup99	A hybrid methodology, PSO-RF, based on PSO and RF. algorithms to select and optimize features simultaneously. RF classifier is used to train the model. The module is validated using KDD99Cup data set	Average IDR and FPR is better than all the other classifiers used. RF algorithm achieved less FPR as compared with all other classifiers, thus PSO-RF selects most appropriate attributes. PSO-RF can be extended to deal with many objectives simultaneously and also many more parameters in PSO can be fine-tuned to obtain more refined results
2	Jankowski D., Amanowicz M. (2016)	On Efficiency of Selected Machine Learning Algorithms for Intrusion Detection in Software Defined Networks	IEEE Systems Self-Organizing Maps and Learning Vector Quantization Unknown - SDN network traffic	Parameters and statistics, extracted from the SDN flows Create tuples of features for classification by Machine Learning Algorithm	Hierarchical LVQ1 selects most appropriate features. Future research should focus on improving of features generation and on applicability of other statistical techniques for detection and classification of malware traffic
3	Leu F.-Y., Tsai K.-L., Hsiao Y.-T., Yang C.-T. (2017)	An internal intrusion detection and protection system by using data mining and forensic techniques	Institute of Electrical and Electronics Engineers Inc. Supervised machine learning algorithm implementation in the data Analyzer Unknown	A divide and conquer approach Labelled training data set is used to train the classifier. The classifier is then applied to the unlabeled data set to obtain a membership vector categorized into low, medium and high fuzziness groups. The low and high fuzziness data set are extracted and incorporated into the training data set. The classifier is then trained with the updated training data set.	Average detection accuracy is higher than 94% when the decisive rate threshold is 0.9, indicating that the IIDPS can assist system administrators to point out an insider or an attacker in a closed environment. The further study will be done by improving IIDPS's performance and investigating third-party shell commands
4	Ashfaq R.A.R., Wang X.-Z., Huang J.Z., Abbas H., He Y.-L. (2017)	Fuzziness based semi-supervised learning approach for intrusion detection system	Elsevier Inc. - Information Sciences Neural Network with Random Weight NSL-KDD	Symbolic attributes of the data set is converted to numeric codes. K-means is applied to 10% training data set in feature reduction SVM and ELM are trained with the training data set. The model is evaluated using NSL-KDD data set.	Methodology effectively improves classification accuracy when training is done using NNR w to get the fuzzy vector output and perform the sample categorization on unlabeled samples according to their fuzziness quantity. Future research will be focused on applying this strategy to improve the effectiveness of IDSs for detecting multiple types of attacks
5	Al-Yaseen W.L., Othman Z.A., Nazri M.Z.A. (2017)	Multi-level hybrid support vector machine and extreme learning machine based on modified K-means for intrusion detection system	Elsevier Ltd- Expert Systems With Applications Support vector machine, extreme learning machine, and K-means Classifier KDD Cup99	Hybrid intrusion detection model using SVM and ELM with K-means for feature reduction	Achieves accuracy of up to 95.75% False alarm rate is 1.87%. Detection rate of novel attacks, reaching 40.02%. Construct a more effective model based on efficient classifiers. Exploit the characteristics of multi-agent system to speed up data analysis and facilitate model retraining on new attacks to increase the efficiency of the system
6	Bostani H., Sheikhan M. (2017)	Modification of supervised OPF-based intrusion detection systems using unsupervised learning and social network concept	Elsevier Ltd- Pattern Recognition Modified Optimum-path forest (OPF), k-means clustering NSL-KDD	Data set are normalized using feature scaling to resolve data imbalance. K-means clustering is employed to partition data set Pruning is carried out on each training set to select the most informative samples.	Accuracy rate of MOPF was improved by 14.86%. The training time of MOPF was about 6.9 times less than OPF The total time for training and testing was about 1.5 times lower than the traditional OPF. The DR and FAR of MOPF improved by 5.9% and 2.75%. The DR of low-frequent at tacks, such as U2R and R2L, was improved The CPE of MOPF was about 2.6 times less than the traditional OPF

continued on following page

Table 2. Continued

No.	Authors	Topic Area/Theme/Sub Theme	Journal/ Algorithm/ Data set (RQ1/RQ2/ RQ3)	RQ4 - Methodology Used	Findings/Recommendation
7	Gauthama Raman M.R., Somu N., Kirthivasan K., Liscano R., Shankar Sriram V.S. (2017)	An efficient intrusion detection system based on hypergraph - Genetic algorithm for parameter optimization and feature selection in support vector machine	Elsevier B.V. - Knowledge-Based Systems Hypergraph based Genetic Algorithm (HG - GA), Support Vector Machine (SVM) UNB ISCX NSL - KDD	The fitness function (HG –GA) is used to dynamically adjust kernel parameters and feature subset for SVM. Training and testing data was generated from the input data split by a ratio of 80: 20. The performance of SVM is evaluated using Testing Data based on the fitness function (number of features, detection rate, and false alarm rate). The model was evaluated using the NSL-KDD	Results obtained experimentations carried out under two scenarios (i) Classifiers trained with all features and (ii) Classifiers trained with feature subset obtained from feature selection technique show that HG –GA SVM perform better than the existing techniques with respect to various performance metrics. HG –GA was found to be scalable, adaptive and robust. HG GA –SVM technique achieves improved classification accuracy (approx. 2%), when trained with the optimal feature subset
8	Li W., Meng W., Kwok L.-F., IP H.H.S. (2017)	Enhancing collaborative intrusion detection networks against insider attacks using supervised intrusion sensitivity-based trust management model	Academic Press- Journal of Network and Computer Applications K- Nearest Neighbor, Back propagation neural networks and Decision tree. Unknown	Label data by experts in data labeling and verification of training data set. Labelled data set is then used to train each classifier New data from newly joined nodes is input and the classifier assigns the values of intrusion sensitivity to each node based on the pre-built model. The model is evaluated by sending out a set of alarms for ranking classification over a 10 level band. Comparison of the classifiers are done based on classification accuracy and time consumption.	Intrusion sensitivity enhances the impact of expert nodes on trust evaluation, while packets-based trust improves the sensitivity of proposed model to traffic betrayal. Validate model with more complex and sophisticated attacks other classifiers including supervised and semi-supervised learning algorithms can be considered to validate results Semi-supervised learning could be considered by leveraging both labeled and unlabeled data items
9	Domb M., Bonchek-Dokow E., Leshem G. (2017)	Lightweight adaptive Random-Forest for IoT rule generation and execution	Elsevier Ltd - Journal of Information Security and Applications Random- Forest Unknown	A balanced model using simple rules for basic type while compound and multi-stage rules use machine learning method. Rules are extracted from training data collected from sensors using "IF THEN ELSE" form. Random forest algorithm is used to build multi-staged rule by training the model with the training data set. Simulations were done using a set of pre-classified 3350 samples data set with 95 attributes each, and a set of 500 unclassified/ anonymous records.	Demonstrated the ability to build a lightweight, simple and handy framework for extracting security rules given a sizable training data For future work, further exploration of the optimized machine learning technology
10	Siddique K., Akhtar Z., Lee H.-G., Kim W., Kim Y. (2017)	Toward bulk synchronous parallel-based machine learning techniques for anomaly detection in high-speed big data networks	MDPI AG Feature selection and classification using machine learning algorithms ISCX-UNB	Feature selection Classification apply Big data tools Validate performance with contemporary data sets	Vital characteristics of anomaly detection system. Feature selection Employment of classification schemes. Utilizing specialized big data computing engines Conduct performance evaluations of the proposed systems. Future research will focus on devising more novel NIDSs techniques using deep learning methods.
11	Ahmad I., Basheri M., Iqbal M.J., Rahim A. (2018)	Performance Comparison of Support Vector Machine, Random Forest, and Extreme Learning Machine for Intrusion Detection	Institute of Electrical and Electronics Engineers Inc. Support vector machine, random forest (RF), and extreme learning machine NSL-KDD	**Preprocessing** of data is done to eliminate or replace symbolic or non-numeric features in the data set. **Classification** of data: Done to categories features as normal or intrusive **Evaluation** of the design based on NSL-KDD	ELM outperforms other approaches in accuracy, precision when used to analyze huge data sets. SVM indicated better results in smaller data sets. In future, ELM will be explored further to investigate its performance in feature selection and feature transformation techniques
12	Muller S., Lancrenon J., Harpes C., Le Traon Y., Gombault S., Bonnin J.M. (2018)	A training-resistant anomaly detection system	Elsevier Ltd- Computers and Security NSL-KDD Digital Corpora, 2009	Threshold strategy where a fix threshold for the monitored quantities is determined in advance. Stream clustering based aimed at learning the different behavioral classes: from a sequence of data points, they group similar (or close) ones together into a cluster	A more stable behaviour with respect to statistical noise Resistant to training attack by considering input at multiple time resolutions, which considerably hardens long-term changes in the behaviour. For future research, the model should be validated with possible tricking techniques, and explore further opportunities for attackers to evade the IDS.

continued on following page

Table 2. Continued

No.	Authors	Topic Area/Theme/Sub Theme	Journal/ Algorithm/ Data set (RQ1/RQ2/RQ3)	RQ4 - Methodology Used	Findings/Recommendation
13	Wang Z. (2018)	Deep Learning-Based Intrusion Detection with Adversaries	Institute of Electrical and Electronics Engineers Inc. Multilayer perceptions (MLPs), Fast Gradient Sign Method, Jacobian-Based NSL-KDD	Data set was split in two, 90% for training data set and 10% as validation set. The models and attack algorithms were implemented using TensorFlow. Training data is fed into Deep Neural Network, then the trained neural network is used as the target of attacks as well as baseline for evaluation of algorithms. The four attack algorithms are used to generate the adversarial examples from the test dataset based on the deep neural networks	An adversary has limited resources and capability to manipulate features therefore altering a large set of features is less practical for an adversary in most cases. JSMA attacks tend to be more attractive for an adversary in terms of usability and applicability as attacks tend to use a limited set of features. The most commonly used features indicate they contribute more to the vulnerability of the deep learning based intrusion detection and therefore they deserve more attention and better protection in the detection and defense efforts. Future work will focus on the transferability of adversarial examples in deep learning based intrusion detection
14	Wang C.-R., Xu R.-F., Lee S.-J., Lee C.-H. (2018)	Network intrusion detection using equality constrained-optimization-based extreme learning machines	Elsevier B.V. – Knowledge-based systems equality constrained-optimization-based ELM (C-ELM) and Least squares support vector ma- chines (LS-SVMs) KDD Cup 99, KDD DoS, NSL KDD, UNSW-NB15	Incremental learning is adopted to compute the output weight of hidden neurons. This approach is used to construct the C-ELM and checked against a pre-specified goal iteratively until the number of hidden neurons in C-ELM matches the goal. A simplified error model is used in each step to help determining an increment of nodes until the desired number of hidden nodes is reached. The final output weights are obtained and the construction of the optimal C-ELM is completed. 10-fold cross-validation is adopted to measure the performance of the classifier.	Experimental results show that the proposed approach is effective in building models with good attack detection rates and fast learning speed. It was also shown that even the attack instances in the minority are not ignored and are well detected.
15	Othman S.M., Ba-Alwi F.M., Alsohybe N.T., Al-Hashida A.Y. (2018)	Intrusion detection model using machine learning algorithm on Big Data environment	Journal of Big Data Spark-Chi-Support Vector Machine for classification KD Cup 99	Preprocessing is done to convert categorical data to numerical. The dimensionality of the data set is reduced by applying ChiSqSelector SVM algorithm (Spark-Chi-SVM) is used for data classification for detection. The model is then tested and validated using KDD Cup 99 Data set.	Experimental results showed that the Spark-Chi-SVM model for intrusion detection out performs other methods such as SVM only and Logistic regression in terms of prediction and time and classification accuracy.
16	Hoang X.D., Nguyen Q.C. (2018)	Botnet detection based on machine learning techniques using DNS query data	MDPI AG – Future Internet KNN, decision trees, random forest and Naïve Bayes Extracted and labeled DNS Query datasets	DNS query data is collected and domain names extracted. The set of domain names is pre-processed to extract the features for the training. KNN, decision trees, random forest and Naïve Bayes algorithms are trained using 3 different training data set (T1, T2, T3) and evaluated and compared for performance using a TESTING data set.	Experimental results show that random forest algorithm gives the best results with the overall classification accuracy of 90.80% whereas others achieved the overall classification accuracy over 85%. Future research work will focus on testing the proposed model with larger data set and exploring new features in order to improve detection accuracy.
17	Lo O., Buchanan W.J., Griffiths P., Macfarlane R. (2018)	Distance measurement methods for improved insider threat detection	Hindawi Limited – Security and Communication Networks Hidden Markov Model, Damerau–Levenshtein Distance, Cosine Distance, Jaccard Distance CERT data set (CERT r4.2)	Preprocessing of data of the files, device.csv, email.csv, file.csv, and logon.csv is done to extract relevant fields. Fields with string description of activity is replaced with numeric values. The machine learning algorithms are then trained and performance compared in evaluation	HMM and distance measurement techniques both have capability of detecting an insider threat when applied against malicious users within the CERT r4.2 dataset in different scenario HMM produces the highest detection ratio By amalgamating the three techniques, system is capable of detecting up to 80% of all insiders threats as opposed to 0.69 for HMM. For future work will focus on experimenting with different time windows of analysis Also experimenting with introduction of threshold when applying technique to benign users in order to reduce false positives

continued on following page

Table 2. Continued

No.	Authors	Topic Area/Theme/Sub Theme	Journal/ Algorithm/ Data set (RQ1/RQ2/ RQ3)	RQ4 - Methodology Used	Findings/Recommendation
18	Li J., Zhao Z., Li R. (2018)	Machine learning-based IDS for software defined 5G network.	Institution of Engineering and Technology Random Forest and K-means ++ with adaptive boosting KDD Cup 99 and NSL-KDD	Random Forest to select features by ranking the significance of different features. K-means++ is used to divide the traffic into two clusters, the normal and abnormal instances. AdaBosst is used to partition anomaly cluster into 4 classes. The model is evaluated using NSL-KDD. Performance of the IDS is evaluated based on precision (P), recall (R), F-score (F), accuracy (AC) and false positive rate (FPR).	Experimental results shows that the proposed system is optimal in achieving higher accuracy and lower overhead without much time consumption. Future research effort will focus on finding the intrinsic relations between features as well as classifiers and adaptively choose the best combination of learning approaches.
19	Kozik R., Chora? M., Ficco M., Palmieri F. (2018)	A scalable distributed machine learning approach for attack detection in edge computing environments.	Academic Press Inc. - journal of Parallel and Distributed Computing. Extreme Learning Machines classifier CTU dataset – CTU University	NetFlows are aggregated within specific time windows. The final feature vector is obtained as a concatenation of the vectors which are calculated for each of the time windows. A distributed Extreme Learning Machines classifier is employed in the training phase using HPC clusters available over the cloud using Apache Spark scalable data processing framework. The performance was evaluated over the CTU dataset	Experimental results show satisfactory precision and accuracy values together with low error rates. Computational time of the ELM training process scales when the number of training samples increase. Adding additional computing resources can decrease the ELM training times. Thus, the proposed model scales for larger training datasets.
20	Zou X., Cao J., Guo Q., Wen T. (2018)	A novel network security algorithm based on improved support vector machine from smart city perspective	Elsevier Ltd - Computers and Electrical Engineering Decision tree learning-iterative dichotomise 3 (DTL-ID3) and one class-support vector machine (OC-SVM). DARPA intrusion detection data set	DTL-ID3 is initially applied to data set to create hub data. OC-SVM is then used to classify data set to the specific class or subset. The model is evaluated using DARPA intrusion detection data set.	Experimental results show that the amalgam DTL-ID3 approach enhances the performance of the classifier when contrasted with an immediate OC-SVM approach. Amalgam A-DT and SVM show the best performance and hence the robustness of the model. Future research efforts will focus on validating the model with more data sets and comparing results across the tests.
21	Cohen A., Nissim N., Elovici Y. (2018)	Novel set of general descriptive features for enhanced detection of malicious emails using machine learning methods	Elsevier Ltd - Expert Systems with Applications J48, Random Forest, Naïve Bayes, Bayesian Network, Logistic Regression, LogitBoost, Sequential Minimal Optimization, Bagging, AdaBoost Private -Email data from VirusTotal	Email data was collected from virusTotal. A Java Feature Extractor module was developed from JavaMail API to parse incoming email. Feature Extractor then outputs a vector of features. Different feature selection algorithms (information gain and Fisher score) are applied on the dataset in order to compare proposed novel features to features that were suggested in other related work. The machine learning classifiers are then applied and performance compared. Evaluation metric used is the area under the receiver operating characteristic (ROC) curve, or the AUC.	Experimental results show that most of the top scoring features are part of the proposed novel set of features. A comparison of the proposed detection model to 60 leading anti-virus engines used in the industry show that the TPR of the Random Forest classifier is significantly higher. The best AV engine achieved a TPR of 0.770 while RF achieved a TPR of 0.875 Future work will focus on exploring most important features to use in training and application of active learning methods to improve detection.

continued on following page

Table 2. Continued

No.	Authors	Topic Area/Theme/Sub Theme	Journal/ Algorithm/ Data set (RQ1/RQ2/ RQ3)	RQ4 - Methodology Used	Findings/Recommendation
22	Al-Jarrah O.Y., Al-Hammdi Y., Yoo P.D., Muhaidat S., Al-Qutayri M. (2018)	Semi-supervised multi-layered clustering model for intrusion detection	Digital Communications and Networks Semi-supervised Multi-Layered Clustering (SMLC), tri-training, Random Forest, Bagging, and AdaboostM1 NSL KDD and Kyoto 2006+	SMLC model is based on the concept of data clustering. K-means is used to generate a diversity of base classifiers by exploiting initialization parameter (seeding). A weighted Euclidean distance measure is used to assign a weight for each attribute based on its significance in distinguishing between class types. Information Gain is used as an attribute's weight. The SMLC is then trained with label and unlabeled instance of data. Base classifiers are initially trained on boot-strapped training datasets from the labeled instances. The final hypothesis is produced via majority voting among all individual decisions of the three base classifier. 10-fold cross-validation is used to evaluate the detection performance. Performance metrics including Acc, DR, FAR, Mcc, Training time and Testing time.	On NSL –KDD, RF achieved the best detection accuracy but has a high training and testing time of 59.045s and 0.374s, respectively. AdaBoostM1 performs better in Training Time and Testing Time compared to RF and Bagging. Detection Accuracy of Bagging is moderate, between that of AdaBoostM1 and RF. SMLC proved to perform better, 99.0264% detection accuracy, with training data having a PLD value of 10%. On the Kyoto 2006+ data set, SMLC achieved a detection accuracy of 99.37711% with a PLD of 50%, whereas the tri-training model requires PLD 70% to achieve the same detection accuracy. Bagging achieved a detection accuracy of 99.39263%, outperforming AdaBoostM1 and RF, 99.37681% and 95.88769%, respectively. SMLC can also achieve a detection accuracy comparable to that of supervised ensemble models using 70% labeled training data (PLD). Future research will be to study the scalability of SMLC, automation of its parameter tuning process and reduction of its testing time.
23	Vinayakumar R., Alazab M., Soman K.P., Poornachandran P., Al-Nemrat A., Venkatraman S. (2019)	Deep Learning Approach for Intelligent Intrusion Detection System	Institute of Electrical and Electronics Engineers Inc. Deep Neural Network. KDDCup 99, NSL-KDD, UNSW-NB15, Kyoto, WSN-DS, and CICIDS 2017.	Experiments were carried out to determine the optimal parameters and the best network topology for DNN. The DNN is trained using the backpropagation mechanism. Datasets were separated into train and test datasets, and normalized using L2 normalization. Train datasets were used to train machine learning model and test datasets were used to evaluate the models.	DT, AB and RF classifiers performed better than the others. The performance of DT, AB and RF classifiers remains the same range across different datasets. In all the cases, DNNs exceeded in performance when compared to the classical machine learning classifiers Future research efforts will explore improvements in execution time via additional processing nodes and optimal feature selection. Also training and validation of proposed model using benchmark IDS data set.
24	Zolanvari M., Teixeira M.A., Gupta L., Khan K.M., Jain R. (2019)	Machine Learning-Based Network Vulnerability Analysis of Industrial Internet of Things	Institute of Electrical and Electronics Engineers Internet of Things SVM, KNN, Naïve Bayes (NB), RF, DT, logistic regression (LR), and ANN. Data set was collected from test bed using Argus and Wireshark network tools	Data collected using Argus and Wireshark from a test bed. SQL injection and command injection attacks were executed in order to have a larger variety of attack records in our dataset. The dataset was created to be imbalanced, to reflect real-world data set, with an attack traffic of 0.2%. Then potential features were reviews and 23 features that are common in network flows and also change during the attack phases were chosen. Machine learning models are then designed to classify traffic sample as attack or normal. Data set was divided into ratio of 80% for training and 20% for testing. Keras library was used to build the ANN, and scikit-learn library was utilized to develop the other learning models	Experimental results show that RF shows the best performance and NB the worst. However accuracy is not the best metric to evaluate the performance as detection algorithms are biased towards estimating all the samples as normal.
25	Aloqaily M., Otoum S., Ridhawi I.A., Jararweh Y. (2019)	An intrusion detection system for connected vehicles in smart cities	Elsevier B.V.- Ad Hoc Networks Deep belief, and Decision tree NS3 – Network Simulated collected traffic and NSL-KDD	Preprocessing of NS3 collected and NSL-KDD data is done such that string features is encoded to numerical ones. The output of the pre-processing, which is a merged data set, undergoes DBN in order to reduce the data dimensionality, select needed features and detect whether there is an attack or not. Finally Decision Tree is used to classify attacks and signal alerts. The proposed D2H-IDS was implemented in Matlab 2017b. The proposed model is evaluated basd on the following criteria: TP, TN and FN.	Simulations have shown the effectiveness of the proposed system in real cyber-security attack scenarios. The proposed solution achieved an overall accuracy of 99.43% with 99.92% detection rate and 0.96% false positive and a false negative rate of 1.53%. For future research efforts, the proposed model will be extended to utilize big data as well as AI models and techniques for data analysis.

continued on following page

Table 2. Continued

No.	Authors	Topic Area/Theme/Sub Theme	Journal/ Algorithm/ Data set (RQ1/RQ2/ RQ3)	RQ4 - Methodology Used	Findings/Recommendation
26	Abusitta A., Bellaiche M., Dagenais M., Halabi T. (2019)	A deep learning approach for proactive multi-cloud cooperative intrusion detection system	Elsevier B.V - Future Generation Computer Systems Deep neural network KDD Cup 99	Experts in intrusion provide assistance in data labeling and verification of training data set. Labelled data set is used to train each classifier to build a classification model. New data from newly joined nodes is input and the classifier assigns the values of intrusion sensitivity to each node based on the pre-built model. The model is evaluated by sending out a set of alarms for ranking classification over a 10 level band. expert (1.0), excellent (0.9), very high (0.8), high (0.7), good (0.6), neural (0.5), not good (0.4), low (0.3), very low (0.2), and lowest (0.1). Comparison of the classifiers are done based on classification accuracy and time consumption.	Average accuracy of the proposed model, with a variety of hidden units (ranging from 70 to 350), was slightly degraded (less than 1.5%). The proposed model (SDAE-IDS) yields increased accuracy compared to SAE-IDS. However for both approaches, SDAE-IDS and SAE-IDS, accuracy and the number of layers increase proportionally. Comparison of the detection accuracy of the proposed model to (MLP)-IDS and VAE-IDS show that the proposed model yields increased accuracy. The reason for better performance of the proposed is the pre-training process which allows the deep network to have better initialization of parameters to be used during backpropagation and fine tuning with denoising autoencoders as a building block for deep neural networks which allow the deep neural network to extract robust features.
27	Shenfield, Alex Day, David Ayesh, Aladdin (2019)	Intelligent intrusion detection systems using artificial neural networks	ICT Express Artificial neural network Unknown/private	A balanced model using simple rules for basic type while compound and multi-stage rules use machine learning method. Rules are extracted from training data collected from sensors using "IF THEN ELSE" form. The Random forest algorithm is then used to build multi-staged rule by training the model with the training data set. Simulations were done using a set of pre-classified 3350 samples data set with 95 attributes each, and a set of 500 unclassified/ anonymous records.	Results show high accuracy, precision and sensitivity with values 0.98, 0.97 and 0.95 respectively. Validated with a mixture of 400,000 random files with yields 1.8% false positive rate. Future research work will focus on online network intrusion detection systems and to test on real-time network data as well as other areas of cyber security (cross-site scripting attacks and SQL injection attacks)
28	Al-Khaleefa A.S., Ahmad M.R., Isa A.A.M., Esa M.R.M., Al-Saffar A., Hassan M.H. (2019)	Feature adaptive and cyclic dynamic learning based on infinite term memory extreme learning machine	MDPI- Applied Sciences (Switzerland) Infinite-term memory online sequential extreme learning machine (ITM-OSELM) UJIndoorLoc, TampereU, and KDD 99	Feature selection Classification Apply Big data tools Validate performance with contemporary data sets	Experimental results show that, for the initial cycle, the ITM-OSELM, FA-OSELM, and OSELM had similar performances because the models did not have previous knowledge to remember. ITM-OSELM was superior to the others in the second and third cycles. FA-OSELM and OSELM had similar performance regardless of repeating the cycle. Future research effort will focus on investigating the effect of the percentage of feature change in consecutive cycles on the performance of ITM-OSELM.
29	Tao, Peiying Sun, Zhe Sun, Zhixin (2018)	An Improved Intrusion Detection Algorithm Based on GA and SVM	IEEE Access Genetic Algorithm and Support Vector Machine KDD Cup 99	Symbolic or non-numeric features were excluded from data set to improve performance since this process add additional overhead and computational complexities. **Classification** is done to categories features as normal or intrusive **Evaluation** of techniques based on the standard dataset NSL–KDD is done.	Experimental results show that feature selection reduces the classification time and increases the classification accuracy. The F-measure fitness function results in SVM final true positive rate of 94.53%, an error rate of 2.4%.
30	Salo, Fadi Nassif, Ali Bou Essex, Aleksander (2019)	Dimensionality reduction with IG-PCA and ensemble classifier for network intrusion detection	Elsevier BV - Computer Networks Information Gain (IG), PCA, SVM, IBK/KNN, and MLP ISCX 2012, NSL-KDD, and Kyoto 2006+	Threshold and Metric based detection schemes. The former is a simple strategy where a fix threshold for the monitored quantities is determined in advance. The major drawback of this approach is vulnerability to training attack. Stream clustering based aim at learning the different behavioral classes: from a sequence of data points, they group similar (or close) ones together into a cluster	Experimental results based on ISCX 2012 data set show that the performance of the proposed ensemble approach achieves the highest accuracy rate of 99.01% with 7 PCAs and outperforms all other individual classifiers. The proposed model exhibits one of the highest scores in DR, precision, and f-measure, and the lowest FAR in comparison with other combined models. Training and testing times were also reduced significantly from 7.36 and 35.58 to 2 and 3.49, respectively. Similar results were obtained for evaluations done with NSL-KDD, and Kyoto 2006+ data sets

Compilation of References

Abdulaziz, A., & Jugal, K. (2016). Authentication of Smartphone Users Using Behavioral Biometrics. *IEEE Communications Surveys and Tutorials*, *18*(3), 1998–2026. doi:10.1109/COMST.2016.2537748

Aburomman, A. A., & Reaz, M. B. I. (2017). A survey of intrusion detection systems based on ensemble and hybrid classifiers. *Computers & Security*, *65*, 135–152. doi:10.1016/j.cose.2016.11.004

Acar, Y., Stransky, C., Wermke, D., Weir, C., Mazurek, M. L., & Fahl, S. (2017). *Developers Need Support, Too : A Survey of Security Advice for Software Developers. In 2017 IEEE Cybersecurity Development IEEE Secure Development Conference Developers* (pp. 22–26)., doi:10.1109/SecDev.2017.17

Adams, M., & Makramalla, M. (2015). Cybersecurity skills training: an attacker-centric gamified approach. *Technology Innovation Management Review, 5*(1).

Afukaar, F. K. (2003). Speed control in developing countries: Issues, challenges and opportunities in reducing road traffic injuries. *Injury Control and Safety Promotion*, *10*(1–2), 77–81. doi:10.1076/icsp.10.1.77.14113 PMID:12772489

Agarwal, A., Maheshwari, S., & Yadav, G. (2014). A review on vein biometric recognition using geometric pattern matching techniques. *Proceedings of the 2014 Conference on IT in Business, Industry and Government: An International Conference by CSI on Big Data, CSIBIG 2014*, *1*. 10.1109/CSIBIG.2014.7056935

Agyemang, O. S. (2019). Linking personal values to investment decisions among individual shareholders in a developing economy. In *Behavioral finance and decision-making models* (pp. 24–45). IGI Global. doi:10.4018/978-1-5225-7399-9.ch002

Agyepong, E., Cherdantseva, Y., Reinecke, P., & Burnap, P. (2019). Challenges and performance metrics for security operations center analysts: a systematic review. *Journal of Cyber Security Technology*, 1–28. Retrieved from https://www.tandfonline.com/doi/full/10.1080/23742917.2019.1698178

Ahmad, I., Basheri, M., Iqbal, M. J., & Rahim, A. (2018). Performance Comparison of Support Vector Machine, Random Forest, and Extreme Learning Machine for Intrusion Detection. *IEEE Access: Practical Innovations, Open Solutions*, *6*, 33789–33795. doi:10.1109/ACCESS.2018.2841987

Ahmed, M., Naser Mahmood, A., & Hu, J. (2016). A survey of network anomaly detection techniques. *Journal of Network and Computer Applications*, *60*, 19–31. doi:10.1016/j.jnca.2015.11.016

Aijaz, L., Aslam, B., & Umar, K. (2015). Security operations center — A need for an academic environment. In *World Symposium on Computer Networks and Information Security (WSCNIS)* (pp. 1–7). 10.1109/WSCNIS.2015.7368297

Ajzen, I. (1991). The theory of planned behavior. *Organizational Behavior and Human Decision Processes*, *50*(2), 179–211. doi:10.1016/0749-5978(91)90020-T

Akbulut, Y., Şendağ, S., Birinci, G., Kılıçer, K., Şahin, M. C., & Odabaşı, H. F. (2008). Exploring the types and reasons of Internet-triggered academic dishonesty among Turkish undergraduate students: Development of Internet-Triggered Academic Dishonesty Scale. *Computers & Education*, *51*(1), 463–473. doi:10.1016/j.compedu.2007.06.003

AlazabM.BroadhurstR. G. (2017). Cyber-Physical Security. doi:10.1007/978-3-319-32824-9

Alfayoumi, I., & Barhoom, T. (2015). Client side pharming attacks detection using authoritative domain name servers. *International Journal of Computers and Applications*, *113*(10), 26–31. doi:10.5120/19862-1820

Alhogail, A. (2015). Design and validation of information security culture framework. *Computers in Human Behavior*, *49*(1), 567–575. doi:10.1016/j.chb.2015.03.054

Ali, M. L., Tappert, C. C., Qiu, M., & Monaco, J. V. (2015). Authentication and identification methods used in keystroke biometric systems. *Proceedings - 2015 IEEE 17th International Conference on High Performance Computing and Communications, 2015 IEEE 7th International Symposium on Cyberspace Safety and Security and 2015 IEEE 12th International Conference on Embedded Software and Systems, H*, 1424–1429. 10.1109/HPCC-CSS-ICESS.2015.66

Ali, M., Shiaeles, S., Clarke, N., & Kontogeorgis, D. (2019). A proactive malicious software identification approach for digital forensic examiners. *Journal of Information Security and Applications*, *47*, 139–155. doi:10.1016/j.jisa.2019.04.013

Alley, C., & Emery, J. (2017). Taxation of cross-border e-commerce: Response of New Zealand and other OECD countries to BEPS Action 1. *Journal of International Taxation*, *28*(9), 38–45.

Alnatheer, M. A. (2015). Information Security Culture Critical Success Factors. 12th International Conference on Information Technology - New Generations, 37–86. 10.1109/ITNG.2015.124

Aloqaily, M., Otoum, S., Al Ridhawi, I., & Jararweh, Y. (2019). An intrusion detection system for connected vehicles in smart cities. *Ad Hoc Networks*, *90*, 101842. doi:10.1016/j.adhoc.2019.02.001

Alshare, K. A., Lane, P. L., & Lane, M. R. (2018). Information security policy compliance: A higher education case study. *Information and Computer Security*, *26*(1), 91–108. doi:10.1108/ICS-09-2016-0073

Alsmadi, I., & Alsmadi, I. (2019). Cyber Threat Analysis. The NICE Cyber Security Framework. doi:10.1007/978-3-030-02360-7_9

Al-Suwaidi, N., Nobanee, H., & Jabeen, F. (2018). Estimating Causes of Cyber Crime: Evidence from Panel Data FGLS Estimator. *International Journal of Cyber Criminology*, *12*(2).

Altawy, R., & Youssef, A. M. (2016). Security, privacy, and safety aspects of civilian drones: A survey. *ACM Transactions on Cyber-Physical Systems*, *1*(2), 1–25. doi:10.1145/3001836

Al-Yaseen, W. L., Othman, Z. A., & Nazri, M. Z. A. (2017). Multi-level hybrid support vector machine and extreme learning machine based on modified K-means for intrusion detection system. *Expert Systems with Applications*, *67*, 296–303. doi:10.1016/j.eswa.2016.09.041

Ampère, A.-M. (1843). *Essai sur la philosophie des sciences, ou, Exposition analytique d'une classification de toutes les connaissances humaines*. Academic Press.

Amsberry, D. (2009). Deconstructing plagiarism: International students and textual borrowing practices. *The Reference Librarian*, *51*(1), 31–44. doi:10.1080/02763870903362183

Anand, P., & Ryoo, J. (2017). Security Patterns As Architectural Solution - Mitigating Cross-Site Scripting Attacks in Web Applications. In *2017 International Conference on Software Security and Assurance (ICSSA)* (pp. 25–31). IEEE. 10.1109/ICSSA.2017.30

Anderson, B. & Anderson, B. (2010). USB-based virus/malicious code launch, seven deadliest usb attacks. Doi:10.1016/B978-1-59749-553-0.00003-2

Anna, P. S., Cooney, M., Pashami, S., Anna, A. S., Fan, Y., & Nowaczyk, S. (2018). Pitfalls of Affective Computing: How can the automatic visual communication of emotions lead to harm, and what can be done to mitigate such risks? *WWW'18 Companion: The 2018 Web Conference, 2018*, 1563–1566.

Antal, M., & Egyed-Zsigmond, E. (2019). *Intrusion detection using mouse dynamics*. IET Biometrics. doi:10.1049/iet-bmt.2018.5126

Anwar, Z. (2019). A new framework for preventing cyber attacks. *Security: Solutions for Enterprise Security Leaders*, *56*(7), 34–36.

Apau, R., Koranteng, F. N., & Adu, S. (2019). Cyber-crime and its effects on e-commerce technologies. *Journal of Information*, *5*(1), 39–59. doi:10.18488/journal.104.2019.51.39.59

Apurva, A., Ranakoti, P., Yadav, S., Tomer, S., & Roy, N. R. (2018). Redefining cyber security with big data analytics. *2017 International Conference on Computing and Communication Technologies for Smart Nation, IC3TSN 2017*, 199–203.

Arachchilage, N. A. G., & Love, S. (2014). Security awareness of computer users: A phishing threat avoidance perspective. *Computers in Human Behavior*, *38*, 304–312. doi:10.1016/j.chb.2014.05.046

Ariyaluran Habeeb, R. A., Nasaruddin, F., Gani, A., Targio Hashem, I. A., Ahmed, E., & Imran, M. (2019). Real-time big data processing for anomaly detection: A Survey. *International Journal of Information Management*, *45*, 289–307.

Arpaci, I. (2016). Understanding and predicting students' intention to use mobile cloud storage services. *Computers in Human Behavior*, *58*, 150–157. doi:10.1016/j.chb.2015.12.067

Arteaga-Falconi, J. S., Al Osman, H., & El Saddik, A. (2016). ECG Authentication for Mobile Devices. *IEEE Transactions on Instrumentation and Measurement*, *65*(3), 591–600. doi:10.1109/TIM.2015.2503863

Ashby, W. R. (1957). An Introduction to Cybernetics (2nd ed.). London: Chapman & Hall Ltd.

Aslam, M. M. H., Shahzad, K., Syed, A. R., & Ramish, A. (2013). Social capital and knowledge sharing as determinants of academic performance. *Journal of Behavioral and Applied Management*, *15*(1), 25–42.

Assarut, N., Bunaramrueang, P., & Kowpatanakit, P. (2019). Clustering cyberspace population and the tendency to commit cyber crime: A quantitative application of space transition theory. *International Journal of Cyber Criminology*, *13*(1).

Aurigemma, S., & Mattson, T. (2017). Deterrence and punishment experience impacts on ISP compliance attitudes. *Information and Computer Security*, *25*(4), 421–436. doi:10.1108/ICS-11-2016-0089

Aurigemma, S., & Panko, R. (2011). A composite framework for behavioral compliance with information security policies. *Proceedings of the Annual Hawaii International Conference on System Sciences*, 3248–3257. 10.1109/HICSS.2012.49

Ayala, L. (2016). *Cybersecurity for hospitals and healthcare facilities: A guide to detection and prevention*. Apress.

Azmi, R., Tibben, W., & Win, K. T. (2016). Motives behind Cyber Security Strategy Development: A Literature Review of National Cyber Security Strategy. In *Australasian Conference on Information Systems*. Wollongong: University of Wollongong.

Badie, N., & Lashkari, A. H. (2012). A new evaluation criteria for effective security awareness in computer risk management based on AHP. *Journal of Basic and Applied Scientific Research*, *2*(9), 9331–9347.

Badu-Marfo, G., Farooq, B., & Patterson, Z. (2019). A perspective on the challenges and opportunities for privacy-aware big transportation data. *Journal of Big Data Analytics in Transportation, 1*(1), 1–23. doi:10.100742421-019-00001-z

Bagozzi, R. P., Yi, Y., & Phillips, L. W. (1991). Assessing construct validity in organizational research. *Administrative Science Quarterly, 36*(3), 421–458. doi:10.2307/2393203

Bakare, A.K., Junaidu, S.B., & Kolawole, A.R. (2018). Detecting Cross-Site Scripting in Web Applications Using Fuzzy Inference System. *Journal Computer Networks and Communications, 2018*, 8159548:1-8159548:10.

Balandin, S., & Waris, H. (2009). Key properties in the development of smart spaces. *Lecture Notes in Computer Science, 5615*(2), 3–12. doi:10.1007/978-3-642-02710-9_1

Balozian, P., & Leidner, D. (2017). Review of IS Security Policy Compliance. *ACM SIGMIS Database: The DATABASE for Advances in Information Systems, 48*(3), 11–43. doi:10.1145/3130515.3130518

Bamford, J., & Sergiou, K. (2005). International students and plagiarism: An analysis of the reasons for plagiarism among international foundation students. *Investigations in University Teaching and Learning, 2*(2), 17–22.

Banin, S., & Dyrkolbotn, G. O. (2018). Multinomial malware classification via low-level features. *Proceedings of the Digital Forensic Research Conference, DFRWS 2018 USA*. 10.1016/j.diin.2018.04.019

Ban, L., & Heng, G. (1995). Computer security issues in small and medium-sized enterprises. *Singapore Management Review, 17*(1), 15–30.

Bansal, G., Green, W., Hodorff, K., & Marshall, K. (2016). *Moral Beliefs and Organizational Information Security Policy Compliance : The Role of Gender*. Academic Press.

Barlette, Y., Gundolf, K., & Jaouen, A. (2017). CEOs' information security behavior in SMEs: Does ownership matter? *Systemes D'information Management, 22*(3), 7–45.

Bayuk, J. L., Healey, J., Rohmeyer, P., Sachs, M. H., Schmidt, J., & Weiss, J. (2012). Cyber Security Policy Guidebook. doi:10.1002/9781118241530

Beek, C., Frosst, D., Greve, P., Kay, B., Lenaerts-Bergmans, B., & McFarland, C. … Sun, B. (2016). *McAfee Labs Quarterly Threat Report December 2016*. Retrieved from www.mcafee.com/us/mcafee-labs.aspx

Benfratello, L., & Di Francesco, F. (2019). *Software License Compliance A quantitative study on software piracy in Italy*. Academic Press.

Berdichevsky, D., & Neuenschwander, E. (1999). *Toward an Ethics of Persuasive Technology*. Academic Press.

Bhatt, S., & Santhanam, T. (2013). Keystroke dynamics for biometric authentication-A survey. *Proceedings of the 2013 International Conference on Pattern Recognition, Informatics and Mobile Engineering, PRIME 2013*, 17–23. 10.1109/ICPRIME.2013.6496441

Binyamin, S. S., Rutter, M. J., & Smith, S. (2018). The Influence of Computer Self-Efficacy and Subjective Norms on the Students' Use of Learning Management Systems at King Abdulaziz University. *International Journal of Information and Education Technology (IJIET), 8*(10), 693–699. doi:10.18178/ijiet.2018.8.10.1124

Bisson, D. (2019). *The State of Security*. Retrieved from https://www.tripwire.com/state-of-security/security-awareness/5-social-engineering-attacks-to-watch-out-for/

Black, C. (2016). *Ransomware on the rise: An enterprise guide to preventing ransomware attacks*. New York: Carbon Black.

Blaike, N. (2009). *Designing social research*. Cambridge: Polity Press.

BMI (Bundesministerium des Innern - Germany). (2011). *Cyber Security Strategy for Germany*. Berlin: Federal Ministry of the Interior.

Bo, C., Zhang, L., Li, X.-Y., Huang, Q., & Wang, Y. (2013). SilentSense : Silent User Identi fi cation Via Touch and Movement Behavioral Biometrics. *MobiCom'13,* 187–189.

Boateng, R., Longe, O., Isabalija, R. S., & Budu, J. (2011). Sakawa - Cybercrime and Criminality in Ghana. *Journal of Information Technology Impact, 11*(2), 85–100.

Boateng, R., Longe, O., Mbarika, V., Avevor, I., & Isabalija, R. S. (2010). Cyber Crime and Criminality in Ghana:Its Forms and Implications. *Americas Conference on Information Systems (AMCIS), Proceedings of the Sixteenth Americas Conference on Information Systems*, Lima, Peru.

Borky, J. M., & Bradley, T. H. (2019). Effective Model-Based Systems Engineering. Effective Model-Based Systems Engineering. doi:10.1007/978-3-319-95669-5

Botta, D., Werlinger, R., Gagné, A., Beznosov, K., Iverson, L., Fels, S., & Fisher, B. (2008). Towards understanding IT security professionals and their tools. In *Proceedings of the 3rd symposium on Usable privacy and security* (p. 100). ACM.

Boyes, H. (2003). *Resilience and cyber security of technology in the built environment*. Institute of Engineering and Technology.

Boyes, H. A. (2013). Cyber security of intelligent buildings: a review. *8th IET International System Safety Conference Incorporating the Cyber Security Conference 2013*, 1.1-1.1. 10.1049/cp.2013.1698

Brenner, S. W. (2004b). Toward a criminal law for cyberspace, Distributed Security. *Boston University Journal of Science & Technology Law, 10*(2).

Brooks, W. J., Warren, M. J., & Hutchinson, W. (2002). A security evaluation criteria. *Logistics Information Management, 15*(5/6), 377–384. doi:10.1108/09576050210447064

Brown, J. M., Greenspan, S., & Biddle, R. (2016). Incident response teams in IT operations centers: The T-TOCs model of team functionality. *Cognition Technology and Work, 18*(4), 695–716. doi:10.100710111-016-0374-2

Buabeng-Andoh, C., Yaokumah, W., & Tarhini, A. (2019). Investigating students' intentions to use ICT: A comparison of theoretical models. *Education and Information Technologies, 24*(1), 643–660. doi:10.100710639-018-9796-1

Buczak, A. L., & Guven, E. (2016). A Survey of Data Mining and Machine Learning Methods for Cyber Security Intrusion Detection. *IEEE Communications Surveys and Tutorials, 18*(2), 1153–1176. doi:10.1109/COMST.2015.2494502

Bulgurcu, B., Cavusoglu, H., & Benbasat, I. (2010). Information security policy compliance: An empirical study of rationality-based beliefs and information security awareness. *Management Information Systems Quarterly, 34*(3), 523–548. doi:10.2307/25750690

Burgess, R. L., & Akers, R. L. (1966). A Differential Association-Reinforcement Theory of Criminal Behaviour. *Social Problems, 14*(2), 128–147. doi:10.2307/798612

Buriro, A., Gupta, S., Crispo, B., & Frari, F. D. (2018). Dialerauth: A motion-assisted touch-based smartphone user authentication scheme. CODASPY 2018 - Proceedings of the 8th ACM Conference on Data and Application Security and Privacy, 2018-Janua, 267–276. 10.1145/3176258.3176318

Burmeister, O. K. (2013). Achieving the goal of a global computing code of ethics through an international-localisation. *Ethical Space: The International Journal of Communication Ethics, 10*(4), 25–32.

Business Software Alliance. (2012). *Shadow market 2011*. Retrieved from https://globalstudy.bsa.org/2011/downloads/study_pdf/2011_BSA_Piracy_Study-Standard.pdf

Bustard, J. D. (2018). Improving Student Engagement in the Study of Professional Ethics: Concepts and an Example in Cyber Security. *Science and Engineering Ethics, 24*(2), 683–698. PMID:28401507

Callegati, F., Cerroni, W., & Ramilli, M. (2009). Man-in-the-Middle Attack to the HTTPS Protocol. *IEEE Security and Privacy, 7*(1), 78–81. doi:10.1109/MSP.2009.12

Cameron, S. (1988). The Economics of Crime Deterrence: A Survey of Theory and Evidence. *Kyklos, 41*(2), 301–323. doi:10.1111/j.1467-6435.1988.tb02311.x

Campbell, T. (2016). Practical Information Security Management. *Practical Information Security Management*, 155–177.

Carl, G., Kesidis, G., Brooks, R. R., & Rai, S. (2006). Denial-of-service attack-detection techniques. *IEEE Internet Computing, 10*(1), 82–89. doi:10.1109/MIC.2006.5

Cassiman, A. (2019). Spiders on the World Wide Web: Cyber trickery and gender fraud among youth in an Accra zongo. *Social Anthropology, 27*(3), 486–500. doi:10.1111/1469-8676.12678

CCDCE (Cooperative Cyber Defence Centre of Excellence). (2017). *Cyber Definitions*. https://ccdcoe.org/cyber-definitions.html

Chaim, M. L., Santos, D. S., & Cruzes, D. S. (2019). What Do We Know About Buffer Overflow Detection? *International Journal of Systems and Software Security and Protection, 9*(3), 1–33. doi:10.4018/IJSSSP.2018070101

Chamiekara, G. W. P., Cooray, M. I. M., Wickramasinghe, L. S. A. M., Koshila, Y. M. S., Abeywardhana, K. Y., & Senarathna, A. N. (2017). AutoSOC: A low budget flexible security operations platform for enterprises and organizations. In *2017 National Information Technology Conference, NITC 2017* (pp. 100–105). 10.1109/NITC.2017.8285644

Chan, S. (2001). Complex Adaptive Systems. In ESD.83 Research Seminar in Engineering Systems (Vol. 31). doi:10.1002/cplx.20316

Chandarman, R., & Van Niekerk, B. (2017). Students' cybersecurity awareness at a private tertiary educational institution. *African Journal of Information and Communication, 20*(20), 133–155. doi:10.23962/10539/23572

Chan, M., Woon, I., & Kankanhalli, A. (2005). Perceptions of information security at the workplace : Linking information security climate to compliant behavior. *Journal of Information Privacy and Security, 1*(3), 18–41. doi:10.1080/15536548.2005.10855772

Charoensukmongkol, P., Daniel, J. L., Sexton, S., & Kock, N. (2012). Analyzing software piracy from supply and demand factors the competing roles of corruption and economic wealth. *International Journal of Technoethics, 3*(1), 28–42. doi:10.4018/jte.2012010103

Chatole, V. (2018). Buffer overflow : Mechanism and countermeasures. *International Journal of Advanced Research. IDeas And Innovations In Technology, 4*(6), 526–529.

Chen, S., Pande, A., & Mohapatra, P. (2014). *Sensor-Assisted Facial Recognition : An Enhanced Bio- metric Authentication System for Smartphones*. Academic Press.

Cheng, J., Goto, Y., Morimoto, S., & Horie, D. (2008). A Security Engineering Environment Based on ISO / IEC Standards : Providing Standard, Formal, and Consistent Supports for Design, Development, Operation, and Maintenance of Secure Information Systems. In *2008 International Conference on Information Security and Assurance* (pp. 350–354). 10.1109/ISA.2008.106

Cheng, L., Li, W., Zhai, Q., & Smyth, R. (2014). Understanding personal use of the Internet at work: An integrated model of neutralization techniques and general deterrence theory. *Computers in Human Behavior*, *38*, 220–228. doi:10.1016/j.chb.2014.05.043

Cheng, L., Li, Y., Li, W., Holm, E., & Zhai, Q. (2013). Understanding the violation of IS security policy in organizations: An integrated model based on social control and deterrence theory. *Computers & Security*, *39*, 447–459. doi:10.1016/j.cose.2013.09.009

Chen, R., Sun, C., Helms, M. M., & Jih, W. (2008). Aligning information technology and business strategy with a dynamic capabilities perspective: A longitudinal study of a Taiwanese semiconductor company. *International Journal of Information Management*, *28*(5), 366–378. doi:10.1016/j.ijinfomgt.2008.01.015

Chen, X., Wu, D., Chen, L., & Teng, J. K. L. (2018). Sanction severity and employees' information security policy compliance: Investigating mediating, moderating, and control variables. *Information & Management*, *55*(8), 1049–1060. doi:10.1016/j.im.2018.05.011

Chiew, K. L., Yong, K. S. C., & Tan, C. L. (2018). A survey of phishing attacks: Their types, vectors and technical approaches. *Expert Systems with Applications*, *106*, 1–20. doi:10.1016/j.eswa.2018.03.050

Chin, W. W. (1998). The partial least squares approach to structural equation modeling. In G. A. Marcoulides (Ed.), *Modern Methods for Business Research* (Vol. 295, pp. 295–336). Lawrence Erlbaum Associates, Publisher; doi:10.1016/j.aap.2008.12.010

Choras, M., & Kozik, R. (2012). Contactless palmprint and knuckle biometrics for mobile devices. Pattern Anal Applic, (123), 73–85. doi:10.100710044-011-0248-4

Christensen, L. B., Johnson, B., & Turner, L. A. (2015). *Research methods, design, and analysis*. Edinburgh: Pearson.

Christiansen, L. (2011). Personal privacy and Internet marketing: An impossible conflict or a marriage made in heaven? *Business Horizons*, *54*(6), 509–514. doi:10.1016/j.bushor.2011.06.002

Chuan, B. L. J., Singh, M. M., & Shariff, A. R. M. (2019). APTGuard: Advanced persistent threat (APT) detections and predictions using android smartphone. In *Computational Science and Technology* (Vol. 481, pp. 545–555). Singapore: Springer Verlag. doi:10.1007/978-981-13-2622-6_53

Cichonski, P., Millar, T., Grance, T., & Scarfone, K. (2012). *Computer Security Incident Handling Guide Recommendations of the National Institute of Standards and Technology*. doi:10.6028/NIST.SP.800-61r2

CO. (2011). *The UK Cyber Security Strategy: Protecting and Promoting the UK in a digital world*. Author.

Cohen, A., Nissim, N., & Elovici, Y. (2018). Novel set of general descriptive features for enhanced detection of malicious emails using machine learning methods. *Expert Systems with Applications*, *110*, 143–169. doi:10.1016/j.eswa.2018.05.031

Cohen, J. (2013). *Statistical power analysis for the behavioral sciences*. Routledge. doi:10.4324/9780203771587

Cohen, L. E., & Felson, M. (1979). Social Change and Crime Rate Trends: A Routine Activity Approach. *American Sociological Review*, *44*(4), 588–608. doi:10.2307/2094589

Collins, E., Lawrence, S., Pavlovich, K., & Ryan, C. (2007). Business networks and the uptake of sustainability practices: The case of New Zealand. *Journal of Cleaner Production*, *15*(8–9), 729–740. doi:10.1016/j.jclepro.2006.06.020

Cook, F. (2016). *Ransomware holds world hostage*. Retrieved from https://www.nzherald.co.nz/business/news/article.cfm?c_id=3&objectid=11604911

Cooke, A., Smith, D., & Booth, A. (2012). Beyond PICO: The SPIDER tool for qualitative evidence synthesis. *Qualitative Health Research*, *22*(10), 1435–1443. doi:10.1177/1049732312452938 PMID:22829486

Cordova, J., Eaton, V., Greer, T., & Smith, L. (2017). A comparison of CS majors and non-CS majors attitudes regarding computer security threats. *Journal of Computing Sciences in Colleges*, *33*(2), 4–10.

Corpus, K. R., Gonzales, R. J. D., Morada, A. S., & Vea, L. A. (2016). Mobile user identification through authentication using keystroke dynamics and accelerometer biometrics. *Proceedings of the International Workshop on Mobile Software Engineering and Systems - MOBILESoft '16*, 11–12. 10.1145/2897073.2897111

Cox, Johnson, & Richards. (2009). Routine Activity Theory and Internet Crime. In F. Schmalleger & M. Pittaro (Eds.), *Crimes of the Internet,* (pp. 302-316). Pearson-Prentice Hall.

Cram, W. A., Proudfoot, J. G., & D'Arcy, J. (2017). Organizational information security policies: A review and research framework. *European Journal of Information Systems*, *26*(6), 605–641. doi:10.105741303-017-0059-9

Crawford, H., & Renaud, K. (2014). Understanding user perceptions of transparent authentication on a mobile device. *Journal of Trust Management*, *1*(1), 7. doi:10.1186/2196-064X-1-7

Cruz, S., Fabio, Q. B., & Fernando, L. (2015). Forty years of research on personality in software engineering : A mapping study. *Computers in Human Behavior*, *46*, 94–113. doi:10.1016/j.chb.2014.12.008

D'Arcy, J., & Greene, G. (2014). Security culture and the employment relationship as drivers of employees' security compliance. *Information Management & Computer Security*, *22*(5), 474–489. doi:10.1108/IMCS-08-2013-0057

D'arcy, J., & Herath, T. (2011). A review and analysis of deterrence theory in the IS security literature: Making sense of the disparate findings. *European Journal of Information Systems*, *20*(6), 643–658. doi:10.1057/ejis.2011.23

D'Arcy, J., Hovav, A., & Galletta, D. (2009). User awareness of security countermeasures and its impact on information systems misuse: A deterrence approach. *Information Systems Research*, *20*(1), 79–98. doi:10.1287/isre.1070.0160

da Costa, K. A. P., Papa, J. P., Lisboa, C. O., Munoz, R., & de Albuquerque, V. H. C. (2019). Internet of Things: A survey on machine learning-based intrusion detection approaches. *Computer Networks*, *151*, 147–157. doi:10.1016/j.comnet.2019.01.023

Da Veiga, A. (2007). An information security governance framework. *Information Systems Management*, *24*(4), 361–372. doi:10.1080/10580530701586136

Da Veiga, A. (2016). A cybersecurity culture research philosophy and approach to develop a valid and reliable measuring instrument. *Proceedings of 2016 SAI Computing Conference, SAI 2016*, 1006–1015. 10.1109/SAI.2016.7556102

Da Veiga, A. (2016). Comparing the information security culture of employees who had read the information security policy and those who had not Illustrated through an empirical study. *Information and Computer Security*, *24*(2), 139–151. doi:10.1108/ICS-12-2015-0048

Da Veiga, A., & Eloff, J. H. P. (2010). A framework and assessment instrument for information security culture. *Computers & Security*, *29*(2), 196–207. doi:10.1016/j.cose.2009.09.002

Da Veiga, A., & Martins, N. (2015). Information security culture and information protection culture: A validated assessment instrument. *Computer Law & Security Review*, *31*(2), 243–256. doi:10.1016/j.clsr.2015.01.005

Dankwa, K., & Nakata, K. (2016). Making sense of non-compliance: A semiotic approach. In M. Baranauskas, K. Liu, L. Sun, V. Neris, R. Bonacin, & K. Nakata (Eds.), *Socially Aware Organisations and Technologies. Impact and Challenges. ICISO. IFIP Advances in Information and Communication Technology, 477*. Cham: Springer. doi:10.1007/978-3-319-42102-5_11

Dankwa, K., & Nakata, K. (2018). Getting it right: A model for compliance assessment. In K. Liu, K. Nakata, W. Li, & C. Baranauskas (Eds.), *Digitalisation, Innovation, and Transformation. ICISO. IFIP Advances in Information and Communication Technology, 527*. Cham: Springer. doi:10.1007/978-3-319-94541-5_23

Danquah, P. (2015), *An Assessment of Cyber Criminal Behavioural Patterns* (PhD Thesis). Accra Institute of Technology Institutional Repository.

Danquah, P., & Longe, O. B. (2011). An Empirical Test Of The Space Transition Theory of Cyber Criminality: The Case of Ghana and beyond. *African Journal of Computing and ICT*, 38–48.

Danquah, P., & Longe, O. B. (2011). Cyber Deception and Theft: An Ethnographic Study on Cyber Criminality from a Ghanaian Perspective. *Journal of Information Technology Impact*, *11*(3), 169–182.

Danquah, P., Longe, O. B., & Totimeh, F. (2012). Just another Harmless Click of the Mouse? - An Empirical Evidence of Deviant Cyber Space Behaviour Using an Online Trap. *African Journal of Computing and ICT*, *5*(3), 49–56.

Das, A., Baki, S., El Aassal, A., Verma, R., & Dunbar, A. (2019). SoK: A Comprehensive Reexamination of Phishing Research from the Security Perspective. *IEEE Communications Surveys and Tutorials*, 1–39.

Davis, F. D. (1989). Perceived usefulness, perceived ease of use, and user acceptance of information technology. *Management Information Systems Quarterly*, *13*(3), 319–340. doi:10.2307/249008

Delgado, M., Fajardo, W., & Molina-Solana, M. (2009). Inmamusys: Intelligent multiagent music system. *Expert Systems with Applications*, *36*(3), 4574–4580. doi:10.1016/j.eswa.2008.05.028

DeloitteN. A. S. C. I. O. (2014). *Cybersecurity Study*. http://www.nascio.org/publications/documents/Deloitte-NASCIOCybersecurityStudy

Dharavath, K., Talukdar, F. A., & Laskar, R. H. (2013). Study on Biometric Authentication Systems, Challenges and Future Trends. *RE:view*. doi:10.1109/ICCIC.2013.6724278

Dhillon, G., Syed, R., & Pedron, C. (2016). Interpreting information security culture: An organizational transformation case study. *Computers & Security*, *56*, 63–69. doi:10.1016/j.cose.2015.10.001

DHS. (2017). *Securing Federal Networks*. Accessed April 15, 2017, from https://www.dhs.gov/topic/securing-federal-networks

Diener, E., Fraser, S. C., Beaman, A. L., & Kelem, R. T. (1976). Effects of deindividuation variables on stealing among Halloween trick-or-treaters. *Journal of Personality & Social Psychology*, *33*, 178-183.

Dillon, A., & Morris, M. (1996). User acceptance of new information technology: Theories and models. In M. Williams (Ed.), *Annual Review of Information Science and Technology, 31* (pp. 3–32). Medford, NJ: Information Today.

Dinh, S., Azeb, T., Fortin, F., Mouheb, D., & Debbabi, M. (2015). Spam campaign detection, analysis, and investigation. *Proceedings of the Digital Forensic Research Conference, DFRWS 2015 EU*. 10.1016/j.diin.2015.01.006

Diver, S. (2007). Information security policy –adevelopment guide for large and small companies, Sans Institute.

DoD. (2015). The DoD Cyberstrategy. doi:10.1017/CBO9781107415324.004

Doherty, N., Anastasakis, L., & Fulford, H. (2009). Institutional repository the information security policy unpacked : A critical study of the content of university policies. *International Journal of Information Management, 29*(6), 449–457. doi:10.1016/j.ijinfomgt.2009.05.003

Domb, M., Bonchek-Dokow, E., & Leshem, G. (2017). Lightweight adaptive Random-Forest for IoT rule generation and execution. *Journal of Information Security and Applications.*

Donalds, C., & Osei-Bryson, K. M. (2020). Cybersecurity compliance behavior: Exploring the influences of individual decision style and other antecedents. *International Journal of Information Management, 51*, 102056. doi:10.1016/j.ijinfomgt.2019.102056

Drass, K. A. (1982). Negotiation and the structure of discourse in medical consultation. *Sociology of Health & Illness, 4*(3), 320–341. doi:10.1111/1467-9566.ep10487982 PMID:10260462

Drystek, D. (2016). Security awareness: The "people part" of information systems. In M. Behan (Ed.), *Beginner's guide to information security.* San Francisco: Peerlyst.

Dua, S., & Xian, D. (2011). Data Mining and Machine Learning in Cybersecurity. Auerbach Publications.

Egermann, H., & McAdams, S. (2013). Empathy and Emotional Contagion as a Link Between Recognized and Felt Emotions in Music Listening. *Music Perception, 31*(2), 139–156. doi:10.1525/mp.2013.31.2.139

Eid, M. I. M., & Al-Jabri, I. M. (2016). Social networking, knowledge sharing, and student learning: the case of university students. *Computers & Educationand Education, 99*, 14–27. Retrieved from http://ssrn.com/abstract=2780765

Eisenhardt, K. M., Gioia, D. A., & Langley, A. (2016). Theory-Method Packages: A Comparison of Three Qualitative Approaches to Theory Building. In Academy of Management Proceedings (Vol. 2016, p. 12424). Academic Press.

Elbaz, L. (2016). *Essentials of cybersecurity.* San Francisco: Peerlyst.

ENISA Threat Landscape. (2013). *ENISA Threat Landscape Report 2013.* Retrieved from https://www.enisa.europa.eu/

Ercegovac, Z. (2006). What students say they know, feel, and do about cyber-plagiarism and academic dishonesty? A case study. *Proceedings of the American Society for Information Science and Technology, 42*(1). doi:10.1002/meet.1450420142

Ernest and Young (EY). (2014). *Security Operations Centers — helping you get ahead of cybercrime.* Retrieved from www.ey.com/GISS2014

Ernst & Young. (2012). *Fighting to close the gap.* Retrieved from https://www.ey.com/Publication/vwLUAssets/GISS2012/$FILE/EY_GISS_2012.pdf

Faircloth, J. (2017). Client-side attacks and social engineering. Penetration Tester's Open Source Toolkit. doi:10.1016/B978-0-12-802149-1.00008-7

Falk, E., Repcek, S., Fiz, B., Hommes, S., State, R., & Sasnauskas, R. (2017). VSOC - A Virtual Security Operating Center. *2017 IEEE Global Communications Conference, GLOBECOM 2017 - Proceedings, 8*, 1–6.

Fanelli, R., & Conti, G. (2012). A methodology for cyber operations targeting and control of collateral damage in the context of lawful armed conflict. *2012 4th International Conference on Cyber Conflict (CYCON)*, 1–13.

Farlow, M. (2016). *Ransomware: Protect your network.* Graham, NC: Comtech Solution.

Farooq, A., Isoaho, J., Virtanen, S., & Isoaho, J. (2015). *Information security awareness in educational institution: An analysis of students' individual factors. In 2015 IEEE Trustcom/BigDataSE/ISPA* (Vol. 1, pp. 352–359). IEEE.

Farris, K. A., Cybenko, G., College, D., Ganesan, R., & Jajodia, S. (2018). VULCON: A System for Vulnerability Prioritization, Mitigation, and Management. *ACM Trans. Priv. Secur, 21*(4), 28. doi:10.1145/3196884

Feledi, D., Fenz, S., & Lechner, L. (2013). Toward web-based information security knowledge sharing. *Information Security Technical Report, 17*(4), 199–209. doi:10.1016/j.istr.2013.03.004

Felson, M., & Clarke, R. V. (1998). *Opportunity makes the thief: Practical theory for crime prevention* (Police Research Series Paper No. 98). London: Research, Development and Statistics Directorate, Home Office. Retrieved from http://www.homeoffice.gov.uk/rds/prgpdfs/fprs98.pdf

Feng, C., Wu, S., & Liu, N. (2017). A user-centric machine learning framework for cyber security operations center. In *2017 IEEE International Conference on Intelligence and Security Informatics (ISI)* (pp. 173–175). Beijing, China: IEEE. 10.1109/ISI.2017.8004902

Fieldera, A., Panaousisb, E., Malacariac, P., Hankina, C., & Smeraldi, F. (2016). Decision support approaches for cyber security investment. *Decision Support Systems, 86*, 13–23. doi:10.1016/j.dss.2016.02.012

Fink, A. (2010). Conducting Research Literature Reviews: From the Internet to Paper (3rd ed.). SAGE.

Finland. (2013). *Finland´s Cyber security Strategy*. Academic Press.

Fishbein, M., & Ajzen, I. (1977). *Belief, attitude, intention and behavior: An introduction to theory and research*. Reading, MA: Addison-Wesley.

Folino, G., & Sabatino, P. (2016). Ensemble based collaborative and distributed intrusion detection systems: A survey. *Journal of Network and Computer Applications, 66*, 1–16. doi:10.1016/j.jnca.2016.03.011

Follner, A., & Bodden, E. (2016). ROPocop - Dynamic mitigation of code-reuse attacks. *Journal of Information Security and Applications, 29*, 16–26. doi:10.1016/j.jisa.2016.01.002

Foltz, C. B., Newkirk, H. E., & Schwager, P. H. (2016). An empirical investigation of factors that influence individual behavior toward changing social networking security settings. *Journal of Theoretical and Applied Electronic Commerce Research, 11*(2), 1–15. doi:10.4067/S0718-18762016000200002

Fornell, C., & Larcker, D. F. (1981). Evaluating structural model with unobserved variables and measurement errors. *JMR, Journal of Marketing Research, 18*(1), 39–50. doi:10.1177/002224378101800104

Fox, R., & Crawford, R. (2016). A hybrid approach to automated music composition. *Advances in Intelligent Systems and Computing, 464*, 213–223. doi:10.1007/978-3-319-33625-1_20

Frauenstein, E. D., & Flowerday, S. V. (2016), Social network phishing: Becoming habituated to clicks and ignorant to threats, Information Security for South Africa. *Proceedings of the 2016 ISSA Conference*, 98-105.

Galbally, J., Marcel, S., & Fierrez, J. (2014). Biometric antispoofing methods: A survey in face recognition. *IEEE Access: Practical Innovations, Open Solutions, 2*, 1530–1552. doi:10.1109/ACCESS.2014.2381273

Gallegos, F., & Cook, C. (2000). Software piracy: Some facts, figures, and issues. *Information Systems Security, 8*(4), 1–23. doi:10.1201/1086/43307.8.4.20000101/31078.5

Gartner. (2018, August). Gartner forecasts worldwide information security spending to exceed $124 billion in 2019. *Gartner Newsroom.*

Gauthama Raman, M. R., Somu, N., Kirthivasan, K., Liscano, R., & Shankar Sriram, V. S. (2017). An efficient intrusion detection system based on hypergraph - Genetic algorithm for parameter optimization and feature selection in support vector machine. *Knowledge-Based Systems, 134*, 1–12. doi:10.1016/j.knosys.2017.07.005

Gazet, A. (2010). Comparative analysis of various ransomware virii. *Journal in Computer Virology, 6*(1), 77-90.

Gcaza, N., Von Solms, R., & Van Vuuren, J. (2015). An ontology for a national cyber-security culture environment. *Proceedings of the 9th International Symposium on Human Aspects of Information Security and Assurance, HAISA 2015*, 1–10.

GCSCC (Global Cyber Security Capacity Centre). (2014). Cyber Security Capability Maturity Model (CMM) (Version 1). Oxford: Global Cyber Security Capacity Centre (GCSCC), University of Oxford.

Gibbs, S. (2020, December). Bitcoin: $64m in cryptocurrency stolen in "sophisticated" hack, exchange says. *The Guardian Online*. https://www.theguardian.com/technology/2017/dec/07/bitcoin-64m-cryptocurrency-stolen-hack-attack-marketplace-nicehash-passwords

Gibson, W. (1984). Neuromancer. New York: Ace Books.

Gibson, W. (1982). *Burning Chrome*. Omni.

GoB (The Government of Belgium). (2012). *Cyber Security Strategy: Securing Cyberspace*. Author.

Goel, S., Williams, K., & Dincelli, E. (2017). Got phished? Internet security and human vulnerability. *Journal of the Association for Information Systems, 18*(1), 22–44. doi:10.17705/1jais.00447

GoJ (The Government of Japan). (2015). *Cybersecurity Strategy (Provisional Translation)*. Author.

GoM (The Government of Montenegro). (2013). *National Cyber Security Strategy*. Author.

Gong, N. Z., Moazzezi, R., Payer, M., & Frank, M. (2016). Forgery-Resistant Touch-based Authentication on Mobile Devices. ASIA CCS '16, 499–510.

Gong, Z., Han, Z., Li, X., Yu, C., & Reinhardt, J. D. (2019). Factors influencing the adoption of online health consultation services: The role of subjective norm, trust, perceived benefit and offline habit. *Frontiers in Public Health, 7*, 286. doi:10.3389/fpubh.2019.00286 PMID:31637229

Goo, J., Yim, M. S., & Kim, D. J. (2014). A path to successful management of employee security compliance: An empirical study of information security climate. *IEEE Transactions on Professional Communication, 57*(4), 286–308. doi:10.1109/TPC.2014.2374011

Gottemukkula, V., Saripalle, S., Tankasala, S. P., & Derakhshani, R. (2015). *Method for using visible ocular vasculature for mobile biometrics*. doi:10.1049/iet-bmt.2014.0059

Granitz, N., & Loewy, D. (2007). Applying ethical theories: Interpreting and responding to student plagiarism. *Journal of Business Ethics, 72*(3), 293–306. doi:10.100710551-006-9171-9

Green, E. (2019). The logic bomb: What it is and how to prevent it. *NordVPN*. Retrieved from https://nordvpn.com/blog/logic-bomb/

Gregory, P. (2010). *CISSP Guide to Security Essentials*. Course Technology, Cengage Learning.

Grimes, R. A. (2001). *Malicious Mobile Code: Virus Protection for Windows*. O'Reilly & Associates, Inc.

Gross, R., & Acquisti, A. (2005). Information revelation and privacy in online social networks. In Workshop On Privacy In The Electronic Society (pp. 71–80). doi:10.1145/1102199.1102214

Guliani, N., Shukla, M. K., Dubey, A. K., & Jaffery, Z. A. (2018). Analysis of multimodal biometrie recognition using Iris and sclera. *2017 6th International Conference on Reliability, Infocom Technologies and Optimization: Trends and Future Directions*, 472–475. 10.1109/ICRITO.2017.8342473

Gurusamy, V., & Hirani, B. (2018). *Cyber security for our digital life*. https://www.researchgate.net/publication/323605373_Cyber_Security_for_Our_Digital_Life

Hair, J. F., Hult, T. M., Ringle, C., & Sarstedt, M. (2014). *A Primer on Partial Least Squares Structural Equation Modeling (PLS-SEM)*. Sage Publications. doi:10.1016/j.lrp.2013.01.002

Hair, J. F., Risher, J. J., Sarstedt, M., & Ringle, C. M. (2019). When to use and how to report the results of PLS-SEM. *European Business Review*, *31*(1), 2–24. doi:10.1108/EBR-11-2018-0203

Hajli, N., & Lin, X. (2016). Exploring the security of information sharing on social networking sites: The role of perceived control of information. *Journal of Business Ethics*, *133*(1), 111–123. doi:10.100710551-014-2346-x

Halder, P., Pietarinen, J., Havu-Nuutinen, S., Pöllänen, S., & Pelkonen, P. (2016). The Theory of Planned Behavior model and students' intentions to use bioenergy: A cross-cultural perspective. *Renewable Energy*, *89*, 627–635. doi:10.1016/j.renene.2015.12.023

Halfond, W. G., Viegas, J., & Orso, A. (2006, March). A classification of SQL-injection attacks and countermeasures. In *Proceedings of the IEEE International Symposium on Secure Software Engineering* (Vol. 1, pp. 13-15). IEEE.

Hall, C., & Rusher, K. (2004). Risky lifestyles? Entrepreneurial characteristics of the New Zealand bed and breakfast sector. In R. Thomas (Ed.), *Small forms in tourisms: International perspective* (pp. 83–98). Amsterdam: Elsevier. doi:10.1016/B978-0-08-044132-0.50009-5

Hall, M. (2016). Realising the richness of psychology theory in contingency-based management accounting research. *Management Accounting Research*, *31*, 63–74. doi:10.1016/j.mar.2015.11.002

Hámornik, P. B., & Krasznay, C. (2017). *A Team-Level Perspective of Human Factors in Cyber Security: Security Operations Centers* (pp. 224–236). Cham: Springer. Retrieved from https://link.springer.com/content/pdf/10.1007%2F978-3-319-60585-2_21.pdf

Hampton-Sosa, W. (2017). The impact of creativity and community facilitation on music streaming adoption and digital piracy. *Computers in Human Behavior*, *69*, 444–453. doi:10.1016/j.chb.2016.11.055

Han, H., Lu, X. L., Lu, J., Bo, C., & Yong, R. L. (2002). Data mining aided signature discovery in network-based intrusion detection system. *Operating Systems Review*, *36*(4), 7–13. doi:10.1145/583800.583801

Han, J., & Tan, H. T. (2009). Investors' reactions to management earnings guidance: The joint effect of investment position, news valence, and guidance form. *Journal of Accounting Research*, *48*(1), 81–104. doi:10.1111/j.1475-679X.2009.00350.x

Hardy, G. (2006). Using IT governance and COBIT to deliver value with IT and respond to legal, regulatory and compliance challenges. *Information Security Technical Report*, *11*(1), 55–61. doi:10.1016/j.istr.2005.12.004

Harrison, D. A., Mykytyn, P. P. Jr, & Riemenschneider, C. K. (1997). Executive decisions about adoption of information technology in small business: Theory and empirical tests. *Information Systems Research*, *8*(2), 171–195. doi:10.1287/isre.8.2.171

Harris, S. (2013). *CISSP Exams Guide (All-In-One)*. McGraw-Hill Companies.

Hazeyama, A., & Shimizu, H. (2012). Development of a Software Security Learning Environment. In *2012 13th ACIS International Conference on Software Engineering, Artificial Intelligence, Networking and Parallel/Distributed Computing* (pp. 518–523). IEEE. 10.1109/SNPD.2012.65

Hedström, K., Kolkowsa, E., Karlsson, F., & Allen, J. P. (2011). Value conflicts for information security management. *The Journal of Strategic Information Systems*, *20*(4), 373–384. doi:10.1016/j.jsis.2011.06.001

Henseler, J., Hubona, G., & Ray, P. A. (2016). Using PLS path modeling in new technology research : Updated guidelines. *Industrial Management & Data Systems*, *116*(1), 2–20. doi:10.1108/IMDS-09-2015-0382

Hepler, J. (2015). A good thing isn't always a good thing: Dispositional attitudes predict non-normative judgments. *Personality and Individual Differences*, *75*, 59–63. doi:10.1016/j.paid.2014.11.016

Herath, T., & Rao, H. R. (2009a). Encouraging information security behaviors in organizations: Role of penalties, pressures and perceived effectiveness. *Decision Support Systems*, *47*(2), 154–165. doi:10.1016/j.dss.2009.02.005

Herath, T., & Rao, H. R. (2009b). Protection motivation and deterrence: A framework for security policy compliance in organizations. *European Journal of Information Systems*, *18*(2), 106–125. doi:10.1057/ejis.2009.6

Herath, T., Yim, M. S., D'Arcy, J., Nam, K., & Rao, H. R. (2018). Examining employee security violations: Moral disengagement and its environmental influences. *Information Technology & People*, *31*(6), 1135–1162. doi:10.1108/ITP-10-2017-0322

Hernandez, P. (2017). Microsoft Hardens Windows Cloud Instances With AI-Enabled Controls. *EWeek*, 1–4.

Hewlett-Packard. (2013). *5G/SOC: SOC Generations -HP ESP Security Intelligence and Operations Consulting Services - Business white paper*. Retrieved from http://www.cnmeonline.com/myresources/hpe/docs/HP_ArcSight_WhitePapers_5GSOC_SOC_Generations.PDF

Higgins, G. E., Wilson, A. L., & Fell, B. D. (2005). An application of deterrence theory to software piracy. *The Journal of Criminal Justice and Popular Culture*, *12*(3), 166–184.

Hilburn, T. B., & Mead, N. R. (2013). Building Security In. *IEEE Security and Privacy*, *11*(October), 89–92. doi:10.1109/MSP.2013.109

Hill, C. W. L. (2007). Digital piracy: Causes, consequences, and strategic responses. *Asia Pacific Journal of Management*, *24*(1), 9–25. doi:10.100710490-006-9025-0

Hina, S., & Dominic, P. D. D. (2018). Information security policies ' compliance : A perspective for higher education institutions. *Journal of Computer Information Systems*, 1–11. doi:10.1080/08874417.2018.1432996

Hirsch, B., Reichert, B. E., & Sohn, M. (2017). The impact of clawback provisions on information processing and investment behavior. *Management Accounting Research*, *37*, 1–11. doi:10.1016/j.mar.2016.12.001

Hirschi, T. (1969). *Causes of Delinquency*. Berkeley, CA: University of California Press.

Ho, G., Cidon, A., Gavish, L., Schweighauser, M., Paxson, V., Savage, S., . . . Wagner, D. (2019). Detecting and characterizing lateral phishing at scale. In *28th {USENIX} Security Symposium ({USENIX} Security 19* (pp. 1273-1290). USENIX.

Hofstede, G. (1983). National cultures in four dimensions: A research-based theory of cultural differences among nations. *International Studies of Management & Organization*, *13*(1–2), 46–74. doi:10.1080/00208825.1983.11656358

Hofstede, G. (2001). *Culture's Consequences: Comparing Values, Behaviours, Institutions, and organizations across nations* (2nd ed.). Thousand Oaks, CA: Sage Publications, Inc.

Hofstede, G. J. (2001). Adoption of communication technologies and national culture. *Information Systems Management*, *6*(3), 55–74. doi:10.9876im.v6i3.107

Horne, C. A., Ahmad, A., & Maynard, S. B. (2016). A Theory on Information Security. *Australasian Conference on Information Systems*.

Hovav, A., & D'Arcy, J. (2012). Applying an extended model of deterrence across cultures: An investigation of information systems misuse in the US and South Korea. *Information & Management*, *49*(2), 99–110. doi:10.1016/j.im.2011.12.005

Hsieh, H.-F., & Shannon, S. E. (2005). Three Approaches to Qualitative Content Analysis. *Qualitative Health Research*, *15*(9), 1277–1288. doi:10.1177/1049732305276687 PMID:16204405

Huang, N., Huang, S., & Chang, C. (2019). Analysis to Heap Overflow Exploit in Linux with Symbolic Execution. *IOP Conference Series: Earth and Environmental Science, 252*(4). 10.1088/1755-1315/252/4/042100

Hu, L., & Bentler, P. M. (1999). Cutoff criteria for fit indexes in covariance structure analysis: Conventional criteria versus new alternatives. *Structural Equation Modeling*, *6*(1), 1–55. doi:10.1080/10705519909540118

Humaidi, N., & Balakrishnan, V. (2017). Indirect effect of management support on users' compliance behaviour towards information security policies. *The HIM Journal*, *47*(1), 17–27. doi:10.1177/1833358317700255 PMID:28537207

Hu, Q., Dinev, T., Hart, P., & Cooke, D. (2012). Managing Employee Compliance with Information Security Policies: The Critical Role of Top Management and Organizational Culture. *Decision Sciences*, *43*(4), 615–660. doi:10.1111/j.1540-5915.2012.00361.x

Hwang, I., Kim, D., Kim, T., & Kim, S. (2017). Why not comply with information security? An empirical approach for the causes of non-compliance. *Online Information Review*, *41*(1), 2–18. doi:10.1108/OIR-11-2015-0358

IEEE. (2014). *Software Engineering Competency Model (SWECOM)*. IEEE. Retrieved from http://www.dahlan.web.id/files/ebooks/SWECOM.pdf

Ifinedo, P. (2012). Understanding information systems security policy compliance: An integration of the theory of planned behavior and the protection motivation theory. *Computers & Security*, *31*(1), 83–95. doi:10.1016/j.cose.2011.10.007

Ifinedo, P. (2014). Information systems security policy compliance: An empirical study of the effects of socialization, influence, and cognition. *Information & Management*, *51*(1), 69–79. doi:10.1016/j.im.2013.10.001

IMCCS (Inter-Ministerial Committee for Cyber Security - the Republic of Trinidad & Tobago National). (2012). *Government of the Republic of Trinidad & Tobago National Cyber Security Strategy*. Author.

Information Commissioner's Office (ICO). (2016). *A practical guide to IT security – ideal for the small business*. Retrieved from https://ico.org.uk/media/for-organisations/documents/1575/it_security_practical_guide.pdf

Islam, A., Tedford, D., & Haemmerle, E. (2017). *Risk determinants of small and medium sized manufacturing enterprises (SMEs) – an empirical investigation in New Zealand*. Retrieved from https://www.anzam.org/wp-content/uploads/pdf-manager/1874_ISLAMMD_235.PDF

Islam, M. R. U., Islam, M. S., Ahmed, Z., Iqbal, A., & Shahriyar, R. (2019, July). Automatic Detection of NoSQL Injection Using Supervised Learning. In *2019 IEEE 43rd Annual Computer Software and Applications Conference (COMPSAC)* (Vol. 1, pp. 760-769). IEEE. 10.1109/COMPSAC.2019.00113

ISO/IEC (International Organization for Standardization/International Electrotechnical Commission). (2012). *ISO/IEC 27032:2012 Information technology — Security techniques — Guidelines for cybersecurity*. Geneva: ISO.

ISO/IEC (International Organization for Standardization/International Electrotechnical Commission). (2013). *ISO/IEC 27001:2013 - Information Security Management*. Geneva: ISO.

ISO/IEC 27032 (2012). *Information technology — Security techniques — Guidelines for cybersecurity*. Retrieved from https://www.iso.org/standard/44375.html

ITU (International Telecommunication Union). (2009). *Definition of cybersecurity*. ITU.

ITU (International Telecommunication Union). (2012). ITU National Cybersecurity Strategy Guide (F. Wamala, Ed.). Geneva: ITU.

Jacobs, P., Arnab, A., & Irwin, B. (2013). *Classification of Security Operation Centers. In 2013 Information Security for South Africa* (pp. 1–7). IEEE. Retrieved from https://ieeexplore.ieee.org/document/6641054/

Jagadeesh, N., & Patil, C. (2017). A B rief R eview of the I ris R ecognition S ystems for D eveloping a U ser- F riendly B iometric A pplication. *International Conference on Energy, Communication, Data Analytics and Soft Computing (ICECDS-2017) A*, 3309–3312.

Jaishankar, K. (2008). Space Transition Theory of Cyber Crimes. In F. Schmalleger & M. Pittaro (Eds.), *Crimes of the Internet* (pp. 283–301). Upper Saddle River, NJ: Pearson-Prentice Hall.

Jalali, M. S., Siegel, M., & Madnick, S. (2019). Decision-making and biases in cybersecurity capability development: Evidence from a simulation game experiment. *The Journal of Strategic Information Systems, 28*(1), 66–82. doi:10.1016/j.jsis.2018.09.003

Jamal, A., Ferdoos, A., Zaman, M., & Hussain, M. (2015). Cyber-ethics and the perceptions of internet users: A case study of university students of Islamabad. *Pakistan Journal of Information Management and Libraries, 16*, 8–20.

János, F. D., & Dai, P. H. N. (2018). Security concerns towards Security Operations centers. *2018 IEEE 12th International Symposium on Applied Computational Intelligence and Informatics (SACI)*, 273–278.

Jansen, J., & Leukfeldt, R. (2016, January – June). Phishing and Malware Attacks on Online Banking Customers in the Netherlands: A Qualitative Analysis of Factors Leading to Victimization. *International Journal of Cyber Criminology, 10*(1).

Janssen, M., & van den Hoven, J. (2015). *Big and Open Linked Data (BOLD) in government: A challenge to transparency and privacy?* Elsevier.

Jegede, A. E., Elegbeleye, A. O., Olowookere, E. I., & Olorunyomi, B. R. (2016). Gendered alternative to cyber fraud participation: An assessment of technological driven crime in Lagos State, Nigeria. *Gender & Behaviour, 14*(3), 7672–7692.

Jenkyn, T., & Stephenson, B. (2013). *Fundamentals of discrete math for computer Science a problem-solving primer.* London: Springer-Verlag. doi:10.1007/978-1-4471-4069-6

Johnson, C. (2015). "French" cybernetics. *French Studies, 69*(1), 60–78. doi:10.1093/fs/knu229

Johnson, J. C., Leeds, B. A., & Wu, A. (2015). Capability, Credibility, and Extended General Deterrence. *International Interactions, 41*(2), 309–336. doi:10.1080/03050629.2015.982115

Johnston & Warkentin. (2010). Fear Appeals and Information Security Behaviors: An Empirical Study. *MIS Quarterly, 34*(3), 549. doi:10.2307/25750691

Jones, B. H., Chin, A. G., & Aiken, P. (2014). Risky business: Students and smartphones. *TechTrends, 58*(6), 73–83. doi:10.100711528-014-0806-x

Jones, K. (1981). Compositional Applications of Stochastic Processes. *Computer Music Journal, 5*(2), 45. doi:10.2307/3679879

Jyotiyana, J. P., & Mishra, A. (2016). Secure Authentication: Eliminating Possible Backdoors in Client-Server Endorsement. *Procedia Computer Science, 85*, 606–615. doi:10.1016/j.procs.2016.05.227

Kals, S., Kirda, E., Kruegel, C., & Jovanovic, N. (2006, May). Secubat: a web vulnerability scanner. In *Proceedings of the 15th international conference on World Wide Web* (pp. 247-256). ACM. 10.1145/1135777.1135817

Kant, I. (1998). Critique of Pure Reason (P. Guyer & A. Wood, Trans. & Eds.). Cambridge University Press.

Kaptelinin, V. (2014). Activity Theory. In M. Soegaard & R. F. Dam (Eds.), *The Encyclopedia of Human-Computer Interaction* (2nd ed.). Aarhus, Denmark: The Interaction Design Foundation. Retrieved from https://www.interaction-design.org/encyclopedia/activity_theory.html

Kara, I. (2019). A basic malware analysis method. *Computer Fraud & Security*, 6(6), 11–19. doi:10.1016/S1361-3723(19)30064-8

Karlin, N. J., & Weil, J. (2019). Exploring Cultural Similarity and Cultural Diversity: A Cross-National Study of Nine Countries. *Journal of Aging Science*, 7, 204. doi:10.35248/2329-8847.19.07.204

Karlsson, M., Denk, T., & Åström, J. (2018). Perceptions of organizational culture and value conflicts in information security management. *Information and Computer Security*, 26(2), 213–229. doi:10.1108/ICS-08-2017-0058

Kasanagottu, S., & Bhattacharya, S. (2017). Significant IT adoption factors by small enterprises in the auto ancillary industry. *International Journal of Applied Business and Economic Research*, 15, 367–379.

Kaspersky. (2016). *IT threat evolution in Q1 2016 report.* San Francisco: Kaspersky Labs.

Kataria, A. N., Adhyaru, D. M., Sharma, A. K., & Zaveri, T. H. (2013). A survey of automated biometric authentication techniques. *2013 Nirma University International Conference on Engineering, NUiCONE 2013*, 1–6. 10.1109/NUiCONE.2013.6780190

Katyal, N. K. (2001). Criminal Law in Cyberspace. *University of Pennsylvania Law Review*, 149.

Kaur, N., & Kaur, P. (2016). Modeling a SQL Injection Attack. In *2016 3rd International Conference on Computing for Sustainable Global Development (INDIACom)* (pp. 77–82). Bharati Vidyapeeth.

Kc, G. S., Keromytis, A. D., & Prevelakis, V. (2003, October). Countering code-injection attacks with instruction-set randomization. In *Proceedings of the 10th ACM conference on Computer and communications security* (pp. 272-280). ACM.

Keith, M., Shao, B., & Steinbart, P. (2009). A behavioral analysis of passphrase design and effectiveness. *Journal of the Association for Information Systems*, 10(2), 2. doi:10.17705/1jais.00184

Kemper, K. J., & Danhauer, S. C. (2005). Music as therapy. *Southern Medical Journal*, 98(3), 282–288. doi:10.1097/01.SMJ.0000154773.11986.39 PMID:15813154

Kemp, S., Miró-Llinares, F., & Moneva, A. (2020). The Dark Figure and the Cyber Fraud Rise in Europe: Evidence from Spain. *European Journal on Criminal Policy and Research*, 1–20. doi:10.100710610-020-09439-2

Kerlinger, F. N. (1979). Behavioral research: A conceptual approach. New York: Academic Press.

Kerner, S. M. (2017). Cisco Cyber-Security Report Finds Server Threats Increased in 2016. *EWeek*, 1.

Kerner, S. M. (2018). How IBM Helps Organizations to Improve Security with Incident Response. *EWeek*, 1–2.

Kestle, R. (2013). *The role of IS assurance & security management.* Derbyshire: University of Derby.

Khatoun, R., & Zeadally, S. (2017). Cybersecurity and privacy solutions in smart cities. *IEEE Communications Magazine*, 55(3), 51–59. doi:10.1109/MCOM.2017.1600297CM

Khatwani, S. (2017, November). Biggest Bitcoin Hacks Ever. *CoinSutra*.

Kim, D. J., Chung, K. W., & Hong, K. S. (2010). Person authentication using face, teeth and voice modalities for mobile device security. *IEEE Transactions on Consumer Electronics*, 56(4), 2678–2685. doi:10.1109/TCE.2010.5681156

Kim, E. B. (2014). Recommendations for information security awareness training for college students. *Information Management & Computer Security*, 22(1), 115–126. doi:10.1108/IMCS-01-2013-0005

Kim, S. H., Yang, K. H., & Park, S. (2014). An integrative behavioral model of information security policy compliance. *TheScientificWorldJournal*, 2014, 2014. doi:10.1155/2014/463870 PMID:24971373

Kitchenham, B. (2004). *Procedures for performing systematic reviews*. Keele University, UK and National ICT Australia.

Kitchenham, B., & Charters, S. (2007). Guidelines for performing Systematic Literature reviews in Software Engineering Version 2.3. Engineering (Vol. 45). doi:10.1145/1134285.1134500

Kokulu, F. B., Bao, T., Doupé, A., Shoshitaishvili, Y., Ahn, G.-J., & Zhao, Z. (2019). *Matched and Mismatched SOCs : A Qualitative Study on Security Operations Center Issues*. Association of Computing Machinery. ACM. doi:10.1145/3319535.3354239

Kolkowska, E., Karlsson, F., & Hedström, K. (2017). Journal of Strategic Information Systems Towards analysing the rationale of information security non- compliance : Devising a Value-Based Compliance analysis method. *The Journal of Strategic Information Systems*, 26(1), 39–57. doi:10.1016/j.jsis.2016.08.005

Koranteng, F. N., & Wiafe, I. (2018). Factors that Promote Knowledge Sharing on Academic Social Networking Sites: An Empirical Study. *Education and Information Technologies*, 1–26. doi:10.100710639-018-9825-0

Koranteng, F. N., Wiafe, I., Katsriku, F. A., & Apau, R. (2019). *Understanding trust on social networking sites among tertiary students: An empirical study in Ghana*. Applied Computing and Informatics; doi:10.1016/j.aci.2019.07.003

Koranteng, F. N., Wiafe, I., & Kuada, E. (2019). An Empirical Study of the Relationship Between Social Networking Sites and Students ' Engagement in Higher Education. *Journal of Educational Computing Research*, 57(5), 1131–1159. doi:10.1177/0735633118787528

Koscher, K., Czeskis, A., Roesner, F., Patel, S., Kohno, T., Checkoway, S., & ... . (2010). Experimental security analysis of a modern automobile. *2010 IEEE Symposium on Security and Privacy*, 447–462. 10.1109/SP.2010.34

Kozik, R., Choraś, M., Ficco, M., & Palmieri, F. (2018). A scalable distributed machine learning approach for attack detection in edge computing environments. *Journal of Parallel and Distributed Computing*, 119, 18–26. doi:10.1016/j.jpdc.2018.03.006

Kuada, E., Wiafe, I., Addo, D., & Djaba, E. (2017). *Privacy enhancing national identification card system. In 2017 IEEE AFRICON: Science, Technology and Innovation for Africa*. AFRICON. doi:10.1109/AFRCON.2017.8095596

Kumah, P., Yaokumah, W., & Buabeng-Andoh, C. (2018). Identifying HRM Practices for Improving Information Security Performance: An Importance-Performance Map Analysis. *International Journal of Human Capital and Information Technology Professionals*, 9(4), 23–43. doi:10.4018/IJHCITP.2018100102

Kumar, G., & Kumar, K. (2014). Network security – an updated perspective. *Systems Science & Control Engineering*, 2(1), 325–334. doi:10.1080/21642583.2014.895969

Kuusisto, T., & Kuusisto, R. (2015). Cyber World as a Social System. In M. Lehto & P. Neittaanmäki (Eds.), *Cyber Security: Analytics* (pp. 31–44). Technology and Automation. doi:10.1007/978-3-319-18302-2_2

Kwok, E. (2015). *Understanding the new cyber reality: Information Security Study 2015*. London: Deloitte.

Kwon, T., Song, J., Choi, S., Lee, Y., & Park, J. (2018). VISNU: A Novel Visualization Methodology of Security Events Optimized for a Centralized SOC. *2018 13th Asia Joint Conference on Information Security (AsiaJCIS)*, 1–7. Retrieved from https://ieeexplore.ieee.org/document/8453754/

Kwon, J., & Johnson, M. E. (2014). Proactive versus reactive security investments in the healthcare sector. *Management Information Systems Quarterly*, *38*(2), 451–471. doi:10.25300/MISQ/2014/38.2.06

Kwon, J., Ulmer, J. R., & Wang, T. (2012). The association between top management involvement and compensation and information security breaches. *Journal of Information Systems*, *27*(1), 219–236. doi:10.2308/isys-50339

Lacey, D. (2010). Understanding and transforming organizational security culture. *Information Management & Computer Security*, *18*(1), 4–13. doi:10.1108/09685221011035223

Lai, P. C. (2017). The literature review of technology adoption models and theories for the novelty technology. *Journal of Information Systems and Technology Management*, *14*(1), 21–38. doi:10.4301/S1807-17752017000100002

Landers, J. (2016). *Preventing ransomware: Enterprise malware defense – 39 technical and administrative best practices for 2016*. New York: Amazon Digital Services.

Langfield-Smith, K., Thorne, H., Smith, D., & Hilton, R. (2015). *Management accounting: Information for creating and managing value*. McGraw-Hill Education.

Larson, D. (2016). Distributed denial of service attacks - Holding back the flood. *Network Security*, *2016*(3), 5–7. doi:10.1016/S1353-4858(16)30026-5

Lathrop, A., & Foss, K. (2000). Student cheating and plagiarism in the Internet era. *A Wake-up Call*.

LBMC. (2020). *Three Categories of Security Controls*. Retrieved from https://www.lbmc.com/blog/three-categories-of-security-controls/

Lee, C., Lee, C. C., & Kim, S. (2016). Understanding information security stress: Focusing on the type of information security compliance activity. *Computers & Security*, *59*, 60–70. doi:10.1016/j.cose.2016.02.004

Lee, G., Lee, W. J., & Sanford, C. (2011). A motivational approach to information providing: A resource exchange perspective. *Computers in Human Behavior*, *27*(1), 440–448. doi:10.1016/j.chb.2010.09.006

Lee, J., & Lee, Y. (2002). A holistic model of computer abuse within organizations. *Information Management & Computer Security*, *10*(2), 57–63. doi:10.1108/09685220210424104

Lee, M. G. (2012). *Securing the human to protect the system: human factors in cyber security. In 7th IET International Conference on System Safety, incorporating the Cyber Security Conference 2012* (pp. 41–41). IET. Retrieved from https://digital-library.theiet.org/content/conferences/10.1049/cp.2012.1519

Lee, S. M., Lee, S. G., & Yoo, S. (2004). An integrative model of computer abuse based on social control and general deterrence theories. *Information & Management*, *41*(6), 707–718. doi:10.1016/j.im.2003.08.008

Lee, T. K., Kim, T. G., & Im, E. G. (2016). User Authentication Method using Shaking Actions in Mobile Devices. *Proceedings of the International Conference on Research in Adaptive and Convergent Systems - RACS '16*, 142–147. 10.1145/2987386.2987411

Lehto, M. (2013). The Cyberspace Threats and Cyber Security Objectives in the Cyber Security Strategies. *International Journal of Cyber Warfare & Terrorism*, *3*(3), 1–18. doi:10.4018/ijcwt.2013070101

Lehto, M. (2015). Phenomena in the Cyber World. In M. Lehto & P. Neittaanmäki (Eds.), *Cyber Security: Analytics* (pp. 3–29). Technology and Automation. doi:10.1007/978-3-319-18302-2_1

Lemos, R. (2016). Government Surveillance Poses Cyber-security Threats, ISPs Say. *EWeek, 1*.

Lenberg, P., Feldt, R., & Wallgren, L. G. (2015). Behavioral software engineering: A definition and systematic literature review. *Journal of Systems and Software, 107*, 15–37. doi:10.1016/j.jss.2015.04.084

Leon, E., & Bruda, S. D. (2016). Counter-Measures against Stack Buffer Overflows in GNU/Linux Operating Systems. *Procedia Computer Science, 83*, 1301–1306. doi:10.1016/j.procs.2016.04.270

Lewis, K. (2008). Small firm owners in New Zealand: In it for the 'good life' or growth? *Small Enterprise Research, 16*(1), 61–69. doi:10.5172er.16.1.61

Liddell, H. G., & Scott, R. (1940). *A Greek-English Lexicon.* Oxford: Clarendon Press.

Li, H., Zhang, J., & Sarathy, R. (2010). Understanding compliance with internet use policy from the perspective of rational choice theory. *Decision Support Systems, 48*(4), 635–645. doi:10.1016/j.dss.2009.12.005

Li, J., Zhao, Z., & Li, R. (2018). Machine learning-based IDS for softwaredefined 5G network. *IET Networks, 7*(2), 53–60. doi:10.1049/iet-net.2017.0212

Lim, J. S., Chang, S., Maynard, S., & Ahmad, A. (2009). Exploring the Relationship between Organizational Culture and Information Security Culture. *7th Australian Information Security Management Conference.*

Liu, K., (2000). *Semiotics in Information Systems Engineering.* Retrieved from doi:10.1017/CBO9780511543364

Li, W., Meng, W., Kwok, L. F., & Ip, H. H. S. (2016, June). Enhancing collaborative intrusion detection networks against insider attacks using supervised intrusion sensitivity-based trust management model. *Journal of Network and Computer Applications, 77*, 135–145. doi:10.1016/j.jnca.2016.09.014

Lopez-Rincon, O., & Starostenko, O., & Ayala-San Martin, G. (2018). Algoritmic music composition based on artificial intelligence: A survey. *2018 International Conference on Electronics, Communications and Computers (CONIELECOMP)*, 187–193. 10.1109/CONIELECOMP.2018.8327197

Lucas, C. (2004). *Cybernetics and Stochastic Systems. The Complexity & Artificial Life Research Concept for Self-Organizing Systems.* http://www.calresco.org/lucas/systems.htm

Lucas, M., Prowle, M., & Lowth, G. (2013). Management accounting practices of (UK) small-medium-sized enterprises (SMEs): Improving SME performance through management accounting education. *Chartered Institute of Management Accountant, 9*(4), 1–14.

Luiijf, E., Besseling, K., & de Graaf, P. (2013). Nineteen national cyber security strategies. International Journal of Critical, 2–31. doi:10.1504/IJCIS.2013.051608

Lyons-Burke, K. (2013). *Office Instruction Title: Malicious Code Protection Guidance Revision Number: 1.0.* Academic Press.

Maathuis, C., Pieters, W., & Van Den Berg, J. (2017). Cyber weapons: A profiling framework. *2016 IEEE International Conference on Cyber Conflict*, CyCon U.S. 10.1109/CYCONUS.2016.7836621

Mackenzie, S. B., & Podsakoff, P. M. (2012). Common method bias in marketing : Causes, mechanisms, and procedural Remedies. *Journal of Retailing, 88*(4), 542–555. doi:10.1016/j.jretai.2012.08.001

MADISA (Ministry of Administration and Digitisation, Internal Security Agency - Republic of Poland). (2013). *Cyberspace Protection Policy of the Republic of Poland.* Warsaw, Poland: Author.

Mahdavifar, S., & Ghorbani, A. A. (2019). Application of deep learning to cybersecurity: A survey. *Neurocomputing, 347*, 149–176. doi:10.1016/j.neucom.2019.02.056

Maheshwari, R. (2018). Ideology of Buffer Overflow Exploits. *International Research Journal of Engineering and Technology, 5*(5).

Mahfouz, A., Mahmoud, T., & Eldin, A. (2017). Poster: A Behavioural Biometric Authentication framework on Smartphones. *ASIA CCS '17 April 02-06, 2017,* 923–925. 10.1074/jbc.272.22.14115

Mahjabin, T., Xiao, Y., Sun, G., & Jiang, W. (2017). A survey of distributed denial-of-service attack, prevention, and mitigation techniques. *International Journal of Distributed Sensor Networks, 13*(12). doi:10.1177/1550147717741463

Mahmood, Z. (2009). Contract cheating: A new phenomenon in cyber-plagiarism. *Communications of the IBIMA, 10*(12), 93–97.

Majid, M. A., & Ariffi, K. A. Z. (2019). Success Factors for Cyber Security Operation Center (SOC) Establishment. In *International Conference on Informatics, Engineering, Science and Technology*. Bandung: European Alliance for Innovation (EAI). 10.4108/eai.18-7-2019.2287841

Makani, R., & Reddy, B. V. R. (2018). Taxonomy of Machine Leaning Based Anomaly Detection and its suitability. *Procedia Computer Science, 132,* 1842–1849. doi:10.1016/j.procs.2018.05.133

Makris, D., Kaliakatsos-Papakostas, M. A., & Cambouropoulos, E. (2015). Probabilistic Modular Bass Voice Leading in Melodic Harmonisation. *ISMIR,* 323–329.

Mančić, Ž. (2010). Cyber piracy and morality: Some utilitarian and deontological challenges. *Filozofija i Drustvo, 21*(3), 103–117. doi:10.2298/FID1003103M

Mano, C. D., Duhadway, L., & Striegel, A. (2006). A Case for Instilling Security as a Core Programming Skill. In *Proceedings. Frontiers in Education. 36th Annual Conference* (pp. 13–18). IEEE. 10.1109/FIE.2006.322347

Mansfield-Devine, S. (2016). Ransomware: Taking businesses hostage. *Network Security, 10*(10), 8–17. doi:10.1016/S1353-4858(16)30096-4

Marotta, A., & McShane, M. (2018). Integrating a proactive technique into a holistic cyber risk management approach. *Risk Management & Insurance Review, 21*(3), 435–452. doi:10.1111/rmir.12109

Martin, P. Y., & Turner, B. A. (1986). Grounded Theory and Organizational Research. *The Journal of Applied Behavioral Science, 22*(2), 141–157. doi:10.1177/002188638602200207

Martins, E. (2012). Organizational and behavioural factors that influence knowledge retention. *Journal of Knowledge Management, 16*(1), 77–96. doi:10.1108/13673271211198954

Matić, D. (2010). A genetic algorithm for composing music. *Yugoslav Journal of Operations Research, 20*(1), 157–177. doi:10.2298/YJOR1001157M

Mayer, P., Kunz, A., & Volkamer, M. (2017). Reliable behavioural factors in the information security context. In *Proceedings of the 12th International Conference on Availability, Reliability and Security* (pp. 1–10). 10.1145/3098954.3098986

MBIE. (2015). *Small businesses in New Zealand. How do they compare with larger firms?* Wellington: MBIE.

McAlaney, J., Frumkin, L. A., & Benson, V. (2018). *Psychological and Behavioral Examinations in Cyber Security. IGI Global book series Advances in Digital Crime.* Forensics, and Cyber Terrorism. doi:10.4018/978-1-5225-4053-3

Mcclain, J., Silva, A., Emmanuel, G., Anderson, B., Nauer, K., Abbott, R., & Forsythe, C. (2015). Human Performance Factors in Cyber Security Forensic Analysis. *Procedia Manufacturing, 3,* 5301–5307. doi:10.1016/j.promfg.2015.07.621

McCumber, J. R. (1991). Information System Security: A Comprehensive Model. *14th National Computer Security Conference*. Washington, DC: National Institute of Standards and Technology, National Computer Security Center.

Mcevatt, P. (2019). Advanced Threat Centre and Future of Security Monitoring. *Fujitsu Scientific and Technical Journal*, *55*(5), 16–22.

McGraw, G. (2004). *Software Security*. IEEE Security & Privacy. doi:10.1109/MSECP.2004.1281254

McGraw, G. (2013). Cyber War is Inevitable (Unless We Build Security In). *The Journal of Strategic Studies*, *36*(1), 109–119. doi:10.1080/01402390.2012.742013

MCIT (Ministry of Information and Communications Technology - India). (2013). *National Cyber Security Policy 2013 (NCSP-2013)* (No. 2(35)/2011-CERT-In). Author.

MED (Ministry of Economic Development - New Zealand). (2011). *New Zealand's Cyber Security Strategy*. Author.

Medeiros, F. A., & Bygrave, L. A. (2015). Brazil's Marco Civil da Internet: Does it live up to the hype? *Computer Law & Security Review*, *31*(1), 120–130. doi:10.1016/j.clsr.2014.12.001

Meeuwisse, R. (2016). *Cybersecurity: Home and small business*. Hythe: Cyber Simplicity Ltd.

Menard, P., Bott, G. J., & Crossler, R. E. (2017). User motivations in protecting information security: Protection motivation theory versus self-determination theory. *Journal of Management Information Systems*, *34*(4), 1203–1230. doi:10.1080/07421222.2017.1394083

Meng, W., Wong, D. S., Furnell, S., & Zhou, J. (2015). Surveying the development of biometric user authentication on mobile phones. *IEEE Communications Surveys and Tutorials*, *17*(3), 1268–1293. doi:10.1109/COMST.2014.2386915

Meng, X., Qian, K., Lo, D., & Wu, F. (2018). Secure Mobile Software Development with Vulnerability Detectors in Static Code Analysis. *2018 International Symposium on Networks, Computers and Communications (ISNCC)*, 1–4. 10.1109/ISNCC.2018.8531071

Menninger, M. (2016). *Information security for small businesses*. Chicago: Security Elements.

Merriam-Webster. (2020). Cyber. In *Merriam-Webster.com dictionary*. Retrieved January 14, 2020, from https://www.merriam-webster.com/dictionary/cyber

Messier, R. (2016). Malware. Operating System Forensics, 265–299. doi:10.1016/b978-0-12-801949-8.00010-6

Microsoft. (2013). Developing a National Strategy for Cybersecurity: Foundations for Security, Growth, and Innovation (C. F. Goodwin & J. P. Nicholas, Eds.). Redmon: Microsoft.

MICT (Ministry of Information and Communications Technology - Kingdom of Qatar). (2013). *National Cyber Security Strategy*. Author.

MICT (Ministry of Information Communications and Technology - Republic of Kenya). (2014). *Cybersecurity Strategy*. Author.

Milgrom, P., & Roberts, J. (1982). Predation, reputation, and entry deterrence. *Journal of Economic Theory*, *27*(2), 280–312. doi:10.1016/0022-0531(82)90031-X

Miller, B. P., & Heymann, E. (2018). *Tutorial: Secure Coding Practices, Automated Assessment Tools and the SWAMP. In 2018 IEEE Cybersecurity Development (SecDev)* (pp. 124–125). IEEE; doi:10.1109/SecDev.2018.00025

Miller, P., & Power, M. (2013). Accounting, organizing and economizing: Connecting accounting research and organization theory. *The Academy of Management Annals*, *7*(1), 557–605. doi:10.5465/19416520.2013.783668

Miloslavskaya, N. (2016). Security operations centers for information security incident management. In *Proceedings - 2016 IEEE 4th International Conference on Future Internet of Things and Cloud, FiCloud 2016* (pp. 131–138). 10.1109/FiCloud.2016.26

Miloslavskaya, N. (2018). Information security management in SOCs and SICs. *Journal of Intelligent & Fuzzy Systems, 35*(3), 2637–2647. doi:10.3233/JIFS-169615

Mirza, M. B., Arslan, M., Tahseen, S., Bokhari, F., Zafar, R., & Raza, M. (2014). Malicious Software Detection, Protection & Recovery Methods. *Survey (London, England), 2*(5), 14–23.

MOD (Ministry of Defence - Republic of Latvia). (2014). *Cyber Security Strategy of Latvia 2014 - 2018*. Riga, Latvia: Ministry of Defence - Republic of Latvia.

Moher, D., Liberati, A., Tetzlaff, J., & Altman, D. G. (2009). Preferred reporting items for systematic reviews and meta-analyses: The PRISMA statement. *BMJ (Clinical Research Ed.), 339*. PMID:19622551

Monteverde, S. (2014). Undergraduate healthcare ethics education, moral resilience, and the role of ethical theories. *Nursing Ethics, 21*(4), 385–401. doi:10.1177/0969733013505308 PMID:24311237

Moore, K. S. (2013). A systematic review on the neural effects of music on emotion regulation: Implications for music therapy practice. *Journal of Music Therapy, 50*(3), 198–242. doi:10.1093/jmt/50.3.198 PMID:24568004

Moores, T., & Dhillon, G. (2000). Software piracy: A view from Hong Kong. *Communications of the ACM, 43*(12), 88–93. doi:10.1145/355112.355129

Moore, T., & Clayton, R. (2007, June). An Empirical Analysis of the Current State of Phishing Attack and Defence. WEIS.

Moor, J. H. (1997). Towards a theory of privacy in the information age. *ACM Sigcas Computers and Society, 27*(3), 27–32. doi:10.1145/270858.270866

Moulton, R., & Coles, R. S. (2003). Applying information security governance. *Computers & Security, 22*(7), 580–584. doi:10.1016/S0167-4048(03)00705-3

Moustafa, N., Hu, J., & Slay, J. (2019). A holistic review of Network Anomaly Detection Systems: A comprehensive survey. *Journal of Network and Computer Applications, 128*, 33–55.

Moustroufas, E., Stamelos, I., & Angelis, L. (2015). Competency profiling for software engineers: Literature review and a new model. In *Proceedings of the 19th Panhellenic Conference on Informatics* (pp. 235–240). Athens, Greece: ACM. 10.1145/2801948.2801960

MPS. (2010). *Canada's Cyber Security Strategy*. Ottawa: Ministry of Public Safety.

Muckin, M., & Scott, C. F. (2019). A Threat-Driven Approach to Cyber Security. *Lockheed Martin Corporation*. Retrieved from https://pdfs.semanticscholar.org/dc7e/99de96c622dea52701a1a70172e532969b89.pdf

Mutemwa, M., Mtsweni, J., & Zimba, L. (2019). Integrating a security operations centre with an organization's existing procedures, policies and information technology systems. In *2018 International Conference on Intelligent and Innovative Computing Applications, ICONIC 2018* (pp. 1–6). IEEE.

Nasir, A., Arshah, R. A., & Ab Hamid, M. R. (2018). The Significance of Main Constructs of Theory of Planned Behavior in Recent Information Security Policy Compliance Behavior Study: A Comparison among Top Three Behavioral Theories. *International Journal of Engineering & Technology, 7*(2.29), 737–741.

Nasir, A., Arshah, R. A., & Hamid, M. R. A. (2018). The Significance of Main Constructs of Theory of Planned Behavior in Recent Information Security Policy Compliance Behavior Study : A Comparison among Top Three Behavioral Theories. *IACSIT International Journal of Engineering and Technology*, 7(29), 737–741. doi:10.14419/ijet.v7i2.29.14008

National Cyber Security Centre. (2018). *The cyber threat to UK business*. Retrieved from https://www.nationalcrime-agency.gov.uk/publications/785-the-cyber-threat-to-uk-business/file

National Cyber Security Framework Manual. (2012). The NATO Science for Peace and Security Programme.

NCKB (National Cyber Security Centre - The Czech Republic). (2015). *National Cyber Security Centre of The Czech Republic for the Periode from 2015 to 2020*. Czech: National Cyber Security Centre (NCKB) - The Czech Republic.

Needle, D. (2017). Oracle Cloud Security Suites Automatically Detect, Foil Cyber-Threats. *EWeek, 6*.

Ngo, F., & Jaishankar, K. (2017, January – June). Commemorating a Decade in Existence of the International Journal of Cyber Criminology: A Research Agenda to Advance the Scholarship on Cyber Crime. *International Journal of Cyber Criminology*, 11(1).

Ngoqo, B., & Flowerday, S. (2014). Linking student information security awareness and behavioural intent. In HAISA (pp. 162–173). Academic Press.

Ngoqo, B., & Flowerday, S. V. (2015). Exploring the relationship between student mobile information security awareness and behavioural intent. *Information & Computer Security*, 23(4), 406–420. doi:10.1108/ICS-10-2014-0072

Nicula, S., & Zota, R. D. (2019). Exploiting stack-based buffer overflow using modern day techniques. *Procedia Computer Science*, 160, 9–14. doi:10.1016/j.procs.2019.09.437

NIST (National Institute of Standards and Technology). (2014). Framework for Improving Critical Infrastructure Cybersecurity. In National Institute of S (Version 1). New York: National Institute of Standards and Technology.

Novotney, B. A., Academy, U. S. N., & Diego, S. (2011). *Beat the cheat Beat the cheat*. Academic Press.

Nye, J. S. Jr. (2013). From bombs to bytes: Can our nuclear history inform our cyber future? *Bulletin of the Atomic Scientists*, 69(5), 8–14. doi:10.1177/0096340213501338

NZentrepreneur. (2017). *Kiwi small-and medium-sized businesses lucrative targets for cybercrime, ransomware*. Retrieved from https://nzentrepreneur.co.nz/kiwi-small-medium-sized-businesses-lucrative-targets-cybercrime-ransomware/

O'Gorman, L. (2003). Comparing passwords, tokens, and biometrics for user authentication. *Proceedings of the IEEE*, 91(12), 2021–2040. doi:10.1109/JPROC.2003.819611

OAS (Organization of American States). (2004). A Comprehensive Inter-American Cybersecurity Strategy: a Multidimensional and Multidisciplinary Approach to Creating a Culture of Cybersecurity. In Inter-Americaan Committee Against Terrorism (CICTE) (Ed.), AG/RES. 204 (XXXIV-O/04) on Adoption of Comprehensive Inter-American Strategy to Combat Threats to Cybersecurity: A Multidimensional and Multidisciplinary Approach to Creating a Culture of Cybersecurity. Montevideo, Uruguay: Organization of American States (OAS).

Oberly, D. J. (2019). Best practices for effectively defending against ransomware cyber attacks. *Intellectual Property & Technology Law Journal*, 31(7), 17–20.

Oinas-Kukkonen, H., & Harjumaa, M. (2009). Persuasive systems design: Key issues, process model, and system features. *Communications of the Association for Information Systems*, 24(1), 28. doi:10.17705/1CAIS.02428

Ojo, S. O., Zuva, T., & Ngwira, S. M. (2016). Survey of biometric authentication for e-Assessment. *2015 International Conference on Computing, Communication and Security, ICCCS 2015*. 10.1109/CCCS.2015.7374150

Okereke, A. O., & Chukwunonso, C. E. (2018). Malware analysis and mitigation in information preservation. *Journal of Computational Engineering*, *20*(4), 53–62. doi:10.9790/0661-2004015362

Okutan, A., & Çebi, Y. (2019). A framework for cyber crime investigation. *Procedia Computer Science*, *158*, 287–294. doi:10.1016/j.procs.2019.09.054

Oliver, A., & Smiley, T. (2013). *Plural logic*. Oxford: University Press. doi:10.1093/acprof:oso/9780199570423.001.0001

Onwubiko, C. (2015). *Cyber security operations centre: Security monitoring for protecting business and supporting cyber defense strategy*. In *2015 International Conference on Cyber Situational Awareness, Data Analytics and Assessment (CyberSA)* (pp. 1–10). London, UK: IEEE. Retrieved from https://ieeexplore.ieee.org/document/7166125/

Onwubiko, C., & Onwubiko, A. (2019). Cyber KPI for Return on Security Investment. In *2019 International Conference on Cyber Situational Awareness, Data Analytics And Assessment (Cyber SA)* (pp. 1–8). Oxford, UK: IEEE. 10.1109/CyberSA.2019.8899375

Onwubiko, C., & Ouazzane, K. (2019a). Cyber onboarding is "broken." In *2019 International Conference on Cyber Security and Protection of Digital Services (Cyber Security 2019)* (pp. 1–13). Oxford, UK: Institute of Electrical and Electronics Engineers Inc.

Onwubiko, C., & Ouazzane, K. (2019b). SOTER : A Playbook for Cyber Security Incident Management. *IEEE Transactions on Engineering Management*, 1–22.

Onyancha, O. B. (2015). An informetrics view of the relationship between internet ethics, computer ethics and cyberethics. *Library Hi Tech*, *33*(3), 387–408. doi:10.1108/LHT-04-2015-0033

Ortner, J., Velthuis, L., & Wollscheid, D. (2017). Incentive systems for risky investment decisions under unknown preferences. *Management Accounting Research*, *36*, 43–50. doi:10.1016/j.mar.2016.09.001

Ottis, R., & Lorents, P. (2010). Cyberspace: Definition and Implication. In *Proceeding of the 5th International Conference Information Warfare and Security*, (pp. 267–269). The Air Force Institute of Technology.

Öugütçü, G., Testik, Ö. M., & Chouseinoglou, O. (2016). Analysis of personal information security behavior and awareness. *Computers & Security*, *56*, 83–93.

OWASP. (2017). *OWASP Top 10 - 2017 The Ten Most Critical Web Application Security Risks*. OWASP.

Owens, J., & Matthews, J. (2008, March). A study of passwords and methods used in brute-force SSH attacks. *USENIX Workshop on Large-Scale Exploits and Emergent Threats (LEET)*.

Oxford Dictionary. (2020). Cyber. In *OxfordEnglishDictionary.com*. Retrieved January 14, 2020, from https://www.lexico.com/definition/cyber

Padayachee, K. (2012). Taxonomy of compliant information security behavior. *Computers & Security*, *31*(5), 673–680. doi:10.1016/j.cose.2012.04.004

Pahnila, S., Siponen, M., & Mahmood, A. (2007). Employees' behavior towards IS security policy compliance. In *2007 40th Annual Hawaii International Conference on System Sciences (HICSS'07)* (p. 156b-156b). Academic Press.

Pahuja, G., & Nagabhushan, T. N. (2015). Biometric authentication & identification through behavioral biometrics: A survey. *Proceedings - 2015 International Conference on Cognitive Computing and Information Processing, CCIP 2015*. 10.1109/CCIP.2015.7100681

PandaLabs. (2012). *2012 annual report pandalabs*. Retrieved September 23, 2013, from http://press.pandasecurity.com/wp-content/uploads/2013/02/PandaLabs-Annual-Report-2012.pdf

Pangaro, P. (2013). *Cybernetics - A Definition.* Accessed January 14, 2020, from https://www.pangaro.com/definition-cybernetics.html

Pangaro, P. (2017). Cybernetics as Phoenix: Why Ashes, What New Life. In L. C. Werner (Ed.), *Conversations. Cybernetics: State of the Art.* doi:10.1007/978-3-642-01310-2_2

Papadopoulos, A., Roy, P., & Pachet, F. (2016). Assisted lead sheet composition using flowcomposer. *International Conference on Principles and Practice of Constraint Programming,* 769–785. 10.1007/978-3-319-44953-1_48

Park, C. S., Lee, J. H., Seo, S. C., & Kim, B. K. (2010). Assuring software security against buffer overflow attacks in embedded software development life cycle. In *2010 The 12th International Conference on Advanced Communication Technology (ICACT)* (Vol. 1, pp. 787–790). IEEE.

Park, J., Kim, T., & Im, E. G. (2016). Touch Gesture Data based Authentication Method for Smartphone Users. RACS'16, 136–141.

Parker, F., Ophoff, J., Van Belle, J.-P., & Karia, R. (2015). Security awareness and adoption of security controls by smartphone users. In *2015 Second international conference on information security and cyber forensics (InfoSec)* (pp. 99–104). 10.1109/InfoSec.2015.7435513

Parker, C., & Castleman, T. (2007). New directions for research on SME-eBusiness: Insights from an analysis of journal articles from 2003–2006. *Journal of Information Systems and Small Business, 1*(1), 21–40.

Park, J., & Jung, W. (2003). The operators' non-compliance behavior to conduct emergency operating procedures - Comparing with the work experience and the complexity of procedural steps. *Reliability Engineering & System Safety, 82*(2), 115–131. doi:10.1016/S0951-8320(03)00123-6

Parsons, K. M., Young, E., Butavicius, M. A., McCormac, A., Pattinson, M. R., & Jerram, C. (2015). The influence of organizational information security culture on information security decision making. *Journal of Cognitive Engineering and Decision Making, 9*(2), 117–129. doi:10.1177/1555343415575152

Parsons, K., Mccormac, A., Butavicius, M., & Ferguson, L. (2010). *Human factors and information security : Individual, culture and security environment.* Science And Technology. doi:10.14722/ndss.2014.23268

Patchin, J. W., & Hinduja, S. (2018). Deterring teen bullying: Assessing the impact of perceived punishment from police, schools, and parents. *Youth Violence and Juvenile Justice, 16*(2), 190–207. doi:10.1177/1541204016681057

Paternoster, R., & Piquero, A. (1995). Reconceptualizing deterrence: An empirical test of personal and vicarious experiences. *Journal of Research in Crime and Delinquency, 32*(3), 251–286. doi:10.1177/0022427895032003001

Patil & Gudasalamani. (2015). *A Survey on Iris Recognition Systems.* Academic Press.

Patil, D. R., & Patil, J. B. (2015). Survey on Malicious Web Pages Detection Techniques. *International Journal of U- and e-Service. Science and Technology, 8*(5), 195–206.

Paul, C. C. L. (2014). Human-Centered Study of a Network Operations Center: Experience Report and Lessons Learned. In *Proceedings of the ACM Workshop on Security Information Workers* (pp. 39–42). Retrieved from https://dl.acm.org/citation.cfm?id=2663899

PCM (Presidency of the Council of Ministers - Italian Republic). (2013). *The National Plan for Cyberspace Protection and ICT security.* Rome, Italy: Presidency of the Council of Ministers - Italian Republic.

Petrescu, M., Gironda, J. T., & Korgaonkar, P. K. (2018). Online piracy in the context of routine activities and subjective norms. *Journal of Marketing Management, 34*(3–4), 314–346. doi:10.1080/0267257X.2018.1452278

Pisani, P. H., & Lorena, A. C. (2013). A systematic review on keystroke dynamics. *Journal of the Brazilian Computer Society*, *19*(4), 573–587. doi:10.100713173-013-0117-7

Plato. (2014). *The First Alcibiades (B. Jowett, Trans.)*. Bloomsbury Academic.

Pluijmers, Y., & Weiss, P. (2002). *Borders in cyberspace: Conflicting public sector information policies and their economic impacts*. Citeseer.

PMO (Prime Minister's Office of Israel). (2011). *Advancing National Cyberspace Capabilities: Resolution No. 3611 of the Government of August 7, 2011*. Author.

Podsakoff, P. M., Mackenzie, S. B., & Podsakoff, N. P. (2003). Common method biases in behavioral research: A critical review of the literature. *The Journal of Applied Psychology*, *88*(5), 879–903. doi:10.1037/0021-9010.88.5.879 PMID:14516251

Posner, R. A. (1978). Economic theory of privacy. *Regulation*, *2*, 19.

Puhakainen, P. (2006). *A design theory for information security awareness*. Faculty of Science. University of Oulu. Retrieved from http://en.scientificcommons.org/13922630

Pulakanam, V., & Suraweera, T. (2010). Implementing accounting software in small businesses in New Zealand: An exploratory investigation. *Accountancy Business and the Public Interest*, *9*, 98–124.

Pusey, P., & Sadera, W. A. (2011). Cyberethics, Cybersafety, and Cybersecurity: Preservice Teacher Knowledge, Preparedness, and the Need for Teacher Education to Make a Difference. *Journal of Digital Learning in Teacher Education*, *28*(2), 82–85. doi:10.1080/21532974.2011.10784684

Qamar, A., Karim, A., & Chang, V. (2019). Mobile malware attacks: Review, taxonomy & future directions. *Future Generation Computer Systems*, *97*, 887–909. doi:10.1016/j.future.2019.03.007

Qian, K., Lo, D., Parizi, R., & Wu, F. (2018). Authentic Learning Secure Software Development (SSD) in Computing Education. *2018 IEEE Frontiers in Education Conference (FIE)*, 1–9.

Qian, K., Parizi, R. M., & Lo, D. (2018). OWASP Risk Analysis Driven Security Requirements Specification for Secure Android Mobile Software Development. In *2018 IEEE Conference on Dependable and Secure Computing (DSC)* (pp. 1–2). IEEE. 10.1109/DESEC.2018.8625114

Quackenbush, S. L. (2011). Deterrence theory: Where do we stand? *Review of International Studies*, *37*(2), 741–762. doi:10.1017/S0260210510000896

Rafique, S., Humayun, M., Hamid, B., Abbas, A., Akhtar, M., & Iqbal, K. (2015, June). Web application security vulnerabilities detection approaches: A systematic mapping study. In *Software Engineering, Artificial Intelligence, Networking and Parallel/Distributed Computing (SNPD), 2015 16th IEEE/ACIS International Conference on* (pp. 1-6). IEEE. 10.1109/SNPD.2015.7176244

Rahman, R. U., & Tomar, D. S. (2018). Botnet Threats to E-Commerce Web Applications and Their Detection. In Improving E-Commerce Web Applications Through Business Intelligence Techniques (pp. 48-81). IGI Global.

Rahman, R. U., Wadhwa, D., Bali, A., & Tomar, D. S. (2020). The Emerging Threats of Web Scrapping to Web Applications Security and Their Defense Mechanism. In Encyclopedia of Criminal Activities and the Deep Web (pp. 788-809). IGI Global. doi:10.4018/978-1-5225-9715-5.ch053

Rahman, R. U., & Tomar, D. S. (2018). Security Attacks on Wireless Networks and Their Detection Techniques. In *Emerging Wireless Communication and Network Technologies* (pp. 241–270). Singapore: Springer. doi:10.1007/978-981-13-0396-8_13

Rahman, R. U., Verma, R., Bansal, H., & Tomar, D. S. (2020). Classification of Spamming Attacks to Blogging Websites and Their Security Techniques. In *Encyclopedia of Criminal Activities and the Deep Web* (pp. 864–880). IGI Global. doi:10.4018/978-1-5225-9715-5.ch058

Rajab, M., & Eydgahi, A. (2019). Evaluating the explanatory power of theoretical frameworks on intention to comply with information security policies in higher education. *Computers & Security*, *80*, 211–223. doi:10.1016/j.cose.2018.09.016

Ramanto, A. S., Nur, U., & Maulidevi, S. T. (2017). *Markov Chain Based Procedural Music Generator with User Chosen Mood Compatibility*. Academic Press.

Ramirez, R., & Choucri, N. (2016). Improving Interdisciplinary Communication With Standardized Cyber Security Terminology: A Literature Review. *IEEE Access: Practical Innovations, Open Solutions*, *4*, 2216–2243. doi:10.1109/ACCESS.2016.2544381

Rash, W. (2015). IT Managers Struggling to Keep Up With Cyber-Threats: Security Experts. *EWeek, 1*.

Rash, W. (2019). *Five Things Enterprises Need to Know About Threat Landscape. EWeek, N.* PAG.

Raymond, D., Conti, G., Cross, T., & Fanelli, R. (2013). A Control Measure Framework to Limit Collateral Damage and Propagation of Cyber Weapons. *5th International Conference on Cyber Conflict (CyCon)*, 1–16.

Raymond, D., Cross, T., Conti, G., & Nowatkowski, M. (2014). Key terrain in cyberspace: Seeking the high ground. *International Conference on Cyber Conflict, CYCON*, 287–300. 10.1109/CYCON.2014.6916409

Read, A. D., West, R. J., & Kelaher, B. P. (2015). Using compliance data to improve marine protected area management. *Marine Policy, 60*, 119–127. Retrieved from https://linkinghub.elsevier.com/retrieve/pii/S0308597X15001670

Refsdal, A., Solhaug, B., & Stølen, K. (2015). *Cyber risk management* (1st ed.). SpringerBriefs. doi:10.1007/978-3-319-23570-7

Reimers, K., Andersson, D. (2017). Post-secondary education network security: the end user challenge and evolving threats. *ICERI Proceedings,* 1787-1796.

Republic of Turkey. (2013). *National Cyber Security Strategy and 2013-2014 Action Plan*. Author.

Research and Markets. (2019, May 22). *SOC as a Service Market - Global Forecast to 2024*. Retrieved March 25, 2020, from https://www.globenewswire.com/news-release/2019/05/22/1840685/0/en/SOC-as-a-Service-Market-Global-Forecast-to-2024.html

Reynolds, G. W. (2015). *Ethics in Information Technology* (5th ed.). Cengage Learning Boston.

Rhode, J., Richter, S., Gowen, P., Miller, T., & Wills, C. (2017). Understanding Faculty Use of the Learning Management System. *Online Learning*, *21*(3), 68–86. doi:10.24059/olj.v21i3.1217

Richiardi, J., & Kryszczuk, K. (2011). *Biometric Systems Evaluation*. Academic Press.

Riehle, D., & Nürnberg, F.-A.-U. E. (2015). How Open Source Is Changing the Software Developer's Career. *Computer Practice*, *48*(5), 51–57. doi:10.1109/MC.2015.132

Roads, C., & Wieneke, P. (1979). Grammars as Representations for Music. *Computer Music Journal*, *3*(1), 48. doi:10.2307/3679756

Rocha Flores, W., Antonsen, E., & Ekstedt, M. (2014). Information security knowledge sharing in organizations: Investigating the effect of behavioral information security governance and national culture. *Computers & Security*, *43*(1), 90–110. doi:10.1016/j.cose.2014.03.004

Rodafinos, A. (2018). Plagiarism Management: Challenges, Procedure, and Workflow Automation. *Interdisciplinary Journal of E-Skills and Lifelong Learning*, *14*, 159–175. doi:10.28945/4147

Rodrigues, A., Costa, E., & Cardoso, A. (2016). *Evolving l-systems with musical notes*. Springer. https://link.springer.com/chapter/10.1007/978-3-319-31008-4_13

Roger, O., Begonya, G.-Z., & Roman, Y. (2017). *Multimodal Biometric Systems : a systematic review*. Academic Press.

Rogerson, A. M. (2017). Detecting contract cheating in essay and report submissions: Process, patterns, clues and conversations. *International Journal for Educational Integrity*, *13*(1), 10. doi:10.100740979-017-0021-6

Rogers, R. (1983). Cognitive and physiological processes in fear-based attitude change: A revised theory of protection motivation. In J. Cacioppo & R. Petty (Eds.), *Social psychophysiology: A sourcebook* (pp. 153–176). New York: Guilford Press.

Rokach, L., & Maimon, O. (2010). *Data Mining and Knowledge Discovery Handbook*. Boston, MA: Springer.

Sadasivam, G. K., Hota, C., & Anand, B. (2018). Honeynet Data Analysis and Distributed SSH Brute-Force Attacks. In *Towards Extensible and Adaptable Methods in Computing* (pp. 107–118). Singapore: Springer. doi:10.1007/978-981-13-2348-5_9

Sae-bae, N., & Jakobsson, M. (2014). *Hand Authentication on Multi-Touch Tablets*. Academic Press.

Saevanee, H., Clarke, N. L., & Furnell, S. M. (2012). Multi-modal behavioural biometric authentication for mobile devices. *IFIP Advances in Information and Communication Technology*, *376*, 465–474. doi:10.1007/978-3-642-30436-1_38

Safa, N. S., Maple, C., Furnell, S., Azad, M. A., Perera, C., Dabbagh, M., & Sookhak, M. (2019). Deterrence and prevention-based model to mitigate information security insider threats in organizations. *Future Generation Computer Systems*, *97*, 587–597. doi:10.1016/j.future.2019.03.024

Safa, N. S., Sookhak, M., Von Solms, R., Furnell, S., Ghani, N. A., & Herawan, T. (2015). Information security conscious care behavior formation in organizations. *Computers & Security*, *53*, 65–78. doi:10.1016/j.cose.2015.05.012

Safa, N. S., & Von Solms, R. (2016). An information security knowledge sharing model in organizations. *Computers in Human Behavior*, *57*, 442–451. doi:10.1016/j.chb.2015.12.037

Safa, N. S., Von Solms, R., & Furnell, S. (2016). Information security policy compliance model in organizations. *Computers & Security*, *56*, 70–82. doi:10.1016/j.cose.2015.10.006

Salo, F., Injadat, M., Nassif, A. B., Shami, A., & Essex, A. (2018). Data mining techniques in intrusion detection systems: A systematic literature review. *IEEE Access: Practical Innovations, Open Solutions*, *6*, 56046–56058. doi:10.1109/ACCESS.2018.2872784

Salter, A., & Liu, K. (2002). Using Semantic Analysis and Norm Analysis to Model Organizations. *ICEIS 2002 - Proceedings of the 4th International Conference on Enterprise Information Systems*, *2*, 847-850.

Sametinger, J. (2013). Software Security. In *2013 20th IEEE International Conference and Workshops on Engineering of Computer Based Systems (ECBS)* (p. 216). IEEE. 10.1109/ECBS.2013.24

Sang, S. K., & Yong, J. K. (2017). The effect of compliance knowledge and compliance support systems on information security compliance behavior. *Journal of Knowledge Management*, *21*(4), 986–1010. doi:10.1108/JKM-08-2016-0353

SANS Institute. (2018). *SEC504: Hacker Techniques, Exploits, and Incident Handling*. Boston: The SANS Institute.

Saunders, M., Lewis, P., Thornhill, A., & Wilson, J. (2009). Business research methods. *Financial Times*.

Scarfone, K., & Mell, P. (2010). *The common configuration scoring system (ccss): Metrics for software security configuration vulnerabilities*. NIST interagency report, 7502.

Schatz, D., & Wall, J. (2017). Towards a More Representative Definition of Cyber Security. *Journal of Digital Forensics, Security and Law, 12*(2).

Schatz, D., Bashroush, R., & Wall, J. (2017). Towards a more representative definition of cyber security. *Journal of Digital Forensics, Security and Law, 12*(2). doi:10.15394/jdfsl.2017.1476

Scheffler, S. (1988). *Consequentialism and its Critics*. Oxford University Press on Demand.

Schinagl, S., Schoon, K., & Paans, R. (2015). A framework for designing a security operations centre (SOC). In *2015 48th Hawaii International Conference on System Sciences* (Vol. 2015-March, pp. 2253–2262). IEEE.

Scirea, M., Barros, G. A. B., Shaker, N., & Togelius, J. (2015). SMUG. *Scientific Music Generator, 299*, 204–211.

Scott, J. (2016). *The ransomware report*. New York: ICIT.

SecurityMagazine. (2019). *Cyber Attacks Cost $45 Billion in 2018*. Retrieved from https://www.securitymagazine.com/articles/90493-cyber-attacks-cost-45-billion-in-2018

Shah, A., Ganesan, R., & Jajodia, S. (2018). A methodology for ensuring fair allocation of CSOC effort for alert investigation. *International Journal of Information Security, 18*, 1–20. doi:10.100710207-018-0407-3

Shah, A., Ganesan, R., Jajodia, S., & Cam, H. (2018). Adaptive reallocation of cybersecurity analysts to sensors for balancing risk between sensors. *Service Oriented Computing and Applications, 12*(2), 123–135. doi:10.100711761-018-0235-3

Shahriar, S., Das, S., & Hossain, S. (2018). Security threats in Bluetooth technology. *Computers & Security, 74*, 308–322. doi:10.1016/j.cose.2017.03.008

Shah, S., & Mehtre, B. M. (2015). An overview of vulnerability assessment and penetration testing techniques. *Journal of Computer Virology and Hacking Techniques, 11*(1), 27–49. doi:10.100711416-014-0231-x

Shankar, V., Singh, K., & Kumar, A. (2016). IPCT : A scheme for mobile authentication ☝. *Perspectives on Science, 8*, 522–524. doi:10.1016/j.pisc.2016.06.009

Shih, S. P., & Liou, J. Y. (2015). Investigate the Effects of Information Security Climate and Psychological Ownership on Information Security Policy Compliance. In PACIS (p. 28).

Shin, A., Crestel, L., Kato, H., Saito, K., Ohnishi, K., Yamaguchi, M., . . . Harada, T. (2017). *Melody generation for pop music via word representation of musical properties*. ArXiv Preprint ArXiv:1710.11549

Shin, Y. H., & Hancer, M. (2016). The role of attitude, subjective norm, perceived behavioral control, and moral norm in the intention to purchase local food products. *Journal of Foodservice Business Research, 19*(4), 338–351. doi:10.1080/15378020.2016.1181506

Shreeve, A., Boddington, D., Bernard, B., Brown, K., Clarke, K., Dean, L., ... Shiret, D. (2002). Student perceptions of rewards and sanctions. *Pedagogy, Culture & Society, 10*(2), 239–256. doi:10.1080/14681360200200142

Shunmugam, S., & Selvakumar, R. K. (2015). Electronic transaction authentication - A survey on multimodal biometrics. *2014 IEEE International Conference on Computational Intelligence and Computing Research, IEEE ICCIC 2014*, 1–4. 10.1109/ICCIC.2014.7238509

Siegfried, R. M. (2004). Student Attitudes on Software Piracy and Related Issues of Computer Ethics. *Ethics and Information Technology*, *11530*(516), 215–222. doi:10.100710676-004-3391-4

Sikolia, D. (2013). "A thematic review of user compliance with information security policies literature" Annual ADFSL. *Conference on Digital Forensics, Security and Law, 2*. Retrieved from https://commons.erau.edu/adfsl/2013/tuesday/2

Silveira, P., Rodríguez, C., Birukou, A., Casati, F., Daniel, F., D'Andrea, V., ... Taheri, Z. (2012). Aiding Compliance Governance in Service-Based Business Processes. In S. Reiff-Marganiec & M. Tilly (Eds.), *Handbook of Research on Service-Oriented Systems and Non-Functional Properties: Future Directions*. doi:10.4018/978-1-61350-432-1.ch022

Singh, V., & Pandey, S. K. (2019). *Revisiting Cloud Security Threat: Dictionary Attack*. Available at SSRN 3444792.

Singh, J., & Nene, M. J. (2013). A Survey on Machine Learning Techniques for Intrusion Detection Systems. *International Journal of Advanced Research in Computer and Communication Engineering*, *2*(11), 4349–4355.

Sinnott-Armstrong, W. (2003). *Consequentialism*. Academic Press.

Siponen & Vance. (2010). Neutralization: New Insights into the Problem of Employee Information Systems Security Policy Violations. *MIS Quarterly, 34*(3), 487. doi:10.2307/25750688

Siponen, M., Adam Mahmood, M., & Pahnila, S. (2014). Employees' adherence to information security policies: An exploratory field study. *Information & Management*, *51*(2), 217–224. doi:10.1016/j.im.2013.08.006

Sitren, A. H., & Applegate, B. K. (2012). Testing Deterrence Theory with Offenders: The Empirical Validity of Stafford and Warr's Model. *Deviant Behavior*, *33*(6), 492–506. doi:10.1080/01639625.2011.636685

Slusky, L., & Partow-Navid, P. (2012). Students information security practices and awareness. *Journal of Information Privacy and Security*, *8*(4), 3–26. doi:10.1080/15536548.2012.10845664

Smith, A. D., & Rupp, W. T. (2002). Issues in cybersecurity; understanding the potential risks associated with hackers/crackers. *Information Management & Computer Security*, *10*(4), 178–183. doi:10.1108/09685220210436976

Solomon, D. (2007, August). Back From the Future: Questions for William Gibson. *The New York Times Magazine*.

Solomon, M. G., & Chapple, M. (2005). *Information Security Illuminated*. Jones and Bartlett Publishers, Inc.

Sommestad, T., & Hallberg, J. (2013). A review of the theory of planned behaviour in the context of information security policy compliance. In *IFIP International Information Security Conference* (pp. 257–271). 10.1007/978-3-642-39218-4_20

Sommestad, T., Hallberg, J., Lundholm, K., & Bengtsson, J. (2014). Variables influencing information security policy compliance. *Information Management & Computer Security*, *22*(1), 42–75. doi:10.1108/IMCS-08-2012-0045

Son, J. Y. (2011). Out of fear or desire? Toward a better understanding of employees' motivation to follow IS security policies. *Information & Management*, *48*(7), 296–302. doi:10.1016/j.im.2011.07.002

Soomro, Z. A., Shah, M. H., & Ahmed, J. (2016). Information security management needs more holistic approach: A literature review. *International Journal of Information Management*, *36*(2), 215–225. doi:10.1016/j.ijinfomgt.2015.11.009

Souppaya, M., & Scarfone, K. (2013). NIST Special Publication 800-83 Revision 1 Guide to Malware Incident Prevention and Handling for Desktops and Laptops. *NIST Special Publication, 800*, 83. doi:10.6028/NIST.SP.800-83r1

SpamLaws. (2019). *What is Malicious Mobile Code and How Does It Work?* Retrieved from https://www.spamlaws.com/how-malicious-mobile-code-works.html

Srinivasan, M. L. (2008). *CISSP in 21 Days*. Packt Publishing.

Stafford, M. C. (2015). Deterrence Theory: Crime. In International Encyclopedia of the Social & Behavioral Sciences: Second Edition (pp. 18–168). doi:10.1016/B978-0-08-097086-8.45005-1

Stamper, R.., Liu, K., Hafkamp, M., & Ades Y. (2000). Understanding the Roles of Signs and Norms in Organizations. *Journal of Behaviour & Information Technology, 19*(1), 15–27.

Stanciu, V., & Tinca, A. (2016). Students' awareness on information security between own perception and reality--an empirical study. *Accounting and Management Information Systems, 15*(1), 112–130.

Stibe, A., & Wiafe, I. (2018). *Beyond Persuasive Cities: Spaces that Transform Human Behavior and Attitude.* Persuasive Technology.

Stocker, M. (1969). Consequentialism and its complexities. *American Philosophical Quarterly, 6*(4), 276–289.

Straub, D., Boudreau, M.-C., & Gefen, D. (2004). Validation guidelines for IS positivistic research. *Communications of the Association for Information Systems, 13*(1), 380–427.

Sudhamani, M. J., Venkatesha, M. K., & Radhika, K. R. (2012). Revisiting feature level and score level fusion techniques in multimodal biometrics system. *Proceedings of 2012 International Conference on Multimedia Computing and Systems, ICMCS 2012*, 881–885. 10.1109/ICMCS.2012.6320155

Sulphey, M. M., & Jnaneswar, K. (2013). A study on the academic dishonesty, anomia and unethical behaviour among business graduates. *The Journal of Contemporary Management Research, 8*(2), 57–72.

Su, N., Levina, N., & Ross, J. W. (2016). The long-tail strategy of IT outsourcing. *MIT Sloan Management Review, 57*(2), 81.

Sundaramurthy, S. C., Florida, S., Mchugh, J., Ou, X., Florida, S., Wesch, M., … Bardas, A. G. (2016). Turning Contradictions into Innovations or : How We Learned to Stop Whining and Improve Security Operations In *Proceedings of the Turning Contradictions into Innovations or : How We Learned to Stop Whining and Improve* (pp. 237–251). USENIX.

Sundaramurthy, S., Ou, X., Bardas, A. G., Case, J., Wesch, M., … Rajagopalan, S. R. (2015). A Human Capital Model for Mitigating Security Analyst Burnout. In *Symposium on Usable Privacy and Security* (pp. 347–359). Academic Press.

Sundaramurthy, S. C., Case, J., Truong, T., Zomlot, L., & Hoffmann, M. (2014). A Tale of Three Security Operation Centers. In *Proceedings of the 2014 ACM Workshop on Security Information Workers - SIW '14* (pp. 43–50). Scottdale, AZ: ACM. doi:10.1145/2663887.2663904

Suraj, M. V., Kumar Singh, N., & Tomar, D. S. (2018). Big data Analytics of cyber attacks: A review. *2018 IEEE International Conference on System, Computation, Automation and Networking, ICSCA 2018*, 1–7. 10.1109/ICSCAN.2018.8541263

Swartz, L. B., & Cole, M. T. (2013). Students' perception of Academic Integrity in Online Business Education Courses. *Journal of Business and Educational Leadership, 4*(1), 102.

Tadda, G. P. (2008). *Measuring Performance of Cyber Situation Awareness Systems. In 2008 11th International Conference on Information Fusion* (pp. 1–8). IEEE. Retrieved from https://ieeexplore.ieee.org/stamp/stamp.jsp?tp=&arnumber=4632229

Taghavi, M., Bentahar, J., Bakhtiyari, K., & Hanachi, C. (2017). New insights towards developing recommender systems. *The Computer Journal, 61*(3), 319–348. doi:10.1093/comjnl/bxx056

Tamjidyamcholo, A., & Baba, M. S. (2014). Evaluation model for knowledge sharing in information security professional virtual community. *Computers & Security, 43*, 19–34. doi:10.1016/j.cose.2014.02.010

Tan, S. A., Nainee, S., & Tan, C. S. (2019). Filial Piety and Life Satisfaction Among Malaysian Adolescents in a Multi-Ethnic, Collectivist Society. In *2nd International Conference on Intervention and Applied Psychology (ICIAP 2018)* (pp. 1–5). Academic Press.

Tang, J.-H., Chung, T.-Y., & Chen, M.-C. (2018). Plagiarism Cognition, Attitude and Behavioral Intention: A Trade-Off Analysis. *International Conference on Information and Knowledge Engineering*, (1), 149–144. Retrieved from https://csce.ucmss.com/cr/books/2018/LFS/CSREA2018/IKE9002.pdf

Tantawi, M. M., Revett, K., Tolba, M. F., & Salem, A. (2012). On the use of the electrocardiogram for biometrie authentication. *2012 8th International Conference on Informatics and Systems (INFOS)*.

Tao, Q., & Veldhuis, R. (2010). Biometric authentication system on mobile personal devices. *IEEE Transactions on Instrumentation and Measurement*, *59*(4), 763–773. doi:10.1109/TIM.2009.2037873

Taylor, S. A. (2012). Evaluating digital piracy intentions on behaviors. *Journal of Services Marketing*, *26*(7), 472–483. doi:10.1108/08876041211266404

Ten, C. W., Liu, C. C., & Manimaran, G. (2008). Vulnerability assessment of cybersecurity for SCADA systems. *IEEE Transactions on Power Systems*, *23*(4), 1836–1846. doi:10.1109/TPWRS.2008.2002298

Tene, O., & Polonetsky, J. (2013). A theory of creepy: Technology, privacy and shifting social norms. *Yale JL & Tech.*, *16*, 59.

The Republic of Croatia. (2015). *The National Cyber Security Strategy of the Republic of Croatia* (Vol. 2015). Zagreb: Republic of Croatia.

Theoharidou, M., & Gritzalis, D. (2007). Common Body of Knowledge for Information Security. *IEEE Security & Privacy*, 64–67.

Thomas, A. E. (2016). *Security operations center : analyst guide*. London: CreateSpace.

Thompson, R. L., Higgins, C. A., & Howell, J. M. (1994). Influence of experience on personal computer utilization: Testing a conceptual model. *Journal of Management Information Systems*, *11*(1), 167–187. doi:10.1080/07421222.1994.11518035

Thomson, K. L., & Von Solms, R. (2005). Information security obedience: A definition. *Computers & Security*, *24*(1), 69–75. doi:10.1016/j.cose.2004.10.005

Tilley, E. N., Fredricks, S. M., & Hornett, A. (2012). Kinship, culture and ethics in organisations: Exploring implications for internal communication. *Journal of Communication Management (London)*, *16*(2), 162–184. doi:10.1108/13632541211217588

Tipton, H. F., & Henry, K. (2007). *Official (ISC)² Guide to the CISSP CBK*. Taylor & Francis Group, LLC. Retrieved from https://books.google.com.gh/books?id=RbihG-YALUkC&lpg=PA139&dq=object%20reuse%20attack&pg=PP1#v=onepage&q&f=false

Tomczyk, Ł. (2019). The Practice of Downloading copyrighted files among adolescents in Poland: Correlations between piracy and other risky and protective behaviours online and offline. *Technology in Society*, *58*, 101137. doi:10.1016/j.techsoc.2019.05.001

Tsai, H. S., Jiang, M., Alhabash, S., LaRose, R., Rifon, N. J., & Cotten, S. R. (2016). Understanding online safety behaviors: A protection motivation theory perspective. *Computers & Security*, *59*, 138–150. doi:10.1016/j.cose.2016.02.009

Tsohou, A., & Holtkamp, P. (2018). Are users competent to comply with information security policies? An analysis of professional competence models. *Information Technology & People*, *31*(5), 1047–1068. doi:10.1108/ITP-02-2017-0052

Tuglular, T., & Belli, F. (2008). Model-Based Mutation Testing of Firewalls. *Fast Abstracts of TAIC-PART Conference.*

United Nations. (2013). *Comprehensive study on cybercrime: Draft.* New York: United Nations.

ur Rahman, R., Tomar, D. S., & Das, S. (2012, May). Dynamic image based captcha. In *2012 International Conference on Communication Systems and Network Technologies* (pp. 90-94). IEEE.

Ur Rizwan, R. (2012). Survey on captcha systems. *Journal of Global Research in Computer Science*, *3*(6), 54–58.

Uskov, A. V., & Avenue, W. B. (2013). Hands-On Teaching of Software and Web Applications Security. 2013 3rd Interdisciplinary Engineering Design Education Conference, 71–78. 10.1109/IEDEC.2013.6526763

Uskov, A. V. (2013). Software and Web Application Security: State-of-the-Art courseware and Learning Paradigm. In *IEEE Global Engineering Education Conference (EDUCON)* (Vol. 0, pp. 608–611). 10.1109/EduCon.2013.6530168

Valasek, C., & Miller, C. (2013). *Adventures in Automotive Networks and Control Units.* Technical White Paper.

Van der Meer, S. (2015). Enhancing international cyber security: A key role for diplomacy. *Security and Human Rights*, *26*(2-4), 193–205. doi:10.1163/18750230-02602004

Van der Meulen, R., & Rivera, J. (2013). *Gartner predicts by 2017, half of employers will require employees to supply their own device for work purposes.* Gartner.com.

Van Niekerk, J. F., & Von Solms, R. (2010). Information security culture: A management perspective. *Computers & Security*, *29*(4), 476–486. doi:10.1016/j.cose.2009.10.005

Vance, A., Lowry, P. B., & Eggett, D. (2013). Using accountability to reduce access policy violations in information systems. *Journal of Management Information Systems*, *29*(4), 263–290. doi:10.2753/MIS0742-1222290410

Vanhée, L., & Dignum, F. (2018). Explaining the emerging influence of culture, from individual influences to collective phenomena. *Journal of Artificial Societies and Social Simulation*, *21*(4), 11. doi:10.18564/jasss.3881

Vani, Y. S. K., & Krishnamurthy. (2018). Survey: Anomaly detection in network using big data analytics. *2017 International Conference on Energy, Communication, Data Analytics and Soft Computing, ICECDS 2017*, 3366–3369.

Vasiete, E., Chen, Y., Ian, C., Yeh, T., Patel, V., Davis, L., & Chellappa, R. (2014). Toward a Non-Intrusive, Physio-Behavioral Biometric for Smartphones. *MobileHCI*, 501–506.

Veltsos, C. (2016). *Small business cyber security quickstart guide.* New York: Infosec.

Venkatesh, V., Morris, M. G., Davis, G. B., & Davis, F. D. (2003). User acceptance of information technology: Toward a unified view. *Management Information Systems Quarterly*, *27*(3), 425–478. doi:10.2307/30036540

Verdon, D. (2006). *Security Policies and the Software Developer.* IEEE Security & Privacy. doi:10.1109/MSP.2006.103

Verma, R. (2018). Security analytics: Adapting data science for security challenges. *IWSPA 2018 - Proceedings of the 4th ACM International Workshop on Security and Privacy Analytics, Co-Located with CODASPY 2018*, 40–41.

Virtue, T. & Rainey, J. (2015). Information Risk Assessment, HCISPP Study Guide, 131-166. doi:10.1016/B978-0-12-802043-2.00006-9

Vishnubhotla, S. D., Mendes, E., & Lundberg, L. (2018). An Insight into the Capabilities of Professionals and Teams in Agile Software Development A Systematic Literature Review. In *ICSCA 2018* (pp. 10–19). Kuantan, Malaysia: ACM. doi:10.1145/3185089.3185096

Voges, K. E., & Pulakanam, V. (2011). Enabling factors influencing internet adoption by New Zealand small and medium size retail enterprises. *International Review of Business Research Papers, 7*(1), 106–117.

Vogt, P., Nentwich, F., Jovanovic, N., Kirda, E., Kruegel, C., & Vigna, G. (2007, February). Cross Site Scripting Prevention with Dynamic Data Tainting and Static Analysis. *NDSS, 2007*, 12.

Von Solms, R., & Van Niekerk, J. (2013). From information security to cyber security. *Computers & Security, 38*, 97-102.

von Solms, R., & van Niekerk, J. (2013). From information security to cyber security. *Computers & Security, 38*, 97–102. doi:10.1016/j.cose.2013.04.004

Von Solms, S. H. (2005). Information Security Governance - Compliance management vs operational management. *Computers & Security, 24*(6), 443–447. doi:10.1016/j.cose.2005.07.003

Vroom, C., & von Solms, R. (2004). Towards information security behavioural compliance. *Computers & Security, 23*(3), 191–198. doi:10.1016/j.cose.2004.01.012

Wada, F., Longe, O., & Danquah, P. (2012). Action Speaks Louder Than Words - Understanding Cyber Criminal Behavior Using Criminological Theories. *Journal of Internet Banking and Commerce, 17*(1), 1–12.

Wafa, Z. (2014). National Cyber Security Strategy of Afghanistan (NCSA) (2nd ed.). Kabul, Afghanistan: Ministry of Communications and IT - Islamic Republic of Afghanistan.

Walkowski, D. (2019). What Are Security Controls? *Application Threat Intelligence*. Retrieved from https://www.f5.com/labs/articles/education/what-are-security-controls

Wall, J. D., Palvia, P., & Lowry, P. B. (2013). Control-Related Motivations and Information Security Policy Compliance: The Role of Autonomy and Efficacy. *Journal of Information Privacy and Security, 9*(4), 52–79. doi:10.1080/15536548.2013.10845690

Wang, C. R., Xu, R. F., Lee, S. J., & Lee, C. H. (2018). Network intrusion detection using equality constrained-optimization-based extreme learning machines. *Knowledge-Based Systems, 147*, 68–80. doi:10.1016/j.knosys.2018.02.015

Wang, Z. (2018). Deep Learning-Based Intrusion Detection with Adversaries. *IEEE Access: Practical Innovations, Open Solutions*. doi:10.1109/ACCESS.2018.2854599

Warikoo, A. (2014). Proposed Methodology for Cyber Criminal Profiling. *Information Security Journal: A Global Perspective, 23*(4-6), 172-178.

Warner, J. (2011). Understanding Cyber-Crime in Ghana: A View from Below. *International Journal of Cyber Criminology, 5*(1), 736–749.

Watad, M., Washah, S., & Perez, C. (2018). IT security threats and challenges for small firms: Managers' perceptions. *International Journal of the Academic Business World, 12*(1), 23–29.

Watling, C. N., Palk, G. R., Freeman, J. E., & Davey, J. D. (2010). Applying Stafford and Warr's reconceptualization of deterrence theory to drug driving: Can it predict those likely to offend? *Accident; Analysis and Prevention, 42*(2), 452–458. https://www.ncbi.nlm.nih.gov/entrez/query.fcgi?cmd=Retrieve&db=PubMed&list_uids=20159066&dopt=Abstract doi:10.1016/j.aap.2009.09.007 PMID:20159066

Weaver, G. R. (2016). Businesses : Culture ' s Role Ethics Programs in Global in Managing Ethics Gary R. Weaver. *Journal of Business Ethics*, *30*(1), 3–15. doi:10.1023/A:1006475223493

WEF (World Economic Forum). (2012b). *Risk and Responsibility in a Hyperconnected World: Pathways to Global Cyber Resilience*. WEF.

WEF (World Economic Forum). (2014). Risk and responsibility in a hyperconnected world: Implications for enterprises. In J. Kaplan, A. Weinberg, & D. Chinn (Eds.), *World Economic Forum In collaboration with McKinsey & Company*. Geneva, Switzerland: WEF.

WEF (World Economic Forum). (2015). *Partnering for Cyber Resilience: Towards the Quantification of Cyber Threats*. Geneva: World Economic Forum (WEF).

WEF. (2012a). *Partnering for Cyber Resilience: Risk and Responsibility in a Hyperconnected World - Principles and Guidelines*. Geneva, Switzerland: World Economic Forum (WEF).

Wegerer, M., & Tjoa, S. (2016). Defeating the Database Adversary Using Deception - A MySQL Database Honeypot. In *2016 International Conference on Software Security and Assurance (ICSSA)* (pp. 6–10). IEEE. 10.1109/ICSSA.2016.8

Westcott, R., Ronan, K., Bambrick, H., & Taylor, M. (2017). Expanding protection motivation theory: Investigating an application to animal owners and emergency responders in bushfire emergencies. *BMC Psychology*, *5*(1), 13. doi:10.118640359-017-0182-3 PMID:28446229

Whitman, M. E. (2004). In defense of the realm: Understanding the threats to information security. *International Journal of Information Management*, *24*(1), 43–47. doi:10.1016/j.ijinfomgt.2003.12.003

Wiafe, I., Nakata, K., Moran, S., & Gulliver, S. R. (2011). Considering user attitude and behaviour in persuasive systems design: the 3d-rab model. In ECIS (p. 186). Academic Press.

Wiafe, I., & Nakata, K. (2012). *A semiotic analysis of persuasive technology : An application to obesity management*. International Conference on Informatics and Semiotics in Organisations.

Wiafe, I., Nakata, K., & Gulliver, S. (2014). Categorizing users in behavior change support systems based on cognitive dissonance. *Personal and Ubiquitous Computing*, *18*(7), 1677–1687. doi:10.100700779-014-0782-3

Widener, S. (2006). Human capita, pay structure, and the use of performance measures in bonus compensation. *Management Accounting Research*, *17*(2), 198–221. doi:10.1016/j.mar.2005.06.001

Wiener, N. (1948). Cybernetics: Control and Communication in the Animal and the Machine (2nd ed.). Cambridge, MA: The MIT Press.

Willems, C., Holz, T., & Freiling, F. (2007). Toward automated dynamic malware analysis using cwsandbox. *IEEE Security and Privacy*, *5*(2), 32–39. doi:10.1109/MSP.2007.45

Williams, D., Kirke, A., Miranda, E. R., Roesch, E., Daly, I., & Nasuto, S. (2015). Investigating affect in algorithmic composition systems. *Psychology of Music*, *43*(6), 831–854. doi:10.1177/0305735614543282

Williams, D., Kirke, A., Miranda, E., Daly, I., Hwang, F., Weaver, J., & Nasuto, S. (2017). Affective Calibration of Musical Feature Sets in an Emotionally Intelligent Music Composition System. *ACM Transactions on Applied Perception*, *14*(3), 1–13. doi:10.1145/3059005

Williams, K. R., & Hawkins, R. (1986). Perceptual research on general deterrence: A critical review. *Law & Society Review*, *20*(4), 545–572. doi:10.2307/3053466

Willison, R., & Warkentin, M. (2013). Beyond deterrence: An expanded view of employee computer abuse. *Management Information Systems Quarterly*, *37*(1), 1–20. doi:10.25300/MISQ/2013/37.1.01

Wilson, D. (2017). 3 basic types of security controls to protect your business. *Concerned Nerds*. Retrieved from http://concernednerds.com/3-basic-types-of-security-controls-to-protect-your-business/

Wixom, B. H., & Watson, H. J. (2001). An empirical investigation of the factors affecting data warehousing success. *Management Information Systems Quarterly*, *25*(1), 17–41. doi:10.2307/3250957

Wu, Z., Evans, N., Kinnunen, T., Yamagishi, J., Alegre, F., & Li, H. (2015). Spoofing and countermeasures for speaker verification: A survey. In *Speech Communication* (Vol. 66, pp. 130–153). Elsevier. doi:10.1016/j.specom.2014.10.005

Xia, H., & Xu, Y. (2017). Design and Research of Safety Test Model Based on Advanced Evasion Techniques. In *Global Conference on Mechanics and Civil Engineering (GCMCE 2017)* (Vol. 132, pp. 92–96). Atlantis Press. 10.2991/gcmce-17.2017.18

Yaokumah, W. (2016). The influence of students' characteristics on mobile device security measures. *International Journal of Information Systems and Social Change*, *7*(3), 44–66. doi:10.4018/IJISSC.2016070104

Yaokumah, W. (2020). Predicting and Explaining Cyber Ethics with Ethical Theories. *International Journal of Cyber Warfare & Terrorism*, *10*(2), 46–63. doi:10.4018/IJCWT.2020040103

Yaokumah, W., Brown, S., & Dawson, A. A. (2016). Towards modelling the impact of security policy on compliance. *Journal of Information Technology Research*, *9*(2), 1–16. doi:10.4018/JITR.2016040101

Yaokumah, W., Walker, D., & Kumah, P. (2019). SETA and Security Behavior - Mediating Role of Employee Relations, Monitoring, and Accountability. *Journal of Global Information Management*, *27*(3), 102–121. doi:10.4018/JGIM.2019040106

Yar, M. (2005). The novelty of cybercrime: An assessment in light of routine activity theory. *European Journal of Criminology*, *2*(4), 407–427. doi:10.1177/1477370805556056

Yau, H. K. (2014). Information Security Controls. *Adv Robot Autom*, *3*, e118. doi:10.4172/2168-9695.1000e118

Yazdanmehr, A., & Wang, J. (2016). Employees' information security policy compliance: A norm activation perspective. *Decision Support Systems*, *92*, 36–46. doi:10.1016/j.dss.2016.09.009

Yeap, J. A. L., Ramayah, T., & Soto-Acosta, P. (2016). Factors propelling the adoption of m-learning among students in higher education. *Electronic Markets*, *26*(4), 323–338. doi:10.100712525-015-0214-x

Yoo, C. W., Sanders, G. L., & Cerveny, R. P. (2018). Exploring the influence of flow and psychological ownership on security education, training and awareness effectiveness and security compliance. *Decision Support Systems*, *108*, 107–118. doi:10.1016/j.dss.2018.02.009

Yoon, C., Hwang, J.-W., & Kim, R. (2012). Exploring factors that influence students' behaviors in information security. *Journal of Information Systems Education*, *23*(4), 407–415.

Young, J. R., Davies, R. S., Jenkins, J. L., & Pfleger, I. (2019). Keystroke Dynamics: Establishing Keyprints to Verify Users in Online Courses. *Computers in the Schools*, *36*(1), 48–68. doi:10.1080/07380569.2019.1565905

Zabicki, R., & Ellis, S. R. (2017). Penetration Testing. In *Computer and Information Security Handbook*. Elsevier Inc.; doi:10.1016/B978-0-12-803843-7.00075-2

Zagare, F. C., & Kilgour, D. M. (2000). Perfect deterrence. *Cambridge Studies in International Relations*, *24*(1), 15–25.

Zainuddin, H. N., & Normaziah, A. A. (2011). Secure Coding in Software Development. In *2011 Malaysian Conference in Software Engineering* (pp. 458–464). IEEE. 10.1109/MySEC.2011.6140716

Zhang, J., Gardner, R., & Vukotic, I. (2019). Anomaly detection in wide area network meshes using two machine learning algorithms. *Future Generation Computer Systems*, *93*, 418–426. doi:10.1016/j.future.2018.07.023

Zhong, C., Yen, J., Liu, P., & Erbacher, R. F. (2016). Automate Cybersecurity Data Triage by Leveraging Human Analysts' Cognitive Process. In *Proceedings - 2nd IEEE International Conference on Big Data Security on Cloud, IEEE BigDataSecurity 2016, 2nd IEEE International Conference on High Performance and Smart Computing, IEEE HPSC 2016 and IEEE International Conference on Intelligent Data and S* (pp. 357–363). New York: IEEE.

Zhu, H., Hu, J., Chang, S., & Lu, L. (2017). ShakeIn: Secure User Authentication of Smartphones with Single-Handed Shakes. *IEEE Transactions on Mobile Computing*, *16*(10), 2901–2912. doi:10.1109/TMC.2017.2651820

Zilber, N. (2018). Hackers for Hire. *Foreign Policy*, (230), 60–64.

Zimmerman, C. (2014). *Cybersecurity Operations Center*. The MITRE Corporation.

Zolanvari, M., Teixeira, M. A., Gupta, L., Khan, K. M., & Jain, R. (2019). *Machine Learning-Based Network Vulnerability Analysis of Industrial Internet of Things*. IEEE Internet of Things Journal. doi:10.1109/JIOT.2019.2912022

Zou, Y., Zhao, M., Zhou, Z., Lin, J., Li, M., & Wu, K. (2018). *BiLock : User Authentication via Dental Occlusion Biometrics*. Academic Press.

About the Contributors

Winfred Yaokumah is a researcher, cyber security expert and a senior faculty at the Department of Computer Science of the University of Ghana. His research interests are in the areas of Information Systems Security, Cyber Security, Cyber Terrorism and Warfare, and Critical Infrastructure Protection. His work has appeared in several reputable journals, including the International Journal of Cyber Warfare and Terrorism, Information and Computer Security, Information Resources Management Journal, Journal of Information Technology Research, Journal of Global Information Management, IEEE Xplore, International Journal of e-Business Research, International Journal of Enterprise Information Systems, Journal of Information Management and Computer Security, and the International Journal of Information Systems in the Service Sector, among others. He serves on the International Review Board for the International Journal of Technology Diffusion.

Muttukrishnan Rajarajan is a Professor of Security Engineering and Director of Institute for Cyber Security at City University of London. He has supervised more than 25 PhD students in this area and advices several organisations with their cyber security strategy. His areas of research interests are in privacy, blockchain, internet of things and intrusion detection. He is also the founder and CEO of CityDefend Limited. He has published more than 300 journal and conference papers and is a member of the Charted Institute of Information Security.

Jamal-Deen Abdulai is the current HOD of the Department of Computer Science, University of Ghana. He is an academic in computer science with over 10 years of working experience in both industry and academia. He graduated with PhD in Computer Science in 2009 and MPhil in 2006 from University of Glasgow, UK. Prior to that, he received BSc in Computer Science in 2002 from the Kwame Nkrumah University of Science and Technology (KNUST). Prior to his appointment at University of Ghana, Dr Abdulai had worked with the School of Technology, GIMPA as a lecturer from 2009 to 2013 and worked at the University for Development Studies (UDS) as Senior Research Assistant from 2002 to 2004. Dr Abdulai current research interest includes Performance modelling and evaluation of Mobile Wireless Ad hoc and Sensor Networks, Network Security and Management, Embedded Systems, Parallel and Distributed Systems, Artificial Intelligence and its applications. Dr Abdulai has been providing consultancy services to public and private organisations in Ghana over the last 10 years. Among them are the Ministry of Finance and the Ministry of Roads and Highways.

Isaac Wiafe holds a PhD in Informatics and an MSc in Applied Informatics from the University of Reading, UK. He also holds a bachelor's degree in Mathematics, from the Kwame Nkrumah University of Science and Technology, Kumasi, Ghana. His research is focused on human-computer behaviour change. He is the inventor of the 3-Dimensional Relationship between Attitude and Behaviour Model (3D-RAB): a robust model for gathering systems requirement for persuasive technology design. Currently, Dr Wiafe is the head of the Intelligence Spaces and Machine Learning lab at the Department of Computer Science, University of Ghana, where he is leading advance research in AI applications for Human development. He has an interest in Intelligent and Persuasive Spaces, Information Security Behavior, IT for Behavior Change and Knowledge Sharing in Social Networks.

Ferdinad Apietu Katsriku received the MEng with distinction degree in Computer Systems Engineering from the Kharkov Polytechnic Institute, Ukraine in 1989, an MSc in Laser Engineering and Pulsed Power Technology from St Andrews University Scotland, in 1992 and the Ph.D. degree in Electrical and Electronic Engineering from City University of London, UK, in 2000. From 2001 to 2012, he was a Senior Lecturer at Middlesex University, London, UK. Since 2012, he has been with the Computer Science department, University of Ghana, Legon as Senior Lecturer. His research interests include security of wireless sensor networks, IoT, propagation modelling and photonic device modelling using the finite element method. F. Katsriku was a recipient of the Alborada award and spent 6 months at Cambridge University UK as a Caprex fellow.

* * *

Enoch Agyepong is a PhD Researcher at the School of Computer Science and Informatics, Cardiff University. His research interest is in Cyber Security and in particular Cyber Security Operations Centres. He is a Senior Cyber Security Engineer at Airbus and holds a Master's Degree in Advanced Security And Digital Forensics from Edinburgh Napier University.

George Oppong Appiagyei Ampong is a Senior Lecturer in the Management Department and Dean of the Business School at Ghana Technology University College. .He teaches courses in Entrepreneurship, Strategic Management and Research Methods. His research interests include disclosure on social media networks, e-business and the dark side of technology in the workplace. He has published in journals including International Journal of Bank Marketing, Behavioral Sciences, Education Sciences and International Journal of Supply Chain and Operational Resilience.

Hod Anyigba is an innovation management scholar and practitioner with research and consultancy interests in the areas of information systems innovation management, entrepreneurship and economics. Hod has over 10 years of industry and academic experiences both in the African and European contexts. He is also fellow at the Institute of Chartered Economists of Ghana (FCE) - a professional body in charge of regulating and guiding the practice of economics in the field. In industry, Hod has done consultancy works for both national and global organizations such as the International Trade Union Confederation, the European Union (EU), OmniBank -Ghana, Kasapreko (Royal Crown Packaging)-Ghana, the Africa Trade Union Development Network, National Entrepreneurship and Innovation Plan (NEIP) – Ministry of Business Development – Ghana, TenStep – Project management consultants etc. He serves on a number of Boards and Committees both in Ghana and Abroad. He is the current assistant Academic Dean at the prestigious Nobel International Business School (NiBS) – Africa's Premier Doctoral School.

Richard Apau is a PhD Candidate in Computer Science at the Kwame Nkrumah University of Science and Technology. He holds Master of Philosophy (MPhil) and Bachelor of Science (BSc) degrees in Computer Science. Richard also pursued Master of Science (MSc) Cyber Security and Management from The University of Warwick, UK. He has extensive university teaching and research experience. His research interests include cyber security, information security, cryptography and steganography, e-commerce, m-commerce as well as mobile financial technology. He has extensive publication in international peer-reviewed journals.

Ima Apriany holds Master Degree in ICT Strategic Planning with Distinction from University of Wollongong. She was formerly a functional IT staff on Directorate General of Taxation (DGT) Indonesia. She joined IT security policy drafting team for DGT. Her responsibilities were to make sure that IT development and procedure comply with the IT security policy. Her research interest is in IT security regulations and compliance.

Kwame Asante-Offei is an IT professional with over 8 years of industrial experience. He started his working carrier as a software developer, subsequently as an MIS administrator and currently as a database administrator. Kwame holds a Master's degree in Management Information Systems from Ghana Institute of Management and Public Administration and a Bachelor of Science (Computer Science) degree from Kwame Nkrumah University of Science and Technology. His research interests include Financial Technology, Information Systems Management, and Information Security.

Nana Asssyne holds a Master of Science in Information Technology from the Lappeenranta University of Technology – Finland, a bachelor's degree in Business Information Technology from Haaga-Helia University of Applied Sciences – Finland. He also holds a professional certificate in pedagogical studies in vocational teacher education from Haaga-Helia University of Applied Sciences – Finland. Nana has over 5 years teaching experience in software engineering courses at the university level and supervising thesis including supervising thesis at Haaga-Helia University of Applied Sciences – Finland. Nana is currently completing his Ph.D. in computer science at the Faculty of Information Technology of the University of Jyväskylä, Finland. Meanwhile he is a faculty member of Ghana Institute Management and Public Administration (GIMPA) – Ghana. Prior to working at GIMPA, Nana worked with Haaga-Helia University of Applied Sciences – Finland as a student/teacher assistant, at Nsense Oy -Finland as a software developer, and at Sekondi-Takoradi Metropolitan Assembly – Ghana as head of MIS Unit.

Riza Azmi is currently a PhD student in cyber security strategy and policy at the Centre for Persuasive Technology and Society, University of Wollongong. He was formerly a research analyst in the Ministry of Information and Technology, Republic of Indonesia. He is a member of the Indonesia Cyber Security Forum (ICSF) and the Indonesia Honeynet Project (IHP). His research interest is in ICT policy.

Pete Burnap is a Professor of Data Science and Cybersecurity at Cardiff University. He is the Director of Cardiff's NCSC/EPSRC Academic Centre of Excellence in Cyber Security Research (ACE-CSR). He holds a PhD in Computer Science from Cardiff University.

Yulia Cherdantseva is a lecturer at the National Software Academy at Cardiff University. She specialises in Cyber Security, Secure Business Process Design and Risk Assessment. She holds a PhD in Computer Science and an MSc (Hons) in Business Information Systems Design, Russia.

Kwasi Dankwa is currently in their final year of a PhD in Business Informatics, Systems and Accounting at the University of Reading in the United Kingdom. Currently working as a Quality Assurance professional, the author is interested in compliance activities as it relates to Regulations, Standards and Rules. They believe that by ensuring compliance requirements are factored into planning and implementation of projects, effective and efficient outcomes may be achieved that saves time, resources and even save lives when it comes to the Health Sector. They are passionate about understanding user and stakeholder attitude and behavior when it comes to compliance activities, and they strive to understand the reasons behind why users fail to comply with Rules, Regulations and Standards. Driving aim is to come out with processes and systems to improve compliance behavior of users and stakeholders.

Paul Asante Danquah is an Information Technology professional, researcher and lecturer with over 21 years' experience. He holds a BSc HONS in Computing, MSc in Information Security and a PhD in Information Technology (Specialized in Cybercrime) from the University of Greenwich UK, Anglia Ruskin University UK and Open University Malaysia respectively. He has various industry certifications, some of which are Certified Security Operations Center Analyst (CSA),Certified Ethical Hacker (CEH), Certified EC-Council Instructor (CEI), Data Center Infrastructure Expert (DCIE), Cisco Certified Network Professional (CCNP) and Microsoft Certified Systems Engineer (MCSE). Dr. Danquah has worked in various capacities over the years, these range from Programmer, Network Engineer, IT Manager, Deputy Director of IT and Senior Lecturer at various prominent technology companies and Universities in Ghana.Dr. Danquah also independently provides Information Security consultancy services for various organizations ranging from the financial sector to utility provisioning and technology solution companies. He has over fifteen published research articles in internationally refereed journals.

Akon Ekpezu is a Lecturer in the department of Computer Science, Cross River University of Technology (CRUTECH), Nigeria. She holds; a Bachelor of Science (B.Sc) in Mathematics and Statistics from the University of Calabar, Nigeria, a Post Graduate Diploma (PGD) in Computer Science from the same university, a Master of Science (M.Sc.) in Information Technology from the National Open University of Nigeria (NOUN) and is currently pursuing her MPhil/PhD in Computer Science at the University of Ghana. She is interested in the following areas of research; Artificial Intelligence, Health Informatics, Behavioral Support Systems and Information Security.

Eli Fianu is a faculty member of the Informatics Faculty of the Ghana Technology University College (GTUC). His areas of lecturing are Database Systems, Systems Analysis and Design, Computer applications for Management, and E-Commerce. He also works in the non-bank financial sector as credit, savings, and investment manager. He holds a Master of Science degree in Management Information Systems from Coventry University, and a Bachelor of Science Degree in Agricultural Economics from the University of Ghana. He is currently a PhD candidate at UKZN in South Africa. His research interests are Social Media and web 2.0, Technology Adoption, and e-Learning.

Pasi Fränti received the M.Sc. and Ph.D. degrees in science from the University of Turku, in 1991 and 1994, respectively. Since 2000, he has been a Professor of computer science with the University of Eastern Finland. He has published 86 journals and 174 peer review conference papers, including 14 IEEE transaction papers. Significant contributions have also been made in image compression, image analysis, vector quantization, and speech technology. His main research interests include machine learning, data mining, and pattern recognition, including clustering algorithms and intelligent location-aware systems.

Daniel Kobla Gasu received his BSc in Computer Science from the University of Cape Coast in 2012. He has worked with Vatebra Limited since 2014 as Software Engineer. His interests are AI, Cyber Security, and Data Science. He is currently pursuing an MSc in Computer Science at University of Ghana, Legon.

Sydney Kanda is a Senior Information Security Consultant who majors in Cyber Security – both for On-prem and Cloud computing. His work is around assisting organisations build resilient defence strategies to secure the critical information asset. He did his Master of Business Administration (MBA) with Massey University. He has worked for a leading NZ Telco, a large countrywide SME (state-owned-enterprise), a massive government ministry looking after all New Zealand embassies & consulates worldwide. He has consulted for a large energy utility that runs the country's national grid and an aerospace company looking after the NZ army. He has massive experience in all modern security and network technologies – both at LAN, WAN, branch, datacentre, and Cloud levels - designing and maintaining network, security and infrastructure solutions to match the customer's desired level of security, availability, modularity and business continuity.

Kautsarina is a government researcher at Ministry of Communication and Information Technology (MCIT), Republics of Indonesia since 2009. She also works as an ISO 27001 Lead Auditor for public institution since 2011. She is involved in developing policy research and ICT master plan. Now she is full-time PhD student at Faculty of Computer Science, Universitas Indonesia. Her interest is about information security awareness improvement for end-user and internet-of-things.

Felicia Amanfo Kissi is a customer success engineer at a security software company. She holds a Bachelor of Science degree in Animal Biology and Conservation science from the University of Ghana, Legon and is currently pursuing her Master of Science in Information Communication Technology from the Ghana Institute of Management and Public Administration. Felicia has a vast experience in Biomedical research in using medicinal plants to curb growth of various stages of Schistosomiasis, due to her 2-year research assistant role at Noguchi Memorial Institute of Medical Research (NMIMR) and currently her research interest lies in information Security. Information security in Customer relationship management piques her interest so much, her current research focuses on how to use blockchain technology and access control mechanism to prevent the leakage of information to unauthorized persons. She is particularly interested in protecting one's privacy online using blockchain technology.

Felix Nti Koranteng is a research assistant. He holds a Bachelor of Science degree in Computer Science from the Kwame Nkrumah University of Science and Technology (Ghana) and a Master of Science in Management Information Systems from the Ghana Institute of Management and Public Administration. Felix's research interests lie in the areas of persuasive technologies. He is particularly interested in persuasive systems that aims to entertain as well as educate. He is also concerned with issues of collaborative learning technologies, human-computer interaction, social media sentiment analysis and information and knowledge management. His current research focuses on social networking sites and knowledge sharing in academic environments.

Jojo Desmond Lartey is an Assistant Lecturer at the department of Information Technology, Heritage Christian College, Ghana. His main research interest lies within the areas of computational intelligence and dynamical systems. He has a BSc. Mathematics from Kwame Nkrumah University of Science and Technology Ghana, MSc. in Industrial Mathematical Modelling from Loughborough University England, and PGCert. in Advanced Computer Systems Development from University of the West of Scotland, Scotland. He is currently a PhD student and a member of Society for Industrial and Applied Mathematics (SIAM).

Olumide Longe has had a progressive and accomplished academic and professional career demonstrating consistent success in research and development, professional impact, national, regional and global recognition and assuring students success. He holds a PhD degree in Computer Science (Information Systems Security Specialization) from the University of Benin; a Master's degree in Computer Science from the Federal University of Technology Akure, a BSc in Computing from the University of Benin, Benin City, Nigeria and National Diploma in Electrical/Electronics Engineering from the Federal Polytechnic, Ado Ekiti, Nigeria. He also holds several certification in information security and IT. A recipient of several national and international awards and recognitions, he is an alumnus MacArthur Scholar, an alumnus MIT Scholar, a recipient of the prestigious Fulbright SIR Fellowship and the highly coveted Heidelberg Nobel Laureate Forum Fellowship in Germany. He is Seasoned in conceiving management information systems theories (evidenced by scholastic publications), and initiatives in ICT diffusion and uptake. Dr. Longe has been named by Microsoft research as one of the leading experts on privacy and information systems security research. He was a lead researcher on the New Partnership for Africa's Development (NE PAD) Council's Cyber Security Program for Africa. He has won several competitive grants including the highly competitive Google CS4HS grant and the US Government sponsored Fulbright Alumni Innovation Engagement. He is a member of several world class professional bodies which include the ACM, ISACA, IEEE, ISOC, IAENG and the AIS. Prior to joining the American University of Nigeria, Yola, Adamawa State, Nigeria as an Associate Professor and Chair of the Information Systems programme, he had worked at The Federal Polytechnic, Auchi, Nigeria, The University of Ibadan, Ibadan, Nigeria, The Accra Institute of Technology, Southern University, Baton Rouge USA as a Visiting Scholar, Adeleke University and Caleb University, Lagos, Nigeria.

Makafui Nyamadi is a Doctoral Researcher in Information Systems at the University of Ghana Business School. He is currently a Lecturer at Ho Technical University, Ghana. He was an Americas Conference on Information Systems (AMCIS) Doctoral Fellow in 2018 and Hawaii International Conference on Systems Sciences (HICSS) Doctoral Fellow in 2019. His research interests include technology addiction, digital platforms, cyber security, and theory development.

Kwame Simpe Ofori is currently a PhD student at the School of Management and Economics, University of Electronic Science and Technology of China. He has taught courses in areas of Finance and Telecommunications Engineering. He holds a Doctorate Degree in Finance. His research interests are in the areas of consumer behaviour, technology adoption, trust in online systems and PLS path modelling. His papers have appeared in Marketing Intelligence and Planning, International Journal of Bank Marketing, Total Quality Management and Business Excellence and African Journal of Economic and Management Studies.

Osaretin Kayode Omoregie is a senior fellow in finance and strategy at the Lagos Business School. He teaches and carries out research in the areas of corporate financial intelligence, executive compensation and performance, including development of empirical models for incorporating ethics in finance in search of ethic-adjusted financial outcomes. Kayode is widely published in reputable peer-reviewed academic and practice oriented journals. He is a licenced and certified chartered accountant and tax practitioner and a business rescue and insolvency practitioner.

Jones Opoku-Ware is currently a PhD Candidate with the Department of Sociology and Social Work at the Kwame Nkrumah University of Science and Technology (KNUST)-Ghana. He is currently the Programme Coordinator for the MSc Development Management programme at the Institute of Distance Learning, KNUST. His current interests is in Deviance and Criminology especially Crime Studies and Analysis, Spatial Crime Distribution, Ecological Crime Studies, Social Disorganization as well as Social Development.

Radiah Othman is currently a Senior Lecturer with Massey University, New Zealand. Her Masters in Accountancy (with distinction) is from Curtin University of Technology (Australia), and PhD from Aston University (UK). She is an active researcher and has published papers in the area of fraud and forensic accounting, sustainability, public sector auditing and accountability in book chapters and reputable journals such as Journal of Business Ethics, International Journal of Public Sector Management, Accountancy, Business and Public Interest. Her current research interest is fraud examination and forensic accounting topics. She has received research grants to profile fraudsters and to examine the usefulness of forensic detecting tools.

Philipp Reinecke is Researcher and Lecturer in Cybersecurity, Performance, and Dependability at School of Computer Science and Informatics at Cardiff University, UK. He holds a PhD in Computer Science from Freie Universität Berlin and an MSc in Computer Science from Humboldt University of Berlin.

William Tibben is a Senior Lecturer at the University of Wollongong, Australia. His research focusses on ICT use in developing countries, including ICT for Development, e-governance, e-business as well as ICT accessibility for people with disabilities. Will has researched and published in telecommunications policy in the Asia-Pacific and has participated on the Independent Grants Review Panel in ACCAN (Australian Communications Consumers Action Network). Will has also been active in the Pacific Islands chapter of the Internet Society (PICISOC) and held executive positions on its board from 2009 to 2012.

Peter Tobbin is an IT Professional with of 20 years industry experience, he is currently the Director of the Center for IT Professional Development in Accra, Ghana. He hold PhD in Information Technology and Telecommunications from Aalborg University, Denmark, a MSc in Information Security from

Westminster University, UK and a BSc HONS Accounting. Dr. Peter Tobbin also has numerous professional certifications among which are CISSP, CISA, CISM, CEH, CCIE, and MCSE.

Deepak Singh Tomar obtained his B. E., M. Tech. and Ph. D. degrees in Computer Science and Engineering. He is currently Assistant Professor of CSE department at NIT- Bhopal, India. He is co-investigator of Information Security Education Awareness (ISEA) project under Govt. of India. Currently, he is chairman of cyber security center, MANIT, Bhopal. He has more than 21 years of teaching experience. He has guided 30 M Tech and 3 PhD Thesis. Besides this he guided 70 B Tech and 15 MCA projects. He has published more than 54 papers in national & international journals and conferences. He is holding positions in many world renowned professional bodies. His present research interests include web mining and cyber security.

Enoimah Umoh has B.Sc. in Computer Science from University of Uyo, also obtained his M.Sc. and PhD in Computer Science from Ebonyi State University, Abakaliki both in Nigeria.

Rizwan Ur Rahman obtained B.E and M.Tech in Computer Science from Maulana Azad National Institute of Technology (MANIT), Bhopal with Hons grade. His programming experience includes C/C++, C#, SQL, ASP, ASP.NET, VB, VB.NET; Win Forms, Web Forms and Java. He has worked on government projects and R&D department of CRISP. Currently he is an assistant professor in JayPee University Waknaghat, Solan, India. His area of research includes web programming and web security.

Abigail Wiafe is a PhD candidate at the School of Computing, University of Eastern Finland, Finland. Before this, she obtained her BSc degree in Computer Science (2007) at the Valley View University, Ghana and her MSc degree in Business Technology Consulting from University of Reading, Reading, UK (2012). she works at Ghana Technology University College as a lecturer at the Faculty of Computing and Information System (FoCIS). Currently, her research interest is in Affective Music Composition, Genetic Algorithms, Machine Learning and Music Recommendation.

Index

Ensure Quality Research is Introduced to the Academic Community

Become an IGI Global Reviewer for Authored Book Projects

 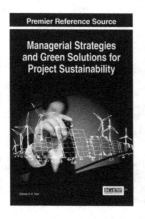  

The overall success of an authored book project is dependent on quality and timely reviews.

In this competitive age of scholarly publishing, constructive and timely feedback significantly expedites the turnaround time of manuscripts from submission to acceptance, allowing the publication and discovery of forward-thinking research at a much more expeditious rate. Several IGI Global authored book projects are currently seeking highly-qualified experts in the field to fill vacancies on their respective editorial review boards:

Applications and Inquiries may be sent to:
development@igi-global.com

Applicants must have a doctorate (or an equivalent degree) as well as publishing and reviewing experience. Reviewers are asked to complete the open-ended evaluation questions with as much detail as possible in a timely, collegial, and constructive manner. All reviewers' tenures run for one-year terms on the editorial review boards and are expected to complete at least three reviews per term. Upon successful completion of this term, reviewers can be considered for an additional term.

If you have a colleague that may be interested in this opportunity, we encourage you to share this information with them.

IGI Global Proudly Partners With eContent Pro International

Receive a 25% Discount on all Editorial Services

Editorial Services

IGI Global expects all final manuscripts submitted for publication to be in their final form. This means they must be reviewed, revised, and professionally copy edited prior to their final submission. Not only does this support with accelerating the publication process, but it also ensures that the highest quality scholarly work can be disseminated.

English Language Copy Editing

Let eContent Pro International's expert copy editors perform edits on your manuscript to resolve spelling, punctuaion, grammar, syntax, flow, formatting issues and more.

Scientific and Scholarly Editing

Allow colleagues in your research area to examine the content of your manuscript and provide you with valuable feedback and suggestions before submission.

Figure, Table, Chart & Equation Conversions

Do you have poor quality figures? Do you need visual elements in your manuscript created or converted? A design expert can help!

Translation

Need your documjent translated into English? eContent Pro International's expert translators are fluent in English and more than 40 different languages.

Printed in the United States
By Bookmasters